Ethics for Public Communication

Defining Moments in Media History

CLIFFORD G. CHRISTIANS
University of Illinois

MARK FACKLER
Calvin College

JOHN P. FERRÉ
University of Louisville

New York   Oxford

OXFORD UNIVERSITY PRESS

Oxford University Press, Inc., publishes works that further
Oxford University's objective of excellence
in research, scholarship, and education.

Oxford   New York
Auckland   Cape Town   Dar es Salaam   Hong Kong   Karachi
Kuala Lumpur   Madrid   Melbourne   Mexico City   Nairobi
New Delhi   Shanghai   Taipei   Toronto

With offices in
Argentina   Austria   Brazil   Chile   Czech Republic   France   Greece
Guatemala   Hungary   Italy   Japan   Poland   Portugal   Singapore
South Korea   Switzerland   Thailand   Turkey   Ukraine   Vietnam

For titles covered by Section 112 of the US Higher Education
Opportunity Act, please visit www.oup.com/us/he for the latest
information about pricing and alternate formats.

Published by Oxford University Press, Inc.
198 Madison Avenue, New York, New York 10016
http://www.oup.com

Oxford is a registered trademark of Oxford University Press

Library of Congress Cataloging-in-Publication Data
Christians, Clifford G.
   Ethics for public communication : defining moments in media history /
Clifford G. Christians, Mark Fackler, John P. Ferré.
      p. cm.
   Includes bibliographical references and index.
   ISBN 978-0-19-537454-4 (pbk. main text : alk. paper)
   1. Mass media—Moral and ethical aspects.   2. Communication—Moral
and ethical aspects.   3. Mass media—History   I. Fackler, Mark.   II. Ferré, John P.   III. Title.
   P94.C4465 2011
   302.23—dc23   2011019139

9 8 7 6 5 4 3 2 1
Printed in the United States of America
on acid-free paper

CONTENTS

✦

PREFACE

Since before humans had written languages to keep records of events and progress (or the opposite), we had each other. People found that company was good, isolation not so good. People learned that hunting together was a better bet against the larger beasts, and singing together a better inspiration to more singing, finer tunes, and greater emotional payoff. Community was good.

But not all community. Some did not work well at all. Some communities became ingrown, isolated, xenophobic. Others became covetous. People fought over land, cattle, gold, or even slaves. Sometimes they fought to defend themselves; sometimes they fought to conquer. Some (like Troy) allowed too easy access to their community and paid dearly. Community is one of the constants of human life, and one of its pitfalls.

Today community is rearranging around communication technology. No longer a geographic phenomenon, community is more and more virtual, less and less physical. "Be a friend" no longer connotes a weekend camping trip. Now it is a click and a text message. If you never meet that friend in person, where is the loss? Some on-line friendships get closer and more transparent than friends of the meet-and-dance variety.

Because we want to know what makes relationships good and what hurts them, this book asks, how have media enhanced or retarded community? We offer in these chapters a vision of community that is proactive, pro-progress, pro-health, and pro-creativity. We present it as a new vision of media ethics in today's complicated world. We call that vision communitarianism.

You will see that word many times in the next pages. We leave to those pages the problem of sorting out what that seven syllable noun means. For now, we acknowledge that a large community of scholars and friends have inspired, critiqued, helped craft this book. We are indebted to them, for without them these chapters would not have come to print, or if they had, the print that you will be reading would have been less lively, less vivid, less telling. So we say "thank you" for keen and open minds to Michael Mandeville, Sam Bultman, Jared Eliason,

Ted Fackler, Jungmo Youn, Kathy Gronendyk, and Kevin Healey. Paul Christians of Open Hand Studios drafted major sections of chapters 4, 7, 12, and 14, and contributed important additions to chapters 8 and 15; his research throughout was indispensable. Professor Melba Velez wrote an early draft of chapter 14, and added good theory to chapter 7. We are indebted to Robert Fortner for his excellent drafts of chapters 3, 5, and 6. He writes with grace and wisdom, leaving little for us to do but change a word here or there, likely obscuring his clear point and muddying his crisp prose.

We three authors are indebted further to our institutions, colleagues, and families for support and encouragement in the work this book required. Indeed, an impressive list of communications scholars who have taken up communitarianism have also pointed the way for us. Our earlier effort, *Good News: Social Ethics and the Press* (1993), showed that we three could harness our lively exchanges into a book that presented a coherent vision of responsible journalism. While that book offered theory for the ethics of journalism, this one approaches the nexus of communitarian theory and media from a different angle. In this book, we use historic case studies to illustrate (sometimes by negative rather than positive example) how people can grow through good communication, how ties that bind us get stronger. We three signed on believing the same would be our own experience, and it has been that way—not all pleasant strolls through violet fields on lofty moorlands, but all to the good. We hope your experience with this book will show the same results.

Clifford Christians
Mark Fackler
John Ferré

✦

Communitarian Ethics

This book is about a moral theory that uses one of those words too long to count as normal spoken English. Sixteen letters will be printed repeatedly in these pages, signaling a theory about people and morality, and how the technologies of mass media help or hurt our effort to live well. That word—the name given to the moral theory elaborated here—is communitarianism.

Before the *-arianism* that English tacks onto nouns to signal grand abstractions, you see embedded in that lengthy word hints of meaning. The word resembles community and commune, communicate and common.[1] In the modern academy, the word stands for a theory of persons and goodness that relocates your center from self to the space between selves, from me to us, from your mind as the focus of identity and being to the relationships you have with others as the centerpiece. Communitarians believe that you have to look away from yourself to understand yourself. Good comes through relationships, not from assertions or moral claims conceived or adopted by your own persona.

It is common knowledge that the starting point of authentic living is "know thyself." (Old English makes an impact still.) And you may still hear, "To thine own self be true" (Polonius in *Hamlet*, Act I). For two hundred years, the self has had the top spot in our reckoning of the good life. Communitarianism reorients our thinking about the good life from self to relation between selves. That is where identity comes from. That is where we find the fuel for ethical action. In relationships, we define our being and become who we are. What if, then, the space we share with others becomes the center of moral attention, and the way that space is changed (better or worse) is how we chart moral progress?

At one level, this book speaks an obvious truth. All human lives are embedded in relationships, some intimate, some efficient, some adversarial or dangerous. Popular culture presumes this truth but rarely reflects upon it. The TV series *Friends* is by title and concept all about the funny, paradoxical, and poignant relationships that give meaning to the day. The acclaimed series *Lost* is nothing without the interplay of all kinds of creatures, some rare and mysterious. Pick your own media favorites. Every story that has ever been told elaborates on the importance and volatility of relationships. Here we intend to reflect upon reasons why relationships define the good, and how relationships shape our ethical problem-solving.

A note of caution: Communitarianism is not a tool to improve your relational skills. It is a way of thinking about the moral life that fixes our attention away from the rights and obligations of the self, and centers instead on the social matrix in which we gather all we know about the true, the good, and the beautiful. In communitarianism, we understand that we are social beings who are constituted through others.

THE AUTONOMOUS INDIVIDUAL

Since the Enlightenment of the eighteenth century, we have been led to believe that we are autonomous individuals. Descartes said it best: "I think, therefore I am" (1637, Part IV). We have grown up to suppose that we make decisions all by ourselves and then live with the consequences. Many are the leaders in Western culture who have taught this lesson.

To understand the Enlightenment mind, both terms are needed, "autonomy" and "individual." What prevailed was the cult of human personality in all its freedom. Human beings were declared a law unto themselves, set apart from everything that claimed their allegiance. Human personality was sovereign, independent of any authority. Individuals were understood as ends in themselves, and self-determination became the highest good. Liberty was the inalienable ingredient that made humans human. While knowing deep down that humans were finite, Jean Jacques Rousseau promoted a limitless, radical freedom—not just liberty from nature, from God and the church, but freedom from any authority. Autonomy became the core of our humanness and the central ideal of life. "Find your autonomy" became life's calling. "Live free" is the lyric of the good life. For the English philosopher and physician, John Locke (1632–1704), the innermost self defined our humanity and must be protected from intrusion by government or any other outside force.

Communication scholars have long understood that autonomy is a concept that arose after the development of movable type in the fifteenth century. Before printed materials were common and many people knew how to read, people understood that everything they knew had come from others. It could not be otherwise. Builders learned their trade through apprenticeships with master craftsmen who gave directions, demonstrated techniques, and supervised the work of their students so it was done to their satisfaction. Artists learned in the same way, following the oral instructions of their teachers. Because knowledge was the direct result of mentoring, builders and artisans may have improved upon what they learned, but they always understood that their own expertise was the result of what others had taught them.

With the rise of printed materials, the direct connection between teacher and student began to disappear, and new ideas about self-taught individuals, or autodidacts, arose. No longer did learning require the physical presence of the teacher. With Bibles, encyclopedias, and manuals of all kinds, people could learn by themselves, or so it seemed. We have often heard statements such as "I taught myself how to cook" or "I passed the bar exam without any help" or "I built this boat all alone." No doubt a lot of individual effort went into all of these endeavors, but they were solitary only in appearance. Chefs wrote the cookbooks, lawyers wrote the legal tomes, and designers wrote the boat-building manuals. Seeing only the words on paper or on screen, we have a tendency to discount the authors of the information we read. We flatter ourselves with the illusion of being autonomous.

Communitarianism is an antidote to this illusion. Instead of a politics of individual rights, it promotes an ethics of the common good. Communitarianism critiques the ideology of individualism. Noted authors Michael Walzer, Michael Sandel, and Charles Taylor argue that individual identities are constituted through a social process that negotiates "the good."[2] Much of what we consider individual effort is really a shared achievement. For communitarians, the liberalism of John Locke and John Stuart Mill isolates persons from their history and culture. Locke's dualism of individual and society is overcome in communitarianism. All moral matters involve the community. Our personal well-being is interlocked with the health and vitality of the people we live and work with. The real cornerstone of the political order is not the bold, solitary decision-maker guiding the political process, but wisdom born of long social struggle. Concepts of the good reflect the values of the community rather than the expertise of theorists removed from everyday affairs. Rather than individual rights as the integrating norm, our obligations to sustain one another define our existence. As Japan taught us with the 2011 Tohoku earthquake and tsunami, the communitarian spirit comes through in times of crisis.

MAINSTREAM ETHICS

Ethical thinking in the Western tradition is rooted in the individual decision-maker, and for good reason. Persons involved in moral decisions must have the freedom to make choices, otherwise they cannot be held accountable for their behavior. From this focus on the decision-maker, three prominent ethical systems have emerged: virtue, consequences, and duty.

Confucius (551–479 B.C.) was the first, known to history at least, to create a morality of virtue. More than a century later, Aristotle developed virtue ethics systematically in the West. Virtue ethics considers moral behavior in terms of the kind of persons who make decisions and the way behavior shapes character. Excellence in virtue, not social position, determines our standing. And virtue requires that we persist in moral behavior until it becomes second nature, habitual, common—the definition of our character. Virtue ethics assumes that when we learn empathy, we will not only understand how our actions affect others but we will feel it. We will become empathetic. Practice makes perfect.

Which virtues are celebrated and practiced depends on one's definition of the hero, the full-grown person, the mature character. Aristotle put courage and generosity high on lists to cultivate. Don Vito Corleone prized loyalty and obedience. Bill Klem liked the consistent, dispassionate ability to see and call baseball's strike zone. Whatever your virtue, it must be widely accepted and admired, or else you are probably using rhetoric to fool yourself into a "feel good" moralism. Virtues are time-tested, popular, celebrated character traits that define the good person fully formed. For students, try effort and perseverance. For media professionals, try honesty and clarity. When we develop our capacities as human beings to the fullest, we achieve what Aristotle in his *Nicomachean Ethics* called *eudaemonia*—our well-being, happiness, flourishing.

Virtue ethics, however, can exaggerate what personal motivation can accomplish. Some critics of broadcasting have suggested that the industry could be morally overhauled if we trained virtuous people to work in all phases of television. Motivated by good intentions, they would transform broadcasting gradually as they reached a critical mass. But highlighting personal motivation while ignoring systemic, structural constraints is troublesome. The practice of piety does make people pious just as the practice of telling the truth makes for honest people, but institutional and systemic structures reduce the choices of virtuous people and therefore limit their influence. As long as the structure of its institutions remains intact, the most virtuous professionals in the world would have minimal impact on the media industry. To be sure, one ought to act as a virtuous person would act, but there are often dilemmas, options that are equally bad, and problems that honesty, loyalty, courage, or the other virtues do not address.

Consequentialism is the most common type of moral decision-making in democratic societies. Philosophers refer to it as teleological ethics, from the Greek word *telos* meaning "goal." Consequentialism asks what goals I want to reach and defines moral behavior as whatever fulfills those aspirations. Consequentialism considers the effects of behavior or policy rather than the intrinsic rightness or wrongness of acts themselves.

The most popular form of consequentialism is utilitarianism, as articulated by Jeremy Bentham in his *Introduction to the Principles of Morals* in 1789. His method of moral decision-making was to compare options by calculating the amount of happiness that each would produce. The best decision was the one that yielded the greatest amount of happiness in the lives of everyone affected. Judged by its beneficial effects, ethics became a type of mathematics for Bentham and its practicality has been immensely attractive.

John Stuart Mill embraced and advanced Bentham's central idea that happiness was the sole end of human action and the test by which all conduct ought to be judged. "Actions are right in proportion as they tend to promote happiness; wrong as they tend to produce the reverse of happiness" (Mill [1861] 1979, 7). With later utilitarians expanding on the notion of pleasure, measuring rightness or wrongness has become a definitive guideline for aiding our ethical choices.

Utilitarianism became an attractive and powerful ethics in democratic societies. It rejects all forms of moral absolutism that claim some actions are always wrong. It does not require belief in God or in a universe of natural laws, and it brings together disparate segments of a diverse society. Moral action based on the degree to which it is helpful or harmful is rooted in the ordinary human motivation to avoid pain and pursue pleasure. Mill's *On Liberty* (1859), written two years before his *Utilitarianism*, is the bible of democratic politics, arguing for the greatest possible liberty, limited only by harm to others. Everyone's well-being is considered equally; the pleasure of the peasant is as important as the pleasure of the king. The difference between democracy and aristocracy hinges on the notion that everyone counts just once.

Utilitarian reasoning pervades North American life, politics, and the professions. Curricula, the policies of media organizations, codes of ethics, and media textbooks are dominated by various strains of it. A utility calculus fits the press's zeal for the public's right to know, as well as with the commitment in public relations and advertising to provide clients with the maximum benefits at the least cost. For the entertainment industry, utility resonates with capitalism's supply-and-demand principle and an institution's risk-benefit calculations.

In some media situations, consequences are a reliable guide. But this theory depends on assessing consequences accurately, when in everyday affairs, the results of our choices are often blurred, especially in the long term. Furthermore, presuming that one factor determines what we morally ought to do is an inadequate framework for navigating such issues as distributive justice, diversity in popular culture, violence in television and cinema, truth telling, social network technology, and conflict of interest. The simplicity of this one-factor model is appealing, but utilitarianism leaves out whatever cannot be measured. We are left with the anomaly that the ethical system most entrenched in the media industry is poorly suited to resolving its most persistent headaches.

A third compelling ethical system, and usually the strongest alternative to consequentialism, is duty. Moral action is considered a duty or obligation always to be obeyed except possibly under rare conditions of extreme crisis. In Immanuel Kant's version (1785, 1788), humans live according to formal laws that must be observed. Moral imperatives are statements of what right and wrong mean. Fundamental moral structures embedded in human nature are as basic to moral theory as cells are to biology. Kant was trained in mathematics and physics, and the moral law was the analog of the unchanging law of gravity. In 1755, Kant's first major book, *Universal History of the Nature and Theory of the Heavens,* explained the structure of the universe exclusively in terms of Newtonian science. Newton's cosmology meant that absolutes were unquestioned.

Lawyers, physicians, plumbers, and big-box cashiers are to follow moral laws as the exercise of their will. Students refuse to cheat even if they can get away with it simply because it is wrong. Because their work in a democracy is so important, media professionals may sacrifice profits to fulfill moral imperatives. It is a person's will, not merely his or her knowledge, that needs nurture and growth. "Good will shines forth like a precious jewel," wrote Kant ([1785] 1964, 62). We are pointed beyond selfish considerations and emotional inclinations to the highest good— living dutifully in accordance with moral absolutes. Everyone ought to keep the promises they make. Telling the truth is always right. We ought to do what is morally right, said Kant, even if the sky should fall, whatever the consequences.

Duty ethics enables us to live beyond subjective approaches that are easily rationalized when convenient or when our moods change. The media's decisions and policies can be self-serving, and practitioners defensive when criticized. Competition and careerism often cloud the application of professional codes or ethical guidelines. Duty ethics encourages faithful and responsible practice whether the circumstances are positive or negative. Duty ethics makes message production more than word-craft or spin. Transparency in communication is nonnegotiable (Plaisance 2007). Deception by the press to get a good story or by advertisers to sell products cannot be excused. Dishonesty in public relations is unacceptable.

Despite its enormous importance in the history of ideas, the Kantian duty tradition is trapped in the rationalist fallacy: Reason determines both the problem and the solution. Reason opens ethical analysis and closes it. Reason is not just an important component in ethics, but determinative of it. Kant assimilated ethics into logic. Supposedly free of contradiction, basic rules of morality are created that everyone is obliged to follow and against which all actions can be evaluated. For ethical rationalists, the truth of all legitimate claims about moral obligation can be settled by formally examining their logical structure.

This tradition of rationalist ethics represents the Enlightenment mind and is correctly criticized as unsuitable for the transnational and intercultural media ethics needed today. The moral being of this tradition is not a universal person as it supposed, but a rational individual defined by a particular time and place. Abstract ethical principles, conceived in the Western mind but presumed true for all cultures, are no longer seen as neutral, but as the morality of a dominant gender and class. Moral absolutes were possible in the age of Newton's cosmology of the universe as a machine, but we live on this side of Darwin, Freud, and Einstein. Defending an abstract good is now considered intellectual imperialism over the moral judgments of diverse communities. We need another kind of ethical principle.

STARTING OVER

The classical canon has been largely monocultural. Despite all of its achievements, the field must become multicultural, gender inclusive, and transnational. Given the power of global media corporations and the high-speed electronic technologies that have come to characterize the media worldwide, it is imperative that ethics be broad enough to match their international scope. Communitarianism is the harbinger of the new day at hand.

In spite of their major differences, these three mainstream ethical systems make individual choice and accountability their centerpiece. Aristotle promoted self-realization, utilitarianism promoted individual autonomy, and Kant promoted rationality. Ethics that depend on the rules, principles, and doctrines of these mainstream approaches is known as formalist ethics, reasoning grounded in prescriptions, norms, and ideals beyond society and culture. In formalist communication ethics, an apparatus of neutral standards is constructed in terms of the major issues that media practitioners face. Moral agents apply these standards consistently and self-consciously. Codes of ethics provide the basic rules of morality that ought to be followed and against them all failures in moral duty can be measured.

Communitarianism insists that we start over. In contrast to commands from the top down, morality is a community product: Moral values unfold through human interaction. Only in community are there ethical formation, action, and accountability.[3]

Moral commitments are embedded in the practices of social groups. They are expressed as a community's values and beliefs. Moral values develop through community formation, not in isolation. The moral life is intelligible as shared human experience rather than abstract theory. Goodness and badness do not merely express subjective attitudes, but are judgments a community together believes to be true about the world. In dialogue, we discover good reasons for acting. More than simply being open to the other party's perspective, we actively listen and contribute with a view to discovering mutual truth we can defend publicly.

Feminist ethics has been explicit about this commitment to contextual values. According to Nel Noddings, an ethics that derives conclusions logically from hierarchical principles is irrelevant: "Moral decisions are, after all, made in real situations; they are qualitatively different from the solution of geometry problems" (1984, 3). Likewise in communitarian ethics, rational calculation and impartial reflection are replaced by communal dialogue. Formalist ethics fails to recognize that while humans do reason morally, they forget and remember, struggle with the past and hope for the future, listen and speak, show remorse and make excuses. It is best not to leave individuals to make difficult choices alone. Without conceptions of the good that they believe with others, there is only moral confusion.

Alasdair MacIntyre's *After Virtue* (2007) offers a similar critique in historical terms. One great mistake of the Enlightenment Project, he says, was "the tendency to think atomistically about human action and to analyze complex actions and transactions in terms of simple components" (204). MacIntyre advocated a new perspective on moral philosophy rooted in the way humans actually experience life and how they interpret it, that is, in community. Our common social and emotional experience helps us make sound moral judgments. Therefore, the teaching, acquisition, and exercise of morality can occur only if we construct "local forms of community within which civility and the intellectual and moral life can be sustained through the new dark ages which are already upon us" (MacIntyre 2007, 263). To MacIntyre, our fragmented society has no conception of the common good and no way to persuade one another about what it may be. For the communications enterprise, therefore, the shift from formal logic to community formation is appealing, and necessary for its future vitality (cf. Borden, 2007).

In making this shift, virtue, duty, and consequences do not disappear from the ethics agenda. They are fundamental components of the moral life. Communitarian ethics rejects the Enlightenment formulation, but the issues remain. Communitarian ethics goes beyond the Enlightenment without forgetting it.

Concepts from the classics enrich moral discourse. Aristotle's "citizen of the polis" is a hint toward communalism, and his notion of practical wisdom needs to be accounted for in theorizing yet today. Mill's concern with the tyranny of the majority is of ongoing importance in moral theory. While Kant's universal model is outmoded, his "principle of humanity" has been unmatched in ethics until now (Plaisance 2009, 50). Communitarianism is a neoclassical theory, fundamentally different than, but enriched by, the intellectual struggles of an earlier time and place.

As a neoclassical theory, communitarianism illustrates a different understanding of theory than the classics represent. Theories are historically situated. They address some issues but not all. Principles are therefore conceived in dramatically dissimilar terms. In the theoretical model of this book, principles are not metaphysical givens, but propositions about human existence. These concepts are provocateurs, not an authoritative canon of self-evident truth. No longer understood as authoritative abstractions, theories empower us to think together by providing conceptual clarity to help us make compelling generalizations. Because our theories are rooted in our core beliefs rather than in scientific certainty, they give us ethical discourse for grounding classroom discussion, professional morality, and public debate. Communitarian ethics is not static and scholastic, but a dynamic body of commitments that release the moral imagination.

WORLDWIDE ETHICS

The mainstream ethics of the North Atlantic has been enormously powerful.[4] But for everything that formalist ethics accomplished historically, it is now seen as parochial, the canon of the old Western tradition that does not fit a multicultural world.

Communitarian ethics is transnational in a way Eurocentric ethics is unable to match. It meets the most stringent tests of non-parochialism. Seeing ethics in terms of human relationships rings true both North and South, and in Western and Eastern cultures. With various versions of it in languages, nations, and groups of people everywhere, communitarian ethics enriches our appreciation of its core values.

In the Jewish tradition, Martin Buber wrote that genuine dialogue ought to be humankind's primary aim (1965, 209–24). Dialogue is to our humanness what blood is to the body: when the flow of blood ceases or becomes diseased, the body dies; when dialogue stops, love disappears, and hate and resentment are born. Buber (1970) calls the dialogic relation a primal notion in his famous lines "In the beginning is the relation" (69) and "The relation is the cradle of actual life" (60). He intends that as a description of being. Relationships, not individuals, have primacy. The one primary word is the combination I-Thou. The relational reality is basic. A person grows only through interaction with others. In Emmanuel Levinas (1985), the infinite is revealed in face-to-face encounters. The Other's presence involves an obligation to which I owe my immediate attention. When I face the Other, I see not only flesh and blood but all humanity. Together Buber and Levinas enable us to endorse the interactive relation as the normative apex of communication. Media are judged by the ultimate test: Do they sustain dialogue, enhance it long term, and thus contribute to human well-being?

Professor Martin Buber in his garden (© David Rubinger/CORBIS).

In Paulo Freire's (1970) language, we become fully human only through dialogue. Through dialogic communication, we can gain a critical consciousness to liberate us from oppression (Freire 1973). Freire summarized the dialogical relation this way:

> There is no longer an "I think" but "we think." It is the "we think" which establishes the "I think" and not the contrary. This co-participation of Subjects in the act of thinking is communication.... Communication implies a reciprocity which cannot be broken.... Communication is not the transference of knowledge, but the encounter of subjects in dialogue in search of the significance of the object of knowing and thinking. (1973, 137–39)

Without dialogue, there is conquest, manipulation, and imprisonment in antagonistic relationships. "Dialogue is the loving encounter of people," according to Freire. "They transform the world and in transforming it, humanize it for all people. This encounter in love cannot be an encounter of irreconcilables" (115). Liberation is a process of self-reflection achieved in public dialogue free of domination.

Ubuntu is an African worldview, an indigenous belief system that represents communitarian ideals (Christians 2004). The word *ubuntu* is a traditional African concept from the Zulu and Xhosa languages that is typically translated as "humanity toward others." The term is derived from the Zulu maxim *umuntu ngumuntu ngabantu* meaning "a person is a person through other persons" or "I am because of others," which "means that a person depends on personal relations with others to exercise, develop and fulfill those capacities that make one a person. …Personhood comes as a gift from other persons" (Schutte 2001, 12).

In Louw's (2004) perspective, *ubuntu* is an indigenous aphorism that "serves as the spiritual foundation of African societies" (2), however diverse Africa is culturally. "Threads of underlying affinity do run through the beliefs, customs, value systems, and socio-political institutions and practices of the various African societies" (2). In this sense, *ubuntu* is the basis for sustainable African values and the African renaissance. Simultaneously, *ubuntu* is understood as a universal value, with humans everywhere able to understand human life according to its terms. Communitarianism as a worldview likewise overcomes the great divisions in the world today, thereby making it congenial with *ubuntu*.

Taoism sees humans as an indivisible whole, a vital organic unity with multisided moral, mental, and physical capacities (Huang 2007). The body, mind, and heart develop together, indivisibly linked. Life is a journey of releasing the sacred power residing within life itself. Taoism recognizes a mysterious power in nature and pursues the harmonious state of being united with nature so that human beings become inwardly certain that they belong to a supersensible world of soul and spirit that both surrounds and animates them. Inner harmony means perceiving one's being in relation to others and our connection to the universe. Harmony within spreads to compassion for others and oneness with the eternal. Within a community the interconnectedness of life is awakened and nourished, and we are exposed to the larger vision of what it means to inhabit the cosmos.

An impressive example of communitarian thinking about American communications was the Commission on Freedom of the Press chaired by Robert Maynard Hutchins, President of the University of Chicago, in the 1940s. Hutchins's work, published as *A Free and Responsible Press,* became known as social responsibility theory. It highlighted the commission's call for media that would serve the public, challenge state control, and give a voice to those on the margins.

Believing that the press was caught in the mystique of its own individual rights, the Commission upended both terms with the label "social responsibility." Responsible journalism neither strengthens the government in power nor insists merely on the individual right to publish and make a profit. Instead, the press must remain free from government and business pressure and be defined by its duties to the community. Reflecting communitarian ideals, socially responsible media serve as "a forum for the exchange of comment and criticism" and "present and clarify the goals and values" of the community in which they operate. Communitarians speaking of media responsibility would consult as a first priority the needs, wants, ambitions, and wisdom of their community. These commonplace recommendations were assailed by mid-century media executives but embraced by subsequent generations around the world.

In social responsibility theory and practice, reflecting communitarian values, the media propel people into democratic participation. Social responsibility theory sees journalism "as democracy's cultivator, as well as its chronicler" (Rosen

1999, 8). A specific version of it, developed in the 1990s, is called public or civic journalism. Public journalism attempts to restyle the press toward greater citizen involvement and a healthier public climate. According to Buzz Merritt, one of its architects, public journalism shifts away from conventional journalism, moving "beyond the limited mission of telling the news to a broader mission of helping public life to go well" (1995, 113).

Although the term "public journalism" has its roots in America, Sam Chege Mwangi identified similar experiments around the world to engage citizens for a healthy democracy. In Kerala, India, journalists and academics use indigenous knowledge, traditional group meetings, oral narrative, and media in local languages to improve the lives of their communities. The Australian Broadcasting Corporation in 1997 developed public forums on government and politics in Brisbane and other municipalities, but broadened the issues to include race and crime. The Swaziland Broadcasting Corporation has a weekly feature on rural communities that arises from the people's concerns and involves them in resolving these issues. And more public journalism projects have been carried out in Latin America than on any other continent (Mwangi 2001).

Inspired by communitarian social philosophy, media around the world have been turned from dependence on business and government, orienting the news media to society instead. Sometimes it comes to expression in the establishment of public broadcasting agencies, independent of government and mandated to public service. In order "to be the world's most trusted news organisation" and "to serve all audiences," BBC News declares that it aspires to "resist pressure from political parties, lobby groups or commercial interests" (BBC Statements of Programme Policy 2005/2006). Long after the end of British colonial control in Asia and Africa, the BBC continues as a media mainstay across those continents.

We need to live as world citizens today. For students and teachers, our common task is the cosmopolitan mind. As Stephen Ward (2010) puts it, media professionals need "a cosmopolitan commitment to humanity" (213); they ought to "pursue the good within the bounds of global justice" (5). Our ways of knowing need to be redirected from our immediate circles and country to a respect for humanity's moral capacity as a whole. As Kwame Anthony Appiah (2006) observes, the idea of a "citizen of the cosmos" has been in vogue since the fourth century B.C., but without meaningful implementation of it across the centuries. Regardless of the past, communitarianism insists that for the twenty-first century we have no alternative but to get it right.

Although world mindfulness is necessary in communitarian ethics, it insists on a home base to give us perspective. Indeed, dealing intelligently with the universal requires a location in time and space. Mahatma Ghandi, as he often does, says it best: "I want the cultures of all the world to blow about my house as freely as possible. But I refuse to be blown off my feet by any." Homelessness means the absence of ethics or moral indifference. But in communitarianism, it is the world that draws, not the individual who pushes. The moral imagination will be stimulated in communitarian terms among those who are bonded with the human race. For the life of the mind, the meaning and purpose of human existence are the context within which professional decisions are made and specific issues resolved. The universal human is at the opposite end of the spectrum from the individual decision maker of classical ethics.

MEDIA AND COMMUNITY

Before we proceed any further, it may be helpful to give an example of communitarianism in media experience. At least in theory, public access television meets communitarian criteria. It is active rather than passive, dialogic rather than monologic, and systemic rather than individual.

In the 1980s cable television companies made handsome profits through their exclusive use of public right-of-ways. This setup bothered citizens in many communities who believed that cable television should offer programming about local issues and concerns, not just movies and commercial programs. So communities began requiring cable companies to use a percentage of the revenue they received from subscription fees to provide channels, equipment, and training for local citizens to produce cable programming. Cable companies broadcast these programs on a first-come, first-served basis as long as they were not pornographic, seditious, or slanderous. Communities with engaged public access television have found it beneficial. More social groups participate in civic discourse and the community reaps the benefits of increased media literacy, which include heightened ability to interpret and critique media productions. The community has the technology for answering objectionable television programs with alternative ones.

Although many public access operations are poorly funded and understaffed, which leads to the kind of low-rent television parodied in the movie *Wayne's World*, there are notable exceptions. One such exception is the Minneapolis Television Network. Founded in 1983, MTN operates three nonprofit, public access channels, mostly scheduled with locally produced programming. MTN does schedule nationally distributed political programs such as *Democracy Now* and *Vets' Visits on TV*, but most of its programming originates locally. Programs based in the various ethnic communities of Minneapolis include *Somali TV*, *Ladha Ya Kenya,* and *Oromo*. Seniors, teens, and gays and lesbians produce shows. Other programs feature local politics, religious faith, and various arts. The *Earth Protector Show* focuses on environmental issues. There are tours of homes, neighborhood gardens, and cultural fairs, videos of court hearings, parades, and neighborhood watch patrols. And in *Video Voices*, students from South High School help produce programs on subjects ranging from libraries and baseball to interracial relationships and Native American languages. Minneapolis Television Network schedules whatever programs local citizens want to make, and it does not have to worry about maintaining political correctness or attracting advertising.

Five more public access channels operate on the adjacent Saint Paul Neighborhood Network (SPNN), each with a particular focus. One channel highlights religious faith; a second focuses on local personalities and a third on education; a fourth broadcasts professional staff productions about local arts, sports, and public affairs; and a fifth explores international issues. Some SPNN programs have even found second life on KTCA, the Twin Cities' PBS affiliate. These include *Kev Koom Siab*, an information program, the first public television program in the Hmong language, and *Mental Engineering*, a weekly program that analyzes television commercials.

The Twin Cities' public access channels do have parallels elsewhere, but they are mostly exceptions to anemic operations. Much of the blame for lackluster public access television has to do with the commercial orientation of cable television companies. Cable companies resist paying for channels over which they have no editorial control and from which they receive no income, so they typically comply minimally with contractual requirements for public access operations. And they have looked for legal reasons to void their commitments to pay for equipment, training, and channels for amateurs to use. Put simply, cable television companies are unhappy with the fact that public access channels reduce their profits.

Communities with lackluster public access channels share the blame for their situation. Motivation is particularly important for public access because all television production, commercial and noncommercial, is labor intensive. Programming even one channel with quality local productions requires many well-trained and reliable volunteers, so the word must get out with imagination and drive. Potential programmers need to believe that what they will undertake is significant. Apathetic communities lack the vision and determination to require adequate funding and to inspire public participation. In such communities, many residents have either not heard of public access cable television or confuse it with PBS. Either way, they end up with anemic public access operations, and this result starts a downward spiral to the termination of public access channels. Amateurish productions, which neither attract audiences nor inspire participants, provide evidence both to cable companies and communities that cable TV would improve by replacing public access with commercial television. That argument can be hard to overcome, but allowing a public access channel to languish is to surrender a potentially powerful medium for community engagement and conversation.

LOOKING AHEAD

This book uses case studies to illustrate how communitarian thinking applies to dilemmas in media production and use. Many of these stories are vintage; a few are current. Typically we find significant moments in the media that signal a democratic "tipping point." We explore communitarian ethics through noteworthy episodes and history-making persons. Rather than a plethora of cases in varying quality and sophistication, episodes are chosen that define the field at critical junctures. The cases that have made a difference are authentic and meaningful for clarifying ethical decision-making.

If reading this book fails to break some of your boundaries or redraw the architecture of your moral map, then its worth to you is a decent grade but no more. We aim for more.

First, this book should challenge moral minimalism. You ask, "Why study ethics? I have a good sense of what is right already." In that you are correct. Adults are not blank moral slates. But neither is the slate full, and often people are satisfied with less, rather than more.

A minimalist says, "I am the sum of my quarks and gluons. If you want moral expertise from me, enable my brain chem to link up in 'right thinking' fashion, and the issue is settled." But of course such a plan is hopelessly naive. Taking a step forward in the moral life is no more a matter of acquiring new quarks than is building a friendship or falling in love. We need a bigger picture of the human person, who is obviously more than the sum of particles and animal adhesive. Biology teaches about the mechanics, but moral education addresses the will, the passions—your hopes and dreams.

Likewise, we need a larger picture of human life than the one provided by atomistic individualism. To speak of character, virtue, duty, or habits of the heart requires more vocabulary than quantum physics, and more also than personal, inner, or mental growth. We cannot, in fact, think about character or virtue apart from the vital social and communal context in which our identity is formed. Growing the moral imagination is a communitarian project. The minimalist will miss moral maturity, not because morality is a phantom, but because the vocabulary of minimalism is inadequate. So the first boundary this book should break is the limit on learning imposed by inadequate views of human experience. To be human means to be in relation. When you understand that, you are ready for moral growth.

Second, this book should challenge moral indifference. Tolerance is a virtue, but today tolerance is often stretched to mean "keep your moral judgments to yourself; do not mess with anyone else's business." Tolerance can become indifference, which isolates the self from others in the name of reducing or avoiding conflict. Before long, you construct a moat around your own moral awareness with "no trespass" signs posted to keep others away. The island you try to construct becomes another face of minimalism—the notion that contending about right and wrong is hopelessly subjective and self-defeating, not to mention annoying.

But indifference is a sign of fatigue, not one of the virtues courageously won by centuries of moral reflection. Indifference is an excuse for inattention, retreat, and sloth. Finding moral wisdom is not a journey in futility. We present here a way to frame moral insights that is not an offense to our neighbors, not a power trip for bigoted egos, not an imposition of "personal values."

Finally, this book aims to challenge technicism as a universal solution to humankind's gaps in prosperity. The French thinker Jacques Ellul used the term *la technique* to describe the modern solution to every dilemma: choose efficiency, get the job done, and move on. Every human institution, Ellul said, is driven by it; every human plan of action bows to it. In all things be efficient and life will be good. If you believe that, we aim (along with Ellul) to convince you it will not hold up.

Communitarianism takes its direction not from industrial planning but from ceremonial and ritual sharing. James Carey (1989, ch. 1) helped us understand that genuine communication is not the transport of information from point A to B, but the maintenance and renovation of human culture through symbol making—always a community ritual.

We acknowledge the strong grip of technicism on every class you take and paper you write, every purchase you make or plan you devise. This book insists that technicism should be understood for what it is—overrated and much less useful than we have been led to believe. We should reconsider technicism as the operating norm in moral decision-making and realize that social transformation requires more than quick fixes.

Now it is time for you to join the conversation. You may not be or become a media practitioner, but you will certainly be a consumer. As you bring your voice and mind to the big questions before us, note that you are acting as a person-in-relation. You are practicing what the long c-word represents.

NOTES

1. Communitarianism is the best umbrella term for this family of concepts rooted in the Latin noun *communis*. Its international usage recommends it also, where it serves as a generic term linking together specific ethical theories from different parts of the world. See, for example, Bell's (2009) review of the way Confucian ethicists connect their theory to communitarian ethics.

2. These philosophical communitarians criticized Rawls' (1971) liberalism for stressing the conditions of individual freedom at the expense of the common good. Along with Alasdair MacIntyre, they have rejected Amitai Etzioni's use of the term as Director of the Center for Communitarian Policy at George Washington University. They have basically ignored Etzioni's program and so do the authors, citing him but once (chapter 5). *Ethics for Public Communication* primarily links Charles Taylor with like-minded theorists across the globe rather than reduce communitarianism to the conservative and American political agenda of Etzioni's "The Communitarian Network." For a history of communitarianism and a review of its international usage, see Bell (2009). *EPC's* website expands on the meaning of this term and our rational for using it.

3. In a historical review of the evolution of normative theories of public communication, "citizen participation" is being affirmed internationally at present as the new norm of public discourse. It is seen as replacing earlier dominant traditions, such as the libertarian paradigm with its core commitment to the individual (Christians et al. 2009, ch. 2). Communitarian ethics puts the "citizen participation" model to work (pp. 58-64; see Christodoulidis 1998).

4. Two books illustrate the worldwide influence of the classical canon: Francis Kasoma's *Journalism Ethics in Africa* (1994) and Venkat Kyer's *Media Ethics in Asia* (2002). Both account for local and regional initiatives in theory and practice, but the concepts of virtue, utility, and duty in Western terms are included throughout.

REFERENCES

Appiah, Kwame Anthony. 2006. *Cosmopolitanism: Ethics in a World of Strangers*. New York: W. W. Norton & Company.

BBC. 2005. "Statements of Programme Policy 2005/2006." <http://www.bbc.co.uk/info/statements2005/pdfs/news.pdf>.

Bell, Daniel. 2005. "Communitarianism." *Stanford Encyclopedia of Philosophy*, pp. 1–25. <http://plato.stanford.edu/entries/communitarianism>

Borden, Sandra. 2007. *Journalism as Practice: McIntyre, Virtue Ethics and the Press*. Adlershot, UK: Ashgate.

Buber, Martin. 1965. "The History of the Dialogic Principle." In his *Between Man and Man*, 209–24. Translated by W. Kaufman. New York: Macmillan.

———. 1970. *I and Thou [Ich und Du]*. Translated by Walter Kaufmann. New York: Scribner.

Carey, James W. 1989. *Communication as Culture: Essays on Media and Society*. Boston: Unwin Hyman.

Christians, Clifford G. 2004. "*Ubuntu* and Communitarianism in Media Ethics." *Ecquid Novi* 25 (2): 235–56.

Christians, Clifford, Glasser, Theodore, McQuail, Denis, Nordenstreng, Kaarle, and White, Robert. 2009. *Normative Theories of the Media: Journalism in Contemporary Societies*. Urbana: University of Illinois Press.

Christodoulidis, Emilios A., ed. 1998. *Communitarianism and Citizenship*. Aldershot, UK: Ashgate.

Descartes, Rene. 1988. *Discourse on Method*, 2d ed. Translated by D. A. Cress. London: Hackett. [originally published 1637]

Ellul, Jacques. 1964. *The Technological Society*. Translated by J. Wilkinson. New York: Random Vintage. [originally published 1954]

Freire, Paulo. 1970. *Pedagogy of the Oppressed*. New York: Seabury.

———. 1973. *Education for Critical Consciousness*. New York: Seabury.

Iyer, Venkat, ed. 2002, *Media Ethics in Asia: Addressing the Dilemmas in the Information Age*. Singapore: Stamford Press Pte Ltd.

Kant, Immanuel. 1964. *Groundwork of the Metaphysic of Morals*. Translated by H. J. Paton. New York: Harper Torchbooks. [original work published 1785]

Kasoma, Francis P., ed. 1994. *Journalism Ethics in Africa*. Nairobi: African Council for Communication Education.

Levinas, Emannuel. 1985. *Ethics and Infinity: Conversations with Philippe Nemo*. Translated by R. A. Cohen. Pittsburgh, PA: Duquesne University Press.

Louw, D. J. 2004. "*Ubuntu:* An African Assessment of the Religious Other" [Online]. <http://www.bu.edu/wcp/Papers/Afri/AfriLouw.htm>.

MacIntyre, Alasdair. 2007. *After Virtue: A Study in Moral Theory*, 3d ed. Notre Dame, IN: Notre Dame University Press.

Merritt, Davis. 1995. *Public Journalism and Public Life: Why Telling the News Is Not Enough*. Hillsdale, NJ: Erlbaum.

Mill, John Stuart. 1975. *On Liberty*. New York: Norton. [original work published 1859]

———. 1979. *Utilitarianism*. Indianapolis, IN: Hackett. [original work published 1861]

Mwangi, Sam Chege. 2001. "International Public Journalism." *Kettering Foundation Conversations* 21 (1): 23–27.

Noddings, Nel. 1984. *Caring: A Feminine Approach to Ethics and Moral Education.* Berkeley: University of California Press.

Plaisance, Patrick. 2007. "Transparency: An Assessment of the Kantian Roots of a Key Element in Media Ethics Practice." *Journal of Mass Media Ethics* 22 (2–3): 187–207.

Plaisance, Patrick. 2009. *Media Ethics: Key Principles for Responsible Practice.* Thousand Oaks, CA: Sage Publications.

Rawls, John. 1971. *A Theory of Justice.* Cambridge, MA: Harvard University Press.

Rosen, Jay. 1999. *What Are Journalists For?* New Haven, Conn.: Yale University Press.

Schutte, A. 2001. *Ubuntu: An Ethic for a New South Africa.* Pietermaritzburg, SA: Cluster Publications.

Ward, Stephen J. A. 2010. *Global Journalism Ethics.* Montreal: McGill-Queens University Press.

PART I

News

CHAPTER 1

✍

Edward R. Murrow and Public Information

"The End of News" was the essay's title, and its view of American journalism anticipated a fizzle-out ending: "Newspapers find themselves less popular than ever before, at a time when the newspaper industry itself is losing readers.... Today's journalists...often seem less willing to resist political pressure....News organizations, rather than push back against the forces confronting them, have too often retreated and acquiesced" (Massing 2005). Bad news for American democracy. Bad news for an informed electorate and community of citizens. Perhaps most troubling was David Mindich's study, published the same year, which found that young adults just did not care.

(Mindich 2005)

The first medium for the first human was voice. It still is, for nearly every human, the first means of signaling need, happiness, want, discomfort, and the elusive, conflicted appetite for human company. We speak to identify ourselves and listen to others as a first round at clarifying what's out there moving about. And just as early in life, we listen and hear what's moving about, reacting with fright, excitement, gladness, attachment, desire, and suspicion, to name just a few of the emotions that sound evokes. The great commentator on oral culture, Walter Ong, said of sound, "Communication, like knowledge itself, flowers in speech" (Ong 1967, 1).

Today, speech is much less a taken-for-granted good. We listen to leaders orate on a chronic social ill, often with intensity and the appearance of the will to act, knowing that the most important speeches are vetted by professional writers, public relations counsel, maybe lawyers, and frequently by those consultants whom we call, derisively, spin doctors. We begin to wonder who we are listening to—the speaker or a focus group that has assured whatever powers want more of it that the message will sell. To take a speaker's words at face value is naïve. We are being suckered by rhetoric. We have learned that messages from leaders are fluffy frosting covering a block of concrete. Words pile up, nothing changes.

That is especially problematic when speech tries to inform us about world events. To be a thinking citizen, we need to know what leaders in Pakistan or the United Kingdom, Beijing or Buenos Aires, are doing, plotting, and planning. The most gripping world news is about war, and there too, few of us will ever see it firsthand. We need thoughtful professionals whom we trust to tell us what is changing in places we cannot go. We call them journalists. And they are under pressure today, together with the minions in business and government on whom they report.

This chapter, similar to those that follow, focuses on a "tipping point" case that illustrates freer, deeper talk between people committed to mutual well-being. That kind of talk can bring positive change. It can galvanize political and social will. Rhetoric will show up, but so will wisdom, in most cases where wide-spread participation is free and dialogical. What we do almost by nature—talk, think together, analyze, and compose scenarios for progressive action—this book argues, we can do better. The case in this first chapter, which illustrates our need for trustworthy speech, is the story of a pioneer in radio news, Edward R. Murrow. His story is set during World War II and in the years following, as Murrow became one of the most trusted voices in America. Although he never had a class in studio performance or news writing, Murrow was uniquely able to catch the passion and context of the moment. To many listeners, even beyond American shores, Murrow was a trusted voice of truth, as best a person could grasp it. The communitarian impulse we describe in this book helped Murrow stick to his responsibility, and it continues to inspire news providers to tell stories with capacity and courage, artistry and accuracy.

Murrow was born in a low-tech world. The Murrow cabin near Greensboro, North Carolina, had no electricity or plumbing in 1908. Egbert (his given name) was the third child, and the youngest to transplant when his family moved to a homestead near Blanchard, Washington, thirty miles from the Canadian border.

Ed (his preferred teen years' name) excelled at talking. He was president of his high school class and a top debater. He majored in speech at Washington State University in Pullman; he became president of the National Student Federation of America (and changed his name to Edward). Working in New York after gradua-tion, he helped displaced German scholars, mostly Jews, find a new life in America. Much talk came from young Edward, most of it serious. Still, he had not yet begun to establish his legacy (Kendrick 1969, passim).

As he did fix that legacy, his skill set combined with world history and tech-nological growth to create something no one had ever heard (or seen) before. But headlines and programs, historic as they were, should not obscure the point of tell-ing his story—which illustrates the universal human need for trustworthy talk, for information we can count on, for illuminating narratives that engage our passions and expand our minds. Murrow was a master storyteller.

From Europe in 1938, Murrow's legendary "tellings" began. A year earlier he had arrived in London to direct CBS's European operations. He had no on-air role and no training as a journalist when he arrived. He was a talent scout of sorts, finding continental leaders to provide monologues on the state of Europe for the American network. But his segues and introductions, his "take it to the next step" questions to guests, soon became a new kind of sound and voice from beleaguered Britain. Howard K. Smith, another broadcast legend, said of

Murrow: "Ed didn't know how to write as a newsman, which freed him to write with his own fresh eye and ear. I went through the files of his first broadcasts and they were just notes on paper. The man was ad-libbing transatlantic broadcasts!" (Seib 2006, 4).

Murrow was in Poland when Hitler, in March, annexed Austria in what became known as the *Anschluss*. When news of Hitler's move into Austria arrived, Murrow and his CBS partner in Vienna, William Shirer (who would later write a definitive history of the Third Reich), seized the competitive edge over rival NBC. Shirer went to London where he could freely transmit the story, and Murrow chartered a plane from Warsaw to Vienna to continue news gathering on site. On March 13, Murrow, Shirer, reporter Frank Gervasi in Rome, and others broadcast the "European News Roundup," the most innovative broadcast storytelling effort to its time: several voices located in different cities all bringing their intelligence and analyses to bear on the dangerous tidings of Nazi expansion. Murrow began this historic broadcast with words that all Americans would soon recognize: "This is Edward Murrow speaking from...". He shortened his opener, on the advice of his Washington State speech instructor Ida Lou Anderson, to "*This* is London" (emphasis on *This*, with no pause but a slight downbeat on *is London*; Seib 2006, 86). Apart from these tags, Murrow and his team had no formula to follow; they created their own as CBS nurtured its broadcast voices into reporting roles (Seib 2006, 8). Murrow's approach followed the successful "fireside talks" used by Franklin Roosevelt, becoming nearly a guest around the tables of American families. Murrow wanted naturalness in his reports on the war in Europe, not talk-at the audience but talk-with. He once advised colleagues: "Give the human side of the news; be neutral; be honest; talk like yourself... if you feel like coughing, go ahead and cough" (Seib 2006, 9). "Never sound excited," Murrow advised his European staff. "Imagine yourself at a dinner table back in the United States, with the local editor, a banker, and a professor, talking over the coffee. You try to tell what it was like, while the maid's boyfriend, a truck driver, listens from the kitchen. Talk to be understood by the truck driver while not insulting the professor's intelligence" (Kendrick 1969, 246).

Typical of his eye for the commonplaces, Murrow reported on a working-class district early in the London blitz:

> It's about the people I'd like to talk, the little people who live in those little houses, who have no uniforms and get no decoration for bravery.... About an hour after the "all clear" had sounded, people were sitting in deck chairs on their lawns, reading the Sunday papers. The girls in light, cheap dresses were strolling along the streets. There was no bravado, no loud voices, only a quiet acceptance of the situation. To me those people were incredibly brave and calm. They are the unknown heroes of this war. (Smith 1978, 58)

During the blitz (beginning September 1940) Murrow went to the rooftops. His bravado in the presence of falling bombs and antiaircraft fire offered Americans an unprecedented sense of the struggle. Philip Seib quotes from broadcasts delivered in late September:

Edward R. Murrow at work (© Bettmann/CORBIS).

Four searchlights reach us, disappear in the light of the three-quarter moon. . . . Just overhead now the burst of the anti-aircraft fire . . . the searchlights now are falling almost directly overhead. Now you'll hear two bursts a little nearer in a moment. There they are! That hard stony sound. (2006, 80)

Permission to risk himself on the tops of buildings during the night bombing raids had to come from Winston Churchill himself.

Murrow knew his was not the only voice attracting American attention. The Nazi-leaning priest from Detroit, Father Charles Coughlin, was heard by forty million listeners in the 1930s. His anti-Semitism fit with Hitler and Mussolini's early strategies and worked against American support for Europe. Another Charles, the famous aviator Lindbergh, was also a popular isolationist whose views enjoyed immense public support. By contrast, Murrow's admiration for the British grew by the day. He walked streets filled with fire and rubble; he knew firsthand the British resolve never to negotiate with Hitler; and he grew to greatly admire the British prime minister, who famously offered his people, in May 1940, "blood, toil, tears, and sweat."

Murrow wanted the United States to support the British; he wanted Roosevelt to declare the end of "America alone." And Murrow worked to make that happen, helping the British Foreign Office set up a bureau to measure the effectiveness of international broadcasts on public opinion. The Royal Institute of International Affairs (RIIA), now known as Chatham House, continues today as a top-tier think tank on international politics.

Did Murrow cross a line, take sides, become an actor more than a reporter? Seib (2006, 58, 73) surmises:

> If there was a political purpose behind his reporting, it was a desire to let the world know about the evil of Hitler's Germany. . . . A purist ethical argument could be made that a journalist should not be so closely involved with the subject of his coverage [but] ethical flexibility is necessary when the stakes are so high.

And Murrow himself advised:

> Occasionally, in reporting this war, the reporter is obliged to express his personal opinion, his own evaluation of the mass of confusing and contradictory statements, communiques, speeches by statesmen, and personal interviews. It has always seemed to me that such statements of personal opinion should be frankly labeled as such without any attempt to cloak one's own impressions in an aura of omnipotence. (Smith 1978, 63)

SOUND AND SIGHT

Humankind's first saved messages were not sounds, of course. Before audio tape, there were rock walls and pigment. Magdalenians (18,000 to 10,000 B.C.) produced the oldest surviving two-dimensional representations of humans and animals. Historian Paul Johnson (2003, 7) states: "Art came before anything. . . . before writing . . . almost certainly before speech, at least forms of speech expressing notions which were at all complex." But Johnson's enthusiasm outruns his logic. Surely the production of early art required cooperation, reflection, selection, negotiated space, audience reaction, and a contest winner to take home the bacon. Surely these arrangements were not achieved in silence. What stories were told, what accolades bestowed, what interpretive arguments ensued, what prehistoric celebrities were created, we cannot know. But humans do little without talking about whatever it is. We can reasonably surmise that Magdalenian drawings and the artisans producing them were "lead news" everywhere stories were being told.

In Thomas Cooper's (1998) study of indigenous cultures, the word is to human life what blood is to the body. In Polynesian tribes, among the Navaho Indians in the United States and the Shuswap in Canada, speech is treasured, even given sacred status. Language is native to everyone, learned without effort and the distinctive mark of belonging to one's home community and not another. All cultures and beliefs are grounded in words. Speech and hearing are the human activities that generate oneness. In Cooper's terms, oral-aural cultures teach us "full-spectrum communication" (1998, 187): the refined art of listening to nature, telling stories that speak to the heart, healing therapy for the soul, mystical communion with the divine. Deception, slander, and inaccuracy do not just break the community's rules, but violate one's very being. Authentic communication is essential for society to survive, certainly to flourish.[1]

Humans tell stories to understand the past and clarify the future. Perhaps the impulse arises from fear of what may lie beyond our horizons. Risk management may have motivated human community and language. Even today we will pay generously for accurate predictions of tomorrow's threats and opportunities. Futurology is, finally, the story of trajectories—economic, natural, social, mystical. Murrow's innovation was to organize the best stories of the war years and transmit them to the eventual winners of World War II conflict. Winners also gain the privilege of explaining how history turns, so Murrow's analysis stuck and the rightness of his observations were finally widely recognized. Such explanatory privilege is one way we humans control the chaos around us.

Murrow's reports brought some order to a chaotic world during Hitler's Reich. Language is our common tool for controlling the roiling universe. We make distinctions by naming one orb Neptune and another Mars, one hard place Normandy and another Stalingrad. We build trust through ritual exchanges like "Pleased to meet you" or "lovely day," terms called *phatic communion* by anthropologist Bronislaw Malinowski (1923), who noted that all humans need to signal friendship (or enemy-ship). Language seeks to control reality directly through ancestral prayers. For example, the Igbo of Nigeria use a formula curse, *Kwo, uno, kwosi okiro* (wash, all of you, wash down upon all of our enemies). Trobriand Islanders chant formulae to charm their axes, making them effective gardening tools. Words said by priests at the Catholic Mass turn wine into blood, which then carries spiritual power to overcome evil. In many ways, we humans pave our way through a dense social jungle of threats, mayhem, and jeopardy merely by speaking.

Likewise, Murrow brought a distant war into American homes through a quite personal combination of voice, tenacity, courage, and conviction. Murrow made Europe's story in the 1940s required hearing for every American citizen. At a dinner in New York in 1941, Archibald MacLeish, Librarian of Congress, gave this tribute:

> You [Murrow] burned the city of London in our houses and we felt the flames.... You laid the dead of London at our doors and we knew that the dead were our dead...were mankind's dead without rhetoric, without dramatics, without more

emotion than needed be....You have destroyed the superstition that what is done beyond 3,000 miles of water is not really done at all. (Starr 2004, 379)

LANGUAGE AND COMMUNITY

The most successful touring band ever, made their music into a "space of hope" amid a culture "dominated by crushing uniformity, familiarity, and repetition," claims a grateful historian (Drabinski 2007, 27). Yet the brilliant musicians in the Grateful Dead were only half the show. Outside their venues—first the bars, then the auditoria—were fans called Deadheads who developed their own artistic and social forms, their own legendary intimacy. Jerry Garcia reflected on the Dead's creation of a musical space where modernity's sense of alienation disappeared: "The Grateful Dead have been the most intimate kind of relationship I've ever experienced...that's what we're after—a kind of community. And we have it" (Fairlamb 2007, 24). The jumping, yelling, tossing fans inside, and the t-shirt sellers outside, knew what Jerry meant. What community the Dead created grew from musical talent and experimentation, from creativity's release, committed and disciplined artistic integrity, but then from a corps of support personnel who moved the Dead through modernity's airport terminals and recording contracts, necessary alienations all. Without the Deadheads, would the Dead have lived?

Why is Deadhead community still celebrated years after Garcia's death? Why is democracy still the world's choice, given its different forms and customs and the constant struggle to maintain it? Perhaps in answering we come to recognize two universal human needs: empowerment and connectedness. We humans simply want to achieve our peace together. Significance is not won in isolation. Gold is no antidote to loneliness. A dungeon of brothers seems a fairer home than a State House run by an isolated tyrant. We want to have our say; we want the company of other voices. Both desires—framing our environment and bonding with it—require communication skills. We need reliable information about the world; we need constant interactive contact with its near points and outposts; we need to sense mutual concern. Shared meanings are the vital ingredients. We express ourselves in symbols that say who we are; we move toward one another to survive, but more, to prosper through shared stories and hopes held in common. To be the object of another's love may be all too rare but eminently human.

Communication creates relationships and empowers people to shape environments. The late James Carey (1989, 18) urged scholars to this wider vision of communication: "If the archetype case of communication under a transmission view is the extension of messages across geography for the purpose of control, the archetype case under a ritual view is the sacred ceremony that draws persons together in fellowship and commonality."

Ed Murrow, at first glance, seems a perfect representative of the narrow transmission view. He sent important information from place to place; listeners knew more as a result of his newscasts. No doubt his listeners gained a sense of empowerment as news of the war came nightly into their homes. But something much deeper was happening in the Murrow era and through his entrepreneurship: a community was forming, understanding itself, defining its purpose, and transforming from isolationist into activist, from Me to We. Murrow was doing what Carey's theoretical claim said must be done: a meaningful culture is created when speakers construct, maintain, and transform it. Carey moved the study of communication from measuring sound bites to understanding community celebrations. Murrow used the best transmission medium of his time to help create a community that knew its identity and could focus its resources and mission.

War requires sacrifice. People need reasons to do that. No one treasures death, much less the extinction of home and culture. People need a stratagem, an intelligent moral base, to put life and future on the line against a determined enemy. In prior wars, news from the front came slowly via newspaper correspondents or personal letters. During the 1940s—and long before the United States was committed to the European war—Murrow was "on air." His opener introduced a city burning, and his closer told something of a peoples' tenacity: "Good night and good luck." Murrow opened the American listener to the courage and fear of Britain's struggle. Vivid descriptions of Allied bombing raids, battles, and later, the liberation of Buchenwald, exposed Americans to war's brutality and clarified for many the reasons for winning it. Americans heard the war in his voice. At the root of Murrow's success, Philip Seib (2006, 86) suggests, was "good fundamental reporting" and hard work. This itself would have been sufficient reason to remember him. Little did the nation, or Murrow, know that his best work was yet to come.

COMMUNITY AND PERSONHOOD

In preliterate cultures, people found their identity in a matrix of ritual and story, passed down by elders and fortified by tribal tradition. But a massive shift in identity occurred with the invention of alphabets and the printing press. Using a printed page, a single person for the first time could learn independently—learn to think personally, without anyone's oversight. For the first time, a person could develop apart from surrounding tradition. A person might even enjoy the privilege of criticizing tradition. Jean Jacques Rousseau was the most outspoken advocate of this radical new sense of freedom. For him, freedom was our human purpose, and escape from tradition and elders' control was history's natural trajectory. "I long for a time," he wrote ([1762] 1961, 350), "when...I shall be myself, at one with myself...when I myself shall suffice for my own happiness." Civilization's artificial controls make us vicious, he wrote, but in the state of nature—free of tradition and social obligation—we "noble savages" live in harmony and peace.

Rousseau worked the romantic ideal of individual sovereignty, free of divine oversight, kings, and empires. From this loam and clay emerged the Autonomous Self. New distinctions between fact (knowledge) and values (morals) led Enlightenment minds toward a rationalism that relegated tradition to the backwaters while science moved to the center. Real human progress, the kind that enables human autonomy, comes through examining the facts of reality by the ultimate human tool, reason. No longer would explanatory narratives include the odd reference to unverifiable pseudo-certitudes taught by priests or embraced by ancestors. Reason was sufficient to explain the world; indeed, reason was all we had.

From that time to this, the Enlightenment ideal was the autonomous individual, alert to the world through observation and reason, choosing his or her goals with an eye to long-term self-interest, believing that history brings human progress and that technology (the fruit of reason) lights the way to human happiness. Today we disconnect fact from value as readily as we study biology and poetry in separate classes. We tend to believe that the past is benighted and the future hopeful, that human reason, if given its way, can master our most complex troubles. In Enlightenment terms, DNA may be a roadmap, but reason and calculus can find the detour that sweeps us past sickness or temper rages and helps us engineer a future of peaceful though competitive abundance.

If this description sounds anything like common sense, it is because so much of our life today is shaped by the Enlightenment paradigm. Yet its frailty forces us to consider a third way between the undifferentiated collective (a culture like ants in a hive) and the individualism of modernity's ideal (akin to the male lion—capable but isolated). That third way we call communitarianism. Although the term is sometimes used to identify a political orientation, we use it to identify a state of reality. We humans are beings in mutuality, drawn to the other by nature, such that relationships between us are the primary way we define ourselves. Who are we? Beings in relation. How do we know that? By communicating together. Is communication often good but sometimes bad? Indeed, or maybe the pendulum tilts to bad often and good only sometimes. Can we know what morally good communication is? Yes, it is symbolic interaction that enhances who we are—our relationships, our shared life, our inherent mutuality.

Mediated communication, then, is morally weighted to build life-affirming relationships. Enlightenment freedom is the absence of constraints, in Rousseau's ideal, the "noble savage" living out his natural selfhood. Communitarian freedom is the affirmation of life, talk for the sake of relationship's prosperity. Of course, these are general guidelines, but the generalizations play out well in particular cases—news stories and information being the focus of this chapter. Carey's cultural view of communication is a better explanatory model than the bare transfer of data bites characterized in the transportation model. Moral guidance is best derived from our situation in relationships. Mediated stories do their important work of shaping culture when they are truthful, just, and compassionate, for those are universal components of human thriving. We need models that reflect these ideals and social policies that lead to opportunities for creating mutuality.

WHAT MURROW DID

Following World War II, the Cold War was raging internationally (Korea) and internally (the Red Scare). Murrow wanted to produce radio and television that addressed the political hot spots. But he himself pondered the rightness of his own best work.

See It Now was invented by Fred Friendly and Ed Murrow, both with CBS, in September 1951. The new program was to provide personal and international reports, biographical features, human interest and documentary—the pulse of the day in 30 minutes, with visuals. On November 18, the show first aired with Murrow's understated promise to "not get into your light any more than I have to, to lean over the cameraman's shoulder occasionally and say a word" (Sperber 1986, 355). His reticence no doubt reflected his lifelong sense that radio, not television, was a more fitting medium for public enlightenment (Conway 2009, 167). That first half-hour included shots from London, Paris, and Korea, and the topics were serious and varied. Particularly moving was the closing sequence with soldiers pulling together their supplies before moving out to take a hill in the Korean conflict. Murrow closed with terse and terrible realism: "They may need some blood. Can you spare a pint?"

Murrow was not a "natural" at this new medium. He simply believed it was the future—how people would thereafter get insight and information about the world. Murrow's biographer described the tension he felt, his lack of fit for the job (Sperber 1986, 356):

> Murrow hated everything about television. The mike fright that beset him in radio intensified before the camera. The hot lamps exacerbated his nervous sweats, and the head-on lighting made him want to squint. His makeup ran. He needed coaching and the nonstop chain of cigarettes to get him past the nervous gesticulation that didn't matter on the radio, and the machine-gun jogging of his right knee.

The Aluminum Company of America, Alcoa, had agreed to sponsor the show, even after Murrow responded to their query about his politics: "Gentlemen, that is none of your business."

When *See It Now* produced the famous half-hour on Senator Joseph McCarthy on March 7, 1954, Murrow had doubts about using a television network to attack a single person. He worried over television news presuming to know, then reporting, motives and schemes that could hardly be fully known even by the one creating news. "Most news is made up of what happens in men's minds, as reflected in what comes out of their mouths. How do you put that in pictures?" Murrow wondered. (Kendrick 1969, 318) While McCarthyism is now a term for reckless and unfounded public accusations, in 1954 he was a prominent senator from Wisconsin during a period of intense suspiciousness inspired by the Cold War. He had risen to national fame in 1950 by claiming to have a list of members of a Communist Party spy ring employed by the U.S. State Department. William Paley, the indomitable chief of the CBS network, had warned Murrow and others that he was not favorable to a show that would expose the bitter anti-communism of the senator and call his integrity into question. In fact, the CBS network ran no promos or ads for this show, one of the most memorable half-hours in television history. Only later in 1954 did McCarthy's popularity fade when the Senate voted censure, 67 to 22.

Murrow's programs were information rich, sponsor poor. Murrow was no idealist with respect to the financial realities CBS faced. When some markets began pre-empting *See it Now* with *Amos 'n Andy*, Murrow knew he would have to "play the game" if quality journalism were to survive (Hewitt 2001, 105). That game in the mid-1950s meant Murrow would host a celebrity-based show called *Person to Person*, weekly visits to homes of the rich and famous. From 1953 to 1959, Murrow interviewed an impressive range of popular Americans: John F. and Jacqueline Kennedy (father Joseph, the isolationist ambassador to the United Kingdom when Murrow was in London, had been recalled on Murrow's recommendation), Frank Sinatra, Groucho Marx, Margaret Mead, Marilyn Monroe, and Harry Truman. TV critic John Horne called this show "low Murrow" in contrast to the "high Murrow" of *See It Now*. But *Person to Person* was still pioneer television, and celebrity interviews done without scripts drew audiences. A few years later Don Hewitt saw potential in combining the best of both and designed the legendary *60 Minutes* to bring audiences back to serious, Murrow-like reporting.

The onset of the quiz-show era spelled doom for controversial commentaries like *See It Now*. Indeed, that program ended as a weekly telecast in 1955 when sponsor Alcoa withdrew its advertising. CBS never found a regular replacement, though *See It Now* continued as an occasional TV special until July 7, 1958.

Off screen, Murrow's big moment was October 15, 1958, at the Radio and Television News Directors Association in Chicago. There he famously blasted TV's emphasis on commercialism at the expense of public service: "This instrument can teach, it can illuminate; yes, and it can even inspire. But it can do so only to the extent that humans are determined to use it to those ends. Otherwise, it is merely wires and lights in a box." The cost of that speech was the loss of Paley's support at CBS, who considered the speech to be a personal attack, the betrayal of a long relationship (Sperber 1986, 542).

Murrow contributed the first episode to *CBS Reports*, where his last major reporting milestone was aired, in November 1960, following Thanksgiving Day. Called "Harvest of Shame," it described the plight of migrant farmworkers in the United States. Murrow personally visited labor camps near Palm Beach to get the story. Although his cough was worsening, Murrow insisted. Why? "Because I hoed corn in a blazing sun," he replied (Sperber 1986, 595). In communitarian terms, Murrow understood that we have obligations to one another. Tears flowed in the screening room after the first exhibition. But Murrow wanted deep understanding, not pity, so he reworked the final scenes consistent with a documentary format: "Is it possible we think too much in terms of Christmas baskets and not in terms of eliminating poverty?... The people you have seen do not have the strength to influence legislation. Maybe we do. Good night and good luck" (Moss 1987, 43). Murrow knew that great television news does not end with pity or fear but furthers community life by promoting the mutual trust and partnership that makes it possible.

Murrow resigned from CBS in 1961 when President Kennedy asked him to head the U.S. Information Agency, to provide new legitimacy to the Voice of America. A friend to the President, Murrow took ill during the Bay of Pigs planning and later, when the invaders were repulsed and abandoned by CIA strategists, he called the entire incursion "a stupid idea." Kennedy took Murrow's counsel during the next high-stakes showdown, the Cuban Missile Crisis. But already Murrow was weakened by the cancer that would kill him in 1965 after an adult lifetime of five dozen cigarettes a day. On the day he died, Eric Sevareid, old friend and colleague on *The CBS Evening News*, said, "He was a shooting star and we shall not see his likes again."

Murrow had lived a public version of the American dream—not riches in his case, but influence and innovation. Born among small-plot farmers in Polecat Creek, North Carolina, raised among lumberjacks in rural Washington, sometimes shy, sparse with small talk, generous to friends, he was smart but not brilliant, and ambitious. NPR broadcaster Bob Edwards wrote (2004, 151–55): "Most of all, Murrow was absolutely fearless.... Nothing scared Murrow—not bombs, dictators, generals, members of Congress, sponsors, corporate executives.... Murrow could not be muscled, bullied, bought, corrupted, or intimidated." His moral code was "rooted in populism and justice," always for the underdog and always deflating the arrogant. Edwards comments that Murrow would not likely be welcome today on the channels that once carried his voice—corporatism and profit now firmly dominating the broadcast spectrum.

As with many pioneers, the legacy edits itself. Murrow's discontent at CBS and indifference to Congress during his term at the USIA tend to be overlooked as the courage of his reporting and the foresight of his call to public service (the RTNDA speech) live through others who claim to march to his cadence.

COMMUNITARIAN LINKAGES

The French philosopher Emmanuel Levinas set the "world of thought" aflame with his 1969 book, *Totality and Infinity*. Until his death on Christmas Day 1995, Levinas's flame lit fires among people unsatisfied with visions of reality—ontologies and cosmologies—making pronouncements about nature, being, existence, etc., absent the role of persons whose discernment and life histories were at the center of such elemental entanglements. Levinas put mutuality at the center of his description of human reality. Relationship to the Other was his core. Meet the Other, he urged. Take responsibility for the Other regardless of the cost. See the good (all that ethics hunts for) in the Other. Find freedom not in retreat to autonomy, but in engagement with the Other. Resist moral abstractions. Principles divorced from lived experience are bludgeons of oppression. See the Other and learn.

"The first word from the Other's face is 'Thou shalt not kill.' It is an order," Levinas writes. "There is a commandment in the appearance of the face, as if a master spoke to me" (Levinas 1985, 89). The Other's presence obligates me. Ethics is turned around—from individual decision-making to beginning and ending with the Other. From Levinas's experience as a POW in Hitler's camps, from his horror at the Holocaust (he was spared by the French army uniform he wore at his capture, but his parents perished), from his study of Husserl and Heidegger, Levinas found a philosophic breakthrough in ultimate regard for the person before you.

Murrow's professional service illustrates and exemplifies this regard for the Other. Not perfectly, certainly. Saints do not work in journalism. But Levinas never required sainthood of the Other. Being was enough. Murrow clearly opposed movements and people bent to diminish the life of the common citizen. Hitler dropped bombs on London; Murrow was there to tell about it. McCarthy's deceit tore at the fabric of social trust; Murrow exposed it. Corporate rapaciousness devastated the environment; Murrow described the problem. Even as entertainment and profit began to warp his own corporation's vision of public service, Murrow signaled the dangers of the trend by calling his profession to account.

Levinas and Murrow were deployed in different rhetorical worlds with similar passions and themes. We doubt either knew the other. We imagine each would have recognized the other. Murrow's seminal contribution was truth told with passionate reserve—never a charismatic call to action, always a courageous confrontation with the brutal facts.

Management guru Jim Collins describes contemporary corporate leaders unable to see "the brutal facts" of their business enterprise and so unable to lead (2001, 65). Confront the brutal facts, Collins urges as part of his six-point agenda (now world famous) for taking a company from good to great. Murrow was a brutal-facts confronter par excellence. As much as any journalist in American history, he opened the ears and eyes of a nation to see its vulnerabilities and take stock of its reservoir of virtue and problem-solving skills.

Utilitarians may invoke Murrow's problem-solving orientation and claim his story as theirs. Utility loves solutions that work, if only to tilt the happiness dial of the majority toward some desired end.

But utilitarians count the majority as the whole. Small pockets of people can be lost to utility's happiness principle. All strides toward "the greater good" require some surrender to the lesser bad. Murrow knew that small injustices grow. Untended gardens in a fortnight show weeds, in a month are worthless to edible plants. For the sake of the whole, even the pockets that comprise the whole, the journalist should tell stories that illuminate and refine, cast light on the shadowed corners, present the minority view. Murrow was communitarian in this sense—the long view of historical change, the short view of intolerance for incompetent leaders, and the direct view for confronting power and holding it accountable to public service. CBS news correspondent Eric Sevareid said of Murrow: "He was a great moralist, you know. He expected individuals, and his government, to live up to high moral standards. He believed in a kind of foreign policy based...on moral principles, which few people really believe in anymore" (Smith 1978, 145).

What are the options today? Is news a simple business—information wrapped around commercial appeals, the ultimate endgame a measured uptick in a corporation's bottom line? In many cases, news providers reflect the common corporate mentality of "infallible and omnipotent, glorying themselves in imposing build-ups and elaborate displays" (Bakan 2004, 5). Workers who once felt a sense of calling now face two "points of pessimism": growing demands to comply with the business goals of the industry and a decline in moral standards in the field (Gardner, Csikszentmihalyi, and Damon 2002, 128, 163). One news broadcaster told researchers: "I see the country drifting in this mindless direction [that] has invaded television news.... these forces of infotainment... are crashing through the door" (ibid., 126). Ratings rule. Personality (or bombast or just plain good looks) wins an audience. Wisdom, integrity, insight, and fairness are the stuff of ethics codes but not needed in most American news shows. Often, these qualities dampen the conflictual, emotional, and ideological reporting that seeks its niche audience and rides its ratings wave.

Not without reason, the open web has filled the gaps. Reviewing the amazing new Kool-Aid Acid Test of storytelling—the web—grassroots journal-ist Dan Gillmor points to "the wider phenomenon of citizen-generated media: a global conversation that is growing in strength, complexity, and power. When people can express themselves, they will" (2006, p. xv). The stories come from the lives of people in neighborhoods, not corporate boardrooms. This is news turned toward city streets and county parks, away from power centers, toward neighborhoods and associations, small scale by traditional news standards but immediate to the lived experience of "ordinary citizens" (the term carries both a pejorative indifference and celebrative relevance). Veteran editors and reporters and influential federal-level spokespersons do not set the agenda, but the people do. Such empowerment has always been the hope of democratic governance, a hope often buried under special interests or hidden by journalism following the dollars. Gillmor's Center for Citizen Media illustrates those who are reshaping old traditions and reviving citizen participation. People are repossessing responsibility for shaping their world.

To university readers, this grassroots participation should be common sense. Raised with the Internet, nearly all have linked-up global chains of story-sharers and friends whose actual eyes have never met. At the same time, college students have largely chosen to "tune out" of public life, as David Mindich (2005, 2) describes it.

Mindich examines what 20-somethings know. His survey includes questions such as: "Who is (celebrity name)?" And "Who are your state's senators?" "Who is (athlete name)?" and "Who is the U.S. Attorney General?" You can guess which questions score highest. Mindich's findings, published in his grimly titled book, *Tuned Out*, document that "young people have abandoned traditional news," which he defines as "general interest and political news... from newspapers, mag-azine, television, and the Web." Mindich urges that news professionals and educa-tors "make politics meaningful again" (2005, 119).

The press Murrow served is reinventing itself and refurbishing its mission. Even as Murrow did his best work in the 1940s and 1950s, American journalism was trying to find its way between the rowdy press wars of the late nineteenth century and the chilling prospect of state-controlled media arising in Asia and parts of Europe. The social responsibility theory of the press was developed in fact by scholars who wanted to reduce government influence over editorial processes. While Murrow practiced broadcast news, Robert Hutchins and his Commission on Freedom of the Press conceived a new paradigm for the press in postwar America. The Commission published its results in a little book still relevant today, *A Free and Responsible Press* (1947), made popular in the small classic *Four Theories of the Press* (1956), and now modernized as a basis for press ethics in *Normative Theories of the Media* (2009). The luminaries on Hutchins's team included Harvard philosopher William Ernest Hocking, New York educator George Shuster, and theologian Reinhold Niebuhr, among others. These formative voices were searching for new models of community, new ways to invigorate the public.

The legacy of the Hutchins Commission was a new vision of cross-cultural news coverage and citizen involvement. "Project a representative picture of the constituent groups in the society," the Report demanded of American media. "Present our corporate goals and clarify our values," it urged, asking media professionals to step into roles typically reserved for professors or priests. Give us "a truthful, comprehensive, and intelligent account of the day's events in a context which gives them meaning," the Report pled. "Public discussion...is essential to the building...of a self-governing society," to put it simply (Leigh 1947, p. xi). Bottom line: we depend on media to know our world.

Storyteller, newscaster, and commentator, Ed Murrow was part of the "greatest generation" of wartime and postwar Americans who took us from the precipice and led the nation to confront, in following decades, its failure at race and social equity. His was a career of courage and clarity, fearless storytelling, and public service. Murrow's sense of press responsibility and the Hutchins Commission Report gave common expression to identical virtues.

Where can we find such expressions today? Where does a corporate commitment to great news reporting and the competence of professionals to bring news to informed people meet? Some may cite CNN's coverage of Hurricane Katrina in 2005, or Christiane Amanpour's fearless coverage of international news (her standup to President Clinton in 1994 over Bosnia, for instance), or occasional stellar coverage of the Macondo oil spill in 2010, the courageous coverage of Egypt's popular uprising in 2011. Sheri Fink at the on-line news source ProPublica won the 2010 Pulitzer for investigative reporting. Is she and her newsroom, devoted to exposing "abuses of power and betrayals of the public trust by government, business, and other institutions, using the moral force of investigative journalism to spur reform through the sustained spotlighting of wrongdoing"[2] the new wave, recovering the Murrow legacy?

SUMMING UP

"Listening is an act of love" is the motto of StoryCorps, a New York based organization that collects personal narratives and now has the largest bank of oral histories in America. StoryCorps gets people talking. We apply that "act of love" to news journalists. Some news stories have such broad public importance that they warrant the widest possible distribution for the sake of informed people making wise decisions. This chapter describes one storyteller whose career illustrates the virtues of communitarianism. The story told here of an exceptional broadcaster and communitarian theory provides a fuller picture of roles and responsibilities born by everyone who makes, manages, and consumes mediated information. Communitarianism contends that information is purposeful, that its presentation is morally bounded, and that people are served well when these purposes and boundaries become lighthouse metaphors for journalists. We will know better who we are, what directions will serve a world community, and how to manage change, if example and theory take hold.

The purpose of news reporting is political literacy—the capacity to understand and guide cultural change. Moral boundaries enrich mutuality with truthfulness and fairness. Moral responsibility is neither rigid rule-keeping nor naïve wonderment at every faddish idea. Edward R. Murrow pursued news as aggressively as any broadcaster before or since and treasured the culture of impartiality that American journalism prizes. In 1941 he said, "It is no part of a reporter's function to advocate policy. The most that I can do is to indicate certain questions facing America. You [citizens] must supply the answers" (Seib 2006, 149). Words so glowing with virtue were spoken by a journalist whose work was pretty far from this neutral ideal. Listeners and viewers had little doubt where Murrow stood on issues, policies, and persons. At least this much must be given to the man: his message always carried a challenge (Seib 2006, 150).

Murrow distinguished himself in another way. After the declaration of war, he went on a speaking junket, earning substantial speaking fees, keeping none. Seib (2006, 102) reports that he gave the money away to the RAF fund and to Washington State University because he wanted to be believed. The message was paramount. Murrow reflected after the war: "I reported what I saw and heard, but only part of it. For most of it I have no words" (Seib 2006, 171). Journalism is not omniscient.

President Roosevelt said of him, "Ed Murrow has kept faith with the truth-loving peoples of the world by telling the truth when he tells the news. I doubt whether in all history there has been a time when truth in the news [has] ever been more needed" (Seib 2006, 147). FDR's words exaggerate only a little. Every time in every history, reliable and purposeful information is both public need and nurture. Journalism must deliver.

NOTES

1. Rather than ignoring indigenous societies, their experience with oral-aural communication is of ongoing value. According to the United Nations Working Group on Indigenous Populations, they number over 350 million people, speaking 5,000 languages in more than 70 countries. For up-to-date research on communications among today's First Peoples, see Alia (2010).
2. ProPublica's Mission is taken from its website, accessed July 19, 2010. <http://www.propublica.org/about/>.

REFERENCES

Alia, Valerie. 2010. *The New Media Nation: Indigenous Peoples and Global Communication.* New York: Berghahn Books.

Bakan, Joel. 2004. *The Corporation: The Pathological Pursuit of Profit and Power.* New York: Free Press.

Carey, James W. 1989. *Communication as Culture: Essays on Media and Society.* Boston: Unwin Hyman.

Christians, C., Glasser, T., McQuail, D., Nordenstreng, K., and White, R. 2009. *Normative Theories of the Media: Journalism in Democratic Societies.* Urbana: University of Illinois Press.

Collins, Jim. 2001. *Good to Great: Why Some Companies Make the Leap – and Others Don't.* New York: Harper Collins.

Conway, Mike. 2009. *The Origins of Television News in America: The Visualizers of CBS in the 1940s.* New York: Peter Lang.

Cooper, Thomas W. 1998. *A Time Before Deception: Truth in Communication, Culture, and Ethics.* Santa Fe, NM: Clear Light Publishers.

Drabinski, John. 2007. "The Everyday Miracle of the Occasional Community." In S. Gimbel, ed., *The Grateful Dead and Philosophy: Getting High Minded about Love and Haight.* Chicago: Open Court, 27–36.

Edwards, Bob. 2004. *Edward R. Murrow and the Birth of Broadcast Journalism.* Hoboken, NJ: Wiley and Sons.

Fairlamb, Horace L. 2007. "Community at the Edge of Chaos." In S. Gimbel, ed., *The Grateful Dead and Philosophy.* Chicago: Open Court, 13–26.

Fuller, Jack. 2010. *What Is Happening to News? The Information Explosion and the Crisis in Journalism.* Chicago: University of Chicago Press.

Gardner, H., Csikszentmihalyi, M., and Damon, W. 2002. *Good Work: When Excellence and Ethics Meet.* New York: Basic.

Gillmor, Dan. 2006. *We the Media: Grassroots Journalism by the People, for the People.* Sebastopol, CA: O'Reilly Media.

Hewitt, Don. 2001. *Tell Me a Story: Fifty Years and 60 Minutes in Television.* New York: Public Affairs.

Johnson, Paul. 2003. *Art: A New History.* London: Weidenfeld and Nicolson.

Kendrick, Alexander. 1969. *Prime Time: The Life of Edward R. Murrow.* Boston: Little, Brown.

Leigh, Robert, ed. 1947. *A Free and Responsible Press.* Chicago: University of Chicago Press.

Levinas, Emmanuel. 1985. *Ethics and Infinity: Conversations with Philippe Nemo.* Pittsburgh, PA: Duquesne University Press.

Malinowski, Bronislaw. 1923. "The Meaning of Meaning in Primitive Languages." In C. K. Ogden and I. A. Richards, eds., *The Meaning of Meaning.* London: Routledge.

Massing, Michael. 2005. "The End of News?" *The New York Review of Books* 52 (19) (December 1): 23–27.

Mindich, David T. Z. 2005. *Tuned Out: Why Americans Under 40 Don't Follow the News.* New York: Oxford University Press.

Moss, Michael. 1987. "The Poverty Story." *Columbia Journalism Review* 26 (2) (July/August): 43–54.

Ong, Walter J. 1967. *The Presence of the Word: Some Prolegomena for Cultural and Religious History.* New Haven, CT: Yale University Press, 27–36.

Rousseau, Jean Jacques. [1762] 1961. *Emile*. London: Dent.

Seib, Philip. 2006. *Broadcasts from the Blitz: How Edward R. Murrow Helped Lead America into War*. Washington, D.C.: Potomac Books.

Smith, R. Franklin. 1978. *Edward R. Murrow: The War Years*. Kalamazoo, MI: New Issues Press.

Sperber, A. M. 1986. *Murrow: His Life and Times*. New York: Freundlich Books.

Starr, Paul. 2004. *The Creation of the Media: Political Origins of Modern Communications*. New York: Basic.

Thigpen, Robert. 1972. *Liberty and Community: The Political Philosophy of William Ernest Hocking*. The Hague: Martinus Nijhoff.

CHAPTER 2

✦

Al-Jazeera English

Building a world news powerhouse has its challenges. Certainly that has been Al-Jazeera's experience. Its broadcast of the 2010 World Cup soccer games was disrupted in Jordan. Al-Jazeera accused the Jordanian government of jamming its signals to get even for Al-Jazeera demanding too high a price for the broadcasts, to which it had exclusive pay-TV rights. The Jordanian government called this claim "absolutely baseless and unacceptable" (BBC Monitoring, October 4, 2010). Earlier that same year, Yemeni authorities confiscated Al-Jazeera broadcast equipment after Al-Jazeera defied government prohibitions against reporting public demonstrations opposing the government, demonstrations that ended with security forces wounding and killing protesters. A government spokesperson said, "I believe that this measure by the Information Ministry serves Al-Jazeera and protects it from future problems" (BBC Monitoring, March 15, 2010). In May 2008, the government of Morocco blocked the Al-Jazeera television channel and al-jazeera.net after the network aired a news report critical of the President. The communication minister explained that the government's action concerned technical issues, not politics (BBC Monitoring, May 9, 2008). And on January 27, 2011, Sunni political factions in Lebanon, who were outraged by Al-Jazeera's coverage, attacked and burned the channel's offices and vans (Worth and Kirkpatrick 2011, A1). During the protest in Egypt, the government condemned Al-Jazeera as the chief culprit in fueling the unrest. Al-Jazeera's office in Cairo was burned down; its Cairo bureau chief and 7 correspondents were arrested (Lucas 2011).

These challenges are to be expected for an aggressive news operation working in a politically charged world. Al-Jazeera has muscled its way from its home on the Persian Gulf to a presence known internationally. After coming on the scene in dramatic fashion on November 15, 2006, and with the financial backing and audience strength of parent network Al-Jazeera Arabic, the English-language Al-Jazeera (AJE) nearly equals the size and influence of BBC World and CNN International. AJE is redefining international news, and as a consequence it has to contend with strong opposition, some deserved, some not.

HISTORY AND BACKGROUND

Al-Jazeera appeared as a belated answer to calls for a New World Information and Communication Order that were formalized in the 1980 proposal by the United Nations Educational, Social, and Cultural Organization (UNESCO). Developing nations had complained for decades that the dominant international news services either ignored them or parachuted in to report violence and natural disasters. Such reporting left international audiences with the misimpression that developing nations as a class were primitive, unstable, and dangerous—curiosities to be pitied and avoided, certainly not countries worthy of capital investment.

Before Al-Jazeera, world news had been gathered and reported primarily by northern hemisphere wire services such as Agence France-Presse, ITAR-TASS, Reuters, and the Associated Press. Reuters and the Associated Press also provided television stations with most of their international news footage. Developing nations wanted a viable alternative to these northern hemisphere news services, one that would report peacetime as well as war, progress as well as calamity, comfort as well as poverty, and decency as well as corruption. The major impediment, of course, was money. UNESCO's New World Information and Communication Order called for northern hemisphere subsidies for a southern hemisphere news service, as well as a formalized system of journalist accreditation (International Commission for the Study of Communication Problems 1980). The United States interpreted these two proposals as assaults on economic and political press freedoms, the final straws in a long history of America bashing. The United States withdrew from UNESCO, effectively killing any chances for a New World Information and Communication Order.

Or so it seemed until 1996, when Al-Jazeera Arabic was established by the Emir of Qatar, Sheikh Hamad bin Khalifa al-Thani. An effective business manager surrounded by Western-educated technocrats, Sheikh Hamad runs the country like a modern executive. His motto from the beginning has been: "Qatar will be known and noticed." He sees it as a "regional hub, a kind of Arab version of Switzerland: rich, neutral, and secure" (Miles 2005, 16). To stand tall among its wealthy Gulf neighbors Dubai, Bahrain, and Abu Dhabi, Qatar has focused on education and technology. Several American universities have built branches in Qatar and the think tank, the Rand Corporation, has an outlet there. Its science and technology park in Doha is approaching world-class status.

Modernizing the media has been one of Sheikh Hamad's means of moving the country forward. In his first year, the new Emir upgraded Qatar state television and began transmitting it by satellite. He decided at that time also on a new channel shielded from his control, commissioning a committee of three to implement it and a seven-person editorial board of directors to supervise it. The new channel was called Al-Jazeera, "the peninsula," after the ground on which it was located protruding from Doha into the sea. In 1998, the Ministry of Information was terminated, ending official press, radio and television censorship. Freedom of the press was written into the new Qatari constitution.

Al-Jazeera was the first satellite TV network independent of government control among the twenty-two nations of the United Arab League. AJA broadcasts from an Arab country, is managed by Arabs, and uses classical Arabic for its programming. Arabs discovered it was possible to have an Arab media system that they could respect and that news professionals had to take seriously.

After its founding in 1996, the Al-Aqsa Intifada, and the U.S.-led invasions of Afghanistan and Iraq, solidified AJA's position in international news. During the Second Palestinian Intifada (2000–2004), 50 percent of the audience deserted local state-run stations and chose AJA instead. AJA's intrusion shocked Israel. For the first time, Israeli military operations were beamed directly from the field to millions of Arab homes. The sophisticated Israeli news machine now had a competitor within Middle Eastern borders (Al-Jaber, 2004).

> Israel's traditional hegemony over the media came to an end and they realized they had to develop new strategies to win world public opinion. ... Israel could no longer claim to be using reasonable force to suppress the Palestinians, when Al-Jazeera showed otherwise. The Israelis no longer looked like the underdog; they looked like bullies, and a week after the fighting started the UN Security Council condemned Israel for its use of excessive force. ... As the Arab public followed the events of the Intifada hour by hour, Al-Jazeera became a household name throughout the Arab world. (Miles 2005, 68, 80)

During the Second Intifada, AJA outworked the competition. From its location in Ramallah, AJA covered Israeli missile attacks. Broadcasts featured the terrified voices of the suffering across the Arabic-speaking world instead of emphasizing official news conferences by military authorities. A dying Palestinian boy in his father's arms became the icon of Israel's brutality (Bakho 2007, 21–23). When Egypt sponsored a summit of neighboring nations, the state-owned press reported official news releases. AJA, however, hosted experts from across the political spectrum. AJA was the only broadcast station in Arabic that included commentary from Israel's leaders and people. AJA reported public outrage over the hesitancy of its governments to defend the Palestinians that was boiling in the streets. The deep-seated frustration and rebellion among the Palestinian rank-and-file was not only aimed at Israel's occupation but also centered on inept and corrupt leadership. For several years already, AJA had criticized Palestinian leader Yassar Arafat, winning credibility for itself that carried into its covering the Intifada violence. Across the Middle East, AJA became the channel to watch.

The extremist Taliban regime established its rule of Afghanistan in 1996, the year that Al-Jazeera was launched, and it allowed Osama bin Laden to form a base of operations for al-Qaeda there. Al-Qaeda's bombing of the World Trade Center in New York in 1993 was the first of a series of attacks on the United States, including bombings of U.S. embassies in Tanzania and Kenya in 1998, plots on the Los Angeles International Airport in 2000, and in October 2000 the bombing of the USS Cole anchored at Aden, Yemen, which killed 17 American service personnel. After the attacks of September 11, 2001 on the World Trade Center and the

Pentagon, President George W. Bush on September 20 issued an ultimatum to the Taliban regime to turn over Osama bin Laden and the al-Qaeda leaders. The Taliban demanded evidence of al-Qaeda's link to the 9/11 attacks and insisted on an Islamic Court trial if such evidence warranted further action. The U.S. policy after 9/11 would not distinguish between al-Qaeda and nations that harbor them.

On October 7, 2001, the United States, Great Britain, and coalition allies began a serial bombing campaign (Operation Enduring Freedom) to destroy al-Qaeda's headquarters and remove the Taliban regime, which controlled 90 percent of the country. In December 2001, the U.N. Security Council established an International Security Assistance Force (ISAF) to stabilize Kabul and its surroundings, with NATO members providing the core of the force.

AJA was the only foreign news service in Afghanistan on October 7. It had negotiated an agreement with the Taliban in 1999 to open a news bureau, with the Taliban conceding that it needed an outlet to state its case to the world. AJA had the sole uplink technology for live two-way communications with its headquarters in Doha. With one correspondent in Kandahar and another in Kabul, AJA used its monopoly on televised information coming out of Afghanistan to report America's first major offensive in its War on Terrorism.

After the first air assault from RAF and U.S. Air Force bombers and Tomahawk missiles, AJA's reporter in Kabul filmed the damage on the ground and interviewed the injured and those whose homes had been destroyed. During the second night of bombing, AJA's reporter stayed on the air, "estimating how many planes or missiles there were and what they might be targeting" (Miles 2005, 143). AJA's images of young Afghan children burned and suffering in Kabul hospital beds became one of the defining interpretations of the war—not only for AJA's audience but through its footage, with its logo superimposed, rebroadcast around the world. Its unrelenting pictures of death and injury, of massive shelling of villages, homes, and public buildings portrayed not a legitimate war on terror, but a hate-mongering superpower destroying a small country. And no amount of counter-publicity could reverse this interpretation. The civilian casualties took a heavy toll on the morale of coalition allies and undermined support for the war in both the United States and Britain.

During the war, AJA transmitted several video messages from al-Qaeda and Osama bin Laden. Typically they would arrive in Doha via courier from Pakistan, though on one occasion an AJA reporter went blindfolded to speak with bin Laden directly.

> The carefully staged videotapes suggest that, while totally outgunned by his opponents, bin Laden was fully aware of the importance of the propaganda battle that would accompany the military conflict.... The ensuing events changed the Western perception of AJA from a "phenomenon of democracy" to a "mouthpiece of bin Laden." (Bessasio 2005, 153)

From the beginning, AJA's motto has been to "present the opinion and the other opinion." It explained its bin Laden airings in those terms, as offering an alternative viewpoint essential to understanding the conflict. Its bureau in Kabul (bin-Laden's home territory) and its sharing the same language made AJA an appropriate outlet.

Three weeks and more than three thousand bombs after the war began, the Taliban were on the run. As the North Alliance finally approached Kabul, supported by U.S. Special Forces, scores of television journalists brought AJA's monopoly on Afghanistan war reporting to an end. But the Western media now recognized AJA as a leading source of breaking news. Setting up a bureau outside the international media mainstream proved to be a smart decision. Its presence in Afghanistan for nearly two years had given the network unique access to Afghanistan's factions and warlords, and enabled the network to understand how the Taliban authorities operated. Management decided to open other bureaus around the globe, such as in Ethiopia, potential hotspots where it could send exclusive reports in the future. In America, AJA had become a household word.

The war in Iraq provided Al-Jazeera with a worldwide exclusive. In the final hours before the Iraq war began on March 20, 2003, then President Bush told all journalists and foreign nationals to leave Baghdad "for their own safety." ABC and NBC had already left. Saddam Hussein had ejected Fox News from the country in February, angry over an Iraqi journalist's expulsion from the United States. CBS left with the warning. Having remained in Baghdad during the first Gulf War, CNN wanted to stay for this one, but the Iraqis threw CNN out two days after the invasion started. That left AJA with the only open bureau in Iraq. American network executives were concerned about retaliation from the Iraqi regime and Baghdad crowds, but AJA's decision to stay made leaving easier. All the major Western media had usage agreements with AJA and assignments with freelancers for coverage within the country. The U.S. military worked out arrangements with the news media to embed reporters with the military operations, and over the three-week offensive, 3,000 foreign reporters visited the country in these terms (Aday, Livingston and Hebert 2004).

While Western networks traveled to Washington, London, and New York, AJA focused on the war's reception in the Middle East. Quality reporting on the war was easier for Arab networks than it was for Western and Eastern ones. Most of them had Iraqis on the staff who knew the places being bombed, and they were able to see events from a native perspective. For AJA, the Iraq invasion was not simply about freedom from tyranny, like the Allies' liberation of countries in World War II. It was also about ordinary citizens caught in the middle. AJA sought to highlight their suffering. AJA's unlimited access to hospitals, bombed bridges, neighborhoods on fire, and interviews with Iraqi officials gave it the appearance of being pro-Saddam (cf. Seib 2005, 603).

Press conferences were given twice daily at Coalition Naval Command in Bahrain, and Al-Jazeera's reporters attended. These sessions were carried live, as were speeches by coalition commanders around the world, from Defense Secretary Rumsfeld and President Bush in the United States, as well as from Prime Minister Tony Blair and Foreign Secretary Jack Straw in Britain. AJA also televised live all the press conferences given by the Iraqi Minister of Information, in addition to irregular broadcasts by other Iraqi ministers and intermittent announcements by Saddam Hussein. Following its own code of ethics, AJA separated news from such commentators as Ba'athists, neoconservatives, antiwar Europeans, and Kurdish and Arab nationalists (el-Oifi 2005).[1]

During the war, AJA was the most popular television news channel in the Arab world. Its audience increased to 50 million. Many new viewers came from Indonesia, the world's most populous Muslim country, where local channel TV7 began to broadcast AJA's signal. But impressive also were the two million new European subscribers to AJA satellite or Internet during the first week of the war. The stage was set for adding an English channel.

WHAT IS AL-JAZEERA ENGLISH?

AJE's broadcast center is Doha, Qatar as with AJA, but other coequal centers include Kuala Lumpur, Washington, D.C., and London. The daily news hour is hosted from these four locations linked together live, "the news essentially following the day around the planet" (Rushing 2007, 205).[2]

AJE's *Everywoman* is the first program originating from the Middle East that makes women's issues central with stories from women around the world. The British television interviewer Sir David Frost moved to AJE in 2006 to host his weekly current affairs show, *Frost Over the World*. *101 East* covers business and politics from the East and *Inside Story* gives background and context on the day's top story from anywhere on the globe. While 24-hour current affairs are AJE's defining feature, sports and business news are included, too. In 2008 AJE won the Golden Nymph award for the "Best 24 Hour News Program" at the Monte Carlo Television Festival, and it has received nominations in other categories such as the "Best News Documentary" award. Within two years (2008), AJE reached 100 million households.

The channel is available mostly via satellite, sometimes through cable. It is also live-streamed on-line to subscribers and available on "Al-Jazeera English YouTube." It is the first global high-definition television network. It explains the world through the eyes of real people and in order to produce people-driven stories, it limits its in-house producers to 300, and commissions programs from freelancers and independents. AJE encompasses the globe with the goal it inherited from AJA—fearless journalism that sets the world news agenda.

Reversing the North-to-South flow of information is one objective. The AJE network includes areas of the world that are not on the mainstream media map. "On the day AJE launched, it ran a live report delivered by Farai Sevenzo from Zimbabwe, where no Western media had been in seven years." It was a "challenging dispatch about Mugabe's failed policies. . . . When his report was over on launch day, everyone in the Washington studio cheered because we were proud of the coverage and what it said about AJE: a network that could go where others could not, and that could speak truth to power" (Rushing 2007, 212). AJE aims to decentralize

Al-Jazeera's newsroom in Doha, Qatar (AFP/Getty Images).

the global news flow (see Wojcieszak 2007). "The fact that Doha, Qatar's capital, is not the headquarters of a great power liberates Al-Jazeera English to focus equally on the four corners of the Earth rather than on just the flash points of any imperial or post-imperial interest" (Kaplan 2009, 55).

Financial stability is a primary reason for AJE's successful entry into international news. Rather than following a strictly commercial model, AJE depends on both patronage and advertising. Ian Davis (2010) demonstrates that

> hybrid funding models lower traditional economic barriers to entry and create new potential for underrepresented voices to be heard in global venues. ... Start-up networks generally have a hard time convincing cable and satellite providers to make room on channel space already crowded with upstart networks and established content providers. ... Establishing a revenue base through the sale of airtime to advertisers requires a massive infusion of start-up capital. (3, 6–7)

Global news services must compete for a relatively select set of pan regional and global advertising campaigns such as international airlines and financial services.

Davis's analysis is correct (2010, 8–9): AJE can challenge existing global news operations because of its funding model. Industry observers estimate that the ruling royal family has supplied $1 billion to AJE in start-up costs. Such subsidy frees Al-Jazeera from the limitations of the corporate media. From newsgathering budgets to network growth, commercial broadcasters limit their business operations to the economic cycles that rise and fall. Expansion plans for commercial networks are premised on favorable demographic advertising value. Qatari finances underwrite the development of new markets by paying operational costs while AJE establishes its audience.

Besides its subsidies from Qatar, AJE has three major sources of revenue: $70 million from two sports channels with 1.7 million subscribers paying $40 a year, licensing fees for exclusive footage, and advertising income from Qatari-based companies like Qatar Petroleum. New media technologies also contribute: AJE provides video news feed services to the leading British newspapers, and its mobile phone podcasts and YouTube news channel to others. Mobile technologies have made news and entertainment programming available to Symbian and Windows phones worldwide. AJE has negotiated an on-line television package with software specialist, Global Digital Broadcast (GDBTV). According to the *Financial Times*, over 20,000 viewers in the United States pay $6 per month for on-line streaming of AJE's broadcasts. During the three weeks of fighting in Gaza in January 2009, AJE's on-line audience for Gaza coverage increased 500 percent by its broadcasts via the Livestation platform.[3]

Asia's enthusiastic reception of cable and satellite media has helped make AJE successful there. In 2008, AJE was granted distribution rights on Hong Kong cable systems and gained access to more than one million viewers. With 326 million pay-TV subscribers in 2009, Asian subscriptions exceed the rest of the world combined. The Cable & Satellite Broadcasting Association of Asia considers broadcasting and on-line video to be equally important in market planning, and AJE's membership in the association has aided network expansion eastward, as well as strengthening its digital outreach (see Davis 2010, 15–16). It has bolstered its credibility with regional viewers by establishing an editorial branch based in Kuala Lumpur rather than filing reports through Doha, London, or Washington.

Contrary to AJE's success elsewhere, the U.S. market remains elusive. "The murky image of its sibling channel" has forced AJE developers to wrestle with "a maelstrom of controversy and preconceptions" (Murphy 2007, 15). "After spending tens of millions to build high-definition broadcast facilities in the U.S., Britain, Qatar, and Malaysia, AJE found cable and satellite providers reluctant to add it to their channel packages due to its parent company's" perceived anti-Americanism and association with terrorism (Davis 2010, 16).

The war of information over U.S. intervention in the Middle East has engendered an atmosphere of mutual suspicion. "By the time the Iraq invasion was *fait accompli*, U.S. forces had twice bombed AJA facilities and held AJA cameraman Sami Al Hajj as an enemy combatant in Guantanamo Bay. ... George W. Bush's 2004 State of the Union Address maligned the network as a source of 'hateful propaganda'" (Davis 2010, 18). U.S. media-industry publications and news outlets actively perpetuate AJA's negative image. Fox News erroneously reported that AJA aired beheadings. It hosted American journalists working for AJA with the provocative caption "Traitor?" (Ackerman 2006, 20–21). Katie Couric of CBS News reported on AJE's new headquarters in Washington using the label, "Osama bin Laden's favorite network" (Rushing 2007, 202). Accuracy in Media produced the documentary *Terror Television: The Rise of Al Jazeera and Hate America Media*.

AOL and Yahoo cancelled its ad campaigns. "AJA's virtual space has also come under attack from hackers, redirecting traffic to porn sites or overwriting the channel's homepage with messages like 'Let Freedom Ring' to disrupt page viewing" (Davis 2010, 20).

Such hostility has made U.S. cable operators reluctant to carry the channel. Paul Maxwell of the cable industry guide *CableFAX*, summed up the cable distributors' hesitation: "With the [negative] climate in the U.S. for Al Jazeera ... who needs the bother?" (Halloran 2006, 38). Four years after its launch, AJE had only three American cable distributors: Buckeye Cablesystem, with an audience of 147,000 homes in Northern Ohio; municipally-owned Burlington Telecom of Vermont, with only 1,000 homes; and MHz Networks in Washington, D.C., with 2.3 million subscribers.[4]

INTERNATIONAL NEWS

After becoming the premier Arabic-language television network, AJE aims to provide both a regional voice and a global perspective. For AJE, the potential world audience is one billion English speakers. But unlike the BBC and CNN, it does not present an Anglo-American worldview. AJA revolutionized the Arab mediascape by giving rise to a new "Arab voice." By letting Arab people speak without censorship, AJA has been able to separate "what Arabs think" from government policies. AJA emerged at an opportune time to help galvanize and give power to an Arabic language public sphere. AJA's staff is representative of Arab nationalities rather than limited to the headquarters' country. While the United Arab League is fragmented politically, its common language and homogeneity in culture have made Arab solidarity possible. AJA has been committed to a pan-Arab identity and to local events at the same time.

AJE represents the same one-and-many philosophy. It understands the universal, not as a single-layer whole, but a composite of different entities. More than an aggregate of individuals, the global is a mosaic of different communities stitched into one overall pattern without the parts losing their identity. The whole is multicultural rather than a unified system held together by information. AJE's vision of providing a regional voice and global perspective at the same time resonates with communitarian thinking.

Ghanaian philosopher Kwasi Wiredu explains that communities are constituted by language, but while we are rooted in language and culture, humans are trans-cultural, too. In his words, "human beings cannot live by particulars or universals alone, but by some combination of both" (Wiredu 1996, 9). All 6,500 known languages are complex. All humans learn languages at the same age. All languages can be learned and translated by native speakers of other languages. Some human beings in every language are bilingual. We are therefore distinctive in ourselves and sympathetic to the whole. We recognize that our own survival is intertwined with the viability of the human species. Even when our relations with others are confrontational and antagonistic, on the deepest level we recognize our oneness with other humans as cultural beings. Thus, we develop rules of warfare to avoid annihilation and to care for the injured. Those same rules urge that military battles avoid civilian losses as much as possible. Apart from war, the relatively recent existence of transnational NGOs, of United Nations' agencies, and widespread diplomatic efforts suggest unequivocally that people of all languages and culture understand and nurture respect for each other. Together we recognize the need to cooperate for food, security, energy, for clean air and water. In communitarian terms, the world is indeed varied, but one.

The one-and-many problem is huge in history and difficult to implement. Is there an underlying unity behind the multiple ways in which the world appears to us, or are things as varied as appearances suggest (Christians 2008b)? Media technology and commerce and finance have globalized the planet while at the same time local identities have reasserted themselves. Taking these contradictory trends into account—homogenization and cultural resistance—while complicated, is essential for communitarianism. AJE's insistence on both local identity and a global vision is laudable, even though it may not always get the balances and relationships exactly right.

Although AJE has the technological capacity for a global audience of one billion, AJE does not call that audience its empire. It aims

> to provide new and productive fora for cross-cultural communication. According to its proponents, AJE presents a tremendous opportunity for a new direction in the discourse of global news flows. With its avowed promise of giving a "voice to the voiceless," AJE represents a new style of news media that challenges existing research regarding transnational media organizations, and media and conflict scholarship more broadly. (el-Nawawy and Powers 2008, 8)

Having over twenty-five news bureaus worldwide, it is touted as the "voice of the South," as Ibrahim Helal, AJE's deputy manager for news and programs, explains: "The 'South' here is not meant to be geographical. It is symbolic. It is a lifestyle because in the West, you have a lot of South as well. The South denotes the voiceless in general." In the words of Waddah Khanfar, Al-Jazeera's director general: "Our philosophy of reporting is the human sentiment paradigm rather than the power center" (el-Nawawy and Powers 2008, 31, 33).

AJE not only covers stories that have been underrepresented in the traditional mainstream media but also multiplies perspectives through the diversity of its staff. As Nahedad Zayed, AJE's Washington news editor, puts it,

> We are so diverse and so varied and it gives you a sense of yes, that's the voice of the voiceless. I see people from Africa. I see people from the jungles of Brazil, Indigenous Indians in Bolivia, Palestinians in the West Bank. ... More than forty ethnic backgrounds and nationalities [are] represented on the staff. (el-Nawawy and Powers 2008, 32)

Early research on AJE indicates that its approach to news differs significantly from CNN International and noticeably from BBC World. "Content analysis points to a repeated and thorough effort at producing programming that has more depth than most contemporary televised news, as well as an agenda that empha-sizes issues of particular importance to those living outside the post-industrialized Western world" (el-Nawawy and Powers 2008, 33). AJE focuses less on being first with "breaking news" and less on the "sound bite culture" that characterizes many of its Western counterparts. It does not follow the "attack mode" philosophy of most American media. News items on AJE "are generally longer and snappier, while documentary-style shows abound. Its stories seem to introduce more angles than would be the case with 'conventional' all-news networks" (el-Nawawy and Powers 2008, 33). In Robert Kaplan's review, AJE reports not only on a wider range of issues but in more depth than anyone else (2009, 55–56).

Because relationships between social groups are often antagonistic, commu-nitarianism seeks mediation between contending cultures and political entities. An early study of AJE viewers found that they understood AJE "as a conciliatory medium ... likely to cover contentious issues in a way that contributes to creating an environment that is conducive to cooperation, negotiation, and reconciliation." Including stories from groups historically or currently disenfranchised was "found to be an important step in the process towards reconciling cultural tensions." The research indicates that stories with depth and context, along with reasoned argu-ments about issues, "induce more open thinking when it comes to considering other people's perspectives" (el-Nawawy and Powers 2008, 8).

AJE interprets this finding as a fragile achievement that needs ongoing atten-tion. Its parent network often produced a non-communitarian divisiveness, with the United States and Israel typically seen by AJA viewers as enemies of Arabic politics and culture.[5] To guard against this outcome, AJE believes it has adopted the journalistic standards and practices that are "essential for a news outlet to cover contentious issues in socially productive ways" (el-Nawawy and Powers 2008, 9). In its most idealized form, AJE does not merely want a global audience, but one that is oriented toward conflict resolution.

Philip Seib (2008) puts the issues of AJE and international news in a larger context. He coins the term "the Al-Jazeera effect" to examine the ways new media technologies are reshaping international politics. AJA and AJE are the most visible exemplar of the media's impact on world affairs at present.

> Traditional ways of shaping global politics have been superseded by the influence of new media: satellite television, the Internet, and other high-tech tools. What is involved is more than a refinement of established practices. We are seeing a comprehensive reconnecting of the global village and reshaping of how the world works. Al Jazeera is a symbol of this new, media-centric world. (Seib 2008, p. ix)

In varying degrees, media connections are reordering the traditional political rela-tions that have structured global affairs. Al-Jazeera's aggressive coverage of the protests in Tunisia, Egypt, and Yemen galvanized the media's role as a political force. Al-Jazeera's Tunisian-born news anchor, Mohammed Krichen, used inter-nal connections to put grainy Facebook images from the streets of Tunisia on the air. From Twitter to as-ansar.com to radio and Al-Jazeera's satellite network, the people's revolt made democratic reform in the Middle East inescapable (Worth and Kirkpatrick 2011, A1, A10).[6] That is "the Al-Jazeera effect"—a dramatically expanding universe of communication providers that is changing the relationship between citizens and their homelands.

Greater access to information in multiple formats is giving ethnic communities an identity, and individuals an unprecedented chance at autonomy. But communitarianism recognizes that abundant information does not magically produce democratic societies. In Al-Jazeera's Middle East region, in fact, making the case for democracy is nearly impossible at present. Gilles Kepel has observed that Abu Ghraib and similar scandals have so tarnished the image of Western democratic nations that "the word 'democracy', preceded by the adjective 'Western,' has negative connotations" even among middle-class Muslims who would benefit from it. "The Arabic word *damakrata*, which designates the democratic process, is frequently used pejoratively, signifying a change imposed from without" (2004, 293).

In communitarian terms, democratic reform is more than freedom to vote and electing officials. International news preoccupied with nation-state policies fails to address community formation with the depth it deserves. Democracies are a composite of groups of people and not merely an aggregate of individuals. With human life rooted in community, communities give us identity and a voice that makes political participation meaningful. Communication is vital for these communities to flourish and when their cultures are empowered, participatory politics results.

TRUTH VS. PROPAGANDA

Community life requires truthfulness, so we need to resolve the question of whether AJE is a propaganda arm of the Arab world. The accusations that AJA is biased have been unrelenting, and AJE is seen as following in the mode of its parent network. Critics note that AJA reported no positive news about Iraq's reconstruction—no new hospitals or schools functioning well or government officials making good decisions. In Afghanistan, AJA depicted the Taliban as the noble underdog and America as the vengeful aggressor; how else, critics ask, could AJA have stayed in Afghanistan when other news agencies were banned? The U.S. State Department accused AJA of misinforming Arabs with its one-sided approach to every issue, and this skepticism has carried over to AJE. Islamic extremist clerics who give religious sanction to terrorism are included, such as Yusuf al-Qaradwi hosting the weekly program, *Sharia and Life* (Pearl 2007, A23). From various sources, AJE's news coverage continues to be seen as hardening the Arab and Islamic positions against Israel and the United States.

AJE recognizes that it has an agenda—to resonate with and represent Arab public opinion. But it does not believe this mission invalidates the network's news. Anti-Semitism and anti-Americanism may emerge from their talk shows, call-in programs, and features, but their news coverage is different. According to AJE's defenders, its journalists understand the need to be balanced, even when its guests, callers, and government spokespersons do not. Bigotry is heard regularly. "Islam is the solution" is a frequent slogan. But AJE itself claims no responsibility for strident opinions. It does solicit polemical guests, but includes several sides, rather than the more sanitized discussions and panels that are typical of BBC World Service and CNN International. AJE's "Code of Ethics" parallels its Western counterparts, and Item Nine explicitly distinguishes news and opinion "to avoid the pitfalls of speculation and propaganda."

To answer the claims and counterclaims about truth or propaganda in AJE, Immanuel Kant's duty ethics is typically cited. For Kant, telling the truth is a categorical imperative for all circumstances without exception.

> Truthfulness in statements is the formal duty of an individual to everyone, however great may be the disadvantage accruing to himself or to another. ... To be truthful (honest) in all declarations is a sacred and absolutely commanding decree of reason, limited by no expediency ("On a Supposed Right to Lie"). By a lie a man throws away and, as it were, annihilates his dignity as a man. (Kant [1785] 1964, p. 93)

Kant was trained in physics and mathematics. For him, as the law of gravity in the physical universe is always and everywhere true, so truth is a formal law that holds the social order together without change over time and space.

In Kant, truth has priority, as it does in communitarianism. But for Kant, the ethical duty to tell the truth includes no guidelines for highly contested and complicated situations. It reflects the eighteenth-century rationalism that dominated his era and is ill-fitted to multicultural circumstances. It assumes a sender and receiver model of communication, in which individual senders determine, and are responsible for, the truth of the message. When applied to professional ethics, truth is typically defined as accurate representation and precision with data. Truth and propaganda are disputed largely in terms of objectivity. Facts are said to mirror reality, and propaganda distorts it. Under Kant's Enlightenment ethics, truth in journalism is equivalent to unbiased reporting, and propaganda its opposite.

For communitarianism, this view of truth as accurate information is too narrow, given today's political and social complexities. Truth's deeper meaning for international news is authentic disclosure, to get at the heart of the matter, to explain the context behind the facts. The ethical principle of truth, as communitarianism defines it, means comprehensiveness. The term "interpretive sufficiency" is one way to describe it. A sufficient interpretation opens up public life in all its dynamic dimensions. A newsworthy account that is truthful represents complex cultures and religions adequately. The people involved at all levels are portrayed authentically without stereotype or simplistic judgments (Christians 2008a, 206–11).

The best reporters present an inside picture of events and their meaning; they disclose the attitudes, beliefs, and culture of those they are representing. The task was defined already by the Hutchins Commission as "putting daily evens in their context of meaning." AJE's inside acquaintance with the Arabic language, Islamic religion, and United Arab League politics, arts, and traditions give them a distinct advantage in a world largely marginal to CNN International and BBC World News (Fahmy and Johnson, 2007).

From AJE's perspective, all news operations play to their audiences' sensibilities and concerns. One's own frame of reference needs to be countered by fairness and balance, rather than hidden under appeals to objectivity. Although the American media are not propaganda agents for the government, they are owned and operated by massive businesses of a worldwide scope and need audiences attractive to advertisers. The media watchdog Fairness and Accuracy in Reporting (FAIR) monitored the U.S. nightly news shows during the Iraq invasion—ABC, CBS, NBC, CNN, Fox News, and PBS—and concluded that of the 1,617 sources who spoke about the war on these six, 71 percent supported the war on Iraq and only 3 percent opposed it. Only PBS interviewed spokespersons from the various antiwar organizations during the three-week invasion period.

AJE takes pride in the respect that it receives as a major international news network from journalists around the world. AJE has sharing agreements with broadcast operations East and West. The Israeli satellite system replaced BBC World Service with AJE (Rushing 2007, p. 196). Western and Arab media may still attack Al-Jazeera, but they continue to use its footage as they first did with the Afghanistan invasion of 2001.

While credibility studies in themselves cannot answer the charge of AJE propaganda, the first major research on its perceived credibility ranks it first, with the BBC and CNN second and third. This research puts all three of them in a completely different category than the local Arab media with no believability at all (Johnson and Fahmy 2008, 349–52). AJE, BBC, and CNN scored 4 (on a scale of 5) in expertise, but AJE alone scored 4 in "depth of information," "accuracy," "believability," and "trustworthiness" (Johnson and Fahmy 2008, 349). In recent research on Jordanian media, Al-Jazeera is the most trusted news source: 35 percent rank it the most reliable, with only 13 percent for Jordanian TV; Al-Hurra News funded by the U.S. government had no support (Carlstrom 2010).

For most educators, journalists, and political leaders in the Arab world, hatred toward America has nothing to do with AJA or AJE. The fundamental issue is not anti-American bias, but foreign policy. U.S. military aid to authoritarian governments alienated from the people's agenda. And for decades, Arabs have despised "America's one-sided policy towards the dispute between Israel and Palestinians." Walid al-Omary, AJA's bureau chief for Palestine and Israel, explains it this way: "If the American administration wants Arab support they should change their policy on the Palestinian issue. They have supported an extremist government in Israel. They have supported nothing of the Palestinians. The Arabs have no reason to like America. The Arabs have suffered under the Americans more than any other nation" (Miles 2005, 386). Lest this sound Palestinian, Walid al-Omary's bureau was suspended by the Palestinian authority in July 2009 for allegations that it aired against its President, Mahmoud Abbas. U.S. political ideology is interpreted in the Arab world as derision of its culture and history.

PEACE JOURNALISM

Nonviolence is often reduced to a political strategy or to the rule "no harm to the innocent." But in communitarianism, nonviolence is a philosophy of life. Peace is normative in both community formation and maintenance. Without peace as the standard, families cannot survive or the weak flourish. Violence, both physical and psychological, destroys human relations at the center of our communal existence (Christians 2010).

AJA was born and raised in violence, and on the strength of the notoriety that resulted, AJE had prominence from the beginning. CNN became a 24-hour news channel of record in covering the Gulf War 1991, and AJA's prominence was forged in years 2000 to 2003 from the Second Intifada to Afghanistan and Iraq. With England's history of intervention in Afghanistan and involvement in the formation of Israel, the BBC coverage of military conflicts there had special audience appeal in the United Kingdom. Instead of making truth the first casualty of war, the BBC, CNN, and Al-Jazeera are rightly called to the ethical principle of truthful reporting on war.

However, even when there is legitimate coverage of conflict, the principle of nonviolence is not implemented. Peace journalism recognizes that military coverage as a media event feeds the very violence it reports, and therefore calls for developing the theory and practice of peace initiatives and conflict resolution (Lynch and McGoldrick 2005). Flickers of peace are emerging on our media ethics agenda, but only glimmers here and there in the news media as a whole (Wolfsfeld 2004). Johan Galtung (2004) has developed and applied this principle most systematically with his peace journalism, concerned not simply with the standards of war reporting, but positive peace—creative, nonviolent resolution of all cultural, social, and political conflicts (see Obonyo 2010). The broad task remains of bringing the principle of nonviolence to maturity, and AJE's staff, supporters, and critics share the challenge of transforming the existing cultures of violence into those of peace (Cortright 2006).

Communitarianism is committed to inclusion. Recognizing culturally based art and ritual, communitarianism keeps low walls between neighbors. After all, talk leads more often to an appreciation of differences than to fear, insecurity, or loathing. It believes that injustice is so real and painful that it should be granted no shields, and that publicity is a stronger step toward resolution than secrecy. It affirms that diversity should be celebrated, not feared. The commitment to local languages, religion, culture, and social practice is a communitarian frame of mind that AJE understands and often illustrates for the world (Iskandar 2005).

In this sense, communitarianism is a normative framework. It shows us what ought to be done. It holds up ideals, and when specific practices fail or when a news operation needs improvement overall, communitarianism is the standard to follow. AJE's commitment to covering the people themselves, their suffering and aspirations, reflects communitarian thinking. AJE's rejection of government control and modulation of expert opinion duplicate the same spirit as social responsibility theory and public journalism practice. Perhaps it is blind optimism to imagine that any media network anywhere could embody in its coverage and mission a commitment to global peace, but we gladly notice that AJE already has many of the required tools at hand for working on the impossible.

CONCLUSION

A satellite news network born in war faces with all media—but with special intensity—the challenge of community building, of thriving on cooperative interaction. Communitarian's philosophy of community building is a standard by which practices can begin rising to the level of principle. Should AJE foster community building as a newly powerful international news operation, it will be known as a world leader not in terms of audience size or technological sophistication, but for opening fresh pathways to human flourishing.

AJE is committed to the latest media technology, from satellites to Internet streaming to mobile phone podcasts.[7] Using this high-tech media system responsibly has been the theme of this chapter. Given AJE's dramatic impact on community formation, communitarianism rightly insists on a rigorous social responsibility from it. The burgeoning cyber world connected to AJE, and growing dramatically outside it, calls for a high moral ground among participants not clearly developed to date. It becomes obvious that the challenges from blogs, web technology, and smart phones are worldwide in scope and demand a sophisticated media ethics. Following the growth of on-line technologies since the Drudgereport.com in the next chapter will illuminate the communitarian pathway.

NOTES

1. The documentary film *Control Room* (Magnolia Pictures, 2004) gives detail and Arab-world context on Al-Jazeera's coverage of the Iraq invasion. The Iraq invasion in April 2003 made AJA an international news channel. For a classroom emphasis on this one episode in Al-Jazeera's history, *Control Room* is recommended.
2. TV news is livestreamed online from the AJE website [english.aljazeera.net]. As the basis for class discussion, an assignment could be: Students watch one hour of TV news from the AJE website. On that home page there's a video link to the broadcast stream.
3. See Davis (2010, pp. 11–13) for further details about the political economy perspective on AJE; they are summarized here.
4. For further details, see Davis (2010, p. 21).
5. Lynch (2006) reaches a more positive conclusion. In his view, AJA has helped create a more politically savvy Arab public that is open to change. AJE can build on this questioning of the status quo.
6. For a review of the Web sites and postings in Egypt during the people's revolt, see Leland (2011, p. A11).
7. For the current state of Al-Qaeda and its "high-tech media weapons" (what the book calls "terrorism 2.0"), see Sieb and Jabek (2010).

REFERENCES

Ackerman, Spencer. 2006. "Coming to America." *New Republic* 234 (16) (May 1): 19.

Aday, S, S. Livingston, and M. Hebert. 2004. "Embedding the Truth: A Cross-Cultural Analysis of Objectivity and Television Coverage of the Iraq War," *Harvard International Journal of Press Politics* 10(1): 2–21.

Al-Jaber, K. 2004. *The Credibility of Arab Broadcasting: The Case of Al-Jazeera.* Doha: Qatar National Council for Culture, Arts and Heritage.

Barkho, Leon. 2007. "Unpacking the Discursive and Social Links in BBC, CNN and Al-Jazeera's Middle East Reporting," *Journal of Arab and Muslim Media Research* 1(1): 11–29.

BBC Monitoring. May 9, 2008. "Morocco Says Closing Al-Jazeera was not Political."

BBC Monitoring. March 15, 2010. "Al-Jazeera Discusses Confiscation of Transmission Equipment in Yemen."

BBC Monitoring. October 4, 2010.. "Jordan Agrees to Al-Jazeera TV Jamming Probe."

Bessasio, Ehab Y. 2005. "Al_Jazeera and the War in Afghanistan: A Delivery System or a Mouthpiece?" In Mohamed Zayani, ed., *The Al-Jazeera Phenomenon: Critical Perspectives on New Arab Media,* pp. 153–170. Boulder, CO: Paradigm Publishers.

Carlstrom, Gregg. 2010. "Jordanians Love Al-Jazeera, Nobody Loves Al-Hurra." *The Majlis,* January 6.

Christians, Clifford. 2008a. "Media Ethics in Education." *Journalism and Communication Monographs* 9 (4): 181–221.

———. 2008b. "The One-and-the-Many Problem in Communication Ethics." In Philip Lee, ed., *Communicating Peace: Entertaining Angels Unawares,* 45–62. Penang, Malaysia: Southbound.

Christians, Clifford. 2010. "Non-violence in Philosophical and Media Ethics." In R. Keeble, J. Tulloch, and F. Zollmann, eds., *Peace Journalism, War and Conflict Resolution,* 15–30. New York: Peter Lang.

Cortright, David. 2006. *Ghandi and Beyond: Nonviolence for an Age of Terrorism.* Boulder, CO: Paradigm Publishers.

Davis, Ian K. 2010. "Bad Reception: Al-Jazeera English's Network Expansion and the Plurality of Global News Discourse." Unpublished paper, Institute of Communications Research, University of Illinois-Urbana.

el-Nawawy, Mohammed, and Iskandar, Adel. 2002. *Al Jazeera: How the Free Arab News Network Scooped the World and Changed the Middle East.* Boulder, CO: Westview Press.

el-Nawawy, Mohammed, and Powers, Shawn. 2008. *Mediating Conflict: Al-Jazeera English and the Possibility of a Conciliatory Media.* Los Angeles: Figueroa Press.

el-Oifi, Mohammed. 2005. "Influence without Power: Al-Jazeera and the Arab Public Sphere." In Mohamed Zayani, ed., *The Al-Jazeera Phenomeon: Critical Perspectives on New Arab Media,* pp. 66–79. Boulder, Co: Paradigm Publishers.

Fahmy, Sahira and Thomas J. Johnson. 2007. "Show the Truth and Let the Audience Decide: A Web-Based Survey Showing Support for Use of Graphic Imagery Among Viewers of Al-Jazeera," *Journal of Broadcasting and Electronic Media,* 51(2): 245–264.

Galtung, Johan. 2004. *Transcend and Transform: An Introduction to Conflict Work.* London: Pluto Press.

Halloran, Liz. 2006. "A Major Image Problem." *U.S. News & World Report* 141 (10) (September 18): 38.

International Commission for the Study of Communication Problems. 1980. *Many Voices, One World: Communication and Society, Today and Tomorrow*. New York: Unipub.

Iskandar, Adel. 2005. "Is Al-Jazeera an Alternative? Mainstreaming Alterity and Assimilating Discourses of Dissent," *Transnational Broadcasting Studies Journal*, 15. www.tbsjournal.com/Iskandar.html.

Johnson, Thomas J., and Fahmy, Shahira. 2008. "The CNN of the Arab World or a Shill for Terrorists? How Support for Press Freedom and Political Ideology Predict Credibility of Al-Jazeera Among Its Audience." *International News Gazette* 70 (5): 338–60.

Kant, Immanuel. 1949. "On a Supposed Right to Lie for Altruistic Motives." In his *Critique of Practical Reason and Other Writings in Moral Philosophy*, 346–50. Translated by L. W. Beck. Chicago: University of Chicago Press. [original publication 1788]

——. 1964. *The Doctrine of Virtue*. Translated by M. J. Gregor. New York: Harper & Row. [original publication 1785]

Kaplan, Robert D. 2009. "Why I Love Al Jazeera." *The Atlantic*, October, 55–56.

Kepel, Gilles. 2004. *The War for Muslim Minds: Islam and the West*. Cambridge, MA: Belknap Harvard University Press.

Leland, John. 2011. "A Long-Anticipated Opening in Cairo," *The New York Times*, February 3, p. A11.

Lucas, Ryan. 2011. "Egypt Takes Aim at Al-Jazeera for Protest Coverage." Associated Press, February 10. <http://news.yah0oo.com/s/ap/20110210/ap_on_en_tv/ml_egypt_al_jazeera>.

Lynch, Jake, and McGoldrick, Annabel. 2005. *Peace Journalism*. Glasgow, Scotland: Hawthorn Press.

Lynch, Marc. 2006. *Voices of the New Arab Public: Iraq, Al-Jazeera, and Middle East Politics Today*. New York: Columbia University Press.

Miles, Hugh. 2005. *Al-Jazeera: The Inside Story of the Arab News Channel that is Challenging the West*. New York: Grove Press.

Murphy, James. 2007. "Tackling Misconceptions on a Worldwide Scale." *Media: Asia's Media and Marketing Newspaper*, January 12, 15.

Obonyo, Levi. 2010. "Peace Journalism Training in East Africa." *Media Development*, March, 59–63.

Pearl, Judith. 2007. "Another Perspective, or Jihad TV?" *New York Times*, January 17, A23.

Rushing, Josh. 2007. *Mission Al-Jazeera*. New York: Palgrave Macmillan.

Seib, Philip. 2005. "Hegemonic No More: Western Media, the Rise of Al-Jazeera, and the Influence of Diverse Voices." *International Studies Review* 7: 601–15.

——. 2008. *The Al Jazeera Effect: How the New Global Media are Reshaping World Politics*. Washington, D.C.: Potomac Books.

Seib, Philip and Dana M. Janbek. 2010. *Global Terrorism and New Media: The Post Al-Qaeda Generation*. New York: Routledge.

Wiredu, Kwasi. 1996. *Cultural Universals and Particulars: An African Perspective*. Bloomington: Indiana University Press.

Wojcieszak, Magdalena. 2007. "Al-Jazeera: A Challenge to the Traditional Framing Research." *International Communication Gazette* 69 (2): 115–28.

Wolfsfeld, Gadi. 2004. *Media and the Path to Peace*. Cambridge: Cambridge University Press.

Worth, Robert F., and Kirkpatrick, David D. 2011. "Seizing a Moment, Al Jazeera Galvanizes Arab Frustration." *New York Times*, January 28, A1, A10.

CHAPTER 3

⚜

Drudgereport.com and Civil Society

Rags-to-riches stories are sometimes true. Just ask Matt Drudge. By his own admission, he failed his bar mitzvah, graduated near the bottom of his high school class, and found work in a convenience store and as a telemarketer (Drudge and Phillips 2000). But that was before 1995, when he started an email newsletter of gossip and conservative opinion. A year later, the Drudge Report was the first to disclose Republican candidate Bob Dole's selection of Jack Kemp as his vice-presidential running mate (Kalb 2001, 84). Then, in 1998, Drudge's big break came. As *Newsweek* waited for confirmation about President Clinton's sexual involvement with a White House intern, Drudge named Monica Lewinsky—accurately as it turned out—and the rest was history. The Drudge Report's popularity and political influence began their steep ascent and Drudge became a well-traveled millionaire. Agence France-Presse included Matt Drudge's rise as one of the top ten media events of the twentieth century and *Time* magazine counted him among the 100 most influential people in the world (Cox 2006).

Drudge's story became interesting ethically, not because of what Clinton did, but because of the shortcut Drudge took in reporting this information. *Newsweek* was preparing to break the story, but apparently held back to check facts before publishing. There is some dispute about how this delay occurred, or who was responsible (whether the "leak" came from inside *Newsweek* or not), but Drudge's website (http://www.drudgereport.com) reported that *Newsweek* had killed the story (see Kinsley 1998; Levy 1998; Surber 2007).

Matt Drudge's notoriety spiked as a result of his announced "World Exclusive" concerning Clinton and a then-unnamed 23-year-old intern (who by that time had left the White House for a job in the Pentagon). And no one was quite sure how to peg Drudge's activities. He was not a trained journalist. He might have been a gossip or a muckraker. He was no businessman. He had no business plan and no income, and his only clients were people who checked into drudgereport. com from time to time. In the eyes of many he was already a pariah, having published a "malicious and totally inaccurate story" based on GOP sources claiming that Clinton adviser Sidney Blumenthal had abused his spouse. The day after Blumenthal filed a $30-million libel suit, Drudge retracted the story and apologized to Blumenthal and his wife. Blumenthal accepted Drudge's apology and withdrew his lawsuit. By this time, however, 90,000 people subscribed to Drudge's exclusive feeds (Kalb 2001, 84–86).

In addition to receiving Drudge's emails via subscription, or browsing his site, people in the late 1990s could also access the website via AOL.[1] Drudge was hired by the Fox network to host a talk show in 1998 and left "on good terms" in 1999 after Fox refused to let him "show a photo of a 21-week-old fetus" on this program.[2] ABC Radio hired him for a syndicated talk show in 1999, but fired him a year later (Kurtz 2000). These short-lived positions paid Drudge perhaps as much as $200,000 per year. By 2003, Drudge estimated that he was earning $1.2 million annually from advertisements placed on drudgereport.com, the income a function of the number of visitors who "viewed" the pages on his website (Pachter 2003).[3]

The attraction of the site to advertisers was clear after the series of exposés that Drudge compiled leading up to, and through, Clinton's impeachment proceedings. The number of the site's subscribers climbed and drudgereport.com's place in the pantheon of websites increased. Marty Beard reported that in the period following the presidential election in 2000 the site was so clogged by visitors that "it was all but inaccessible." By 2001 the Drudge Report was attracting half a million visitors a week, and the seven-day period after the 9/11 attacks brought nearly three-quarters of a million visitors there (Beard, 2001).

What is the significance of Matt Drudge and his email list, website, and portal to the news? According to former president of NBC News and PBS, Lawrence K. Grossman, "The Walter Winchell wannabe is the harbinger of the shape of the press to come in the century ahead. With a modem, anyone with no training or credentials, like Drudge, who works on a laptop from his apartment in Los Angeles, can deliver the news of the world to a global audience" (1999, 17). Besides snatching the announcement of Clinton's dalliance away from Michael Isikoff and *Newsweek* in 1998, he was the first to report that Kathleen Willey had been subpoenaed by Paula Jones's lawyers in another Clinton sex scandal. Drudge was the first to report that CBS fired anchor Connie Chung (Bai 1997). *The Guardian* (U.K.) reported in 2007 that Hillary Clinton owed her political career to Drudge. Its logic: "In 1998, the humiliation of her husband's affair with the White House intern led to an outpouring of sympathy for the first lady. Her approval ratings soared, the image of the calculating political spouse blurred" (Goldenberg 2007). But the BBC's profile on Matt Drudge (2008), referencing *Brill's Content*, reported that "of the 51 stories that he claimed as exclusives from January to September 1998, the magazine found that 31 were actually exclusive stories. Of those, 32% were untrue, 36% were true and the remaining 32% were of doubtful accuracy."[4]

Drudgereport.com is an aggregator site—plain, divided into columns, and largely made up of text, photos, and links. Its links send readers to mainstream media sites and columnists, foreign news sites (Pravda, Islamic Republic Wire, Xinhua, etc.), wire services, trade publications, specialty sites (such as wowowow for women), and other news aggregator sites. The site's links cover the entire range of ideological positions from ultra-conservative (Marvin Olasky and Phyllis Schafly) to liberal (Maureen Dowd and Nat Hentoff), including both writers with a religious bent such as Ann Coulter and those who denigrate religion such as Christopher Hitchens. The site is updated dozens of times each day (Drudge says sometimes hundreds of times), so it provides up-to-the-minute news on both serious and trivial events ("City Requires Workers Must Wear Underwear, Deodorant" or a report from London's *Daily Mail* that Sacha Baron Cohen had marched in hot pants to the premier of his new film *Brüno* on June 19, 2009).

Drudge's site is most often compared to politico.com, a conservative news site that carried such headlines as "Obama fails to quell gay uproar" on June 18, 2009 (upon his signing a presidential memorandum that provides benefits to gay partners of those working in the federal government [Gerstein and Smith 2009]). Quantcast lists "anncoulter.com" as the site with the most affinity to Drudge, based on the behavior of his subscribers.

Drudge's political convictions themselves are murky. He was raised by liberal Jewish parents, but most commentators consider Drudge to be conservative (some even referred to him as a mouthpiece of the administration when George W. Bush was in office), and libertarians claim him to be one of their own (Winter n.d., 1).

ETHICS AND MATT DRUDGE

You do not have to be a Clinton supporter to criticize Drudge for his actions or a Clinton opponent to defend him. The ethical issues raised by Drudge, and the many Internet "news" sites that have been created over the past twenty years, are not a result of anyone's political convictions—whether conservative or liberal.

What are the ethical issues? First is the decision Drudge made to publish the claim about Clinton's relationship with Monica Lewinsky based on an email sent to him by... who knows? He provided no evidence that he did any fact-checking or sought any confirmations. A student in Duty Ethics 101 would know that truthfulness is necessary for journalism, not to mention the maintenance of society. To imagine the opposite would be to conceive a world of mistrust and anarchy. Kant would have us do whatever we can to insure telling the truth—including checking and double-checking the facts we report. *Newsweek* may have lost political and economic points for waiting to confirm its facts about Clinton and Lewinsky before going public, but it would have certainly won a blue ribbon in the category of ethical duty for doing so. Drudge's bet that his information was true paid off, but that does not get him off the ethical hook because he cared more about the scoop than about the truth. Having no journalistic training—the closest Drudge ever got to having a media job was working in the coffee shop at CBS studios in Los Angeles—is no excuse for recklessness.

Second, virtually anyone with a laptop can, with questionable morals, adroit marketing, and a little luck, have a global audience. No licenses, training, or adherence to codes of conduct are required. No gatekeepers stand between those who collect and write news and those who read it. No major capital investments are needed in printing presses, transmission towers, or production studios. Internet publishing is a person-to-person affair.

The changes in the way news has been gathered and reported since 1995 were unplanned. One thing merely led to another, spurred by creativity, technological change, and an acrimonious political environment. John F. Harris (2006) referred to this environment as "highly polarized and often downright toxic":

> At first, it was just [Drudge] gathering gossip for the amusement of friends. Yet the Drudge Report was different, because it was universally accessible....Its author could get to anybody, and anybody could instant-message him. And so the nature of news and news-gathering changed. No longer did it take a battalion of producers and editors and lawyers to put together a news product. It took just one man, working by himself in his one-bedroom apartment in Hollywood. (Pinkerton 2003)

The application of the World Wide Web to the process of news gathering and distribution (in addition to making it more difficult for traditional newspapers to survive) changed the news cycle that traditionally had provided opportunities for investigation, fact-checking, and deliberation before stories went to press. "When almost anyone can be a publisher, the result is a tidal wave of 'news' from sources far beyond the trusted, familiar shores of the mainstream press. This influx of fresh voices is a wondrous effect of technology, but no one can know whether such 'news' is propaganda, a spoof, or real reportage" (Caruso 1998). As Alicia Shepard (1998) put it,

> The remarkable ability of personal computers to provide news instantaneously via the Internet, combined with the influence of nonstop cable news networks, has jacked up the pressure on all journalists to get it first and fast—not so much first and right. The unfortunate casualties in this new and highly competitive marketplace are sometimes accuracy, fairness, and balance.

The public sphere in democratic societies depends on "accuracy, fairness, and balance" in the news; for the civil society to function effectively this need is doubly important.

At another level, Drudge's website raises a related—but more profound—ethical issue. Should he be judged by the standards applied to journalists (as mentioned above) or to gossip columnists? Does the distinction between these two types of writers matter in an age of infotainment, happy talk TV, and re-creations of historical events? (Williams and Carpini 2009).

When Grossman called Drudge a "Walter Winchell wannabe," he referred to America's most famous gossipmonger. Winchell's career extended from the 1920s to the 1960s, and he was usually seen and photographed wearing a fedora, a habit that Matt Drudge has also adopted—and which encourages comparisons between Winchell and him. Besides being called a gossip, Drudge has variously been referred to as a "spoiler" (*Vanity Fair* 2008), "the world's most powerful journalist" (Harnden 2008), a "conservative cybercolumnist" (Dowd 2003), a "fedora-wearing grandstander" (Rich 1999), a "self-styled Internet terrorist" (Day 2000), and a "maverick gossip columnist" (Burgunder 2011). Drudge probably

Matt Drudge (© Larry Downing/Sygma/Corbis).

cares little what people call him; notoriously reclusive, he may be taking Rush Limbaugh's advice to "disappear from public life" (*New York Magazine* blog 2009; see also Whitworth 2008).

Journalists are expected to be accurate, fair, and balanced in their reporting. By some accounts, Drudge is none of these. Jules Witcover has argued that the Lewinsky revelation "surfaced in the wildly irresponsible Internet site of Matt Drudge, a reckless trader in rumor and gossip who makes no pretense of checking on the accuracy of what he reports." Robert Lissit has referred to Drudge as inaccurate, self-promoting, and essentially a liar for claiming "exclusives which often aren't." Journalists believe in telling the truth, but gossip is held to no such ideals, so the expectations that anyone has of Drudge's site are in some respects "in the eye of the beholder" (quoted by Lissit 1998).

Based on Drudge's experience and the needs of the booming blogosphere, codes of ethics are emerging to specify the best practices for this new technology. Rebecca Blood (2002, ch. 6) included a "Weblog Code of Ethics" in the first edition of *The Weblog Handbook* and Jonathon Dube, founder of CyberJournalist. net, maintains a code for on-line journalism patterned after the Society of Professional Journalists Code of Ethics. Both of these codes focus on blogs that have been integrated into mainstream media corporations and center on news. The Radio Television Digital News Association (RTDNA) adopted a set of Social Media and Blogging Guidelines on April 12, 2010, summarizing its major principles this way: "As a journalist you should uphold the same professional and ethical standards of fairness, accuracy, truthfulness, transparency and independence when using social media as you do on-air and on all digital news platforms" ("Social Media and Blogging Guidelines," <http://www.rtnda.org/pages/media_items/social-media-and-blogging-guidelines1915.php>).

With a communitarian instinct, Martin Kuhn argues for a broader code that is helpful to political blogs but also credible to bloggers more generally. He surveyed the field of computer-mediated communication and developed a "Code of Blogging Ethics" (C.O.B.E.) that meets the digital world's two most important needs: truth-telling instead of gossip and innuendo, and accountability instead of anonymity (Kuhn 2007; cf. Perlmutter and Schoen 2007). For bloggers who are not professionals in a business or nonprofit network, adopting Kuhn's code enhances credibility and influence. It creates, in effect, an A-list of bloggers who are a resource for both citizens and journalists.[5]

"AND WILD CONFUSION ROUND THEM SEE" (GOETHE)

By 2009 the Internet had begun to do what the news business had long predicted: shut down newspapers. Newspapers in the nineteenth century had attempted to control the spread of wire services for their own protection. They had tried to stop radio from reporting the news when it arrived as a new medium. People predicted that television would put newspapers (as well as movies) out of business. But it was the development of the Internet, with its low barriers to entry and limited capital investment requirements, that provided a platform that could replace the newspaper. U.S. daily newspapers were dying, shrinking, or reducing their publication schedules, while on-line news sites, including drudgereport.com, owned both by media companies and non-media organizations, seemed to thrive. More and more people became "citizen journalists," reporting the events of their day via mobile telephone cameras and videos, text blogs, and cable television channels. (One such cable channel, Current, employed two journalists who were tried and imprisoned in North Korea in 2009 for illegally entering North Korea from China. Political pawns in the North Korea/U.S. dispute over nuclear weapons, they were freed shortly after their arrest as the result of a visit to Pyongyang by former President Bill Clinton.) The advent of "mashups" also allows citizen journalists to use unlikely Internet sites such as Google Earth to file stories on the destruction caused by Israeli warplanes in Lebanon.

In 2009 the *Rocky Mountain News* ceased publication. Although *Time* magazine blamed this demise on poor management as much as the Internet (Diddlebock 2009), several other metropolitan dailies met the same end (http://www.news-paperdeathwatch.com). Obituaries for newspapers as a medium proliferated: "newspapers are at death's door"; "the Internet helped turn that slow puncture [of newspaper readership] into a blowout"; and "it no longer requires a dystopic imagination to wonder who will have the dubious distinction of publishing America's last genuine newspaper" (Rogers 2009; Surowiecki 2008; Alterman 2008).

But the decline of printed news is hardly the same as the decline of journalism. Jack Shafer wrote as early as 2006 that although newspapers were dying, news was thriving (2006). Drudge's success led Arianna Huffington to begin the Huffington Post "as a liberal alternative to the Drudge Report." But it was quickly transformed into "a shared enterprise between its producer and consumers," including "highly opinionated posts of an apparently endless army of.... bloggers—more than eighteen hundred so far" (Alterman 2008). In 2011, AOL acquired the Huffington Post for $315 million, betting that it represents the news business of the future.

The Associated Press on-line has experienced abundant use also. In fact, AP has had so many news aggregators and bloggers using its proprietary material without permission or compensation that it has needed to add a "homing beacon" to its on-line content to "ensure that it is re-used under the agency's terms of use" (Dannen 2009). This beacon automatically notifies AP about every use made of its content. According to the AP's own press release, this system makes it possible to continue providing "original, independent and authoritative journalism at a time when the world needs it more than ever" (AP 2009). Meanwhile, Digital Rights Management was being abandoned in the music business, a system that provided similar protection to recordings.

The need for AP to monitor dissemination is understandable, given the ease of flow for news stories on the Internet. The bankrupt Tribune Company had informed AP of its decision to stop paying for its services in 2010, arguing that its own proprietary content was more valuable to its readers than shared wire content that was available widely. Several other newspapers had already pulled the plug, or announced their intention to do so, when the Tribune announcement came (Rosenthal 2008). Both the nature of news itself and the financial implications of newsgathering were being negotiated in the dynamic environment created by the Internet. According to newspaperdeathwatch.com, a "confidential" Associated Press document (apparently the same one that raised the homing beacon idea) claimed that on-line news searches were fundamentally different following Michael Jackson's death in 2009 compared to those following 9/11. Early web users went to CNN.com and other news sites to get updates by refreshing the pages. Now they "learn of new information on Twitter, they search on Google and then head to Wikipedia" (Gillin 2009).

Changes to on-line journalism have by no means been all Matt Drudge's doing. But by thumbing his nose at the mainstream press, he helped loosen the press's stranglehold that many Americans thought needed to be broken.[6] "The eight-month investigation as to whether President Clinton had a sexual affair...was a central force in the Internet's coming of age. When Matt Drudge broke the news of the Kenneth Starr investigation in January of 1998, Internet news was still in its infancy. By the time the Starr report was released eight months later...the Internet largely dictated how the story played out" (Lasica n.d.). The Clinton scandal and the Starr report changed everything. "It was the first time that official Washington, journalism, and the Internet bumped into one another nose to nose" (Lasica 2000).[7] By 2009 Drudge's website was the sixth most-visited news site on the Internet, well behind industry leader yahoo.com, but ahead of sites produced by the *New York Times*, *USA Today*, and the *Washington Post*. And the Drudge Report led in terms of time spent on the site per month. Its average of close to an hour was five times more than the typical news site (Pew Project 2010).

The decline of the traditional media—including not only newspapers, but radio and TV networks, magazines, and even cable television—is the result of the new freedom for individuals to express themselves factually and ideologically on the web. "Big media" still matter, and they own myriad websites as well as many of the technologies and much of the software that makes the web possible. But average citizens can now express themselves in ways earlier generations could not imagine. Everyone's efforts may not come to something—the sheer volume of material on the Internet makes that impossible—but when someone's site does catch on, as Matt Drudge's certainly did, that site becomes a beacon for the dreams of others.

THE DRUDGE REPORT AND CIVIL SOCIETY

Civil society is especially important to communitarians. Jürgen Habermas describes civil society as "non-governmental and non-economic connections and voluntary associations that anchor communication structures of the public sphere in the society component of the life world" (1996, 366–67). These are the social units in a democratic society located between the private sphere and the government. Outside political institutions and business are communities and organizations that are vital to a healthy nation: school classrooms and parent teacher associations; churches, synagogues, and mosques; town halls; book clubs; professional and academic bodies; neighborhood associations; volunteer groups such as Amnesty International, the League of Women Voters, Doctors Without Borders, and the Audubon Society. Does the Drudge Report and its legacy facilitate thinking and action in civil society (cf. Taylor 1991)?

Certainly the media's links to government and business are of concern to communitarian ethics. Every chapter in this book shows how the media are accountable for those relationships. The press's duty is to root out abuse, expose corruption, evaluate government activities, protect civil liberties from encroachments by government regulators or policy-makers, and represent to political authority the public's needs and desires as they are developed in the public arena. The press is both watchdog and town crier. The mainstream press has not always functioned this way, of course, but the watchdog and the town crier roles form the overarching rationale for the First Amendment's guarantee of a free press.

From a communitarian perspective, it is important that news and information enlighten public debate, elevate the deliberative discourse of civil society, and encourage respect for others (whether institutions or individuals) rather than engage in *ad hominem* attacks (a person is guilty or venal as a result of being a Democrat, a Republican, or LBGT for instance). Truth-telling is a more dependable route to healthy communities than lying, obfuscation, or wishful thinking (Bok 1978; Frankfurt 2006). Presumably, the default position on public communication in any democracy would be "the more information the better." We assume that more information is better for consumer decisions on, say, prescription or over-the-counter drugs, the contents of our prepackaged food or the calorie count and fat content of our fast food, the initial or long-term quality of our automobiles, the ethanol content of gasoline or the type of paint used on children's toys. With more information, we can make more informed purchasing decisions. Knowing how well the mayor has performed in getting potholes fixed, or the police chief in reducing crime, is supposed to help citizens cast better informed votes. Knowing how presidential candidates will handle Supreme Court appointments, or whether they are in favor of balanced budgets and reproductive choice, should enable citizens to exercise the voting franchise in a transparent environment.

But human communication is riddled with bias. Ideologies inform us before the facts do. Our sense of entitlement or disenfranchisement, acceptance or alienation, influences not only what we say but how we hear what others say. So we have to wonder whether more information is always better. Is "raw" unprocessed information—perhaps peppered with innuendo, misinterpretations, unconcealed prejudices—as legitimate as information that has been fact-checked, edited for bias, and balanced by providing different points of view? And how do we distinguish one sort of information from another? Is it a matter of the sources themselves? The quality of the writing? The attention to detail or alternative explanations? The speed with which it is delivered? Its titillating quality? How well it accords with our perspectives and convictions? These are important questions for communitarians.

Nowhere today is the issue of mediated bias more pronounced than in WikiLeaks.org, the website launched by Australian Julian Assange in 2006 that publishes classified data leaked from governments and businesses. WikiLeaks has documented toxic dumping in the African seaport Côte d'Ivoire that caused massive illness and more than a dozen deaths. It has published "Camp Delta Standard Operating Procedures," the U.S. military's 238-page manual for operating the Guantánamo Bay detention facility. Video from a U.S. Army Apache helicopter, dubbed "Collateral Damage," shows the killing of two Reuters reporters and ten unarmed Iraqis (Cohen and Stelter 2010). In November 2010 WikiLeaks released 250,000 secret diplomatic cables from the U.S. State Department, and in March 2011 it leaked one million documents from governments and corporations in Asia, the Middle East, sub-Saharan Africa, and the former Soviet Bloc.

Supporters of WikiLeaks see such publication as truth-telling, pure and simple. "Publishing improves transparency, and this transparency creates a better society for all people," the WikiLeaks website proclaims. "Better scrutiny leads to reduced corruption and stronger democracies in all society's institutions, including government, corporations and other organizations" (http://wikileaks.org/About.html). Upon its debut, WikiLeaks audaciously claimed it would "crack the world open" by becoming a global watchdog more reliable than conventional media (Lynch 2010). WikiLeaks sees itself as publisher of record, providing the world with documents that governments and businesses have tried to keep hidden from public view. Countries such as North Korea and Zimbabwe will no longer be able to maintain total censorship of its political affairs. Defending WikiLeaks on *Fox Business*, Texas Congressman Ron Paul said, "In a free society we're supposed to know the truth. In a society where truth becomes treason, then we're in big trouble" (Barr 2010).

Assange does not work alone. Documents submitted to WikiLeaks go through a review process by volunteers around the world comprised of "journalists, software programmers, network engineers, mathematicians and others," according to the organization's website (http://wikileaks.org/About.html). In the end, though, "if the document is legit," Assange himself makes the decision to publish (Kushner 2010). WikiLeaks uses military-grade encryption to protect anonymity and keeps some of its servers in a "bombproof, underground bunker in Sweden." Assange's decisions of whether and when to publicize information is technically impossible to disrupt (Greenberg 2010).

WikiLeaks' critics raise serious objections to the ethics of its structure and policies. One concerns a double-standard regarding transparency. Assange rejects all calls for privacy except his own. He refuses to name either those who support WikiLeaks financially or those who serve as advisors—not to mention those who leak information to WikiLeaks. Given the sensitive nature of WikiLeaks, such secrecy is understandable—but by the same token, so are many government and business secrets. Why is privacy unacceptable for all organizations other than

WikiLeaks (Kushner 2010)? As Andy Greenberg concluded in his article about Assange in *Forbes* magazine, "The world's most vocal transparency advocate is now one of the world's biggest keepers of secrets" (Greenberg 2010).

Just as important is the issue of news judgment. When WikiLeaks publishes the documents it receives, it does so as an indiscriminate data dump. WikiLeaks does not question the motives of those who leak corporate or government secrets. It does not research the truthfulness of the information in the documents. It does not redact names of innocents who may find themselves in harm's way. According to Russian investigative journalists Andrei Soldatov and Irina Borogan, "What WikiLeaks has done is publish online a massive number of reports without checking the facts, without putting them in context, and without analyzing them" (Soldatov and Borogan 2010). Another reporter says, "Society does set limits on information disclosure in many ways; also in the journalism community there are rules." WikiLeaks raises serious questions for him about "the ethics of quoting anonymous people you can't meet or verify" (Lynch 2010, 6).

In our reflective moments we recognize that computer efficiency and transmission capacity relentlessly multiply the data we receive but not necessarily our knowledge or our understanding. Globally networked digital systems are producing "unmanageable data floods" that make recognizing, ordering, and evaluating relevant information difficult. For the French thinker, Jacques Ellul, the information explosion produces crystallized humans, not the politically informed. He used the analogy for overwhelmed audiences of pricking a frog's muscles incessantly in the laboratory until its body freezes (1967, 57–58). "The production of more knowledge creates more non-knowledge in the form of information overload" (Debatin 2008, 260).

Given today's profusion of electronic information, it is no surprise that communitarians are preoccupied with the vitality of education—learning to think critically, to weigh evidence, and to understand how social institutions operate. Ideally, schools can teach technological citizenship "where the responsibilities and privileges . . . associated with living in a world suffused with technology are a matter of ethical reflection and political practice" (Lyon 2003, 160). With cultural identity understood dialogically, education is central for enriching the human world, by "exposing us to differing cultural and intellectual perspectives, and thereby increasing our possibilities for intellectual and spiritual growth, exploration, and enlightenment" (Gutmann 1994, 9). Dealing with cultural differences and moral disagreements in the classroom by deliberation rather than denunciation contributes to the collective associations of civil society and develops critical distance from racism, sexism, homophobia, and ethnocentrism on-line.

Civil society is composed of interactive modules of deliberation. Does drudgereport.com use interactive technology to create a deliberative community that adds opportunities for democratic participation? To return to Grossman's remarks, the answer to this question does not depend on how we define the difference between a journalist, a gossip, or a blogger (a term Drudge reputedly hates). Discussion in civil society formats is not always civil, but civility is the principle by which such interaction ought to be judged. If the Drudge on-line exchange is rude, salacious, libelous, acrimonious, and deceptive, it does not meet the civil society standard.

COMMUNITARIAN ETHICS IN CULTURAL CONFUSION

The arrival of Web-based reporting accelerated a trend in American communication—a confusion of spheres. Journalists could rightly be accused at various points in U.S. history of arguing for a foolish policy or hyping the truth (as when William Randolph Hearst claimed that his *New York Journal* started the Spanish-American War in 1898). Reporters have taken wildly partisan positions, especially prior to the development of the penny press in the 1830s and 1840s. When newspaper financing broke free from political party subsidies, neutrality became easier, but sensationalism designed to attract audiences escalated, too. Sensationalism helped newspapers attract buyers, justifying higher rates to advertisers as circulation increased. Standardization of news also developed as newspapers were connected through cooperative wire services (see Czitrom 1982, ch.1). Despite these pushes and pulls in newsgathering and reporting, over time the idea of objective news achieved nearly universal recognition in the print media (the *National Enquirer* and its ilk excepted) and also found acceptance with some variation in the electronic media.

By the mid-1990s, however, consensus definitions were breaking down. Television comedy programs, for instance, were making forays into the preserve of news organizations. Bill Clinton appeared on MTV in 1993 and responded to a question about whether he wore boxers or briefs. By the turn of the millennium, comedy and news had become thoroughly mixed. *The Daily Show* premiered in 1996 and Jon Stewart took over as host in 1999. Stephen Colbert spun his own program, *The Colbert Report*, from *The Daily Show* on Comedy Central. Bill Maher hosted *Politically Incorrect* on Comedy Central and then ABC, before beginning *Real Time* on HBO. News became hard to distinguish from satire.

The Drudge Report was an early part of this cultural shift. Although Matt Drudge described his Fox News program as entertainment rather than news, the material he used on it came from the same sources as his website that "is read religiously by Washington's reporters, political operatives, and cable news producers" and thus "retains a striking ability to dictate what appears in the mainstream press" (Sherman 2009; see also Hilden 2003). Drudge also appeared on *Meet the Press*, giving him a further patina of authority. This appearance led media critic Tom Shales to write that Drudge "has no credentials whatever to serve on a panel with professional journalists or even professional pundits.... Drudge's sudden rise to fame, and now [Tim] Russert's implied endorsement of him, may be but one small sign of the new electronic Tower of Babel that the Internet will become" (Bowman 1999). Tara Sonenshine (1997) has argued that paparazzi are also part of this cultural shift because they "consider themselves foot soldiers in a new and growing army of information-gatherers in a media age in which information-gathering has somehow gotten confused with news-gathering."

This cultural shift has resulted in soul searching by the mainstream media. When the National Press Club invited Matt Drudge to address the assembled journalists, he defended himself from the implied criticism of Hillary Clinton that "any time an individual leaps so far ahead of that balance and throws the system. . . . out of balance, you've got a problem. It can lead to all kinds of bad outcomes which we have seen historically." His defense: "Would she have said the same thing about Ben Franklin or Thomas Edison or Henry Ford or Einstein? They all leapt so far ahead out that they shook the balance" (quoted by Lipschultz 2000, 135).

Of course, nothing lasts forever. The Drudge Report is still strong at the moment, but on-line news entrepreneurs, such as Politico and the Huffington Post, are providing stiff competition. Unlike Drudge, they encourage reader interaction and provide ongoing original reporting, not to mention citizen journalism. The Huffington Post, for instance, encourages readers to send in firsthand reports through Twitter. The Drudge Report, by contrast, seems to be more about its CEO than about its constituents, a remarkable feature in an era of rapidly evolving social media. Drudge's site will inevitably become less influential, but its impact among ideologically driven electronic news and gossip shows no immediate sign of abating (Porter 2009).

What conclusion should we reach? Is the cultural shift (and its accompanying confusion of roles in journalistic practice) to be embraced as a great leap forward for democracy or abhorred as a dangerous turn away from democracy? The answer, however uncomfortable, is that it is both. But even though the cultural shift represents a leap forward and dangerous turn at the same time, the ideal remains the same for this technology. According to Friend and Singer, "Online journalism has enormous potential to enhance the democratic purpose that has been the press' social and ethical foundation for centuries" (2007, p. xx).

Understanding such a cultural shift cannot depend upon individuals acting out of personal preference. To reduce the cultural confusion and come to grips with important ethical issues, our discourse and analysis must be rooted in democracy's expectations that the press enhance public life. Even within this communal framework, however, situations can be perplexing. On the one hand, there is certainly an expectation in the American experience that the press will root out the abuse of privilege. Even if the relationship between President Clinton and Monica Lewinsky were consensual, Clinton's position vis-à-vis an intern indicates an unquestionable abuse of power. Abuse is abuse. On the other hand, there is some expectation of personal privacy within a democratic public.

So the pertinent question is this: Were the events triggered by Drudge's report about Clinton's affair necessary for democracy? Did the public have a "right to know"? Indeed, was Drudge obligated to tell the public? Or in more communitarian terms, did this information enhance the public sphere? Was disclosure important for conversations about public policy or for making democratic institutions more productive or inclusive?

The answer to these questions depends on how we evaluate the right to spread rumors (though Monica was no mere rumor). Are secrets permissible in a democracy? On its face, the answer seems obvious: of course secrets are permissible. We protect military secrets, the names of intelligence operatives, anything having to do with national security. But secrets are not always permissible. Public corruption, malfeasance, and incompetence are matters the public needs to know and anyone who reveals them is doing a public service. The Clinton–Lewinsky event is murky, however. Marvin Kalb argues,

> Because of their timing and subject matter, Drudge's reports contributed to the media's preoccupation with sex and sensationalism. They encouraged the publishing and broadcasting of poorly sourced information. And, as much as anything, they highlighted the problems of Internet journalism—an "Open Sesame" to a world of speeding and colliding fragments of unchecked data fired into cyberspace without any assurance of accuracy or reliability. (2001, 97)

Communitarianism reminds us that ethics is informed by people's particular cultural and social context (value system, history, and publicly acclaimed aspirations as a people). Therefore, actions should be judged not on the basis of their ultimate impact on, or their fit within, our own personal biases, but on their accord with the sort of society its members are trying to build and maintain. If a democracy is to be built on truth, then rumor or gossip is unethical. If a society is determined to protect the press from government encroachment (as the United States has done in the First Amendment), then the public has the moral duty to demand that journalistic standards be sacrosanct. Attribution of sources, in-depth investigation, fairness, balance, and facts within a context of meaning should be non-negotiable for all reporting, whatever the medium. Habermas (1996), the founder of discourse ethics, concludes that the quality of public discourse depends on the extent to which the media fulfill their long-standing roles as sounding board, reliable chronicler of events, and watchdog—no matter what technology is used.

Of particular significance is transparency (cf. Plaisance 2009, ch. 3). As Bernhard Debatin puts it, objectivity—traditionally the press's core value—is being replaced by a new norm of transparency. "Each and every increase in complexity causes a loss of transparency" (Debatin 2008, 259). The profusion, anonymity, and decontextualization of digital technology means that deep structures and sources are easily hidden and difficult to recover. Transparency in on-line reporting means exposing hidden agendas and revealing the reasons behind positions taken on matters of public concern.

In the health care debate in the U.S., for instance, people may argue a position based on principle, beliefs, personal experience, fear, or self-interest—or maybe because they have accepted significant contributions from those who have a financial stake in the outcome. A commitment to transparency demands that the public record include the actual reason for any public position taken for or against a particular proposal. Politicians, as well as those who report about them, must be subject to expectations of full disclosure if the commonweal is to flourish.

Is Drudge a journalist? Does it matter? The playing field for journalists is murky because there is no requirement that journalists be trained in reporting, be licensed or bonded, or pass competency examinations. Whether Drudge thinks he is or is not a journalist—and he waffles on this point—is irrelevant. On the most basic level, a journalist is anyone who reports news. But as Debatin argues, professional journalists in the on-line world are changing from gatekeepers to sense-makers. They distinguish themselves from the rest of the Internet environment by focusing on investigative stories and in-depth information.

CONCLUSION

Communitarian ethics asks us to judge news on the basis of the public good. Do the reports we receive promote communal dialogue? Does the on-line information on which citizens rely flaunt their values or treat them respectfully? Is our civil society becoming more deliberative in the digital age, or are prejudices being stoked by hateful speech, unchecked gossip, and falsifications? Can we trust our sources to report the facts, or do they hide behind anonymity to deceive us?

Internet technology enables us to consider multiple points of view, but unless we engage in respectful dialogue with those with whom we disagree, its democratic value is limited. For communitarian ethics, dependence on those who exploit the worst tendencies in the body politic ought to be avoided. Otherwise, the future of communal life and the democracy it serves are seriously at risk.

NOTES

1. Sydney Blumenthal and his wife sued AOL over Matt Drudge's incorrect characterization as a "wife-beater" because AOL had paid Drudge $3,000 per month for his Drudge Report (Corn 1998).

2. Drudge opposed abortion but "wanted to use the picture to talk about why the United States should not help finance U.N. population-control programs." However, Fox Network executives said that would misrepresent the photo, which was shot during a spina bifida operation on the fetus. Brit Hume, Fox's Washington managing editor, said that "what he [Drudge] calls censorship is what the rest of us call editing" (Kurtz 1999).

3. The word "viewed" is in quotation marks because there is dispute about whether the page views reported by Drudge are accurate or manipulated. Intermarkets, Inc., the firm that handles advertising for Drudge's site, reports 500 million page views and 12 million unique visitors monthly (http://www.intermarkets.net). Quantcast, an Internet research company, reports 14.4 million visitors monthly (less than half from the United States), with 78 percent coming from the 17 percent of visitors it labels "addicts" (http://www.quantcast.com). But Tom Crandall of the SEM Report claims that Drudge uses an "underhanded tactic...to manipulate these figures" (<http://www.semreportcard.com>).

4. *Brill's Content*, a magazine concentrating on journalism ethics, got its start by reporting on the Drudge Report in its first edition in 1998. It ceased publication in 2001 when investors "pulled the plug" because its circulation was not meeting their expectations. Stephen Brill, its founder, was a Clinton supporter. Conservative critics continually complained about its accuracy, even as it complained about their distortions.

5. For a helpful review of blogging, in historical and media ecological context, see Levinson 2009.
6. The Gallup organization reports on confidence in American institutions, including the news media. The percentage of Americans who say they have at least a fair level of confidence in the news media has hovered around 53 percent since at least 1997 (see Gallup, Gallup, and Newport 2007, 360).
7. Several periodicals cited in this chapter were accessed on-line via Highbeam Research, which does not provide volume or page numbers for most materials. Highbeam Research is a subscription Internet site located at <http://www.highbeam.com>.

REFERENCES

Alterman, Eric. 2008. "Out of Print." *The New Yorker*, March 31, 48–59.
AP. 2009. "Associated Press to Build News Registry to Protect Content." Press Release, July 23. <http://www.ap.org/pages/about/pressreleases/pr_072309a.html>.
Bai, Matt. 1997. "Whispers on the Web: The Gossipy Matt Drudge Roils the Media Elite." *Newsweek*, August 18, 69.
Barr, Andy. 2010. "Ron Paul Stands Up for Julian Assange." *Politico,* December 3. <http://www.politico.com/news/stories/1210/45930.html>.
BBC News. 2008. "Profile: Matt Drudge." <http://news.bbc.co.uk/2/hi/uk_news/7270685.stm>.
Beard, Marty. 2001. "Matt Drudge's Rise as a Hot Ad Domain." <http://www.medialifemagazine.com/news2001/oct01/oct01/2_tues/news5tuesday.html>.
Blood, Rebecca. 2002. *The Weblog Handbook: Practical Advice on Creating and Maintaining Your Blog*. New York: Basic.
Bok, Sissela. 1978. *Lying: Moral Choice in Public and Private Life*. New York: Pantheon.
Bowman, James. 1999. "Postmodern Journalism." *World and I*, 14, May, 310.
Burgunder, Lee B. 2011. *Legal Aspects of Managing Technology*, 5th ed. Mason, OH: South-Western Cengage Learning.
Caruso, Denise. 1998. "The Law and the Internet Beware." *Columbia Journalism Review* 37 (May–June): 57–59.
Cohen, Noam, and Stelter, Brian. 2010. "Airstrike Video Brings Notice to a Website." *New York Times*, April 7, A1, A9.
Colon, Alicia. 2006. "The Mendacity of the Liberal Press." *New York Sun*, December 15, 2.
Corn, David. 1998. "Cyberlibel and the White House: This Presidential Aides' Suit Against a Critic and AOL Raises More than Eyebrows." *The Nation*, 266, January 12, 23–24.
Cox, Ana Marie. 2006. "Matt Drudge: Redefining What's News." *Time*, May 8, 171.
Crandall, Tom. 2007. "The Drudge Report's Dirty Little Secret—Criminal or Just Unethical?" June 20. <http://www.semreportcard.com/the-drudge-reports-dirty-little-secret-criminal-or-just-unethical.html>.
Czitrom, Daniel. 1982. *Media and the American Mind: From Morse to McLuhan*. Chapel Hill: University of North Carolina Press.
Dannen, Chris. 2009. "AP Adds Homing Beacon to Online News Content." July 23. <http://www.fastcompany.com/blog/chris-dannen/techwatch/ap-adds-homing-beacon-online-news-content>.
Day, Nancy. 2000. "Tabloid Reporter Drudges up Internet Scoops in 'Manifesto.'" *Boston Herald*, November 2, 58.

Debatin, Bernhard. 2008. "The Future of New Media Ethics." In T. Cooper, C. Christians, and A. Babbili, eds., *An Ethics Trajectory: Visions of Media Past, Present and Yet to Come*, 257–63. Urbana: Institute of Communications Research—University of Illinois.

Diddlebock, Bob. 2009. "Who Really Killed the *Rocky Mountain News*?" *Time*, March 6. <http://www.time.com/time/business/article/0,8599,1883345,00.html>.

Dowd, Maureen. 2003. "Let's Blame Canada." *New York Times*, July 20, sec. 4, p. 11.

Drudge, Matt, and Phillips, Julia. 2000. *Drudge Manifesto*. New York: New American Library.

Eddy, Nicholas. n.d. "'Screw Journalism!' Improper Exercise of Personal Jurisdiction in Blumenthal v. Drudge." <http://cyber.law.harvard.edu/fallsem98/final_papers/Eddy.html>.

Ellul, Jacques. 1967. *The Political Illusion*. Translated by K. Kellen. New York: Alfred A. Knopf.

Frankfurt, Harry G. 2006. *On Truth*. New York: Knopf.

Friend, Cecilia, and Singer, Jane B. 2007. *Online Journalism Ethics: Traditions and Transitions*. Armonk, NY: M. E. Sharpe.

Gallup, Alec, Gallup, George Horace, and Newport, Frank. 2007. *The Gallup Poll*. New York: Rowman and Littlefield.

Gerstein, Josh, and Smith, Ben. 2009. "Obama Fails to Quell Gay Uproar." June 18. <http://www.politico.com/news/stories/0609/23868.html>.

Gillin, Paul. 2009. "News Wikification." August 14. <http://newspaperdeathwatch.com/news-wikification/>.

Goldenberg, Suzanne. 2007. "Hillary Clinton Woos Man Who Nearly Ruined Her Husband." *The Guardian*, October 23, 22.

Greenberg, Andy. 2010. "WikiLeak's Julian Assange Wants to Spill Your Corporate Secrets." *Forbes*, 186 (11), December 20, 70–86.

Grossman, Lawrence K. 1999. "From Marconi to Murrow to—Drudge?" *Columbia Journalism Review*, July/August, 17–18.

Gutmann, Amy. 1994. "Introduction." In Charles Taylor et al., eds., *Multiculturalism: Examining the Politics of Recognition*, 3–24. Princeton, NJ: Princeton University Press.

Habermas, Jürgen. 1996. *Between Facts and Norms: Contributions to a Discourse Theory of Law and Democracy*. Translated by W. Rehg. Cambridge, Mass.: MIT Press.

Harnden, Toby. 2008. "Matt Drudge: World's Most Powerful Journalist." February 28. <http://www.telegraph.co.uk/news/worldnews/1580164/Matt-Drudge.html>.

Harris, John F. 2006. "New Media a Weapon in New World of Politics." *Washington Post*, October 6, A1.

Hilden, Julie. 2003. "Matt Drudge Versus 'K Street': Does the Internet Maverick Have a Claim against the Boundary-Testing Show?" November 11. <http://writ.news.findlaw.com/hilden/20031111.html>.

Intermarkets, Inc. "Drudge Report." <http://www.intermarkets.net/advertisers/portfolio/news/drudgeReport.html>.

Kalb, Marvin. 2001. *One Scandalous Story: Clinton, Lewinsky, & 13 Days that Tarnished American Journalism*. New York: Free Press.

Kinsley, Michael. 1998. "In Defense of Matt Drudge." *Time*, February 2, 41.

Kuhn, Martin. 2007. "Interactivity and Prioritizing the Human: A Code of Blogging Ethics." *Journal of Mass Media Ethics* 22 (1): 18–36.

Kurtz, Howard. 1999. "Fox Threatens Matt Drudge with Lawsuit over Walkout." *Washington Post*, November 17, C1.

———. 2000. "ABC Fires Radio Host Matt Drudge." *Washington Post*, November 13, C1.

Kushner, David. 2010. "Click and Dagger: Inside WikiLeaks' Leak Factory." *Mother Jones*, 35 (4), June 2, 62–73.

Lasica, J. D. n.d. "Case Study Teaching Notes." <http://www.jdlasica.com/2000/01/20/case-study-teaching-notes/>.

———. 2000. "Internet Journalism and the Starr Investigation." January 20. <http://www.jdlasica.com/2000/01/20/internet-journalism-and-the-starr-investigation/>.

Levine, Art. 2009. "The Kennedy Legacy vs. Glenn Beck's Lies about Reform 'Murdering' Small Businesses." August 27. <http://www.huffingtonpost.com/art-levine/news-reports-small-business_b_270116.html>.

Levinson, Paul. 2009. *New New Media*. Boston: Allyn & Bacon.

Levy, Steven. 1998. "New Media's Dark Star." *Newsweek*, February 16, 78.

Lipschultz, Jeremy Harris. 2000. *Free Expression in the Age of the Internet: Social and Legal Boundaries*. Boulder, CO: Westview.

Lissit, Robert. 1998. "Internet News: Cybergold or Cybersludge?" *World and I*, 13 (10), October, 94–99.

Lynch, Lisa. 2010. "We're Going to Crack the World Open: WikiLeaks and the Future of Investigative Reporting." *Journalism Practice*, 4 (3), July 8, 309–18.

Lyon, David. 2003. *Surveillance after September 11*. Cambridge, U.K.: Polity.

New York Magazine blog. 2009. "Rush Limbaugh Told Matt Drudge to 'Disappear from Public Life.'" Posted April 21, 2009. <http://nymag.com/daily/intel/2009/04/rush_limbaugh_told_matt_drudge>.

Pachter, Richard. 2003. "Linking News Sites, Matt Drudge Creates Internet Success." *Miami Herald*, September 2.

Perlmutter, David D., and Schoen, Mary. 2007. "If I Break a Rule, What Do I Do, Fire Myself? Ethics Codes of Independent Blogs." *Journal of Mass Media Ethics* 22 (1): 37–48.

Pew Project for Excellence in Journalism. 2010. The State of the News Media. <http://stateofthemedia.org/2010/>.

Pinkerton, James. 2003. "Matt Drudge's Written Words (Editorial)." *Cincinnati Post*, January 20.

Plaisance, Patrick L. 2009. *Media Ethics: Key Principles for Responsible Practice*. Thousand Oaks, CA: Sage.

Popp, Karen A. 2000. "The Impeachment of President Clinton: An Ugly Mix of Three Powerful Forces." *Law and Contemporary Problems* 63 (1–2): 223–43.

Porter, Ethan. 2009. "Drudge has Lost his Touch." *Columbia Journalism Review*, 48 (3), September/October, 14–16.

Quantcast. "Drudgereport Network." <http://www.quantcast.com/drudgereport.com>.

Race, Tim. 2009. "Two Right-Angled Views." *New York Times*, August 27. <http://prescriptions.blogs.nytimes.com/2009/08/27/two-right-angled-views/>.

Rich, Frank. 1999. "The Strange Legacy of Matt Drudge." *New York Times*, December 4, A17.

Rogers, Tony. 2009. "Why Are Newspapers Dying?" <http://journalism.about.com/od/trends/a/dyingpapers.htm>.

Rosenthal, Phil. 2008. "Tower Ticker." October 16. <http://newsblogs.chicagotribune.com/towerticker/2008/10/the-wire-will-t.html>.

Shafer, Jack. 2006. "The Incredible Shrinking Newspaper." *Slate*, June 24. <http://www.slate.com/id/2144201/>.

Shepard, Alicia C. 1998. "The Incredible Shrinking News Cycle." *World and I*, 13, June, 80–86.

Sherman, Gabriel. 2009. "Underground Man." *New Republic*, 240 (7), May 6, 5–6.

Soldatov, Andrei, and Borogan, Irina. 2010. "WikiLeaks Case Highlights Crisis in Journalism." December 2. <http://www.agentura.ru/english/press/wleaks/>.

Sonenshine, Tara. 1997. "Is Everyone a Journalist?" *American Journalism Review*, 19 (8), October, 11–12.

Surber, Don. 2007. "Monica Turned Journalism Inside Out: Matt Drudge Sets the Pace of American News." *Charleston Gazette*, December 22, 5A.

Surowiecki, James. 2008. "News You Can Lose." *New Yorker*, 84 (42), December 22, 48.

Taylor, Charles. 1991. "Civil Society in the Western Tradition." In E. Groffier and M. Paradis, eds., *The Notion of Tolerance and Human Rights*, 117–36. Ottawa: Carleton University Press.

Vanity Fair. 2008. "Matt Drudge." <http://www.vanityfair.com/online/newestablishment/2008/09/matt-drudge.html>.

Whitworth, Damian. 2008. "Matt Drudge—the Secretive Recluse who Keeps America on Its Toes." TimesOnLine, February 29. <http:www.timesonline.co.uk/tol/news/uk/article3460490.ece>.

Williams, Bruce, and Carpini, Michael X. Delli. 2009. "The Eroding Boundaries between News and Entertainment and What They Mean for Democratic Politics." In L. Wilkins and C. Christians, eds., *The Handbook of Mass Media Ethics*, 177–88. New York: Routledge.

Winter, Bill. n.d. "Matt Drudge—Libertarian." The website of Advocates for Self-Government. <http://server.theadvocates.org/celebrities/matt-drudge.html>.

Witcover, Jules. 1998. "Where We Went Wrong." *Columbia Journalism Review*, 36 (6), March–April, 18–25.

CHAPTER 4

๛

Surveillance after September 11

A retired special education teacher on his way to a wedding in Orlando, Fla., said he was left humiliated, crying and covered with his own urine after an enhanced pat-down by TSA officers recently at Detroit Metropolitan Airport.

"I was absolutely humiliated, I couldn't even speak," said Thomas D. "Tom" Sawyer, 61, of Lansing, Michigan.

Sawyer is a bladder cancer survivor who now wears a urostomy bag, which collects his urine from a stoma, or opening in his abdomen. "I have to wear special clothes and in order to mount the bag I have to seal a wafer to my stomach and then attach the bag. If the seal is broken, urine can leak all over my body and clothes."

Sawyer said he went through the security scanner at Detroit Metropolitan Airport. "Evidently the scanner picked up on my urostomy bag, because I was chosen for a pat-down procedure."

Due to his medical condition, Sawyer asked to be screened in private. "One officer looked at another, rolled his eyes and said that they really didn't have any place to take me," said Sawyer. "After I said again that I'd like privacy, they took me to an office."

Sawyer wears pants two sizes too large in order to accommodate the medical equipment he wears. He'd taken off his belt to go through the scanner and once in the office with security personnel, his pants fell down around his ankles. "I had to ask twice if it was OK to pull up my shorts," said Sawyer, "And every time I tried to tell them about my medical condition, they said they didn't need to know about that."

(Baskas 2011)

* * *

September 11, 2001: Just one day in history, but never to be forgotten. Suicide attacks by al-Qaeda. Nineteen terrorists and four hijacked airliners change the mightiest nation on earth. The Twin Towers of the World Trade Center in New York City collapse in two hours; 2,974 people from more than ninety countries die. A third airliner hits the Pentagon, and a fourth—headed to Washington, D.C.—overwhelmed by passengers and crew, slams to the ground in rural Pennsylvania. The United States has been attacked by outside forces for only the third time in history, each in its own century (War of 1812, Pearl Harbor in 1941, and now 9-11).

The President declares a "War on Terrorism"—on both terrorists and the countries that hide them, anywhere on earth. To depose the Taliban with its al-Qaeda sanctuaries, Afghanistan becomes target number one. The aggravated superpower searches the planet to cut off terrorists at their origin. Within its own borders, it commences a relentless campaign to tighten security

Six weeks after September 11, President George W. Bush signed the USA Patriot (Uniting and Strengthening America by Providing Appropriate Tools Required to Intercept and Obstruct Terrorism) Act into law. Written quickly and pushed through Congress in record time, the bill shifted the Department of Justice's goal from prosecuting terrorists to preventing terrorism. Its purpose was to preserve freedom by stopping terrorist activity before it begins. "It's a fundamental and unprecedented shift," says Viet Dinh of the Georgetown University Law Center. "We are fighting guerilla warfare on steroids" (Carnes 2003, 27).

The Patriot Act was a 9-11 response within the provisions of the omnibus Foreign Intelligence Surveillance Act (FISA) ratified in 1978. The law governs information gathering related to foreign powers. Its rulings control surveillance of people and institutions that might prove useful in dealing with U.S. enemies. Warrants can be issued for intercepting foreign-to-foreign communications passing through telecommunication switches on American soil. The Patriot Act gives broad powers to the Executive branch to collect phone and email messages. No longer does the FISA court decide who, what, or where the government will monitor. The Patriot Act also gives retroactive immunity to telecommunications companies that have complied with government requests for information on private persons that turn out to be unconstitutional.

Even with the expanded powers that the Patriot Act provided the government, certain agencies were still accused of reaching beyond the scope of information legally accessible to them, raising concerns about the abuse of power and calling for lawmakers to repeal or revise the Act to restore the appropriate guarantees of privacy and transparency regarding the use of such information. In 2007, the Justice Department's inspector general discovered that the FBI routinely issued national security letters to cull information about Americans suspected of terrorism. An audit found that some letters were written "without proper authority, cited incorrect statutes or obtained information they weren't supposed to" (Arena and Quijano 2007). In several instances, the "emergent situation" cited by investigators to warrant access to private information did not exist (Lichtblau 2008).

Now you already know more about government surveillance than you ever wanted to, and we have just begun. And by the end of this chapter, we will know what you had for breakfast—so pay attention!

Surveillance of a community by those outside it is a crucial issue for communitarianism, and reporters should be vitally involved in promoting awareness of it. The New York Times, which sets the standard for all news media to follow, is constantly vigilant when the Patriot Act is being considered for renewal or revision. It correctly editorializes against the government's excessive powers to search financial records, conduct roving wiretaps, and track terrorist suspects (e.g., "Patriot Act Excesses" 2009, A28; "A Bruise on the First Amendment" 2010, A22).

Beyond understanding the legal dimensions of the Patriot Act and FISA, communities must come to grips with this legislation in ethical terms. Privacy is a moral good because it is a precondition for developing a unique sense of self. Violating privacy violates human dignity. Communitarian ethics puts the moral spotlight on the space between persons, the relation between us, but it does not require that this space be lit for indiscriminate or secret viewing. In fact, communitarian thinking recognizes the universal human need for sanctuary—free of intrusion and measured control of one's own story. As persons, we need privacy both for our individual dignity and for wholesome relationships with others.

Privacy is a moral good in a political sense also. Respect for privacy distinguishes democratic from totalitarian societies. Democracies as a system of rule by the people (*demos*) protect citizens from government encroachment on what they themselves control. Authoritarian societies use the near absence of privacy to produce a servile populace. Good living presupposes enough elbowroom to protect my relationships from unwarranted intrusions, while assuming community safety. The ethics of privacy grounded in human dignity elevates government surveillance above political disputes and legal wrangling case-by-case. It emphasizes the impact of surveillance on healthy communities instead.

We are focusing here on the Patriot Act and FISA for the sake of depth and specificity, but expanded judicial powers to detain and profile also appeared after 9-11 in Canada's Anti-Terrorism Act, in the United Kingdom's counter-terrorism laws (tightened even further after the July 7, 2005, attacks on London), and in France, Germany, Denmark, Sweden, Austria, and Singapore. India's Home Ministry has announced the right to monitor and decrypt digital messages whenever it considers eavesdropping vital to national security (Bajaj and Austen 2010, B1, B8). Aggressive data gathering and law enforcement, considered necessary for the "war on terrorism," vex democratic societies everywhere.

CLIMATE OF FEAR

History turned a corner on 9-11. Airports will forever be high-security zones. Tall buildings, despite luxury and spacious views, will always be inviting targets for people bent on causing disaster. From now on business magnates who occupy top floors in downtown office complexes will flip on their desk lamps in some of the most nervous real estate on earth. Metal detectors in doorways will be as commonplace as elevators. And fear—the knowledge that any stranger may be a threat, any "package left unattended" a potential bomb—will hover wherever people gather. Protection against terror has required that we surrender speed for caution, friendliness for suspicion, and privacy for surveillance. Anyone wearing TSA (Transportation Security Administration) is free to go through your unmentionables and conduct total body scans. The stone-faced scanner technician will see parts of you that you have never seen. And the stakes keep escalating. In December 2009, Umar Farouk Abdulmutallab smuggled explosives in his underwear through airport security in Amsterdam and tried to blow up a plane in Detroit. The 190 nations of the United Nation's International Civil Aviation Organization are working day and night to find solutions. Airport security is adding, beyond its magnetometer strategy, protection against powder and plastics. It is the price we pay to reduce our fear. But reduced fear today is still greater than pre-9-11 fear, which did not contemplate such tragedies as we saw in New York, Washington, and Pennsylvania.

Fear is a dangerous environment in which to work out the ethics of privacy. The pressure to overcompensate, to employ overwhelming force, to escalate the stakes, takes the foreground. Debate, dissent, alternative approaches, and nonviolent resistance are put off for another day. Has America overreacted to the terrorist threat in legalizing unprecedented government surveillance? Have the news media failed to alert readers and citizens to this unparalleled invasion of private space because of allegations of siding with the enemy?

On the side favoring FISA and aggressive intelligence gathering, we hear the argument that the disaster at New York's Twin Towers has not been repeated. Threats and cabals have been interdicted secretly to avoid compromising other investigations. We are, to date, relatively safe. The "relative" part hinges on continued access by security agencies to global communications as our enemies become increasingly sophisticated and determined to breach protective networks and inflict harm. The Patriot Act, an essential mechanism for rooting out terrorists, is said only to amend existing federal laws.

On the opposing side, we hear that FISA and its central pillar, the Patriot Act, compromise, if not distort beyond recognition, our First and Fourth Amendments, the very heart and soul of our legal tradition. Say what you will about a non-falsifiable assertion (i.e., the absence of a second attack is credited to surveillance strategies), we are becoming a democracy that our Founders would not recognize: Orwell's worst nightmare, a nationwide no-hide zone. FISA and the Patriot Act establish a secret information-gathering process that opens confidential records, not for probable cause, but merely on the grounds they are relevant to an investigation into domestic terrorism. In its controversial threats to privacy, the Patriot Act grants the FBI access to medical, financial, and educational records when considered necessary to protect against clandestine intelligence activities. The Act was refined and made permanent in March 2006. Its key provisions were included in a four-year extension (May 2011), such as roving wiretaps on multiple phones and surveillance against noncitizens suspected of insurgency.

The possible consequences of government surveillance were explored in film even before 9-11. In the 1998 movie *Enemy of the State*, corrupt politician Thomas Reynolds (played by Jon Voight) has a congressman murdered. When Reynolds discovers that a tape of the murder exists, he deploys his goons to destroy both the tape and its owner. Shortly before the tape's owner dies, he manages to pass the evidence to main character Robert Dean (played by Will Smith), albeit without

Dean's knowledge. Once Reynolds discovers that the evidence still exists, he uses the surveillance capabilities of the National Security Administration to gather information and destroy the life of Robert Dean. Dean's only hope for survival is to join forces with a man named Brill (played by Gene Hackman) who draws upon his extensive knowledge of surveillance capabilities to beat Reynolds and his men at their own game.

Entertainment media about surveillance, conspiracy, paranoia, and control took on additional heft post 9-11. In 2006, *Matrix* co-director Andy Wachowski followed up the huge success of his franchise with *V for Vendetta*, a none-too-subtle sci-fi allegory about an English totalitarian state created in response to the "war on terror." The cable television show *Rubicon* premiered in August 2010 exploring the intelligence-security complex. The show follows a team of intelligence analysts working for the fictional policy think tank, the American Enterprise Institute. The team is neck deep in conflicting intelligence reports from around the world as they weigh attacks by suspected terrorists based on fragmented and contradictory evidence. *Rubicon* set a ratings record for its cable network with over 2 million people viewing its pilot episode.

COMMUNITIES AND NATIONS

Surveillance has its origins in the perceived need to defend one's possessions. Intelligence directs troop movements against enemy weakness, or in business applications, against competitors or consumer resistance. The more commanders or executives know, the better they can direct effective power. The Civil War might have turned on the chance discovery of Robert E. Lee's orders by a Union corporal before the battle at Antietam Creek (Miller 2008, 184). During the Pacific island campaign of World War II, the U.S. Navy depended on code breakers to decrypt the Japanese system (Haufler 2003, 146 ff.). The widely used Global Positioning System (GPS) and the ubiquitous Internet were military inventions with immediate applications still in effect (Lyon 2006, 14). When the classified U.S. military documents were published on the website WikiLeaks in July 2010, the Army intelligence officer, PFC Bradley Manning, was charged with violating Article 92 of the Universal Code of Military Justice. From ancient eavesdropping to stop-and-search technologies used by police to aggressive control over unauthorized disclosure, surveillance has been an important tool of the state to protect its interests and hold advantage over adversaries.

Indeed, a large part of surveillance's history has involved reinforcing power by enforcing discipline. In 1785, Jeremy Bentham, the father of utilitarianism, proposed a new type of prison, the panopticon. In this prison, individual cells surrounded a central viewing station, enabling guards to watch prisoner movement at all times. For Bentham, the panopticon would reinforce good behavior: not knowing when guards were watching, prisoners would behave as if they were under surveillance constantly (Bentham 1995; see Lyon 2006, ch. 2). The famous twentieth-century social theorist Michel Foucault contended that the basic idea of surveillance represented by the panopticon is in fact the way that the state (or any institution) reinforces discipline and brings individuals under social control (Foucault 1977; see Lyon 2006, chs. 2, 10). We note that Nelson Mandela's success as the political leader of South Africa was directly related to his having sufficient privacy for twenty-seven years at Robben Island prison as he set the stage for the end of apartheid (Mandela 1994, 391).

David Lyon argues that since 9-11, but continuing an overall process beginning in the 1960s, countries around the world have become surveillance societies.[1] For Lyon, the events of September 11 created a powerful impetus to use new information and search technologies for dramatically expanding surveillance. A secure nation, "the safety state" as Lyon calls it, requires personal data set in the "cross-hairs of space and time" by sophisticated digital technologies (Lyon 2007, 9). Biometric and genomic data are especially important for profiling, but so are electronic records of commercial activity, which expose key traits of human behavior.

The investigative series, "Top Secret America," in the *Washington Post*, July 18–21, 2010, documents America's huge buildup of surveillance machinery since 9-11, with little accountability and no time for ethics. At least 854,000 Americans hold top-secret security clearances as of 2010. The National Security Agency near Fort Meade, Florida alone employs about 30,000 people and occupies 6.3 million square feet of offices with 112 acres of parking. The NSA aims to increase those totals to 40,000 workers and 14 million square feet over the next decade and a half. Eighty other agencies and corporations have a presence near the Fort Meade NSA campus, which is only one of a dozen such "nerve centers" around the United States (Priest and Arkin 2010, July 21). In the Washington area alone, over 4,000 separate corporate offices handle classified data and help conduct espionage on terrorist networks (Priest and Arkin 2010, July 20). The investigation estimated that some 1,271 government organizations and 1,931 private companies work on programs related to counterterrorism, homeland security, and intelligence in 10,000 locations across the United States. The enterprise is so huge that no one in government has a full understanding of it (Priest and Arkin 2010, July 19).

Early in the story of American democracy, when citizens considered the state a necessary evil (Wills 1999, 16–17), the very Constitution framing this new nation was created with strong guarantees against state prying into private places and personal thoughts. The Bill of Rights permits the state no control over personal expression, no authority to barge into or occupy private property or to know what is on the mind or conscience of any citizen. We now question whether those rules are effective. The National Security Agency's ECHELON system gathers global intelligence from telecommunications signals at its huge base in the United Kingdom, yet its use of these data is "shrouded in secrecy, with [its] technological capabilities the subject of…guesswork…and rumour" (Lyon 2006, 18). In health, law enforcement, labor, and manufacturing, the hunger for data grows more ravenous every day.

Ever-expanding technological capacity opens up new avenues not only for surveillance systems like ECHELON or the Pentagon's Total Information

Awareness program but also for possible criminal attacks. Cyberterrorism—the idea that terrorists could target computer systems and networks to disable security, wreak havoc on infrastructure, or access confidential data—has become an increasing threat since the 1990s. September 11 heightened these concerns. Previously known mostly for harvest, changing leaves, and Halloween, October is now National Cyber Security Awareness Month. The back-to-school season is also the time for the CyberPatriot program's "National High School Cyber Defense Competition" sponsored by the Air Force Association and defense giant Northrop Grumman.

What is a person to do? Fear is one response, the unfortunate by-product of growing technological capacity. "The fear of random, violent victimization blends well with the distrust and outright fear of computer technology," notes a special report titled "Cyberterrorism: How Real is the Threat?". "Although cyberterrorism does not entail a direct threat of violence, its psychological impact on anxious societies can be as powerful as the effect of terrorist bombs" (Weimann 2004, 2).

Such anxiety is well placed. We are barely ten years away from the "Black Ice" experiment, sponsored by the National Security Agency (NSA), in which thirty-five hired hackers were able to break into the U.S. Pacific military's command-and-control system and, had they been working for a foreign agency and not as "friendlies," cripple it (Weismann 2004, 6). Surveillance data gathered by your own government that profile you may be beyond the government's ability to manage responsibly. That you are no longer a player in the virtual game about you is certain. That your prosperity is vulnerable to a hacker or terrorist is also certain—whatever "certainty" might mean given channels and data banks of uncertain purpose in secret places now absent the obstacles of court review. As Symantec Security warns, "New terrorist organizations are highly funded, technologically articulate groups capable of inflicting devastating damage to a wide range of targets [which] poses significant risk to U.S. infrastructure" (Gordon and Ford, n.d., 9).

A growing number of those fears have been realized on an interstate level. In 2009, media reports (e.g. BBC 2009; Markoff 2009) detailed the discovery of GhostNet, clandestine spying software within a global network of at least 1,295 computers, up to 30 percent of which were "high-value" targets at government installations or other secure sites such as embassies, offices of the Dalai Lama, and even NATO. Researchers involved in the months-long investigation could not identify a culprit, though most of the attacks originated on servers in China. And in the summer and fall of 2010, cybersecurity agencies were rocked again as reports surfaced of the first computer virus to sabotage a control system in the physical world, in this case a Siemens software suite used to regulate nuclear energy and other major industrial facilities. The Stuxnet worm spread around the world, over 60 percent of the malware's infections occurring in Iran (Sanger 2010).

Such threats are ominous, indeed, and there is no retreat to a less technical wilderness. We can never move back. The technologically sublime future envisioned by Marshall McLuhan (1964), who coined "the global village" as a metaphor for tranquil interconnectedness, seems as remote a dream as Jules Verne's journey to the center of the earth. Instead, when talking about surveillance and cyberterrorism in the twenty-first century, we are left with deep uncertainty. Nobody complains that banks require a PIN number to access our accounts at the ATM. When murderers terrorize Virginia Tech and Northern Illinois universities, campus communities welcome tighter restrictions. Most people would concur that safety and security from terrorist acts—in the real world or in cyberspace—are important. But at what costs? What is being eroded, Lyon explains, is "social trust, mutual care, the politics of recognition, due process, and the limits of power. Surveillance is always ambiguous; care and control are always in tension" (Lyon 2003, 11).

COMMUNITARIANISM'S RADICAL DIFFERENCE

Business consultant Peter Block advises that bringing a frightened world back to sanity and humaneness requires us "to transform isolation and self-interest...into connectedness and caring for the whole." That happens through what he calls "associated life": people forming groups to serve the common interest. Block's own work to foster civic engagement in Cincinnati, Ohio, is widely recognized. Yet world populations are another problem, and peoples whose visions of reality are not concordant are less apt than Cincinnatians to prefer cooperation to conquest. Yet the cyberwar we fear, and the unchecked surveillance threatening our privacy, engage differences of geography and history which neither "getting together" or "declaring a right" seem likely to solve (Block 2008, 1, 43).

Communitarianism is frequently compared to the health benefits of good nutrition. We all know that eating greens (antioxidants) is healthier than eating sugars and that green vegetables deliver natural defenses against malignancies. But if you are diagnosed with cancer, a diet of greens is too little, too late. To combat aggressive sickness you take the violent chemicals of chemotherapy and fight to live. Similarly, communitarianism as a mode of public life maintains balance as it builds bonds of human care and webs of social connectedness, creating loyalty where suspicion and distrust had placed a wet blanket on embers of the I-thou. Communitarianism is the ounce of prevention that reduces the unstable edge; it carves a path between boulders, it finds language that leads to common purpose and not long thereafter, to shared laughter. It quiets the anxiety of dealing with an unknown Other.

Communitarian ethics never holds a gun to the head of the Other. Its pace may appear no more effective than any other in our flash-point world. Lincoln once accused his flamboyant General McClellan of having "the slows." Little Mac, as he was called, was disposed more to training an army than to fighting an enemy. Always complaining that he needed more supplies, Mac often seemed to Lincoln as if he had no intention of challenging Lee. To muster force against the Confederacy was next month's action; for Little Mac a dress review was enough sword-swinging for today. Communitarianism's slow-change methods, its low-conflict approach, strike many as its fatal flaw. In the war against terror, we can debate the Fourth Amendment until morning, but sunrise will not come if we fail to interdict those who plot our ruin. Communitarianism appears like the Roman senate conducting decent and good business while Visigoths burn the city. Communitarian music is solace on the sinking *Titanic*, but it will not keep the ship afloat, critics claim.

But such criticism misperceives the radical difference communitarian theory brings to the twin crises of surveillance and cyberterrorism. Indeed, real steps toward peace, security, and justice are more likely when communitarian practice and policy hold the attention of all the players at the table.

Cyberterrorism poses considerable risks. Electronic terrorism's list of targets is long and weighty: the banking industry, military installations, power plants, air traffic control centers, water systems, and emergency services. A successful attack on such critical computer networks would render vast systems dysfunctional. One recent critique suggests that media coverage itself has helped disseminate and construct cyberterrorism as the premier threat to infrastructure in the United States and worldwide. The more the public knows, the better equipped cyberterrorists are (Conway 2008, 4).

Communitarians are not naïve idealists who imagine that committed ideologues and trained (and fanaticized) suicide missioners would pause to discuss their grievances if invited to the conference table. Those who kill civilian populations without warning must be stopped, period. Communitarians hold to a high view of life. Human life should be protected and nourished above all else. Persons who threaten life must be educated or restrained. Life trumps killing except in extreme circumstances, which must be publicly justified.

There is no guarantee that communitarian ethics will win at the end of the day. Communitarians can lose their temper, hyperventilate, or compromise the virtuous upper hand just like anyone else. What communitarians do claim is that proper public policy restrains evildoing without diminishing the humanity of those committing it.

Did we say "evil"? There's a loaded term. Some very smart people doubt there's much value in that medieval word. William Hart has described the work of zealots down through the ages as worse than the evil they have opposed. If we were only sharper in our moral analysis, he writes, we would realize that the concept of "evil" is out of place in an age of science and commerce. Science washes our vocabulary of such terms. In the era of modern medicine, "evil" is replaced by "virus," the "devil" by anti-social development of deficits (Hart, 2004, xi, 61). Yet we claim that evil still fits those with motive and means to kill indiscriminately. Communitarianism provides no tolerance for this death-dealing, but we recognize that incivility in response to evil would hand the future to tyranny. There must be a better way.

INVENTING THE PRIVACY RIGHT

Perhaps George Orwell's *1984* did as much as any book to convince us that privacy was part of a civilized society. Winston Smith, the lead character, can hardly escape the all-seeing eye of Big Brother, the ubiquitous state. The Party controls both the history and culture of its subjects. In an attempt to prevent a possible uprising by its citizens, the ruling Party invents "Newspeak," a language devoid of terms useful to rebels. Even dissenting thoughts are outlawed.

Ayn Rand's novels and essays drove the point home. Rand insists that the "altruist-collective premise"—that people have an obligation inherent in our humanness to regard the Other with care—is insidious and wrong (Rand 1961, 93). The individual is paramount, she insists. Privacy is sacrosanct.

But Orwell and Rand were not the first. In an 1890 *Harvard Law Review*, two Boston attorneys decried the press's prying into citizens' private affairs. Louis Brandeis (appointed to the Supreme Court in 1916) and his law partner Samuel D. Warren articulated for the first time a right to relief from the public gaze, a boundary protecting personal privacy:

> Later, there came a recognition of man's spiritual nature, of his feelings and his intellect. Gradually the scope of these legal rights broadened; and now the right to life has come to mean...the right to be left alone. (Warren and Brandeis 1890, 193)

The long history of the right to privacy working its way into the law of the land peaked in 1972 when Justice Harry Blackmun reckoned privacy as the operative right in childbirth and struck antiabortion laws throughout the United States. That decision and nearly all others invoking privacy rights are based not on explicit wording in the Constitution, but on renderings of commonsense beliefs about what life requires. When Jackie Kennedy Onassis was pestered by photographer Ron Gallela, she sought a court order restraining him. The District Court in Manhattan, trying to square the need for personal privacy and the right to receive public information, opined:

> The essence of the privacy interest includes [a general right] to have moments of freedom from the unremitting assault of the world...in order to achieve some measure of tranquility...without which life loses its sweetness. (353 F. Supp. 196 [SDNY 1972])

These cases preceded Web 2.0, after which technology could remember everything and recall anything. The privacy interest has been smashed by "egalitarian, self-expressing hierarchy-busting, anti-exclusive Internet" technologies that "end up standardizing its users" and make us all alike, wrote Lee Siegel (2008, 65). If technology works its will, we will have little need for privacy in a generation to come. Privacy is unnecessary where idiosyncrasy does not exist.

Communitarians resist that leveled future where cultures look alike and the only food available to travelers comes from kitchens owned and operated by global monopolies. The rainbow of cultural variety is a resource we must preserve, a sign of life itself. That rainbow needs the warm earth of creativity and cultural dignity to give it rootage. Digitize culture, open the shades on every art studio, put a wiretap on every carrier of sound, and the rainbow will never show its colors again.

The individualist theory of privacy from Orwell and Rand through Warren and Brandeis, represents only one model of democracy. The Anglo-American version makes free and autonomous individuals the centerpiece by protecting individual ends and personal preferences from government interference. By contrast, communitarians advocate a civic tradition that emphasizes common goods and shared values.[2] This civic version is a democracy of ends, where we discover goods together we cannot know alone. Thus, the test of democracy is the degree of participation, community consciousness, and cooperation, with the ethics of surveillance seeking to protect these values rather than asserting "the right to be left alone" for its own sake.

Already before 9-11 and unmistakably since, the cult of individual privacy provides no protection against the tendency of bureaucracies to collect and store data when technology makes it possible. Focusing on super-snoop threats to personal freedom leads to a scattershot of reactive policies instead of a coordinated approach rooted in the common good.

David Lyon speaks in communitarian terms when he argues that privacy as an individual issue detracts our attention from the social consequences of surveillance. Humans are organized into categories using "government technologies" like statistics and probabilities:

> To think of surveillance primarily as endangering personal spaces of freedom... misses the point about surveillance contributing to social sorting mechanisms. To possess personal data in order to classify groups is to affect profoundly their choices and their chances in life. This is why the *social* analysis of surveillance is so essential to a proper understanding. And it is even more vital after 9/11. (Lyon 2003, 146; emphasis in original)

Classification binds people into descriptions they cannot easily escape—the category "terrorist" certainly, and those circles of suspects in its wake since September 11 ("Arabs" and "Muslims," for example).[3] Amitai Etzioni makes a strong case for using "combatant civilian" instead of "terrorist" or "criminal" in our nomenclature. The clarity of the name then compels a reasoned and communitarian response in the law (Etzioni 2009, 109).

> Surveillance practices enable fresh forms of exclusion that not only cut off certain targeted groups from social participation, but do so in subtle ways that are sometimes scarcely visible.... This may be exclusion as domination, where the categories of outcast reflect deep and long-term tensions. But it may also be exclusion as abandonment in which the way is eased for some simply to "walk by on the other side." (Lyon 2003, 146)

Although communitarians face fear, they need not surrender to it or allow exclusion-by-category to give them a false sense of protection. They promote life and will not compromise or appease death merchants. They resist the tightening of private space as a threat to cultural diversity and to art, without which life turns grey. Yet important questions remain. In the era of cell phones and spies, body bombs and cyberworms, can communitarians get all they want and still survive? Are privacy and safety wrapped with the same ribbon?

PRIVACY VERSUS SAFETY

You may have noticed that standard moral positions can be used on either side of these twin dilemmas, privacy and safety. A utilitarian might say that "the greatest good" is survival and allow considerable slippage on other points in order to guarantee the survival of the species for another generation. Another utilitarian might argue that the "greatest good" means that civilization is first and foremost human. Beasts survive, but humans live with dignity. Extract dignity/privacy from the scene and our species loses its humanity. Clearly, we need a way to transcend the utility principle's ambiguities if we hope to find a trajectory over the threat of terror and the vulnerability of privacy.

The need for such a trajectory is urgent. The more we depend upon sophisticated communications technology, the more hackers and cyberterrorists threaten our bank accounts, credit cards, identities, and economies. Yet the threat does not lead us to withdraw from technology. The utility principle permits no retreat from the cyber future, sure as we are that the best IT is yet to be. The deontological principle allows no falling back. Pressing ahead is nonnegotiable. Virtue ethics musters on the side of technological progress, displaying the courage to press into the unknown and the patience to get there despite obstacles.

Each of these standard moral positions condemns the data spoilage of cyberterror or the privacy preemption of unfettered government surveillance. But if you may use the principles any which way, how helpful are they, really?

We can agree—relationships are primary and individuals find their identities and happiness through relating to others. But the utility principle cannot move us beyond two contradictory conclusions. On the one hand, technology affords multiple, economical, and very fast ways of building social networks. Social networks escalate overnight. Internet users enjoy more friends at daily reach than ever before. Adding numbers does not build depth, of course, and depth requires more than text-messaging. Nonetheless, global communities are a growth industry.

But utility cannot escape the opposite: Technology is vulnerable to enemies of peaceful community. Our love of Blackberry brings us closer to blackout, that is, grievous loss of relationship through system breakdown.

And utility speaks with a forked tongue on surveillance itself. Surveillance can serve the common good. When an early warning system safeguards coastal populations from hurricanes or medical tests from cancers, it preserves community. Surveillance is quiet, discreet, nonintrusive; we are not distracted or even aware. Given the relative inconvenience for so much security, one is inclined to consent to more surveillance.

At the same time, surveillance can be harmful. It accumulates data that violate our capacity to build relationships by preventing us from leaving mistakes behind and by taking away from us choices on what parts of our story to share and when. Surveillance is voyeurism in ways we cannot even know because no one will

Richard Bartholomew, August 7, 2007 (© Artizans Entertainment, Inc.).

tell us how much data surveyors collect. Surveillance is not community; it is Big-brotherism, the leer of the state.

This dynamic was captured in the surreal British television series from the late 1960s, *The Prisoner*. This program concerned a former British secret agent who found himself confined in a seaside village where his captors tried to determine why he resigned from his job. Everything "Number Six" did was monitored, and the captors resorted to drugs, hypnosis, and other forms of manipulation to get the answers they sought, all to no avail. Number Six, it turns out, could resist the surveillance society, although he was the exception that proved the rule. Indeed, *The Prisoner* fits uncomfortably well as a symbol of our post 9-11 times, not just as a countercultural relic. In the spring of 2010, American TV channel AMC remade it for the United States as a six-episode mini-series. Main title? Still, *The Prisoner*. The new tagline? "You only think you're free."

We cannot turn back the IT clock; neither should we give the state or the market a blank check to gather and store details of our purchases, reading matter, conversations, medicines, or attitudes. The relationships we build constitute a story worth sharing and preserving, but a story punctuated by choices of what community means and how far community reaches. Communitarian ethics recognizes that we prosper in relationships, but it also frames itself in choices: who gets close to me, who does not. The communitarian reality assures us that relationships are a permanent feature of human life, in part a matter of position (family, native culture, mother tongues) and in part a matter of choice (friends, intimates, colleagues, mentors). Relationships use technology to water the social space between selves; relationships retain value only as persons say yes to shared space, which implies also the capacity to say no.

Cyberterror may bring down traffic grids, revenue systems, and tax collection schemes. Surveillance may build a caricature, a two-dimensional "person" whose name and number are mere symbols for a person, but not an actual person. In communitarian logic and life, relationship survives either of the twin terrors. The stronger community is, the less technology can dislodge its weight or surveillance diminish its value.

Cyberterror mistakenly believes that efficiency creates virtual networks. People are thought to crave efficiency. People are complex chemical machines whose databanks (DNA) have survived thus far not because the carrier has greater speed or larger teeth, but by increasingly efficient social networks, the theory goes. Cut the networks, isolate the people, and you have killed them in a bloodless purge.

Surveillance believes that vast pools of data define and delimit personhood such that abnormal or "unlawful" moments (variations from standard) can be assessed, collated, and eventually eliminated, perhaps by some form of incarceration or perhaps through publicity—human society loving sameness as it does. Surveillance builds persons from data and disperses persons with light-speed statistical emanations. Surveillance prefers profiles to personalities, which are too obscure, complete, and soul-like.

Communitarianism's moral claim is that relationships can resist technology's impressive web. Social bonds are made not of data heaps, but shared ritual, purpose, friendship, covenant, and love. Communitarian bonding is pricked by cyberterror's erratic jabs, but not fatally stabbed. Surveillance presents its best case—a data mirage—which turns out to be not a person at all, and so ultimately unconvincing.

Communitarianism will not permit a person to be circumscribed by billions of bits. Persons are richer than that. The interstices of relationships pulsate with life, not quantifiable digits. Privacy invasion and cyberterror mock the best of humanity's moral theories, but against the bond of community, they pull up, unable to do so. What terrors come, come. Love never fails, claims the ancient tradition: it bears all things, believes all things, hopes all things, endures all things. This poetic imagery suggests the resilience of relationship against the worst pressure of efficiency or the most flagrant caricature of humanity that technology can muster. Communitarian ethics upholds nonnegotiable human dignity and the universal solidarity of human care.

Communitarianism does not parcel care on predictions of probable gain, nor does it withhold care to those whose utility is unproven or past prime. All are care-givers and cared-for. This is what we humans are and do. It is our nature, our *telos,* our mission, purpose, and core identity. Aristotle dismissed slaves and

women from the truly happy life; he was wrong. First-world academics pity the
Third World poor; they are wrong. Politicians believe people can be managed
by the tools and messages of public opinion; they are wrong. Being undernour-
ished or illiterate is not a retraction of humanity. Being a slave is not a role fit for
millions of human beings who spent and still spend their lives thus. All are nonetheless our brothers and sisters. This reality is what communitarian ethics presents.
It is not a reality oversold, as if sheer rhetoric supported the claim. The tenacity
of communitarianism is found in the social reality of which each of us is a part.
Our being bears witness. In that light, cyberterrorism is a problem, surveillance an
annoyance. Human dignity holds.

CORRECTIVE MEASURES FOR ACTION

We ought to be about the business of creating institutions and communities that
honor human dignity. When remedial measures are within our power, we are
obliged to act. Here are correctives that esteem humanity:

1. Build tools for conviviality, to use the term described eloquently by Ivan
   Illich just before the dawn of the Internet. Illich would not turn us back;
   neither would he walk naïvely into the technologically sublime. He urged
   a "convivial society" but recognized we could not wait for a "total absence
   of manipulative institutions and addictive goods." Rather, he pointed the
   industrial West to a "balance between those tools which create the specific
   demands they are specialized to satisfy and those...enabling tools which
   foster self-realization" (Illich 1973, 24). The emphasis is on balance, much
   like the argument that humankind is comprised of persons in community.
   Tools for community enable greater reach and depth to the space linking
   selves together. This connection must be made without irreparable damage to nonhuman features of our world, for the sake of community yet
   to come. This feature of communitarianism is understood best in places
   that treasure the bonds across generations, as Bujo (1998) describes his
   native Congo.
2. Safeguard IT networks from misuse and cover catastrophe with alternative
   networks. This strategy, present at the birth of the Internet, has never left
   the party. The Internet was created with multiple paths for point-to-point
   connection. Redundancy is reliable, dependence vulnerable. Let IT networks reflect the spread of voice, not of wire. Ripples and waves cannot be
   snipped or severed. Voice fills the silent void in all directions.
3. Data gathering has its seasons, as does life. Data heaps should live their
   fair lifespan, then pass away. Human dignity requires renewal, the possibility of forgiveness, the lease on life that transcends the past and presses
   forward. Put term limits on data mountains. Hard as it may be to lose what
   is gathered at some cost, let data heaps follow the logic of creative control.
   No copyright is perpetual; all expire into public ownership. Likewise with
   data timed to allow creative intelligence to press for cleaner methods,

better bell curves, more complex comparisons. Community must renew itself.

4. Encourage what Ian Barns (1999) calls "technological citizenship." The new surveillance uses every technology available: heat, light, motion, and olfactory sensors; electronic tagging; biometric access devices; facial and voice recognition hardware; iris and retinal scans; software for assessing hand vision patterns. The more technologically savvy we are, the more sophisticated our ethical reflection and acts of resistance need to be.

5. Control surveillance by custom and law. Structures of accountability must be open, negotiated, and transparent. Communities finally decide how to set boundaries on gathering, storing, using, and deleting their data, and the means of protecting themselves from cyberwar. Community boundaries favor the interests of a future generation, as all communities care for the aged but plan for the young. Bureaucracies resist diminution of their power base, but communities accept the wisdom of collective guidance freely offered. Bureaucracies penalize mistakes, but communities accommodate error and adjust for better futures commonly conceived. Bureaucracies want proof before they act, but communities want consensus, buy-in, trust, interdependence, and Other-regarding care.

6. Cultivate core relationships with real human beings. Virtual reality is no substitute for tactile friendship. Human touch, voice, reciprocity, laughter, even visceral tension and anger—these the Internet cannot replace. Reduce your techno-gear, if only on occasion, to recover the immediate and satisfying human pleasures of actual beaches, sunsets, mountain paths, singing, and long conversations. Try the ear before the iPod. Try listening to the rhythms of community, not merely the phonemes. Try making music with others a more primal satisfaction than downloading it.

7. Seek wisdom over information, though the latter will frequently inform the pathways your wisdom takes. Wisdom is the preservation of bonds that tie us together, the implementation of human value in attitude and action. Wisdom is not to be captured in a capsule, but must be tracked and trailed through the labyrinth of people whose life experience engages the edges of the universe. More than just spatial, this universe is also relational and inquisitively positive, learning from the past and pondering the future. It is the real Holy Road, a book title given to the sequel of a story of community lost and found (Blake 2004). Such stories are many. Find one, consider it, turn it over, plant it in your heart, tell it to your people.

8. Treasure communities that celebrate hope, love, and service. These are often communities of faith. But communities of play, of art, of skill, of observation are also places where relationships are enriched, where people are saved from terror and *ennui*. No one should live as an orphan.

9. Take symbols as the dynamic social sinew by which culture is created, maintained, and transformed (Carey 1989, 110). Symbols extracted from culture are barren. Symbols isolated from content are vacuous. Symbols

thrive in community, and community is fueled by symbols. Symbols are loci of meaning, and meaning is the nucleus of understanding. Symbols are at the center of the human scrum, the centerpiece of the human festival. Be there at the table (Ferrazzi 2005).

This chapter began by highlighting threats to humanity through misuse of technology. It closes by proposing habits of the heart that put those threats in perspective (Schultze 2002). Cyberterrorism and surveillance are significant problems that people of this millennium cannot ignore. Past millennia of human experience can teach us that neither cyberterrorism nor privacy-invading technologies have the power to make us happy or to destroy us, if we consciously withhold that power from them. Communitarianism withholds power from IT and fixes destiny rather on friendship, sharing, and irreproachable dignity.

NOTES

1. While surveillance has been highly developed in most countries of the world before September 11, 2001, the "pendulum swung wildly" toward control with September 11, accelerating at a new level and generating a culture of fear unknown before (Lyon, 2003, 143). While surveillance in this chapter is elaborated within the broad context of the international war on terrorism, September 11, 2001 in the United States is understood as the tipping point, the catalyst toward a new era of high-technology surveillance.
2. Jürgen Habermas (1996) calls these two traditions in modern democratic thought, civic republicanism and procedural liberalism. The former is rooted in the French Revolution and Jean-Jacques Rousseau. The latter is indebted to John Locke and Thomas Hobbes. The former has produced deliberative traditions of democracy; the latter is aggregative and pluralistic. The former defines liberty positively and the latter in regulative terms.
3. Jack Shaheen (2008) studied 100 films post-911 that defile Arabs, while describing a few that appreciate the complexities of the Muslim world. Hollywood tends to lump together Muslims and Arabs into a homogenous body, though only 1/5 of the world's Muslims are Arabs. It ignores the fact that much of the Arab world is secular and there are 20 million Arab Christians worldwide. Sheehan's study of film imagery in shaping public consciousness indicates that only a few positive representations of Arabs break through the wall of ignorance.

REFERENCES

"A Bruise on the First Amendment." 2010. *New York Times,* Editorials, June 22, A22.

Arena, Kelli, and Quijano, Elaine. 2007. "Audit: FBI's Patriot Act Snooping Broke Rules." March 9, CNN.com..

Bajaj, Vikas, and Austen, Ian. 2010. "Privacy vs. National Security: India's Demands for Surveillance Seen as Roadblock." *New York Times,* September 28, B1, B8.

Barns, Ian. 1999. "Technological Citizenship." In Alan Petersen, Ian Barns, Janice Dudley, and Patricia Harris, *Post-Structuralism, Citizenship, and Social Policy.* London: Routledge.

Baskas, Harriet. 2011. "TSA Pat-Down Leaves Traveler Covered in Urine." MSNBC, March 25. <http://www.msnbc.msn.com/id/40291856/ns/travel-news/>.

BBC. 2009. "Major Cyber-Spy Network Uncovered." BBC, March 29. <http://news.bbc.co.uk/2/hi/americas/7970471.stm>.

Bentham, Jeremy. 1995. "Panopticon." In Miran Bozovic, ed., *The Panopticon Writings*, 29–35. London: Verso.

Blake, Michael. 2004. *The Holy Road*. Tucson: Hrymfaxe.

Block, Peter. 2008. *Community: The Structure of Belonging*. San Francisco, CA: Berrett-Koehler.

Bujo, Benezet. 1998. *The Ethical Dimension of Community*. Nairobi, Kenya: Paulines.

Carey, James W. 1989. *Communication as Culture*. Boston: Unwin Hyman.

Carnes, Tony. 2003. "Curbing Big Brother: Christians Urge Ashcroft to Respect Freedom in Surveillance Law." *Christianity Today*, September, 27.

Conway, Maura. 2008. "Media, Fear, and the Hyperreal: The Construction of Cyberterrorism as the Ultimate Threat to Critical Infrastructures." *Working Papers in International Studies Centre for International Studies*, Dublin City University 5.

Etzioni, Amitai. 2009. "Terrorists Neither Soldiers nor Criminals." *Military Review*, July–August, 108–118.

Ferrazzi, Keith. 2005. *Never Eat Alone*. New York: Currency.

Foucault, Michel. 1977. *Discipline and Punish: The Birth of Prisons*. New York: Random House.

Gordon, Sarah, and Ford, Richard. n.d. "Symantec Security Response, White Paper, Cyberterrorism?" <http://www.symantec.com/avcenter/reference/cyberterrorism.pdf>.

Habermas, Jürgen. 1996. "Three Normative Models of Democracy." In *Democracy and Difference*, ed. Seyla Benhabib, pp. 21–30. Princeton, NJ: Princeton University Press.

Hart, William. 2004. *Evil: A Primer*. New York: St. Martin's.

Haufler, Hervie. 2003. *Codebreakers' Victory*. New York: New American Library.

Illich, Ivan. 1973. *Tools for Conviviality*. New York: Harper and Row.

Lichtblau, Eric. 2008. "FBI Made 'Blanket' Demands for Phone Records." *New York Times*, March 13. <http://www.nytimes.com/2008/03/13/washington/13fbi.html?_r=1>.

Lyon, David. 2003. *Surveillance after September 11*. Cambridge, U.K.: Polity Press.

———. 2007. *Surveillance Studies: An Overview*. Cambridge, U.K.: Polity Press.

Lyon, David, ed. 2006. *Theorizing Surveillance: The Panopticon and Beyond*. Cullompton, U.K.: Willan Publishing.

Mandela, Nelson. 1994. *Long Walk to Freedom*. Boston: Little, Brown.

Markoff, John. 2009. "Vast Spy System Loots Computers in 103 Countries." *New York Times*, March 28. <http://www.nytimes.com/2009/03/29/technology/29spy.html#>.

McLuhan, Marshall. 1964. *Understanding Media: Extensions of Man*. New York: McGraw Hill.

Miller, William Lee. 2008. *President Lincoln*. New York: Knopf.

"Patriot Act Excesses." 2009. *New York Times*, Editorials, October 7, A28.

Priest, Dana, and Arkin, William M. 2010. "A Hidden World, Growing Beyond Control" (July 19); "National Security, Inc." (July 20); The Secrets Next Door" (July 21). <http://projects.washingtonpost.com/top-secret-america/articles/secrets-next-door/>.

Rand, Ayn. 1961. *The Virtue of Selfishness*. New York: Signet.

Sanger, David E. 2010. "Iran Fights Malware Attacking Computers." *New York Times*, September 25, A4.

Schultze, Quentin. 2002. *Habits of the High-Tech Heart: Living Virtuously in the Information Age*. Grand Rapids, MI: Baker.

Shaheen, Jack G. 2009. *Guilty: Hollywood's Verdict on Arabs after 9/11*. Northampton, MA: Olive Branch Press.

Siegel, Lee. 2008. *Against the Machine*. New York: Spiegel and Grau.

Warren, Samuel D., and Brandeis, Louis D. 1890. "The Right to Privacy." *Harvard Law Review* 4 (December 15): 193–220.

Weimann, Gabriel. 2004. "Cyberterrorism: How Real Is the Threat?" The United States Institute for Peace, Special Report No. 119, December.

Wills, Garry. 1999. *A Necessary Evil*. New York: Simon and Schuster.

CHAPTER 5

✒

WLBT and Hearing the Public

None of us knew anything about television. All we knew was that this local station was terrible. ... For the black community, I think a major gain was not to have your children walk in front of the TV and worry about them hearing racial slurs or someone calling them apes.

Patricia Derian, who monitored WLBT's programming prior to the lawsuit challenging its license.

(Mills 2004a, 71)

The year 1963 was very significant. President John F. Kennedy was assassinated in November, but other important events dominated that year too. George C. Wallace became Governor of Alabama in January. He was one of the last, and most outspoken, segregationists in the American South. Marvel Comics released the first Iron Man edition. The Southern Christian Leadership Conference initiated a sit-in against segregation in Birmingham, Alabama, and Dr. Martin Luther King wrote his widely reprinted "Letter from Birmingham Jail" in April. The first James Bond film, *Dr. No*, appeared in theaters in April, the same month that the Coca-Cola Company introduced TaB. In June President Kennedy promised to introduce a Civil Rights Bill in Congress, a bill that would become law the following year. The civil rights leader, Medgar Evers, was murdered. In July the United States got zip codes for the first time and NASA orbited the first geosynchronous satellite. In August Dr. Martin Luther King delivered his "I Have a Dream" speech on the steps of the Washington Memorial, with an estimated 250,000 people listening on the Mall. In September the 16th Street Baptist Church in Birmingham, Alabama, was bombed by the Ku Klux Klan, killing four young girls and injuring twenty-two other people. The African American singer, Sam Cooke, and his band were arrested in Louisiana in October for attempting to register at a "whites only" motel. In December the Warren Commission began its investigation into the assassination of President Kennedy and the Beatles released "I Want to Hold Your Hand," beginning Beatlemania.

This seemingly odd collection of events provides a context for understanding how civil rights were presented on television in the Deep South. In 1963, popular culture, with its developing hold on American teens, was still in its infancy. The iconic James Bond films got their start (with two released in one year); the Beatles became a sensation and initiated their first U.S. tour the following year; Coca-Cola began the diet cola phenomenon. It was innocence (despite the Vietnam War that was in its early buildup) and the height of "Camelot."

But African Americans knew no innocence and no Camelot. They were struggling with the continuing legacy of racism still left over from the Civil War. The U.S. Supreme Court had decided *Brown v. Board of Education*[1] in 1954, condemning the practice of "separate but equal" schools that segregated white and black children, but that battle was still being fought in the South. Governor Wallace famously stood at the door of a classroom building at the University of Alabama to protest integration, even while James Meredith became the first African American to graduate from the University of Mississippi. The Ku Klux Klan was a significant force in the South; bombings were occurring while the civil rights movement was heating up. Enter WLBT, a television station in Jackson, Mississippi.

THE REGULATORY AND LEGAL BACKDROP

Broadcasting in the mid-twentieth century was unlike broadcasting today in many ways. For starters, there were three commercial television networks—no satellite television, no cable channels, and no Internet. The vast majority of American households received their television programs via antennas, either the "rabbit ears" on their TV sets or roof-mounted aerials. In most parts of the country, people received fewer than six channels of TV, and in many places no more than three. Because airwave space for television stations to broadcast was limited, each station was expected to act like a steward, concentrating its activities on meeting the needs of its local community, and the Federal Communications Commission regulated broadcasting with a sense of purpose. Its regulations included the 7-7-7 rule: No company could own more than seven AM radio stations, seven FM radio stations, and seven American TV stations, and no more than five of these could be in the VHF spectrum (channels 2–13).

The FCC required all stations to make program choices based on the "public interest, convenience and necessity." In 1960 the FCC had changed the requirements for license renewal by inserting the proviso that licensees "ascertain and serve diverse community programming needs" (Brotman 2006, 14). This proviso highlighted the preference for localism in license renewal proceedings. Owners who lived locally and knew their communities, or who had significant local presence in the communities where their licenses were held, would be preferred over those with no stake in the community in cases of competitive applications for television licenses.

You may be wondering how the national television networks fit into all this. First, the networks were under the same 7-7-7 ownership restrictions as everyone else. So most of the stations that carried the programs of the three networks of that day (ABC, CBS, NBC) were affiliate stations. They were owned by others and agreed, for a percentage of the advertising revenues that were generated by network-fed programs, to air the network's programs. But network affiliates were still obliged to serve their communities, so they always had the choice of whether to carry a particular program if, in their view, it was not in the best interests of their viewers.

American television was still young in the 1960s. The first TV licenses were not issued until 1948 and then only a few as the FCC imposed a freeze on licenses while it devised a fair geographic plan for license allocation. This freeze lasted until 1952. There were no TV stations in Mississippi at all until 1953. Congressional hearings on network TV affiliate relations put the networks on the defensive in the late 1950s, making it difficult for the networks to put pressure on their affiliates for "clearance" (a guarantee that affiliates would carry network programs), which would allow the networks to increase their advertising rates.

By 1963, networks had expanded their evening news shows to a half hour, and this expansion of the powerful visual medium shifted the way Americans consumed news. After 1963, television became the primary source of news for most Americans. This fact gives the WLBT case special importance.

It was routine for southern television stations to refuse to broadcast programs in the interests of their communities if it meant carrying entertainment programs (and especially news reports) that portrayed African Americans in a positive light. The first entertainment program featuring an African American star, *The Nat King Cole Show*, aired in 1956–57, but was cancelled after one season because southern affiliate stations refused to carry it (Pondillo 2005) and advertisers did not want to offend southern audiences (Torres 2003, 22). The Museum of Broadcast Communications (n.d.) summarizes television programs' treatment of minorities prior to the late 1980s this way: "U.S. television perpetuated U.S. cinema, radio, theatre and other forms of public communication and announced people of color overwhelmingly by their absence. It was not that they were malevolently stereotyped or denounced. They simply did not appear to exist."

The broadcasting industry was in a quandary by the end of the 1950s. According to Sasha Torres, the networks wanted to

> strengthen ties to their southern affiliates during this period, but the percolating race trouble in the South threatened those ties....White southern audiences... were likely to balk at black performance in *any* genre, and this tendency—which in some cases grew as the civil rights movement continued—threatened clearance rates....As the civil rights movement was enticing television information workers, many southern affiliates were systematically refusing to clear news and documentaries about civil rights produced by the networks. (2003, 21–22)

WLBT (an NBC affiliate) was among the stations that refused to air positive portrayals of blacks or programs that dealt with civil rights as a legitimate social movement (ibid.). Like many southern television stations, it saw such programs as "integrationist propaganda" (Torres 2003, 22).

This racism could never be justified ethically, not by virtue, consequences, or duty. Virtue ethics would point out that repeated acts of discrimination produce racism. And if good character is the median between excess and deficit, as

Aristotle argued, then we would reject hatefulness, on the one hand, and indifference, on the other, in favor of acceptance. Similarly, the consequentialism of John Stuart Mill, who advocated the most happiness for the aggregate whole, explicitly rejected what he called "the tyranny of the majority." The majority exploiting a minority would produce an inhumane society, surely not the setting of widespread happiness. And the duty of a categorical imperative—follow principles that should be applied to everyone everywhere—would reject acts of racial discrimination because, taken to their universal conclusion, they would lead to a society that was both hurtful and mistrustful.

THE WLBT CASE

The NAACP field secretary for the Mississippi Branch, Medgar Evers, filed a complaint in 1955 against WLBT for presenting local news "in a racially biased manner" that did not serve the public interest (NAACP 2008, 2). This complaint was made only two years after the station originally went on the air and only one year following the Supreme Court's *Brown v. Board of Education* decision to which whites in Mississippi responded by forming so-called "Citizens' Councils" to prevent black and white children from going to the same schools (Mills 2004a, 20).[2] In 1956 WLBT refused to carry any news about the integration of schools in Little Rock, Arkansas, which had resulted in President Eisenhower calling in the 101st Airborne to protect schoolchildren. In 1958 the FCC delayed renewing the station's license for a year because of its reportage but granted it a full license in 1959 (Atkins 2008, 93; Mills 2004a, 29).[3]

Often when news came from NBC, too, the station would replace stories about African Americans (including one portraying Martin Luther King) with a sign declaring "Sorry, Cable Trouble," which would end at the conclusion of the story (Wilson, Gutiérrez, and Chao 2003, 249).[4] The "Sorry, Cable Trouble" sign came in handy when Thurgood Marshall, then director of the Legal Defense fund of the NAACP, was interviewed about *Brown v. Board of Education*. "I don't know how many years of desegregation will take," Marshall said, "but it won't take as long as many die-hard Southern government officials hope." But WLBT's viewers learned of interrupted transmission, not national resolve.

WLBT had more cable trouble in 1963, during NBC's three-hour documentary, *American Revolution*, the first network program to spend an entire evening of prime time on a single issue. As soon as a sequence about a sit-in at the Woolworth store in Jackson began, "Sorry, Cable Trouble" appeared, and the sign did not disappear until the sequence about local civil rights protest ended. Sometimes before the *Today* show, a WLBT voiceover would warn viewers, "What you are about to see is an example of biased, managed, Northern news. Be sure to stay tuned at 7:25 to hear your local newscast" (Friendly 1976, 89–91).

There were other egregious examples of racism:

- In 1962, WLBT ran spot announcements paid for by the Jackson (White) Citizens Council about school integration that claimed that communists were responsible for the "racial agitation."

- WLBT also repeatedly attacked Tougaloo College, a historic black college near Jackson, but it never interviewed administrators from Tougaloo. "We are nursing a viper to our breast," segregationists claimed. "Communists are teeming up there at Tougaloo."
- Only white children were allowed to appear on locally produced children's programs such as *Romper Room*.
- WLBT manager Fred Beard operated the Freedom Bookstore on the premises of WLBT, and he used WLBT airtime to promote its white supremacist literature.

Station Ownership Clearly Had Its Privileges

In 1962 the FCC began an investigation into eight radio and television stations in Mississippi, including WLBT, "concerning their role in instigating violence and broadcasting inflammatory editorials during the enrollment of James Meredith at the University of Mississippi" (Classen 2004, 191; Wade 1998, 316–18; Nossiter 2002, 123–25). WLBT had taken an editorial position against Meredith's admission, arguing that "states, and not the federal government, should determine who could attend their schools and colleges" (Mills 2004b).[5] Despite the Fairness Doctrine, which required radio and television stations to air both sides of controversial issues, and the inquiry into WLBT's editorializing, neither seemed to have much import when WLBT's license came up for renewal two years later. In 1962, after the general manager at WLBT responded to integration at the University of Mississippi at Oxford by urging viewers to "go out to Oxford and stand shoulder to shoulder with Governor Barnett and keep that nigra out of Old Miss," the FCC investigated the editorializing done by WLBT and other stations (Friendly 1976, 90). The FCC issued its report of findings after Medgar Evers had appeared on WLBT to respond to the Jackson, Mississippi, mayor's claims that "when all the agitation is over Jackson will still be prosperous, people will still be happy, and the races will live side by side in peace and harmony" (Mills 2004a, 48). The report "raised serious questions about whether WLBT had complied with the requirement that stations offer reasonable opportunities for the discussion of opposing views" (Mills 2004a, 54). But by then, Medgar Evers had been murdered.

Newton Minow, Chairman of the Federal Communications Commission during the early 1960s, told the story of how he became aware of the WLBT situation. He received a telephone call from Eleanor Roosevelt in 1962 who asked him why he was not doing anything to help Robert L. T. Smith, a black pastor who was running for a U.S. House seat in Mississippi, buy airtime. Smith's campaign manager, Aaron Henry, had approached WLBT to purchase time for the candidate and was told by the station manager: "Nigger are you crazy? Get out of here. We're not going to sell you any time." When Smith himself made the request for airtime he was told that if he appeared on the station "they would find my body floating upside down in the river" (Minow and LaMay 2008, 3–4).[6] Minow discovered from the FCC staff that he was officially powerless, since the "equal time" regulation required

JACKSON, MISSISSIPPI

26

C11-0770

September 17, 1962

This is Fred Beard with a WLBT-WJDX Editorial, an expression of opinion by the management of these stations:

The eyes of the Nation are on Mississippi this week. History is being made in our State. The issue is not only whether the University of Mississippi will remain segregated - - the issue is whether the individual states still have sovereignty. The developments during the next few weeks will be history-making in the survival of the States' Rights. As Governor Barnett said: "If our nation is to survive, we must maintain strong State Governments and unity in matters of national security".

It seems that Washington is more concerned about placing a student in the University of Mississippi, for political purposes, than they are about removing thousands of Communist troops from Cuba. Why must the Federal Government continue to harrass the loyal, patriotic Southern States - states who are more responsible today for this great Nation of ours than any other segment of our Nation. If our Nation is to survive the threats of Socialism from within our country, it will survive through the efforts of the Southern States. The re-establishment of the State Sovereignty is the first step in such a plan.

This is no time for any political clique in our State to oppose our Governor because of political jealousy and past differences. We must all join together in a united front to combat forces from outside our State who would destroy us. This is a time for unity of all of our citizens, working together to re-establish States' Rights.

This is a WLBT-WJDX Editorial.

WLBT station manager Fred Beard delivered this editorial about the admission of James Meredith to the University of Mississippi in 1962 (National Archives and Records Administration).

only stations that sold time to one candidate to provide opponents with an equal opportunity. Because Smith's opponent had not purchased any time, WLBT was technically under no obligation to sell time to him.

Minow called WLBT on the carpet anyway, asking the station in a telegram how it served the public interest not to have any discussion of the congressional race in its area. The station's lawyer told Minow later that day that it would hap-pen, and the station sold 30 minutes of airtime to Smith the day before the primary election, which he lost to segregationist John Bell Williams (Minow and LaMay 2008, 4–5). Minow left the FCC prior to the lawsuit against the FCC by the Office of Communication of the United Church of Christ in 1964.

As WLBT was refusing to sell advertising time to congressional candidate Smith, Medgar Evers was shot down in his driveway by a member of the Ku Klux Klan. These events gave New York minister and media activist Everett Parker all the incentive he needed to make the journey to Mississippi to investigate WLBT's broadcast practices. On behalf of the Office of Communication of the United Church of Christ, Parker coordinated volunteers from Millsaps College in Jackson to monitor a full week of WLBT's broadcasts following careful television monitoring protocols. Then, to demonstrate local African American dissatisfaction with WLBT's broadcasts, Parker collected signatures on a petition—a dangerous move for him, those who helped him, and any local citizen who signed. But under cover of darkness, Parker convinced many local African Americans to sign.

One month after WLBT filed its license renewal application, the United Church of Christ filed a Petition to Intervene and to Deny Application for Renewal with the FCC. It was joined in this suit by the Reverend Smith and by Dr. Aaron Henry, who was the president of the Mississippi chapter of the NAACP. Their petition to deny was based on WLBT's failure to serve the 45 percent of the population in its service area who were African American and for its failure to treat controversial issues as required under the Fairness Doctrine. But the Federal Communications Commission ruled 4–2 against the challengers on May 19, 1965, because the United Church of Christ and its co-filers had no "standing" given that they had no economic interest in the outcome or could not demonstrate economic harm or electrical interference from broadcasting towers. The FCC renewed WLBT's license, albeit only for one year to give WLBT time to demonstrate compliance with the Fairness Doctrine.

We pause for a word about the Fairness Doctrine. Worried that American broadcasters were maximizing their audiences by avoiding controversial issues—and thus avoiding issues of importance to Americans—the FCC in 1949 adopted what became known as the Fairness Doctrine. It required radio and television stations to broadcast issues of public importance in a way that gave fair hearing to their contrasting points of view. Broadcasters could present the various sides of controversial issues in any number of ways—in news reports, editorials, or special documentaries—but they were no longer permitted to play it safe by avoid-ing controversy. The FCC granted licenses to broadcasters that promised to pro-mote the public interest, and the public interest included more than entertainment. It included the divisive issues of the day.

Although the Fairness Doctrine would be challenged by broadcasters who believed that they should have the right to further their point of view without having to account for other perspectives, the Supreme Court never supported this contention. Justice Byron White explained that those with broadcast licenses were permitted to broadcast but that they had no right to monopolize their channels to the exclusion of other citizens. "There is nothing in the First Amendment which prevents the Government from requiring a licensee to share his frequency with others," White wrote in 1969. "It is the right of the viewers and listeners, not the right of the broadcasters, which is paramount" (*Red Lion Broadcasting Co. v. FCC*[7]). Interestingly, it was the FCC that repealed the Fairness Doctrine during a sweep of deregulation in 1987. Periodic efforts to revive it ended in 2011 when the FCC eliminated the last related regulations.

Now back to the story.

Although the Commission found that WLBT had violated the Fairness Doctrine and had ignored the needs of its black audience, it would not go as far as revoking its license (Mills 2004a, 84; see also Classen 2004). The United Church of Christ was denied the hearing it had sought to make its case public. Three weeks later the United Church of Christ appealed the FCC decision to the U.S. Court of Appeals, DC Circuit. The Circuit Court declared that the FCC had erred in not granting standing to the United Church of Christ and failing to hold a hearing in the WLBT case. Historian Kay Mills describes the significance of the Circuit Court's landmark ruling:

> The appeals court profoundly altered the way the FCC would operate over the next several decades. The court had given the public the right to participate in Commission business, a right it would exercise to seek equal employment opportunity rules, to try to improve children's television, and to affect the outcome of other license renewal proceedings and sales of television stations. (Mills 2004a, 104)

There was considerable legal maneuvering prior to the hearings demanded by the Circuit Court. Changes occurred with WLBT's management; among other things Fred Beard lost his job as general manager. And efforts were made to reach a settlement, prompted by FCC legal counsel Henry Geller who agreed with the United Church of Christ's original position. But all such efforts failed. Hearings were held, oral arguments were made, and the FCC voted 5–2 to renew WLBT's license, the majority somehow agreeing "that the challengers had failed to substantiate virtually all of their allegations on which the hearing was based" (Mills 2004a, 157).

The United Church of Christ, which ended up spending $240,000 fighting WLBT and an obstinate FCC, appealed the decision. By now it was 1969. The Court's decision, written by Justice Warren Burger (his last Appellate Court decision before he became Chief Justice of the U.S. Supreme Court), excoriated the FCC for the way it had treated WLBT's challengers and ordered the case to be sent back to the Commission so that other groups could compete for the license. The Court demanded a "comparative hearing" because "the station had yet to demonstrate that it was in the public interest for its license to be renewed" (Mills 2004a, 166). It would allow WLBT's owner, Lamar Life Insurance, to compete against any others desiring the license, but with no presumption of renewal.

WLBT lost its license renewal in the comparative hearing. A new group, incorporated in 1970, Communications Improvement, Inc., won the license on September 8 of that year. WLBT became the first majority black-owned television station in the United States, with Aaron Henry its General Manager.

MEDIA OWNERSHIP AND DIVERSITY

This book is not concerned with the law per se. What is legal and what is ethical are often not the same thing. But it is necessary here to indicate what this case has meant in terms of representing minorities in the years since the decision.

Since the WLBT case was concluded in 1970, minority ownership of both radio and television stations increased along with the number of TV channels available to the average U.S. household as a result of increasing satellite, cable, and fiber optic penetration. But black-owned TV stations faded, dropping from nineteen stations in 2007 to only eight in the following year (Muhammad 2008). (According to the National Association of Black Owned Broadcasters, African Americans own only 245 radio stations today, and its eight TV outlets are 0.6 percent of all stations compared with 13.5 percent of the general population.) In this decline it followed the trajectory of individually owned media outlets generally as media consolidation continued in the United States (Turner and Cooper 2007). Omachonu and Healy (2009, 90–109) use history and data to show that the concentration of media has reduced the diversity of ownership. Bob Johnson, founder of Black Entertainment Television, puts the issue in First Amendment terms as a threat for black Americans and for all America:

> Media concentration is taking place at a rapid place, and…prices are going up for the media. Big companies are getting bigger. The end result is that all of the voices and the control of the editorial content could rest in the hands of a very few people. We must make sure that in this rush to put technology into the hands of a few, we do not forget that the First Amendment can be lost if diversity is denied. (1997, 22)

Congress passed the Telecommunications Act of 1996 to promote competition and deregulation of the "private sector development of advanced telecommunications and information technologies and services to all Americans by opening up all telecommunications markets to competition." Congress also instructed the FCC to "conduct a rulemaking proceeding to determine whether to retain, modify or eliminate" existing local television ownership limitations (from section 202 of the 1996 Act). In its 1998 biennial review of its broadcast ownership rules, the FCC decided to retain its limitation on ownership of television stations, which declared that no single ownership entity could, through the coverage of all its owned stations, reach more than 35 percent of American households. The Fox Network sued the FCC over the restriction and in 2002 the D.C. Circuit Court of Appeals remanded this rule back to the FCC for justification, while vacating (or eliminating) the cable/broadcast cross-ownership rule. At about the same time the Sinclair Broadcast

Group sued the FCC over its "eight independent voices" exception to the owner-ship rules because the eight voices did not include non-broadcast media, such as cable or satellite channels. (The FCC allowed one company to own two broadcast TV stations in the same market as long as that left at least eight broadcast TV stations there with different owners.) Again the appellate court for the D.C. Circuit remanded the rule to the FCC saying that it lacked adequate justification.

After all of this turmoil, the FCC announced that it would review its broad-cast ownership rules. As a result, the Commission reaffirmed its three traditional policy objectives in promoting the public interest—competition, diversity, and localism—even while further altering its TV ownership rules that allowed greater media concentration. Again the FCC was sued, this time by multiple organizations in multiple courts, but the suits were all consolidated before the D.C. Appellate Court. In general the Court upheld the FCC's allowance of greater cross-media ownership and increases in the limits to single-party ownership. The FCC had argued that "the presence of other media sources—such as the Internet and cable—compensate[d] for the viewpoint diversity lost to consolidation" (*Prometheus Radio Project v. Federal Communications Commission,*[8] Part IV.B.). The Court agreed, although it was not entirely sure the extent to which Internet and cable were "complete substitutes for viewpoints provided by newspapers and broadcast stations" (ibid., Part C-1). In essence the Court defined "diversity" as merely the presence of an adequate number of outlets, regardless of ownership. Today's FCC does not consider the type of owners (female or minority, for example) as part of the equation for diversity of station ownership in any particular market.[9]

The original question of WLBT—was a television station doing its job if it systematically excluded nearly half of its potential audience in its programming and when it did portray that audience, it did so in an offensive and demeaning way—has not been addressed in court actions since Communications Improvement took control of WLBT in 1970. Does it matter? Has the reality of television changed since WLBT?

Does it matter? Derald Wing Sue (2003, 205) thinks so. "If you want to under-stand racism, information from White folks may not be the most insightful or accurate sources," he says.

> Acquiring information from minority-run or minority-edited TV stations or publications allows you to understand the perspective of people of color. It also acts as a counterbalance to the worldview expressed by White society about minority groups. Be aware that your perspective is often in marked contrast to the worldview of racial/ethnic minorities. (Sue 2003, 205)[10]

Has the reality changed since WLBT? A 2010 survey conducted by the National Association of Black Journalists found that only 7.8 percent of television newsroom managers were African American (NABJ Communications 2010). Another study of this question was conducted in Chicago where 60 percent of the population is African American or Latino. The research reported that only 35 percent of the African Americans and bilingual Latinos who were questioned thought their race or ethnic group was accurately portrayed on local television news (Linton and LeBailly 1998). The Screen Actors Guild released a study in 2000 concluded that representation of African Americans on television nationwide continued to be skewed (Braxton 2000). In 2005 Chicago Media Action filed a petition to deny relicensing to nine Chicago area television stations because of their failure "to meet the needs of their community of license and, therefore, that renewal of their licenses would not serve the public interest" (2005, 1). This petition was not based on race. The complaint was an alleged failure to report adequately on state and local elections in 2004 so that voters would have the information necessary to cast an informed vote. The FCC denied the petition.

A thesis completed in 2003 at Georgetown University also claimed that despite the absence of legal racism,

> African American stereotypes are still very much a part of the public consciousness. This is, at least partially, a result of sustained exposure to media messages from TV news which reinforces these myths. The overwhelming majority of African American images on television news consist of suspected criminals, homeless beggars, welfare queens, ghetto-dwelling gang members, or drug addicts. (Melone 2003, 1)

In 2006, a Network Brownout Report complained that TV news ignores Latinos except in reports involving crime and undocumented immigration (Montalvo and Torres 2006). And a recent analysis of Asian Americans on reality TV programs found that they were characterized as "technicians who lack creativity," a stereotype that can impede professional advancement (Wang 2010).

THE ETHICS OF INCLUSION

One tradition in mass media research is concerned with the legitimation that is conferred by media representation, especially on television. The human quest for legitimation is one reason that so much attention has been paid to media diversity by minority groups and feminists. Health advocates have emphasized body images on the media, especially for young girls and teenagers.

There are assumptions here, of course, that television matters—that people learn from it, emulate it, and use it as the basis for conversation. Research conducted in different countries on different continents confirms that the legitimacy conferred by media representations is a cross-cultural phenomenon (Hall, 1997; Pettitt, 2000). The explosion of amateur-produced video on YouTube indicates the significance of media portrayal within many groups in the United States. But what are the ethical issues that are raised by what we see? Is seeing also believing?

This question is complicated. Any perusal of the issues that Americans face today will reveal hardened attitudes on both sides of the debates over health care, home foreclosures, financial bonuses for elite executives, the movement of manufacturing to the developing world, NAFTA, abortion, and taxation. If what you see is a function of what you believe and if believing is seeing as much as seeing is believing, how then is a democratic society to correct its ills when the glasses through which people see are so different?

The WLBT case shows one part of the answer: dialogue. In order for Mississippi to change, it was necessary that white citizens see black citizens as legitimate and equal participants in the development of the state: equal partners in education, social change, political engagement, mental health, public safety, that is, in all aspects of life that both races know are necessary to thrive. So long as black Mississippians were portrayed in the media as animals and their heroes ignored by the press, their concerns were illegitimate in the eyes of their white counterparts. Dialogue was impossible. Only military or police forces that were necessary to assure Meredith's enrollment, or civil disobedience embodied in marches, sit-ins, and other similar actions, would get attention. And many times such activities merely elicited the majority's scorn. Demonstrations may have been an important start, but they were not dialogue.

Communitarian ethics insists on dialogue as the means by which people reach their human potential. As Charles Taylor points out, contemporary culture suffers from "soft relativism" about value: "Things have significance not of themselves but because people deem them to have it—as though people could determine what is significant, either by decision, or perhaps unwittingly and unwillingly by just feeling that way" (1991, 34, 36). Segregationists did the very same thing in Mississippi. They decided that their way of life was threatened by change. They took steps to prevent that change to preserve their way of life. Even some black Mississippians spoke in favor of segregation at the time, unwittingly supporting a system that denied the equality of every citizen. Segregation, and the actions of WLBT as part of its legitimizing apparatus, alienated black Mississippians from their own common humanity with the white majority. Taylor calls such actions "crazy" (1991, 36).

In response to these divisions driven by hatred and fear, communitarian ethics calls for "intelligibility." We cannot define for ourselves, in our own personal terms, the character of the communities in which we live. We cannot establish internally the basis for evaluating our individual significance. The "horizon" against which we see ourselves must be larger, or more transcendent, than our individual or local community definitions.

The abolitionist leader Frederick Douglass understood intelligibility's horizons in the nineteenth century as did Martin Luther King, Jr. in the twentieth. Their credibility in their own time, and validity still, is grounded in the larger context to which they appealed. Douglass's fiery rhetoric insisted finally that "America, the land of the free" rise to the occasion. King's "I Have a Dream" oration from the Washington Mall reverberates yet today because our humanity as a people was its anchor. Their calls for inclusion spoke the truth and inspired change. Our all-too-common pinched definitions "recognize few external moral demands or serious commitments to others" (Taylor 1991, 55). Giving ourselves legitimacy only from within is a recipe for trivialization.

The antidote to trivialization is struggle—not against, but with. For people in democratic societies to live together in harmony, mutually discovering their personal needs and the needs of those they care for, the failure to struggle *with* means conflict, often irresolvable without violence. In that respect, the decision of the Court to demand dialogue (in hearings) and to evaluate the result of that dialogue (its good faith and legitimacy) allowed Jackson, Mississippi to dodge a bullet. Continuation of WLBT's policies could have been the catalyst eventually for violence by the disenfranchised half of Jackson's population. The strong action of the Court prevented this course of action and thus must be judged in communitarian terms as ethically laudable.

The "struggle with" of genuine dialogue is a hard lesson. Not much fruitful interaction occurred among the public despite the 1970 ruling that changed WBLT. But "struggle with" remains a lesson relevant to current debates about the disenfranchised—illegal immigrants, Arabs, Muslims, gays, or any other racial or ethnic group that people consider potentially dangerous, threatening, or alien to narrowly defined ways of life.

How people are portrayed in the media, or how they are ignored or labeled, does matter. Media can reinforce or question prejudices. They can serve the interests of unity or disunity. But in no case is what public communication says or ignores inconsequential. The only question is the norm to which the media are held.

To cite just one example, the 2009 film *Amreeka* tells the story of a Palestinian divorcée and her son who emigrate from the West Bank to the American Midwest to pursue the American dream. But the timing of their move—at the beginning of the second Gulf War—means that they encounter post-9/11 fears targeted at Arabs living in America. The mother, ever hopeful and resourceful, finds ways to overcome obstacles that she and her son encounter at work and at school, learning from her mistakes and making friends in the process. This optimistic and inclusive movie, so unlike many movies that portray Arabs as sinister and dangerous (Shaheen 2001), won the prize of the International Federation of Film Critics at the 2009 Cannes Film Festival.

Communitarian ethics argues for an inclusive standard in creating and maintaining community. Inclusion requires common purpose as defined by the inclusive community and legitimation for all who are part of it. There can be no narrow definitions of humanity or personhood. No a priori exclusions based on particular attributes of otherwise legitimate constituent groups are morally acceptable. To legitimate on the basis of race, gender, ethnicity, religion, sexual orientation, disability, education, occupation, or wealth leads to conflict and stunted social development.

It is in everyone's interest to define the horizons by which they judge value and significance as non-individualistically as possible. While any single person may achieve self-defined significance or success (becoming a "legend in his own mind" to quote Dirty Harry), such self-definitions always carry within them the seeds of delusion. If one's community moves on to new definitions of any of these aspects of life, then one's own "victory" can become hollow. But building moral and responsible legitimation within a larger context minimizes such risks. Communitarian ethics measures value and success by the level of inclusion that communities ought to sustain.

NOTES

1. *Brown v. Board of Education of Topeka*, 347 U.S. 483 (1954).
2. Hodding Carter III, then a Greenville, Mississippi, journalist who would eventually serve as Assistant Secretary of State for Public Affairs and State Department spokesman, told the FCC in 1964 that Jackson, Mississippi's TV stations were, "almost without exception, geared to a far right-wing, rigid segregationist approach." He called Fred Beard, who was the WLBT general manager, "an unofficial mouthpiece for the total resistance of the Citizen's Council" (Mills 2004a, 19–20).
3. Atkins also notes that the station was not only racist but also equally venomous toward labor unions, taking editorial positions against union representation for workers and airing "what journalist Bill Barton called 'a terrific propaganda barrage against unionization'" (2008, 93).
4. The Office of Communications of the United Church of Christ filed a lawsuit against the FCC in 1963 after its decision to relicense WLBT. The OC/UCC had conducted a study of the station's programming and reported that between July 1, 1962, and August 31, 1963, although NBC produced seven regularly scheduled news programs, the station had only broadcast one regularly, *The Today Show*. That show had carried twenty-four segments dealing with race, but the station had run just one. It had also only run the program *Meet the Press* once during this period, when Alabama Governor George C. Wallace was a guest. (See Roberts and Klibanoff 2007, 446; see Katagiri 2001, 102–31, for a fuller account of the Meredith enrollment imbroglio.)
5. One of Beard's editorials declared that Mississippi was facing "the final hour in its official fight to maintain segregation in all its public schools. The showdown that has been building up since 1954 is here. Mississippi is fortunate enough in having men at its leadership who have vowed to prevent integration of our schools. The very sovereignty of our state is threatened" (quoted by Mills 2004a, 40).
6. According to Mills (2004a), Beard had told Smith that "his body, and mine, too, would likely be found in the river.... Smith said later that he took Beard's words as a threat. Beard said it wasn't—it was a realistic description of what might happen" (p. 37). Beard's news director, Richard Sanders, recalled that Beard had the front door and windows of the station covered with heavy plywood and painted to protect it from "the rednecks of Rankin County just across the river from WLBT" (ibid.).
7. *Red Lion Broadcasting Co. v. FCC*, 395 U.S. 367 (1969).
8. *Prometheus Radio Project v. Federal Communications Commission*, United States Court of Appeals for the Third Circuit (2004).
9. The Court did not say that one ruling by the FCC, a repeal of the Failed Station Solicitation Rule, was an unreasonable analysis, but that it was the only FCC rule that was aimed at preserving minority ownership as outlined in its 1999 Television Rule Review (*Prometheus Radio Project v. Federal Communications Commission*, Part V.E.).
10. In addition to actions before the FCC, more than 250 advocacy groups were involved in efforts to change prime-time TV programming by 1970. These included African American groups (the NAACP's first objection to TV programming was the *Amos 'n Andy* program that had white actors in blackface portraying the characters), anticommunists, Hispanics, people of Polish descent, antiabortionists, evangelical Christians, Arab Americans, gay rights advocates, Muslims, and "pro-family" groups (see Montgomery 1990, 5–6).

REFERENCES

Amreeka. 2009. Director Cherien Dabis. Virgil Films and Entertainment, DVD.

Atkins, Joseph B. 2008. *Covering for the Bosses: Labor and the Southern Press.* Jackson: University Press of Mississippi.

Braxton, Greg. 2000. "Study Blasts TV's Portrayal of Blacks." *Chicago Sun-Times*, February 28.

Brotman, Stuart N. 2006. *Communications Law and Practice.* New York: Law Journal Press.

Chicago Media Action. 2005. *Petition to Deny Renewal.* Before the Federal Communications Commission. <http://www.chicagomediaaction.org/pdffiles/2005petition.pdf>.

Classen, Steven D. 2004. *Watching Jim Crow: The Struggles over Mississippi TV, 1955–1969.* Raleigh, NC: Duke University Press.

Friendly, Fred W. 1976. *The Good Guys, the Bad Guys and the First Amendment: Free Speech vs. Fairness in Broadcasting.* New York: Vintage.

Hall, Stuart. 1997. *Representation: Cultural Representations and Signifying Practices.* Thousand Oaks, CA: Sage.

Johnson, Bob. 1997. "The First Amendment Speech You've Never Heard Before." *Broadcasting and Cable*, May 19.

Katagiri, Yasuhiro. 2001. *The Mississippi State Sovereignty Commission: Civil Rights and States' Rights.* Jackson: University Press of Mississippi.

Linton, Cynthia C., and LeBailly, Robert K. 1998. "African American and Latino Views of Local Chicago TV News." <http://www.northwestern.edu/ipr/publications/wpS98/tvnews/report.html>.

Melone, Jennifer. 2003. "Holding Network TV News Accountable for the Perpetuation of African American Stereotypes." M.A. thesis submitted to the Faculty of the Graduate School of Arts and Sciences of Georgetown University.

Mills, Kay. 2004a. *Changing Channels: The Civil Rights Case that Transformed Television.* Jackson: University Press of Mississippi.

———. 2004b. "Changing Channels." *Prologue* 36 (3). U.S. National Archives & Records Administration.

Minow, Newton, and LaMay, Craig L. 2008. *Inside the Presidential Debates: Their Improbable Past and Promising Future.* Chicago: University of Chicago Press.

Montalvo, Daniela, and Torres, Joseph. 2006. *National Association of Hispanic Journalists Network Brownout Report.* Washington, D.C.: NAHJ.

Montgomery, Kathryn C. 1990. *Target, Prime Time: Advocacy Groups and the Struggle over Entertainment Television.* New York: Oxford University Press.

Muhammad, Nisa Islam. 2008. "Black-Owned TV Stations Nearly Extinct." January 2. <http://news.newamericamedia.org/news/view_article.html?article_id=e62b69d9845c083523c04dd0d9cda407>.

Museum of Broadcast Communications. n.d. "Racism, Ethnicity and Television." <http://www.museum.tv/archives/etv/R/htmlR/racismethni/racismethni.htm>.

NAACP. 2008. "Out of Focus—Out of Sync Take 4." *NAACP Report.* December. Baltimore, MD: NAACP.

NABJ Communications. 2010. "NABJ Broadcast News Survey: Diversity STILL Lags in TV Management." July 30. <http://www.nabj.org/news/48802/NABJ-Broadcast-News-Survey-Diversity-STILL-Lags-in-TV-Management.htm>.

National Association of Black Owned Broadcasters. 2010. "NABOB Mourns the Sudden Passing of Radio Pioneer Sydney Small." August 10. <http://www.nabob.org/Press_Releases/8-10-10_Sydney_Small.pdf>.

Nossiter, Adam. 2002. *Of Long Memory: Mississippi and the Murder of Medgar Evers.* New York: DaCapo Press.

Omachonu, John O., and Healey, Kevin. 2009. "Media Concentration and Minority Ownership: The Intersection of Ellul and Habermas." *Journal of Mass Media Ethics* 24 (2–3): 90–109.

Pettitt, Lance. 2000. *Screening Ireland: Film and Television Representation.* Manchester, U.K.: Manchester University Press.

Pondillo, Bob. 2005. "Saving Nat 'King' Cole." *Television Quarterly,* 35 (3/4), Spring/Summer, 8–16.

Prometheus Radio Project v. FCC, 373 F. 3d 372 - Court of Appeals, 3rd Circuit 2004.

Roberts, Gene, and Klibanoff, Hank. 2007. *The Race Beat: The Press, the Civil Rights Struggle, and the Awakening of a Nation.* New York: Random House.

Shaheen, Jack G. 2001. *Reel Bad Arabs: How Hollywood Vilifies a People.* New York: Olive Branch Press.

Sue, Derald Wing. 2003. *Overcoming Our Racism: The Journey to Liberation.* Hoboken, NJ: John Wiley and Sons.

Taylor, Charles. 1991. *The Ethics of Authenticity.* Cambridge, MA: Harvard University Press.

Torres, Sasha. 2003. *Black White and in Color: Television and Black Civil Rights.* Princeton, NJ: Princeton University Press.

Turner, S. Derek, and Cooper, Mark. 2007. *Out of the Picture: Minority & Female TV Ownership in the United States.* <http://www.freepress.net/files/otp2007.pdf>.

Wade, Wyn Craig. 1998. *The Fiery Cross: The Ku Klux Klan in America.* New York: Oxford University Press.

Wang, Grace. 2010. "A Shot at Half-Exposure: Asian Americans in Reality TV Shows." *Television & News Media* 11(3), September, 404–27.

Wilson, Clint C., II, Gutiérrez, Féliz, and Chao, Lena M. 2003. *Racism, Sexism, and the Media: The Rise of Class Communication in Multicultural America.* 3d ed. Thousand Oaks, CA: Sage.

PART II

Advocacy

CHAPTER 6

✍

Supersize Me and Marketing Fat

Have you called Jenny yet? Or purchased a book on weight loss, joined WeightWatchers, tried the Atkins diet or the peanut and peanut butter diet (yes, there is one), or followed any of the hundreds of other books, pills, or weight-loss aids available around the world? If so, you have become part of a $30 billion (some estimate as much as $50 billion) industry. You also see yourself as one of the 74 percent of American adults who is overweight, obese, or extremely obese (Ogden and Carroll 2010). But chances are good that you will gain all the weight you lose within three years. More than 95 percent of dieters do.

Who is to blame for our collective failure to maintain a healthy weight? The (Burger) King, Ronald McDonald, Wendy, the Colonel, the Taco Bell Chihuahua who thinks outside the bun? Or should we blame ourselves—our sedentary lifestyles, our automobiles that get us to Sonic or Dairy Queen, or our lack of willpower?

Initial responses to the film *Supersize Me* raised all these questions. Morgan Spurlock wrote and directed this documentary, which premiered at the Sundance Film Festival in 2004, where Spurlock was named "best documentary director" (Strauss 2004). The film was nominated for an Academy Award as "best documentary" as well, but did not win the prize. It did become the twelfth-highest grossing documentary of all time, earning better than $11.5 million, although Spurlock produced the film for only $65,000 (Thorn 2005; "Awards for Supersize Me" 2004).

Spurlock says that his inspiration for eating three meals a day for a month at McDonald's and "supersizing" whenever he was asked (nine times altogether) was a lawsuit that had been filed by attorneys for two teenagers claiming that misleading advertisements had caused their obesity. The advising attorney in this case was John Banzhaf, III, who had successfully sued cigarette companies for misleading consumers in the 1970s. A Federal District Court eventually dismissed the case in 2010 (Harris 2010).

The initial responses to Spurlock's film illustrated the reality of polysemy, multiple interpretations of a text. At first the articles and blogs written about the film saw the major issue as the give-and-take between personal and corporate responsibility. Because Spurlock had chosen to gorge himself on cheeseburgers, Big Macs, and supersized orders of fries, he could not blame McDonald's. But he did suggest that clever marketing (Ronald and the Hamburgler, et al.), playgrounds (often where there were no alternative play areas for children), adver-tising jingles, and slogans had duped thousands of other people into consuming the fat-, salt-, sugar-, and calorie-laden cuisine promoted by fast food restaurants (especially McDonald's). Even schools felt compelled to offer similar fare for student lunches.

The reasoning in *Supersize Me* was utilitarianism through and through. The problem with fast food marketing was not that it exhibited a character flaw in the producers or consumers of Big Macs, fries, and shakes, or that it violated some sort of human duty (say, to feed the hungry). No. *SuperSize Me* faulted fast food marketing with its effects: It led people to make poor food choices, which made them fat.

But other interpretations began to emerge. Some of them were blatantly defensive of fast food emporia. Others took issue with Spurlock's choice of targets, either because they liked the food or because they had eaten it for years without ill effect. These detractors suggested that the real issue was Spurlock's own recklessness for pulling such an obviously unhealthy stunt in the first place.

Soso Whaley, an adjunct fellow at the Competitive Enterprise Institute, began her own McDonald's odyssey to demonstrate that a person who made the right choices could eat at McDonald's, stay healthy, and lose weight (Fields 2004, A21). In two months, after following the same tactic as Spurlock but without supersizing, Whaley lost 18 pounds. She limited herself to 2,000 calories per day rather than Spurlock's 5,000 (Higgins 2004). Whaley made her own documentary, *Mickey D's and Me* (Lopez 2005; Bauman 2005), about another woman who lost 37 pounds eating only at McDonald's for 90 days.

As Erin Murphy explained, "Spurlock says he aimed to educate the public about the obesity 'epidemic,' but if the promotional materials are any indicator, demonizing the world's most popular fast food chain runs a very close second." And Whaley's own aim:

> This anti-corporate, anti-fast food take on the "evil" McDonalds is nothing more than simple junk science and should be relegated to the comedy section at Blockbuster once it is released.... I've had it with all the doom, alarmist, anti-everything attitude of certain individuals and organizations who want to control my life, your life, everyone's life with little regard for individual tastes, freedom of choice and personal responsibility. (Fields 2004, A21)

ETHICAL ISSUES: INTENDED AND UNINTENDED

None of us has the ability to control the responses that may result from our actions or remarks. Spurlock saw the project at least initially as merely an experiment to answer a simple question, "What would happen if?" Whatever he intended in producing his documentary, once he produced it and inserted it into the public sphere, he could not determine how it would be received. Some people got the point that Spurlock wanted to make: the obesity problem of Americans is caused (at least partly) by the number of times that people eat outside the home and the choices they make when they do so. They are encouraged to do so, of course, by the continual drumbeat of promotion on the part of the various sectors of the restaurant industry. The film "uses this multinational chain as a platform from which to address broader questions of America's burgeoning waistline, commercial greed and the lawful ruthlessness of advertising campaigns as it wrestles with issues of personal responsibility" (Lee 2004). The documentary, Lee argued, "taps into a collective consciousness" (Lee 2004).

But others saw a very different—and sometimes sinister—point to the film. Those on the more libertarian side of the political spectrum, such as Whaley, saw Spurlock's intentions as merely another anti-corporate, anti-choice diatribe. Those who were on the conservative side—but not fully libertarian in their views—saw the film as both useful and misguided. David Edelstein wrote in *Slate Magazine* that Spurlock had used a

> terrific gimmick. Did he act irresponsibly? Yes, but what he did is not as far out-side the realm of mainstream American behavior as some would have you believe. Is he a hustler? Maybe. Spurlock is not the most attractive personality: He once made a gross-out reality dare show for MTV. And I think he makes a mistake in the film by putting so much emphasis on lawyers suing McDonald's on behalf of obese people. That's an easy target for libertarians and those "free enterprise" groups that are largely funded by the food industry. (2004)

At first, then, Spurlock's intentions in producing the film seemed to be paying off in communitarian terms. People were talking. The issue of personal responsibility for one's own health and appearance was considered, as well as the alternative view that people's health and appearance were the result of clev-erly packaged, but unhealthy fast food. Some Internet websites that provided ideas for term papers to students picked up on the film and gave examples of how *Supersize Me* could be turned into a paper on an important public issue (see <http://www.oppapers.com/essays/Super-Size-Me/121980> and <http://www.termpaperslab.com/essay-on-rhetoric-documentary-film-super-size-me/31265.html>). Another website (http://www.teachwithmovies.org/samples/super-size-me.html) used the film as the basis for lesson plans that could be used with students 11 years old and older. It said the ethical emphasis of the film was "responsibility." Spurlock himself created a DVD series based on the film that he hoped would be underwritten by a foundation so that poor schools could get it for free (Gillespie 2005). He removed certain portions of the film to make sure it would pass muster in schools.

The film also led to political discussions in the House of Representatives, where the so-called "cheeseburger bill" was passed to block lawsuits by people who blame fast food chains for their obesity ("'Cheeseburger Bill' Puts Bite on Lawsuits" 2005). The Consumers Union weighed in on the issue, opposing the measure before the House Judiciary Committee (http://www.consumersunion.org/pub/core_food_safety/000877.html). Later the Senate failed to go along

Morgan Spurlock outside McDonald's (© Andrew Brusso/Corbis).

with the bill. But the Utah legislature did pass such a measure (Genessy 2004). McDonald's announced shortly after the film was released that it was eliminating the "supersize" option on its menu, although it denied that this move was a result of the film's negative publicity. However, "insiders said the moves are a response to criticisms leveled against the conglomerate" (Jie 2005, 2).

In 2009 the National Bureau of Economic Research issued a report (Currie, DellaVigna, Moretti, and Pathania) that indicted the placement of fast food restaurants within one-tenth of a mile of a school. The field research among ninth graders in California found that "a fast food restaurant within a tenth of a mile of a school is associated with at least a 5.2 percent increase in obesity rates." This research led Eric Gioia, councilman from Queens, New York, to propose a bill to ban new fast food restaurants from locating within a tenth of a mile of New York City schools (Signore 2010).

In *The Omnivore's Dilemma*, author Michael Pollan returned to McDonald's, this time to trace the origins of fast food. Pollan's research ultimately led him to Midwestern cornfields, the source of America's highly processed diet that has so much to do with the country's obesity. Pollan encourages Americans to eat locally grown foods instead of highly processed foods that are rich in calories and poor in nutrition (2006). It turns out, though, that healthy food not only costs more than highly processed food, but poorer people are likely to live in "food deserts," neighborhoods with easy access to fast food and convenience stores but without access to grocery stores and farmer's markets (Shaw 2006).

Public discussions jumpstarted by the film began to wobble and eventually ran off the rails. Flak came from various quarters on issues that Spurlock probably never anticipated when he made the film. Part of the reason for this flak was the politicization that occurred as legislative assemblies debated or took action to protect the fast food industry. Part was the result of the American cultural tradition of spinning profit out of every new cultural phenomenon. Spurlock's film did not spawn any new giveaways at fast food restaurants, or new toys by Mattel or Hasbro, but it did create the climate for a publishing frenzy to solve the American obesity epidemic.

Books dealing with fast food, health, and obesity had been published prior to Spurlock's film. The most prominent were Greg Critser's *Fat Land* (2003) and Eric Schlosser's *Fast Food Nation* (2004). After the film's success, a raft of new titles appeared with various takes on this general subject. These included such titles as *Want Fries with That?* (Ingram 2005), *Fats, Sugars, and Empty Calories* (Libal 2006), *Food Inc.* (Weber 2009), *Generation Extra Large* (Tartamella, Hersher, and Woolston 2006), *The World Is Fat* (Popkin 2008), a children's book, and *The Gulps* (Wells 2007). Such books capitalized on the phenomenon of the film and on American's perennial diets. They provided dozens of solutions to being overweight, including exercise routines, diet pills and supplements, exercise equipment, various diet regimens (Atkins, South Beach, etc.), and psychological explanations of eating disorders, including anorexia and bulimia.

It did not take long for the film to raise the ire of various groups and individuals. The American Council on Science and Health took issue with Spurlock's misleading "perversion of healthful nutritional practices" as early as May 2004. The ACSH nutrition director, Dr. Elizabeth Whelan, claimed that "while the movie may entertain, it certainly does not educate" ("Health Panel: 'Supersize Me' Movie Trivializes Obesity, A Serious Problem" 2004). J. Eric Oliver, who said that he intended to write a book about America's "big, fat problem," decided as he researched his book that the problem was not obesity, the warnings about which were "based on little more than loose statistical conjecture," but "America's public health establishment" (2006, 1–5). As he explained, "contrary to the conventional wisdom, the primary source of America's obesity epidemic is not to be found at McDonald's, Burger King, or Krispy Kreme donuts. Nor is it how little we exercise, our declining smoking rates, a 'fat virus,' or any of the other theories that are often used to explain our rising weights. Rather, America's obesity epidemic originates in far less conspicuous places" (2006, 5). What the public health care establishment that Oliver identified as the culprit had done, according to his analysis, was create a low and arbitrary definition of obesity (and being overweight), and "inflated the dangers and distorted the statistics about weight and health, [and] exaggerated the impact of obesity on everything from motor accidents to air pollution" (ibid.).

Efforts to explain or deal with obesity, while not directed specifically at the film or Spurlock, nevertheless undermined the film's premise: that corporate greed and fancy marketing campaigns had short-circuited Americans' abilities to maintain a healthy weight. Emily Nunn (2007), attending the Obesity Society's annual meeting in New Orleans, quoted the society's founding president, Barbara Hansen: "It's my view that we've taken the lid off the [fat] environment around the world, even those who don't have McDonald's. People are free to express their genes. We have more people becoming obese as the economy improves—when calorie restriction is no longer forced upon them by lack or quality of food or forced labor." Margaret Hughes and Tony Farrow, also quoting American health researchers, claimed that obesity was a cultural concept that differed from one culture to another: "Black Americans believed obesity to be positively related to attractiveness and sexual desirability, which contrasted greatly with Caucasian Americans, who viewed obesity in a negative way" (2007, 14). And *Obesity & Diabetes Week* reported that "the tendency toward obesity is directly related to the brain system that is involved in food reward and addictive behavior, according to a new study. Researchers at Tufts University School of Medicine (TUSM) and colleagues have demonstrated a link between a predisposition to obesity and defective dopamine signaling in the mesolimbic system in rats" (*Obesity & Diabetes Week* 2008). Dr. James Gavin said that although he did think there was too much fast food consumed in the United States, the problem was the lack of physical activity created by an infrastructure "in which it is possible for a child never to be challenged.... except on a voluntary basis.... They don't have to walk to school. They don't do physical education in school. They don't have to walk to the store. In the malls, what is it they do? They go and park themselves in the videogame room and sit there moving only a finger. At home what do they do? They watch television. They don't do outdoor games" (quoted by Goode 2001, 36).

Maybe the problem was on its way to solution, too, some thought. After Schlosser's book and Spurlock's film, Molly Marsh wrote that there had been an incredible jump in the number of people interested in the problem of food and weight. Quoting Anna Lappé: "In the 1970s, there were fewer than 100 farmers markets; now we have 3,700 and counting." Quoting Bryant Terry: "From my experience, so many people want to make a shift [in their eating habits] because they've seen so many suffer. As we see the effects of this failed American diet experiment, it's going to push people to see other ways to think about food" (Marsh 2006).

Finally, the website "Teaching Tolerance" went after the film directly for its visual images of "large stomachs, buttocks and thighs, larger families at the beach, and even images of overweight children. As part of a visual theme of fat bodies as objects, representing both corporate malfeasance and individual poor health, the film's context exaggerates the dehumanization of the faceless 'fatties'" (Maschal 2004) (J. Eric Oliver had written that Spurlock sneered "at the black kids who actually like McDonald's food" [2006, 7].) The website concluded that while Spurlock's film was full of statistics, it "ignores the experience entirely." It asked: "How much stronger would the film have been if the nameless McDonald's patron were included not just as an image, a symbol, or butt of a joke, but a voice?" Its advice—write to Spurlock and consult with the National Association to Advance Fat Acceptance (NAAFA).

While the World Health Organization continued to use the amount of physical activity and measures of obesity as the top two health indicators globally, for *Supersize Me* and the discussion following, the problem could be racially biased and culturally determined or the result of faulty dopamine signaling. Or perhaps it is a conspiracy by health providers (who had the most to gain from artificially low definitions of healthy weight), or even of Spurlock's own prejudice and sly dehumanization of fat people. None of these explanations of the crisis (if it was a crisis) had anything to do with either corporate or personal responsibility. Both parties addressed by Spurlock's film were essentially off the hook. Ethics at either the personal or corporate level was irrelevant.

And the pièce de résistance? Although McDonald's gave up its supersizing option after the film's release—William Grimes (2004) called the decision "a crippling blow to the American lifestyle"—by 2005 "monster meals" had made a comeback (see also Mitchard 2004; Sawer 2005; Shah 2004). And besides, as Tom Murse put it, the elimination of supersizing made little difference at McDonald's anyhow: "I did my own little test on Friday and found there's barely a difference in either calories or fat between the Supersize and the 'large' servings" (2004, B1). In ordering two meals simultaneously (one supersized), Murse claimed the supersize portion only had two French fries more than the large serving. And the drink, ostensibly ten ounces more when supersized, had the same amount of soda—only the quantity of ice cubes differed. In other words, the only thing that was supersized was McDonald's profit.

IS OBESITY A REAL PROBLEM?

Marion Nestle and Michael F. Jacobson wrote in *Public Health Reports* in 2000 that:

> In 1974, an editorial in *The Lancet* identified obesity as "the most important nutritional disease in the affluent countries of the world," yet a quarter century later, its prevalence has increased sharply among American adults, adolescents,

and children. The deleterious effects of obesity on chronic disease risk, morbidity, and mortality; its high medical, psychological, and social costs; its multiplicity of causes; its persistence from childhood into adulthood; the paucity of successful treatment options; the hazards of pharmacologic treatments; and the complexities of treatment guidelines all argue for increased attention to the *prevention* of excessive weight gain starting as early in life as possible. Prevention, however, requires changes in individual behavioral patterns as well as eliminating environmental barriers to healthy food choices and active lifestyles—both exceedingly difficult to achieve. (2000, 1)

In 2001 the Surgeon General of the United States published a "call to action" to fight obesity among Americans.

The Trust for America's Health and the Robert Wood Johnson Foundation released a report in 2009 indicating that every state in the union had an obesity problem, with obese and overweight children at or above 30 percent in 30 states. Likewise, the Institute of Medicine reported that childhood obesity had "skyrocketed in the last three decades" (2009). According to the nationmaster website, the United States leads the world in the number of deaths from obesity per year with more than three times as many deaths from obesity per year as second-place Mexico. Clearly Spurlock's film was not targeting a nonissue.

Other documentaries about obesity have followed in the wake of *Supersize Me. Fast Food Nation* (2006), starring Greg Kinnear and Patricia Arquette, based on Eric Schlosser's book, also looked at the social and health consequences of America's obsession with fast food, including the lack of attention to sanitation by America's teenage "chefs," the treatment of the cattle that provide the beef for burgers, and the artificial flavoring used in fast food. *King Corn*, a documentary released in 2007, looked at the role that corn has in the American diet (it is huge), and its contribution to the U.S. food industry. Its subtitle: *You are what you eat*. And the conclusion: we are corn. More recently, *What's on Your Plate* (2009) followed two 11-year-old friends from New York who investigate where their food comes from, how it is grown, and how far it travels to reach their plates.

Reality television joined the cause when *Jamie Oliver's Food Revolution* went to Huntington, West Virginia, to inspire healthful eating in a place pegged as the most obese city in America. For six weekly episodes in 2010, Oliver spoke in various community settings and worked in a school cafeteria in an effort to change eating habits. But the going was tough. During an interview on a country music morning radio show, the disc jockey said, "We don't want to sit around and eat lettuce all day. Who made you the king?" And presented with a choice of roast chicken, salad, and wild rice or pepperoni pizza, schoolchildren overwhelmingly went for the school pizza. In fact, when Oliver prepared fresh chicken in front of children—detaching the breasts, thighs, legs, and wings and processing the rest into a fatty goo that Oliver battered and fried as chicken nuggets—the children still chose the nuggets over the cuts of meat. Without even taking on food industry lobbying or USDA school lunch guidelines, Jamie Oliver's *Food Revolution* showed just how difficult it can be to persuade people to choose what is best for them (Hale 2010, C17).

Responsibility

Clearly the issues raised by *Supersize Me* were muddled—if not in its original conception, then in the responses it generated. Much of the criticism against the film was true: it did demonize McDonald's and it did blame corporate America rather than individual decision-making (which was, according to the film, made more difficult if not impossible by the cultivation of consumers through McDonald's marketing prowess). The film did pixelate eyes on overweight people used to illustrate the obesity problem and thus imply that there was something very wrong with these people. And the long-term impact of the film is not yet known. Weights in America have reached a plateau. By 2007, the Center for Disease Control and Prevention reported that "after a quarter century of increases, obesity prevalence has not measurably increased in the past few years but levels are still high—at 34 percent of U.S. adults aged 20 and over."

Spurlock makes a strong point about responsibility: both business and consumers are accountable for their actions. But he reflects the individual and society split of liberal democracy that sees individuals as primary and society as derivative. In principle, individuals are responsible, but are they when their freedom is encroached upon or the information they need to make rational decisions is manipulated? Businesses, as social institutions, are accountable internally to the laws governing them, but their moral obligations to society are ambiguous. Debates across the divide typically assign blame to the other rather than resolve the issues constructively. These combination terms—corporate responsibility, individual responsibility, social responsibility—require a deeper understanding of the nature of responsibility, this time in communitarian terms.

Responsibility thinking and responsible action are inherently dialogical. There is no two-step process in which sovereign individuals are first true to themselves and then calculate the risk and benefits of their actions for others. Responsibility is not accountability to oneself while acting out one's preferences, some of which intersect with others. Judgments about being responsible arise from the interpersonal character of our lives together. The I-Thou relationship is both the beginning and end of responsibility. It is determined in community formations, not first of all in the inner sanctum of individuals insisting on their rights while they decide what duties they might have to others.

And responsibility in communitarianism is not a legal and political issue but a moral good. The community's flourishing and one's own are an organic whole. Love your neighbor as yourself in the Judeo-Christian tradition puts moral obligation in these integrated terms. Richard Swinburne (1989) is helpful here. He argues that responsibility concerns the difference between moral goodness and moral badness. Moral goodness requires that "an action must minimally have... overall goodness, of overriding importance, deriving from universal properties" (14). Although he admits that people have differing definitions of what might be allowed or prevented, characterizing actions as morally good or bad is the proper fault line for accountability rather than the self and society.

What if corporate responsibility is understood as goodness and badness? The dualism between individuals and social institutions disappears. Whether corporations have a responsibility to the public good, or only to shareholders who have invested in them, is not the primary question. *Supersize Me* pits McDonald's responsibility against that of consumers. But rather than one or the other, these two forms of responsibility ought to complement each other. Ian Wilson puts the corporation's problem this way: "If business can come up with no better definition of its social purpose than profit, it is little wonder that it is the object of so much public suspicion and skepticism at best and outright hatred at worst" (2000, 35). And, Wilson continues, "It is scarcely surprising that, when profit is positioned as the one true purpose of business, the conflict with social responsibility is most extreme" (42). While Wilson advocates the continuation of profit incentives, he also suggests that they should be calculated within a package of democratic values such as "freedom, the dignity of human beings, equality, pluralism and justice" (46). Once profit-making is considered along with other social values, corporate responsibility will more closely match the goodness–badness standard.

But if our examination stops here, we will have made only partial progress toward dealing with the issue raised by Spurlock. We might ask, how is any fast food franchise responsible for people's eating habits? It is responsible for, among other things, paying its employees, meeting health and sanitation requirements, and paying its taxes. But what responsibility does it have to those who frequent its establishments? Remember the dialogic character of responsibility. Do businesses have a responsibility not to overcharge? Not to serve tainted meat? Not to use beef tallow to cook its French fries (as McDonald's did until it switched to vegetable oil in 1990)? Does it include the responsibility to serve healthy food (low in saturated fat, sugar, and salt)?

On the grounds that responsibility is determined interactively in one step, accountability to employees and to customers is intrinsic to MacDonald's every practice. Even if duty to a nameless public may be difficult to specify, responsible corporations are known for their high-quality people relations. We can debate whether Spurlock's supersize eating at McDonald's is more insightful for customers than, say, Soso Whaley's. We often do apply this simple standard to the fast food chains: Does the food cause pleasure or pain? ("It's a simple question, sir," as the fry cook puts it in the Tums commercial, "do you want heartburn now or later"?) The humans-in-relation model of responsibility raises the ante, expecting a knowledgeable public to engage in the definition of business responsibility (beyond what a public representative on corporate boards can contribute).

Benjamin Barber (2007) correctly complicates the communitarian dialogic ideal. He argues that "we sow as individuals what we would not necessarily choose to reap as a community. We are trapped in an individualistic consumer culture in which the public goods that belong to us as citizens are no longer part of the accounting. The fate of capitalism and the fate of citizens no longer converge"

(18–19). The reason for this divergence, he says, is that our culture has been "infanticized," aimed more and more at the young, the most malleable members of society and the easiest to manipulate. Today's consumerist capitalism is designed for "those whose essential needs have already been satisfied but who have the means to assuage 'new' and invented needs" (9). Now, he continues: "The new religion of shopping with its induction of children into the cathedral of commerce sacralizes these new needs" (48).

Barber's argument suggests that the question of the consumer's responsibility has been made moot by the culture within which we live every day. We have been lured by a materialist culture into consumption habits that short-circuit any effort to exercise personal choice outside its boundaries and values. Yale University's Office of Public Affairs released news of experimental research conducted at the university that found that "food advertising on television increases automatic snacking on available foods in children and adults.... even foods that were not specifically presented in the advertisements." The lead author, Jennifer Harris, summarized the Yale studies this way: "This research shows a direct and powerful link between television food advertising and calories consumed by adults and children.... Food advertising triggers automatic eating, regardless of hunger, and is a significant contributor to the obesity epidemic. Reducing unhealthy food advertising to children is critical." In discussing this tendency to consume, Barber argues that consumer capitalism has convinced us all that we are autonomously empowered individuals making personal choices, when in fact the infantile ethos inculcated in children too young to exercise either liberty or judgment "reinforces consumer market ideology by providing corporate predators with an altruistic ethic to rationalize selfish and patently immoral ends" (2009, 33).

Communitarian ethics is concerned about our collective responsibility for these broad and deep social values that together shape our well-being. All of us are obligated to one another, in the advertising we attend to, the conversations we have, the warnings we issue, the care we show, the choices we make for ourselves or our children in the presence of others. It is not that any one makes choices for others (beyond parents for young children), or that we must picket the local KFC for basting its "grilled chicken" in beef tallow for taste, adding to its fat content while promoting it as a healthy alternative to its normal fried fare. Although each of us is ultimately responsible for our own food choices, these decisions are discussed and made in a context. The current context is one of convenience and taste, defined as what is salty, sugary, and fatty.

From the perspective of communitarian responsibility, however, this context can be changed as the conversation changes about what is "good." And such changes are not impossible. Americans now drink more wine than spirits, more "lite" beers than ever before. We have reduced the amount of red meat in our diets. These new ways of speaking and acting are the result of collective conversations about drunk driving, the health values of red wine, the publically recognized need to reduce caloric intake and the like. It can be done if the collective will to do it can be created through public communication of different food and convenience values. Healthy choices could be made more palatable, too, and more nutrition information could be readily available if the collective will to use the information to make choices existed. This shared responsibility is what communitarian ethics calls for.

AUTHENTICITY

If Barber is correct, then you are not happy to hear that your choices are not your own, that you are not a free and empowered individual. Barber would probably say, "You just made my point." If he is correct, it also means that none of us is who we think we are. We are not, as Charles Taylor (1991) puts it, "authentic."

Authenticity, for Taylor, comes from the "general feature of human life" that is "fundamentally dialogical" (1991, 32–37). Individuals, in other words, best understand themselves in relationship. We know things are important, he says, only against a background of intelligibility. Our authenticity is based on our ability to make significant choices, not just any choices (like choosing steak with baked potato rather than poutine for lunch), but choices whose significance is beyond my personal decision (1991, 39). "To shut out demands emanating beyond the self is precisely to suppress the conditions of significance, and hence to court trivialization" (40).

What does this discussion have to do with *Supersize Me*? If we accept the premise that the film is about the nature of responsibility, then the measuring stick that we should use to come to a conclusion about this issue is the same for both persons and businesses. Recall that under law corporations are "individuals." So we are asking, when it comes to the question of responsibility for health, which individual is responsible: the one who serves the French fries or the one who consumes them? And remember, too, that however we answer this question, the implication for the social obligations of others to the overweight or obese person is the same—they will use health facilities (hospitals and the like) and perhaps other public "goods" to the same extent regardless of who is at fault for their poor health.

Communitarian ethics, as represented by Taylor, argues that who I think I am (a healthy and happy individual, as Spurlock claims to have been before his experiment), a despondent one (as Spurlock became during his experiment), or anything in between, is a function of my identity choices "against the background of things that matter" (1991, 40). "Only if I exist in a world in which history, or the demands of nature, or the needs of my fellow human beings, or the duties of citizenship, or the call of God, or something else of this order matters crucially, can I define an identity for myself that is not trivial. Authenticity is not the enemy of demands that emanate from beyond the self; it supposes such demands" (1991, 40–41).

Society, in other words, determines what is significant. It may be equality, or independence, or progress. These elements transcend persons and constrain their choices. But there is something, too, beyond these social values that constrain our discourse. In Taylor's terms, definitions of significance themselves must be judged against the background "of things that matter" (1991, 40). The history of the human race makes moral demands on us. For instance, international law forbids genocide; societies are expected to protect their citizens from this atrocity. No society has the right to flaunt our right to live. And any society that fails in its obligation to this fundamental right is subject to international sanction—provided countries have the will to act (which, admittedly, they fail to do all too often). There are also duties of citizenship and the call of God (for those who profess faith in a deity). These long-term and overriding obligations have crucial significance. "No man is an island, entire of itself; every man is a piece of the continent, a part of the main.... any man's death diminishes me," as John Donne wrote in "Devotions upon Emergent Occasions" (Meditation XVII).

In this respect, our well-being is dependent on living within the confines of what are socially constructed goods that matter. In collective responsibility, we recognize our accountability for what happens as a result of them. Every time individuals pull into the Burger King drive-through, they encourage others to do likewise. And every time they pass it by, they become a model for others. The collective decisions that we make help construct the society that can battle obesity, physical inactivity, and ignorance of nutrition.

Society is flawed. Individuals are flawed. Nonetheless, communitarian ethics promotes the ideal of responsibility for following, preserving, and advocating the communal values that are forged in relationship and respond to transcendent definitions of the good. These values lead a community away from the greedy pursuit of personal fulfillment or a distorted sense of responsibility to shareholders. The authentic self judges one's conduct against those "things that matter." The culture of authenticity out of which such responsibility emerges is one that gives precedence to "two modes of living together," as Taylor puts it: On the public level, we demand "equal chances for everyone to develop their own identity." In "the intimate sphere, love relationships are identity-forming" (1991, 50). Out of both levels of obligation, collective responsibility makes sense, instead of "I want what I want when I want it."

Without energetic attention to a morally mediated culture of authenticity, a culture of narcissism is likely, especially in affluent societies (Taylor 1991, 55). When "things that matter" are lacking, we have an illusion of choice and freedom in which corporations do whatever is likely to increase their profits and reject anything likely to reduce them. And individuals will follow destructive paths, with that society itself bearing the cost. Responsibility depends on a collective social life made authentic by long-term moral values.

THE COMMON GOOD

Certainly it is important in communitarian ethics that reality shows like *Supersize Me* stimulate public debate and challenge viewers, advertisers, and businesses to act responsibly. But beyond such moral decision-making, communitarianism has an even weightier agenda. The common good is a central concept within this framework. Eating disorders are not just individual pathologies; obesity is a public health problem. The U.S. Surgeon General reports that preventable mortality and morbidity associated with obesity may exceed those caused by cigarette smoking. An ethics centered on the common good wants to ensure that the epidemic of obesity is understood finally in terms of public health.

Although political and moral philosophers have differed on the precise content of the common good and how to promote it, they agree that the welfare of all citizens, rather than that of factions or special interests, should be served impartially. For Aristotle, a common good is the basis for distinguishing Constitutions in the people's interest from illegitimate ones on the rulers' behalf (*Politics*, bk. III, chs. 6–7). Rousseau understood the common good as the object of the general will and the end of the state, in contrast to particular wills of subgroups within the whole (1997, bk. II, ch. 1). In Habermas, discourse in the public sphere must be oriented "toward mutual understanding" (1993, 66).

The common good is a normative concept, not just the majority results of an opinion poll or voting. The common good cannot be understood statistically, but as the basis of social morality. Obesity will not be discussed constructively as a public health issue unless government officials, the medical profession, the media, citizens, schoolteachers, and parents are committed to the concept of the common good. Individual rights are the standard language in democratic societies. The politics of rights is familiar in democracies and give priority to self-gratifying individual liberties. Situating ourselves toward moral goods in common is hard in cultures that prize self-reliance. But when societies are faced with the need for broadly shared values to confront major threats such as obesity, rights language is mute. When the importance of goods-held-in-common is ignored, the political community is only an aggregate of individual preferences without the dynamic of a common purpose. Insisting on my individual autonomy in matters of public health preserves the status quo rather than enabling a society to come to grips with an issue and resolve it constructively.

There is another way to describe the common good as a basis for seeing obesity in terms of public health. Libertarian democracy claims that political obligations are specified in a voluntary contract. The assumption is that public commitments are self-assumed. We enter into them freely and for the length of the contract only. Through the voting process, for example, individuals exercise their duties to the state.

The common good approach starts over intellectually. We assume obligations to others because we consider them to be distinctive as our own species. In acknowledging their human dignity, we carry an obligation to treat them accordingly—in the case at hand, including the obese. Thus, obligations are not directed primarily to the state, but to one another. Duties are constituted by the presumption of dignity, and therefore are owed to fellow members of institutions and participants in social practices. In other words, the common good is accessible to us in living form; it has its ground and inspiration in human being itself, rather than in contract. The reciprocity it considers essential for human existence is itself built on the assumption of a human dignity in which we regard others as basically like ourselves.

In order to build from and nurture a common good perspective, all relevant materials need to enter the discussion, rather than only a documentary or two. Surgeon General reports and World Health Organization documents are essential. The books and films and educational materials sparked by *Supersize Me* are important for cultural transformation around a mutual commitment to the whole. Schools, churches, synagogues, and NGOs with a common good orientation are obvious locations for teaching and learning. Those who participate in articulating common-good alternatives ordinarily develop a commitment to implement them.

CONCLUSION

The moral foundations of our public life are the same for all. The means by which we determine responsibility in cases such as that raised by *Supersize Me* are identical for a society's members and its institutions. It is a false dichotomy to say it is either the consumer's responsibility or McDonald's. Under communitarianism, both are responsible. Judgments about behavior in this case must use the same standards. And the basis for deciding the levels of responsibility for any of the parties must be not what is good for profits, or even individual health, but what is good for the public—for its furtherance, for its moral development, for its continuing care for its members, and ultimately for the well-being of all who live within it.

REFERENCES

Aristotle. 1888. *Politics: A Treatise on Government.* Translated by W. Ellis. London: George Routledge.

"Awards for Supersize Me." 2004. <http://www.imdb.com/title/tt0390521/awards>.

Barber, Benjamin R. 2007. *Consumed: How Markets Corrupt Children, Infantilize Adults, and Swallow Citizens Whole.* New York: W. W. Norton.

Bauman, Valerie. 2005. "A McDonald's Diet Helps Mom Lose Supersize Status and She's Loving It." *Albany Times Union,* August 12, A2.

Center for Disease Control and Prevention. 2007. "New CDC Study Finds No Increase in Obesity among Adults; But Levels Still High." November 28. <http://www.cdc.gov/nchs/pressroom/07newsreleases/obesity.htm>.

"'Cheeseburger Bill' Puts Bite on Lawsuits." 2005. October 20. <http://www.cnn.com/2005/POLITICS/10/20/cheeseburger.bill/index.html>.

Critser, Greg. 2003. *Fat Land: How Americans Became the Fattest People in the World.* Boston: Houghton Mifflin.

Currie, Janet, DellaVigna, Stefano, Moretti, Enrico, and Pathania, Vikram. 2009. "The Effect of Fast Food Restaurants on Obesity and Weight Gain." NBER Working Paper No. 14721. February. <http://www.nber.org/papers/w14721.pdf>.

Edelstein, David. 2004. "Big Mac Counterattack." *Slate Magazine,* May 6. <http://www.slate.com/id/2100114/>.

Fields, Suzanne. 2004. "Downsizing the 'Victim': Personal Responsibility and Health." *Washington Times,* April 26, A21.

Genessy, Jody. 2004. "Supersize Lawsuits No Longer Possible." *Deseret News,* April 2.

Gillespie, Noreen. 2005. "'Supersize Me' Educational Program Heading to Schools." *Charleston Gazette*, February 11, A2.

Goode, Stephen. 2001. "Gavin Preaches Healthy Habits as a Way of Life." *Insight on the News*, April 16, 36.

Grimes, William. 2004. "Supersize, We Knew Thee Too Well." *New York Times*, March 7, sec. 4, p. 2.

Habermas, Jürgen. 1993. *Justification and Application: Remarks on Discourse Ethics.* Translated by C. Cronin. Cambridge, MA: MIT Press.

Hale, Mike. 2010. "Trying to Put Nutrition on the Lunchroom Menu." *New York Times*, March 26, C17.

Harris, Andrew M. 2010. "McDonald's Obesity Case Can't Proceed as Group Suit." October 27. <http://www.bloomberg.com/news/2010-10-27/mcdonald-s-obesity-case-judge-rejects-bid-for-group-suit-status.html>.

"Health Panel: 'Supersize Me' Movie Trivializes Obesity, A Serious Problem." 2004. *PR Newswire*, May 6.

Higgins, Marguerite. 2004. "Downsized at McDonald's; Filmmaker Loses 18 Pounds in Debunking Fast-Food Flick." July 4. <http://cei.org/gencon/019,04100.cfm>.

Hughes, Margaret, and Farrow, Tony. 2007. "Caring for Obese Patients in a Culturally Safe Way: Obesity Is a Culturally Constructed Concept and Nurses Need to be Culturally Safe in their Practice, When Caring for Those Labelled Obese." *Kai Tiaki: Nursing New Zealand*, May 1, 14–15.

Ingram, Scott. 2005. *Want Fries with That? Obesity and the Supersizing of America.* San Francisco: Children's Press.

Institute of Medicine. 2009. *Local Government Actions to Prevent Childhood Obesity.* Committee on Childhood Obesity Prevention Actions for Local Government. Institute of Medicine and National Research Council. Washington, D.C.: National Academies Press.

Jie, Liu. 2005. "McDonald's Bowing to 'Supersize' Critics." *China Daily*, September 29.

Lee, Christina. 2004. "Supersize Me." *Film Journal.* <http://www.thefilmjournal.com/issue9/supersizeme.html>.

Libal, Autumn. 2006. *Fats, Sugars, and Empty Calories: The Fast Food Habit.* Broomall, Penn.: Mason Crest.

Lopez, Kathryn Jean. 2005. "Soso, So Good." June 23. <http://www.nationalreview.com/interrogatory/whaley_200506230747.asp>.

Marsh, Molly. 2006. "Grub for Body and Soul: An Interview with Food Activists Anna Lappé and Bryant Terry." *Sojourners Magazine*, 35 (5), May, 32–34.

Maschal, Laura. 2004. "'Super Size Me' Serves Hefty Dose of Bias." *Teaching Tolerance.* August 18. <http://www.tolerance.org/news/article_print.jsp?id=1051>.

Mitchard, Jacquelyn. 2004. "Supersize Is More Than Simply a Meal Portion." *Milwaukee Journal Sentinel*, February 29.

Montada, Leo. 2001. "Denial of Responsibility." In Ann Elisabeth Auhagen and Hans-Werner Bierhoff, eds., *Responsibility: The Many Faces of a Social Phenomenon*, 79–92. New York: Routledge.

Montague, Mamie C. 2003. "The Physiology of Obesity." *ABNF Journal*, 14 (3), May/June, 55–60.

Morad, Tamar. 2005. "Youthful Obesity Is Epidemic: Declines in Physical Activity and Unhealthy Eating Habits Are Making More and More Children Overweight." *Human Ecology*, 33 (3), December, 18–20.

Murphy, Erin. 2004. "America and Obesity: An Epidemic Obsession." February 12. <http://www.cfif.org/htdocs/freedomline/current/guest_commentary/america_and_obesity.htm>.

Murse, Tom. 2004. "Impressed by the Demise of Supersize? Take a Closer Look." *Lancaster New Era*, March 8, B1.

Nestle, Marion, and Jacobson, Michael F. 2000. "Halting the Obesity Epidemic: A Public Health Policy Approach." *Public Health Reports* 115 (1), January/February, 12 ff.

Nunn, Emily. 2007. "Is Fast Food off the Obesity Hook?" *Sunday Gazette-Mail*, November 4.

Obesity & Diabetes Week. 2008. "Obesity Predisposition Traced to Brain's Reward System." August 11.

Ogden, Cynthia L., and Carroll, Margaret D. 2010. "Prevalence of Overweight, Obesity, and Extreme Obesity among Adults: United States, Trends 1960–1962 through 2007–2008." Centers for Disease Control and Prevention. June. <http://www.cdc.gov/NCHS/data/hestat/obesity_adult_07_08/obesity_adult_07_08.pdf>.

Oliver, J. Eric. 2006. *Fat Politics: The Real Story Behind America's Obesity Epidemic*. New York: Oxford University Press.

Pollan, Michael. 2006. *The Omnivore's Dilemma: A Natural History of Four Meals*. New York: Penguin.

Popkin, Barry. 2008. *The World is Fat: The Fads, Trends, Policies, and Products that are Fattening the Human Race*. New York: Penguin.

Rousseau, Jean Jacques. 1997. *The Social Contract and Other Political Writings*. Edited by V. Gourevitch. Cambridge, U.K.: Cambridge University Press.

Sawer, Patrick. 2005. "Now It's the Supersize Burger: Monster Meals Make a Big Comeback." *Evening Standard* (London, U.K.), January 11.

Schlosser, Eric. 2004. *Fast Food Nation: The Dark Side of the All-American Meal*. New York: Harper Perennial.

Shah, Neepa. 2004. "Goodbye, Supersize!" Knight Ridder/Tribune News Service, March 11.

Shaw, Hillary J. 2006. "Food Deserts: Towards the Development of a Classification." *Geografiska Annaler Series B: Human Geography* 88 (2): 231–47.

Signore, John Del. 2010. "Fast Food Restaurants May Get Zoned Out of Some NYC Areas." March 24. <http://gothamist.com/2010/03/24/fast_food_restaurants_may_get_zoned.php>.

Stout, Martha. 2005. *The Sociopath Next Door: The Ruthless Versus the Rest of Us*. New York: Broadway Books.

Strauss, Gary. 2004. "Moviegoers Show a Big Appetite for 'Supersize Me.'" *USA Today*. June 7. <http://www.usatoday.com/life/movies/news/2004-06-07-super-size-me_x.htm>.

Surgeon General of the United States. 2001. *The Surgeon General's Call to Action to Prevent and Decrease Overweight and Obesity 2001*. Rockville, Md.: Public Health Service. U.S. Department of Health and Human Services.

Swinburne, Richard. 1989. *Responsibility and Atonement*. Oxford, U.K.: Clarendon Press.

Tartamella, Lisa, Hersher, Elaine, and Woolston, Chris. 2006. *Generation Extra Large: Rescuing Our Children from the Epidemic of Obesity*. New York: Basic.

Taylor, Charles. 1991. *The Ethics of Authenticity*. Cambridge, MA: Harvard University Press.

Thorn, Patti. 2005. "A Supersize Survivor." *Rocky Mountain News*, April 29.

Trust for America's Health. 2009. *F as in Fat: How Obesity Policies are Failing in America*. <http://healthyamericans.org/reports/obesity2009/Obesity2009Report.pdf>.

Weber, Karl, ed. 2009. *Food, Inc.: How Industrial Food is Making Us Sicker, Fatter, and Poorer—and What You Can Do About It*. New York: Public Affairs.

Wells, Rosemary. 2007. *The Gulps*. New York: Little, Brown.

Wilson, Ian. 2000. *The New Rules of Corporate Conduct: Rewriting the Social Charter*. Westport, CT: Quorum Books.

Yale University Office of Public Affairs. 2009. "TV Food Advertising Increases Snacking and Potential Weight Gain in Children and Adults." July 1. <http://Opa.yale.edu/news/article.aspx?id=6770>.

CHAPTER 7

✣

Rachel Carson's *Silent Spring*

Time magazine included Rachel Carson on its list of the 100 most important people of the twentieth century—along with Einstein, Freud, and Gandhi. And the Carson buzz continues in the twenty-first century. The Rachel Carson Council is busier than ever. Its 2010 publication, *A Disaster in the Making*, on the hazards of the chemical imidacloprid has been a newsmaker. The Environmental Protection Agency sponsors an annual "Rachel Carson 'Sense of Wonder' Contest."[1] She is EPA's honorary founder whose book, says the EPA, reversed the nation's environmental policy forever.

Greatness also draws opposition, of course. A conservative Washington think tank, the Competitive Enterprise Institute, fights restrictions on food production and "repressive laws against technological progress." Its website (http://www.rachelwaswrong.com) realizes that Carson's name belongs in American folklore, but at every turn condemns what it calls "her extremism."

Silent Spring, a best-seller in its time, is still in print a half century later and read in twenty-two languages worldwide. For the *Columbia Journalism Review,* it is the gift that keeps on giving. *Silent Spring* is included in its "Second Read" series—classics from history whose lessons endure for journalists. As Marla Cone, an environmental reporter for the *Los Angeles Times*, puts it: "Carson's book burns with as much intensity today" as in 1962; "most of Carson's science remains sound and her warnings prescient."[2]

Carson teaches us that social issues need a moral language in the public media before minds are changed and society moves forward. Her extraordinary career demonstrates that when common problems are understood, not just technically but ethically, constructive social action becomes possible.

Silent Spring synthesized a huge body of research on the biological effects of chemicals to show that altering the natural world harms life on earth permanently. Carson explained how the complex interaction of living creatures with each other and with the environment was a delicate balance created over vast time. Powerful synthetic chemicals previously unknown to nature upset its organic balance. Many of these chemicals proved initially effective in controlling pests for increased agricultural production (Carson 1962, 17–19). But Carson insisted on two important questions: What was their long-term impact on the environment? And what were the wider effects of using these chemicals on living creatures, including humans?

Rachel Carson's research showed that chemicals such as DDT gradually built up and silenced the sounds of spring as the poisons worked indiscriminately on the food chain as a whole.[3] With her tart tongue and vivid prose, she called their accretion over time "the chain of evil," and pesticides were "elixirs of death." As chapter 8 ("And No Birds Sing") begins: "Over increasingly large areas of the United States, spring now comes unheralded by the return of the birds, and the early mornings are strangely silent where once they were filled with the beauty of bird song" (Carson 1962, 103).

She illustrated how these chemicals could remain stored in the human body after contact with or consumption of contaminated material. Insects and other targeted pests often adapted quickly, forcing scientists to develop and apply ever-deadlier chemicals to maintain beneficial effects. But instead of advocating a total ban on pesticides and a halt to chemical research, Carson promoted wise solutions. She devoted an entire chapter of *Silent Spring* to reducing pesticide use by balanced, biological techniques (1962, ch. 16). She believed that humans stood at a crossroads with their new capabilities to dominate the environment. It was up to society to determine which direction to travel:

> Only by taking account of such life forces and by cautiously seeking to guide them into channels favorable to ourselves can we hope to achieve a reasonable accommodation between the insect hordes and ourselves. The current vogue for poisons has failed utterly to take into account these most fundamental considerations. (Carson 1962, 161)

Even before *Silent Spring* arrived in bookstores on September 27, 1962, Carson's critique of pesticides and their wider consequences had received months of press attention. Publicists sent advance copies to scientists, nature societies, political organizations, members of Congress, literary outlets, women's groups, and government agencies. In June, the *New Yorker* began serial publication of excerpts from the work, preceding *Silent Spring*'s publication by three months (see Murphy 2005, 9–10, 17–18).

Despite the headlines and its award-winning author, *Silent Spring* was not universally welcomed. The agricultural industry had already "mobilized a substantial public relations effort with a $250,000 war chest" to counter the *New Yorker's* message (Murphy 2005, 4). Velsicol Chemical Company, which held sole rights to heptachlor and chlordane—two chemicals discussed in the book—threatened to sue Carson's publishers at the *New Yorker* and Houghton Mifflin if they completed publication. Government critics tried to discredit Carson, attacking message and messenger alike. Many entomologists, whose research birthed chemical pesticides like DDT, felt their professional reputations impugned and dismissed *Silent Spring* as an emotional rant. Industrialists warned of civilization's decline, asserting that to stop using pesticides would reverse human progress and the American way of life. Monsanto, for example, published a parody of *Silent Spring* called *The Desolate*

Fear, in which disease, famine, and insects take over the world after pesticides are banned (Cone 2005, 66). Others attacked her gender. Ezra Taft Benson, Secretary of Agriculture in the Eisenhower administration, asked "why a spinster with no children was so concerned with genetics" (quoted in Lytle 2007, 175).

But the tide of public opinion began to turn. Two months after its release, *Silent Spring* was the number one best-seller with over 100,000 copies sold. The book received a positive review from the *New York Times* and an interview by *Life* magazine. Rachel Carson, though struggling with cancer, sought to return the debate to her arguments and evidence. An initial well-received appearance on *CBS Reports* was later translated into an April 3, 1963, special show "The Silent Spring of Rachel Carson"—aired "despite withdrawal of advertisements by some sponsors and threats by others to do the same" (Murphy 2005, 5).

Although chemical industry heavyweights such as Dr. Robert White-Stevens, head of American Cyanamid's agricultural research, argued against her position, others responded to her call for reform. The day after publication, Senator Abraham Ribicoff of Connecticut announced that the Government Operations subcommittee would hold hearings on the use and impact of chemical pesticides—and that Rachel Carson would testify. On May 15 the Presidential Science Advisory Committee released its long-awaited report "Use of Pesticides." To conservationists' surprise, it significantly reversed earlier government reports by recommending documentation of pesticide use, monitoring of residues, more research into their effects, and the development of alternatives. The *Christian Science Monitor*'s headline declared "Rachel Carson Stands Vindicated" (Lytle 2007, 176, 183–85). According to Christopher Bosso,

> Carson's original writings were quoted, discussed, and publicized by other media on a scope not previously experienced for an "environmental" matter. The initial *New Yorker* series reached a limited audience, but particularly explosive pieces of journalism tend to have marked multiplier effects—a pattern of attention first on the part of political leaders and the "attentive public," and later the mass audience, as other media organs report on the original story. The first two factors influenced short-term government response; the third helped *Silent Spring* to spark the modern environmental movement. (Bosso 1987, 115; quoted in Murphy 2005, 203)

LIFE AND IMPACT

Rachel Louise Carson was born on May 27, 1907, the youngest of Maria and Robert Carson's three children. Growing up along the Allegheny River in Springdale, Pennsylvania, her mother, a former teacher, took Rachel almost daily to observe the living world in the woods and fields near their home. She felt nature's wonder, later commenting that the source of her life-long passion for the natural world was no surprise (Lytle 2007, 18, 15). An accomplished student, Carson read voraciously and by age 11 she started to send her own stories to publishers. In 1918 *St. Nicholas Magazine*, a well-known periodical for young readers, printed four of her stories inspired by her brother Robert's World War I service in the Army Air Corps.

After graduating first in her class at Parnassus High School in 1925, Carson entered the Pennsylvania College for Women in nearby Pittsburgh (now Chatham University). In college Carson's love for natural science and for writing began to merge. Grace Croff and Mary Scott Skinker, professors in English and Biology, guided Carson toward the works of Alfred Tennyson, John Muir, and other naturalists. Lytle confirms how these writers were reflected in later years: "In embracing those writers as literary models, Carson had begun to confirm her character. No matter how conventional in manner and personal appearance, Rachel Carson was, like the writers she admired, something of a subversive" (Lytle 2007, 31).

After Carson graduated with honors in biology in 1929, she followed her mentor, Professor Skinker, to Johns Hopkins University, where she was accepted into the zoology program on a scholarship. She spent the summer before entry at the Woods Hole Marine Biology Laboratory, which gave her the chance to observe sea environments for the first time. Earning her master's degree in 1932, she continued in the doctoral program until 1934, when she decided to leave the university and look for a teaching job.

On Skinker's recommendation, Carson took civil service exams in biology and scored well. Skinker also pushed her to contact Elmer Higgins of the U.S. Bureau of Fisheries. No job was available, but Higgins commissioned Carson to write a series of scripts for a bureau radio series. Soon after the series concluded, she found a position as a junior aquatic biologist in the science division, becoming one of only two women hired at a professional level in the entire bureau (Lear 1997, 82). She compiled research data of department scientists, wrote reports, and created public brochures based on the conclusions. She also began writing about marine biology for the *Baltimore Sun*. She spent significant time traveling to government research projects and biological stations for her work, getting to know several leading scientific thinkers, and employees of commercial enterprises (Lytle 2007, 39–40). The expertise Carson gained during this period would enhance her ability to synthesize scientific research for a mass audience.

In 1937 Carson published an essay "Undersea" in the *Atlantic Monthly* and responses were encouraging. Scientists and literary figures alike admired her ability to explain scientific research with evocative prose. Simon and Schuster's Quincy Howe and author Hendrik Van Look encouraged her to develop a book from the four-page article. Excited by the challenge, Carson strove to replace the period's conventional anthropocentrism by using her years of oceanic observations and several summers at Woods Hole lab to describe sea life from the animals' point of view (Lytle 2007, 44).

Under the Sea-Wind was published in November 1941 to more acclaim from reviewers. The United States' entrance into World War II, however, curtailed the new author's exposure to the public and she received little commercial success (Brooks 1980, 278). (*Under the Sea-Wind* would become a best-seller when it was re-released a decade later.) While Carson sometimes felt she should contribute more directly to the war effort, she soon managed all publications for the U.S. Fish and Wildlife Service (Lytle 2007, 57–58). Although she published a few more small works in magazines, she yearned to write independently as a career. She continued to hunt for opportunities to engage her passion full time even as her increasing latitude at the Service afforded her access to the latest oceanographic and environmental research compiled during the war. In 1945 she even proposed to *Reader's Digest* a series on DDT. The rejection letter she received foreshadowed later controversies over *Silent Spring*: "The *Digest*... had no appetite for scientific muckraking, especially in the summer of 1945. The triumph of science was the big story in a year in which the United States successfully detonated atomic bombs at Hiroshima and Nagasaki" (Lytle 2007, 60).

By the late 1940s, Rachel Carson proposed a new book project, for which she received an advance from Oxford University Press. Published in 1951, *The Sea Around Us* was met with rave reviews. The *New Yorker* serialized a condensed version of it. The *Saturday Review of Literature* and the *New York Times Book Review* featured her new book over the summer. As other publications followed suit, recognition began flowing in—including the National Book Award for 1951. *The Sea Around Us* spent eighty-six weeks on top of the *New York Times'* best seller list, selling 1.3 million copies. It was translated into thirty-one languages. Carson had met her goal: she could now devote herself full-time to writing (Lytle 2007, 80–83). She continued to offer readers the latest scientific research without losing the grandeur and beauty of her subject.

Rachel Carson's efforts over the next four years jelled into a third book, *At the Edge of the Sea*. Illustrated by Bob Hines, a former colleague at the Fish and Wildlife Service, the new work became a companion to *The Sea Around Us*. This volume explored shorelines as a field and ecological guide, emphasizing the interdependence of all life. *At the Edge of the Sea*'s 1955 publication also met with critical success. Several chapters were condensed or otherwise republished in magazines, and both the American Association of University Women and the National Council of Women of the United States recognized Carson's work.

As time progressed, however, Carson began to think more about the major changes scientific knowledge wrought, especially in the decade following the development of atomic energy. She began to question the assumption in her first three books that humans had relatively little impact on environments as large as Earth's oceans. She still found her subject to be life and its interaction with the environment, but Carson was losing "confidence in the enduring capacity of 'life' to withstand human assaults. She discovered within herself a new skepticism toward the dominant faith of postwar America in science and human progress" (Lytle 2007, 120).

A 1958 letter from a friend in Boston, Olga Owens Hutchins, began to crystallize Carson's growing concern with the impact of synthetic pesticides on the environment. Hutchins reported that a state spraying program to eliminate mosquitoes ended up killing denizens of a nearby bird sanctuary. Rachel Carson investigated the problem, along with the U.S. Department of Agriculture's new fire ant eradication program in much of the Southeast and a similar USDA program for gypsy moths in the Northeast. Although she and her agent worried about the implications of such a book, Carson had found her topic. In May 1958 she signed a contract with Houghton Mifflin for what a friend referred to as the "poison book" (Lytle 2007, 129).

Research on a vast—and often just emerging—scientific literature occupied much of Rachel Carson's next four years, even as her health declined. She scrutinized dozens of contacts from her decade and a half with the federal government, as well as many others she had read over the years. She continued to send the relevant book chapter to experts with whom she had conferred, to make sure she interpreted their work accurately. She knew that only the strongest evidence would help her work endure the criticism sure to follow from powerful government, corporate, and trade interests. Yet neither did she intend to let the facts speak for themselves. As Lytle perceptively notes, indignation was key to the enterprise:

> Such a case required more than gathering evidence. She undertook her research as a partisan, not a neutral observer. In that sense, Carson violated the canons of scientific objectivity. Those who supported the cause were allies; those opposed, enemies.... She was out to win. (2007, 133–34)

The same persuasive skills that allowed Carson to hone the reputation of a trained scientist and talented writer in her previous projects proved central to the conflict over *Silent Spring* upon its publication in 1962.

> Carson's writing did not simply evoke the dangers of science run amok. A reverence for the mysteries of life linked her to the romantics. With their idealism, passion, and fascination with the unknown world, romantics often flaunt convention. Empirical science has routinely dismissed them as "shrill," "irrational," and "emotional." These same terms distinguished the masculine from the feminine. In that way, Carson's critics could use both her passion and her gender to discredit her ideas. (Lytle 2007, 134)

The ensuing battle proceeded predictably. Opponents criticized Rachel Carson on all fronts. Too often they left the actual text of *Silent Spring* unexamined and ignored the 55 pages of bibliography and source material. Very few detractors acknowledged, as supportive scientists continually reminded the public, that Carson did not advocate the eradication of biocides. Instead, she promoted the judicious application of all chemicals with appropriate concern for their long-range impact.

Carson's careful research and her passionate writing style soon won over a sizeable number of Americans. The momentum generated by positive coverage in the spring of 1963 continued during her May testimony to both the Senate Government Operations subcommittee and the Senate Commerce committee. In November further support for her argument appeared when Washington's Public Health Service determined that the pesticide endrin caused a massive fish die-off in the Mississippi River. Eventually investigators traced the endrin contamination to a waste treatment plant in Memphis operated by chemical giant Velsicol (Lytle 2007, 190). In December, Carson received the National Audubon Society's medal

Rachel Carson appearing before a Senate Government Operations subcommittee studying pesticides (Library of Congress).

and the American Geographic Society's Cullum medal, and she was inducted into the American Academy of Arts and Letters. The following spring, cancer having spread throughout her body, she suffered a heart attack and died.

Rachel Carson's legacy lived on. Throughout the rest of the 1960s, the burgeoning environmental movement gained wide public support (cf. Murphy 2005). In 1969, Congress adopted the National Environmental Policy Act (NEPA). The Council on Environmental Quality, and the Occupational Safety and Health Administration (OSHA) soon followed. In 1970, the Nixon administration consolidated the federal government's rapidly expanding environmental agencies into the new Environmental Protection Agency (EPA). Two years later the EPA reversed an earlier commission's decision and banned DDT spraying on crops (but allowed exports to other countries and emergency use within the United States). The decision to ban DDT was upheld in a 1973 appeal.[4]

Creating the EPA and banning DDT encouraged American discussion about the proper relationship of science, industry, and the environment. Both Carson's backers and her opponents also utilized the language of democracy to add weight to their attempts to define a good society (Buhs 2002, 379). Further counterattacks ensued, beginning with the Reagan administration of the 1980s and continuing until now. At different times various causes have pushed the issue to the fore, with justifications as diverse as economic deregulation and global health. But regardless of public discourse pro and con, *Silent Spring* and Rachel Carson remain an enduring part of the debate.[5]

COMMUNITARIAN ETHICS

In communitarian ethics, human communities are held together by common values. Rachel Carson's massive influence results from aligning her work with social life's moral axis. Many people of Carson's time—and even today—assumed an anthropocentric view of human supremacy over the natural world as a justification for intervention into the environment. But Rachel Carson recognized that making good decisions about any environmental issue required reconceiving the relationship between *homo sapiens* and the rest of nature. The rational self of Enlightenment hubris needed turning—from supremacy to partnership, from hegemony to care. Carson did not diminish the human gifts of reason and reflection, nor conflate all life forms as equally worthy of the investment required to preserve them. She advocated a view of the rational mind that respected the processes of nature, but not as a substitute for reason. Humans were to conserve nature, not merely consume it. They were to be stewards, not merely users.

This biocentric conviction had deep consequences for *Silent Spring*. It moved her argument beyond mere partisan politics. Viewing humans as making choices within a larger system downplayed political differences, but highlighted the importance of long-range public policy without appealing to political stereotypes or partisan rhetoric. As Lytle comments:

> In *The Sea Around Us* and the books that followed, Carson embraced the cooperative ideal. She could do so because she had little concern with the political implications of ecology for human society. The moral condemnations that appeared in her writing had ecological, rather than political, import. (2007, 90)

Her ideas gained traction in both Republican and Democrat administrations and political climates, and throughout American society. Her perspective has survived repeated challenges, precisely because she framed her fundamental argument in moral terms rather than in party politics. The highest achievement of *Silent Spring* was not the creation of the EPA or the banning of DDT (which are excellent ends in themselves), but its fostering the public conversation around morality (cf. Craig 2009, 210).

In the communitarian perspective, humans are selves-in-relation with a moral commitment for orienting the social space they share together. According to Charles Taylor, "Developing, maintaining and articulating" their moral intuitions and reactions are as natural for humans as learning up and down, left and right (1989, 27–29). Public life cannot be facilitated in technical terms only; it needs moral discourse and ongoing attention to common values. In communitarianism, identifying and defending a culture's normative base amplifies our deepest humanness. Moral discourse provides the overall context for thinking through and acting upon shared issues such as the environment.

Carson's view of communication combined moral fervor with hard evidence to motivate both the mind and heart. Communitarian ethics recognizes that will and knowledge, conviction and intelligence, passion and reflection are human impulses that move us to decision and action. As Martha Nussbaum argues, emotions "shape the landscape of our mental and social lives." They are not "alien forces" but "highly discriminating responses to what is of value and importance;" they "form part of our system of ethical reasoning" and we need to take account of their role in "our thinking about the good and the just" (2001, p. i).

Carson knew how to stir the public conscience while explaining scientific facts. But Vera Norwood places her nature writing within a larger context—the philosophy of science taking shape during the 1950s and 1960s. A paradigm shift was occurring, away from pure scientific theorems to scientific theories as historically conditioned and value laden. Indeed, Carson's *Silent Spring* and Thomas Kuhn's first edition of *The Structure of Scientific Revolutions* were published in the same year and share perspectives on scientific epistemology. Carson illustrated this shift in scientific knowledge—depending as she does on laboratory discovery, mathematics, and expertise. But she communicates at the same time the values of the people whom knowledge empowers. As Norwood concludes: "One of Carson's least appreciated contributions is to have made available to a general readership new ideas about the nature of knowledge" (Norwood 1987, 759).

ENVIRONMENTAL COMMUNICATION

The modern history of environmental communication studies typically begins with Carson, who influenced a wide range of media from interpersonal communication to virtual communities. Standing on the shoulders of this giant and others such as John Muir and Henry David Thoreau, environmental communication has grown into a significant academic specialty with these components: conceptual perspectives, media production, and citizen participation.

Conceptual Perspectives

Regarded as the father of modern ecology, naturalist and forester Aldo Leopold proposed a land ethic that extends "the boundaries of the community to include soil, water, plants, and animals, or collectively: a land" (1987, 204).[6] Healthy human communities make room for other forms of life. They are committed to the vitality of natural communities (biota), nurturing their productivity and insuring their capacity for self-renewal. Human communication and political deliberation are integral components of a land ethic, which calls on human communities to negotiate its specific meaning using the best scientific knowledge available to meet biotic community needs that include human beings. Land health reflects the dynamic and broad set of contexts in which conservation can provide ethical norms in trying to adjudicate between the one and the many.

Another theoretical alternative is Arnold Pacey's (2003) environmental philosophy developed in terms of technological progress. Materialism, driven by technological innovation and market forces, results in environmental degradation and crisis. Rather than material growth being the master value, social development is reconceived at a slower pace to include sustainability, conservation, and machines that do not "injure and destroy plant and human life" (126).

Media Production

Rachel Carson's ability to combine factual evidence with moral fervor is the basis for major documentaries, books, and exhibits on environmental concerns today. Albert Gore's film *An Inconvenient Truth*, for instance, demonstrates that global warming is a premier moral issue of the twenty-first century. Winner of the Academy Award for Best Documentary Feature, the film reviews scientific evidence on climate change, greenhouse gases, water salinity, and carbon dioxide concentrations in Antarctic ice core samples. Its purpose is to refute critics who claim global warming is unproven or insignificant, and calls on viewers to learn more and take action.

Sandra Steingraber is a contemporary biologist and author, whom the Sierra Club calls "the new Rachel Carson." A survivor of bladder cancer when only 20 years old, Steingraber's *Living Downstream: An Ecologist's Personal Investigation of Cancer and the Environment* (2010) blends scientific analysis and personal memoir. For the first time in a public text, she relates toxins with data from the U.S. cancer registries. *Living Downstream* was featured on Bill Moyers's PBS program, *Kids and Chemicals*, and is now a documentary film. Steingraber's investigation of fetal toxicology demonstrates that chemically poisoned environments threaten each crucial stage of human development. Reflecting communitarian principles, she describes community efforts to reverse the impact of carcinogenic toxins, such as an Iowa farming group's decision to use natural methods of pest control rather than chemical herbicides.

Citizen Participation

Carson's activism is an inspiration for citizens groups, all of whom depend on media marketing and coverage. These include the Natural Resource Defense Council, Consumers' Union, the Rachel Carson Council, Tanzania Environmental Society, Worldwide Fund for Nature, Earth First, Greenpeace, Clean Up the World, Audubon Society, Alliance for Climate Protection, BirdLife International, Wildlife Conservation Society, and Wetlands International. Environmental organizations provide special projects for learning awareness and grassroots organizing.

Wendell Berry's "Think Little" is the classic statement on environmental activism (1975). The editorial in the first *Whole Earth Catalog*, "Think Little," has been quoted, debated, and acted on ever since. As an alternative to fads, crowds, and slogans, Berry maps out a strategy of sustainable action for long-term transformation. Instead of using emotional appeals to blame others and motivating us by guilt and fear, Berry wants the people's voice to be knowledgeable and rooted in personal change. Following the communitarian impulse, involvement springs from below. Rather than waiting for political and business leaders to educate a public they consider uninformed, the people themselves recognize the problems and find mechanisms to shape policy and resolve conflicts. Instead of relying on technological solutions, what matters most is crafting durable human and natural communities

(Berry 2001). Robert Cox calls this "community or place-based collaboration" grounded in the "principles of participatory democracy" (2010, 125–26).

PROFESSIONAL ETHICS

Carson's lasting gift to the environment was her communitarian vision, which ranked political and economic concerns behind moral concerns. She described ecosystems with a moral focus that came alive, a focus that inspires the evidence-driven energy sciences, natural resources, forestry protection, and food safety government agencies. The environmental professions need detailed guidelines, codes of ethics that are taken seriously, and practical training in moral decision-making. For example, the "Land Ethic Canon" is placed first in the Society of American Foresters (SAF) Code of Ethics—the most famous formulation of our ideals for sustaining the earth's ecosystems followed by specific provisions and practices for technically trained people to act on it (Irland 2007, ch. 14). Lloyd Irland, Yale University Senior Scientist in Environmental Studies, emphasizes ethical reflection above all, that is, the exercise of ethical thinking that helps people make the right choices (Irland 2007, 7–10). When the environmental professions develop "the highest personal and organizational standards of ethical behavior" (p. 10), then the legacy of Rachel Carson will finally be fulfilled.

With the news media providing the public voice for environmental professionals, reporters need to know these standards themselves. Reporters hold workers in environmental management accountable on behalf of the public, and professional ethics serves as a standard for evaluating their performance. The Code of Ethics of the National Association of Environmental Professionals is one general code worth knowing. It pledges duty to the public welfare and integrity in all the members' responsibilities. Knowing what is expected in land and water management, monitoring land trusts, community education, stewardship, contingency plans, and enforcement make the reporter's role more intelligent (Perschel 2004). Of particular help to news professionals, several codes include major sections on communication policies and procedures (Irland 2007, 32–33). Working knowledgeably within the ethical framework of environmental professionals themselves, the media will not become tiresome moralizers full of abuse and accusation, but rather fulfill the communitarian ideal of empowering the public to act on the problems and solutions themselves.

To insure that professional ethics is communitarian requires some hard thinking.[7] Utilitarianism tends to dominate business and government and the media in a democratic society. Making the best consequences the determining issue, as utilitarianism does, fits comfortably with democracies where each person gets one vote and the majority sets public policy. John Stuart Mill's *On Liberty*, written two years before *Utilitarianism* has been enormously influential in shaping democratic politics. A theory based on promoting happiness and preventing pain—as developed by the British philosopher Jeremy Bentham (1806–1873)—certainly reflects an important dimension of our humanness. When working out a professional ethics for environmental communication, it is natural that we emphasize the best results for the overall social welfare, the greatest balance of good over harm.

Robert Cox (2010) illustrates utilitarian ethics at work when a dam was recommended for the Hetch Hetchy Valley in Yosemite National Park. In 1901, the city of San Francisco proposed to dam the river running through this valley in the park as its water supply. After years of controversy, the dam was approved in 1913 following the utilitarian ethics of Gifford Pinchot, the director of what would become the U.S. Forest Service, who understood conservation as "the wise and efficient use of natural resources" (p. 49). When logged, timberlands should be reforested so environmental damage is limited. Water use meant benefiting the most without harming the landscape. Conservation in Pinchot's sense was pitted against the preservation approach of John Muir and like naturalists who argued for a ban on commercial use of wilderness areas and preserving them for recreation and study, for their wildlife and the rhythms of nature (pp. 48–49).[8]

And here in the preservation movement, one sees communitarian ethics take shape. Knowing the consequences for the long term is nearly impossible. How should benefits to the City of San Francisco be balanced against environmental harm for future generations? Relying on one criterion—the best results—typically reduces complexities and leads to ongoing disputes over the legitimacy of actions taken in the name of the majority's benefit.[9] Communitarian ethics is broader in scope; it includes the philosophy of John Muir and Aldo Leopold as it develops its morality of human flourishing.

Environmental justice is the best label for the communitarian alternative. The term connects "the safety and quality of the environments where people live" with concerns for social and economic justice (Cox 2010, 55).[10] In policy statements from various locations around the world, environmental justice refers to "the basic right of all people to be free of poisons and other hazards." At its communitarian core is "a vision of the democratic inclusion of people and communities in the decisions that affect their health and well-being" (55). Rather than decisions made by the business and political elite, those directly affected by environmental hazards, toxic wastes, and polluted water need to participate meaningfully (see Cox, 2010, ch. 8).[11]

In communitarian terms, news does not focus just on environmental crises and tragedies. The issues of justice need to weave their way in and out of news stories, editorials, and investigative reports. The disproportionate use of the world's resources by industrial countries requires ongoing reporting:

> If everyone lived the same way as the average American, we would need 5.3 planets with the resources of Earth.... Even though the number of people living in utter poverty does not seem to budge, an increasing number are consuming like developed countries. (Jamieson 2008, 197)

With a world population of 6.5 billion and increasing, the inequities are not sustainable and are morally indefensible. Media that represent the communitarian agenda challenge the resource-intensive polluting model of development, but they are not simply negative. Communities are shown how to live with reduced consumption and sustainable technologies as their responsibility for "healing the global environment" (Jamieson 2008, 199).

Aidan Msafiri (2007), head of the Philosophy Department at St. Augustine University of Tanzania, has written a book-length treatment of the communitarian approach with justice its central theme. Tanzania faces major local and regional problems—massive pollution and overharvesting of Lake Victoria, deforestation, biodiversity depletion at Mt. Kilimanjaro, and urban garbage in Dar es Salaam (1–20). International issues are abundant, too: imported toxic waste, unfriendly tourism, global climate changes, and genetically modified crops (21–34). In addressing this broad range of issues, Msafiri rejects technical, functional utilitarian approaches as reductionist and too easily applied in the interests of the powerful.

He grounds his framework within the human community itself. He appeals to the indigenous African vision of the interdependence between humanity, nature, and the Supreme Being. He takes seriously the holism of African spirituality. From African Christianity he develops the principle of solidarity as the centerpiece of environmental justice, that is "active unity and cooperation among all humans, particularly with the weakest and poorest" (Msafiri 2007, 94). He agrees with John Pobee, Professor of Theology at the University of Ghana, that the West's individualism is "responsible for an exploitative approach to creation" (174). Therefore, Msafiri is radically communal in orientation instead (174).

Theological ethics enables Msafiri to develop a systematic treatment of environmental issues, but he roots all of his elaborations in the common humanity of *ubuntu,* "I am because you are, and you are because we are" (pp. xix, 184–85). Global ethics needs not only an African worldview but also the global one called "*ubuntu* communitarianism" (Christians 2004). As Msafiri defines it, "This community-based worldview has not only humanistic and communitarian dimensions but ecological overtones as well, that is, being-together with the entire universe" (185).[12] Promoting and protecting human life inevitably means the human habitat, all of life. Instead of seeking one alternative policed by the state, or pessimistically concluding there are no alternatives, the "*ubuntu* communitarian" model sees a thousand alternatives.[13] Strategies of community action that arise from human ingenuity are compatible with local cultures and are therefore sustainable.

ENVIRONMENTAL JOURNALISM

News and editorials tackle issues ranging from genetically modified crops to mad cow disease and biofuels. The list of newsworthy materials continues to grow: rain forests, coral reef depletion, the ozone layer, ecosystems management, and world famine. The Kyoto Protocol (1997), an international treaty on curbing greenhouse gas emissions, stays in the news and will move to the front pages when it faces ratification again in 2012. Journalists from around the world covered the Copenhagen Climate Summit in December 2009. The worst oil spill disaster in human history in the Gulf of Mexico dominated media news in the spring and summer of 2010, though without changing public opinion about our dependence on fossil fuels. Global warming, carbon-trapping gases, and comprehensive energy legislation will continue as contentious issues.[14]

Reporting about the effects of mountaintop removal is a good example of daily journalism that highlights human costs of environmental damage. From William S. Doyle's *Strip Mining of Coal* (1976) to Shirley Stewart Burns's *Bringing Down the Mountains* (2007), two dozen books have documented the effects of mountaintop removal on the environment and on mountain communities. In 2005, Wendell Berry invited several Kentucky writers to observe mountaintop removal operations with him, and they reported on the subject in national periodicals and edited the book, *Missing Mountains*. The subtitle expresses their lament: *We Went to the Mountaintop But It Wasn't There* (Johannsen, Mason, and Taylor-Hall, 2005). Erik Reece's 2006 contribution, *Lost Mountain*, followed a similar path. He visited a mountaintop removal site every month for a year, chronicling the devolution of the site from lush to lunar and the perpetuation of a debilitated population left to live in a denuded landscape devoid of minerals.

The issue of mountaintop removal is both straightforward and vexing. To feed America's ravenous appetite for electricity, mining companies supply coal-burning power plants by clearing the forests and then blasting through the soil and rock to expose seams of coal that can be scooped out with a huge machine called a dragline excavator. Mountaintop removal is safer than traditional mining because it does not require miners to work underground; and using dynamite and large machines to extract coal from above is faster, less labor intensive, and cheaper than digging coal from shafts.

If only mountaintop removal did not harm the environment. Each mountain subjected to this process is first stripped of its vegetation and topsoil. The rock underneath, called overburden, is then blasted and pushed into drainage valleys where it buries streams. As the coal is removed, the accompanying sludge is dumped into deep lakes of slurry the size of a few thousand Olympic swimming pools. The earthen dams that hold the slurry sometimes leak or even give way altogether, poisoning waterways and flooding nearby towns. Finally, when all the coal has been mined, what is left of the mountain is bulldozed, covered with backfill, seeded with grass, and planted with seedlings. Such reclamation results in land that is neither biodiverse nor suitable for farming. Reflecting these devastating results, Robert F. Kennedy, Jr. calls mountaintop removal mining, "the greatest environmental tragedy ever to befall our nation" (McMorris-Santoro 2010, 1).[15]

Then there are the human costs. As Ken Ward, the environmental reporter for the Charleston, West Virginia *Gazette*, explains, "The real legacy of mountaintop removal is not just the scarred land and buried streams—or the battle of jobs vs. the environment—but the missed opportunities that proper regulation of the post-mining development rules would have provided to America's coalfields and to those who mined them" (2004, 14). Ward explains that lawmakers have conceived of mountaintop removal as a social compact between mining companies and local communities: mining companies are permitted to destroy mountains as long as they replace them with community resources such as factories, schools, shopping centers, or parks. Ward's reporting, based on extensive reviews of federal mining regulations, permits, and reports, shows that mining companies strip mountain communities of their natural resources with impunity, selling the coal and leaving behind flat grassland only.[16]

Despite illuminating news coverage, mountaintop removal continues unabated. In fact, economic interests are such that Ward's reporting has generated protests from the United Mine Workers and criticism from business leaders that his environmental reporting hurts the local economy. Such complaints have been endemic to environmental reporting in general. Philip Shabecoff, a former business reporter who covered environmental issues for the *New York Times*, recalls editors fretting that his environmental reports focused too much on how this business activity was harming the economy. However, when he was a business reporter, nobody ever complained that he said nothing about business harming the environment (2002, 36). Shabecoff eventually left the *New York Times* to found Greenwire, a website that reports news about energy and environmental policy.

The agricultural industry is another major topic for reporting, with 99 percent of Illinois farmland, for example, treated annually with 54 million pounds of synthetic pesticides. Factory farming now dominates food production—3 percent of hog farms produce 50 percent of today's pork, and "2% of the nation's feedlots finish 40% of all cattle" (Jamieson 2008, 122). "In 1996 the US cattle, pork, and poultry industries produced 1.4 billion tons of animal waste, 130 times more than was produced by the entire human population—most of it stored in lagoons where it poses serious threats to land, air, and water quality" (Jamieson 2008, 122). Agriculture uses 87 percent of the fresh water consumed in the United States, with 2,500 gallons needed to produce one pound of meat (Jamieson 2008, 124). Chemical run-offs from agriculture and industry create algae blooms that suck oxygen from streams and rivers, suffocating marine life. "There is a 'dead zone' the size of New Jersey at the mouth of the Mississippi River in the Gulf of Mexico that was created by this process" (Jamieson 2008, 124).

Food safety is a serious concern around the world; food contamination and such agencies as the U.S. Food and Drug Administration (FDA) are frequently in the news. The Centers for Disease Control and Prevention estimate that each year there are 76 million cases of food-borne illness in the United States resulting in 325,000 hospitalizations and 5,000 deaths. Quality environmental reporting is more urgent than ever.[17]

CONCLUSION

Rachel Carson got the nation talking in terms not heard before her work. With *Silent Spring* she challenged the traditional view of nature as existing primarily for our convenience with a view of the earth as a living web of interrelations.

American conversation on the environment, pre-Carson, could aptly be called the silent era.[18] For this reason *Silent Spring* is regarded as a culture-changing book (Killingsworth and Palmer 1992, 65). America in the 1950s was building a military-industrial complex (to use a term from that period), but doing so without due diligence to the extent its burgeoning economy was ruining nature's delicate balance.

Carson's dramatic prose reminds us that environmental problems are, in her words, those of "ecology, of interrelationships, of interdependence" (1962, 169). Humans are part of nature and to presume otherwise is an unfortunate consequence of a Neanderthal paradigm of science and philosophy fixated on domination and control. She exposes chemical salesmen, eager contractors, and perhaps more damningly what she calls "scientists for hire," for selling their secrets to the chemical industry. In doing so, she makes the role of the scientist, developer, and average citizen, a moral one as she calls for social action guided by an enlightened sense of the communitarian "we."

Carson introduced care for the environment into the national conversation about progress and international power. From backwater to mainstream, conserving nature would never again be regarded as the irrelevant chatter of peripheral politics. For that communitarian gain, Rachel Carson's courage stands as a model, her perseverance as a tipping-point. The dialogue that will fashion social life for the next century will owe her this debt: She saw a gap in the public intelligence and did her best to energize a human conversation of the highest order.

NOTES

1. The award's name comes from Rachel Carson's *Sense of Wonder*. Thoughtware TV's documentary, "Rachel Carson's *Silent Spring*" is an excellent review of Carson's life and work. It includes photos of Ms. Carson and explains how her work initiated environmental legislation. The documentary is divided into six, ten-minute segments, and useful for classroom discussion.

2. Cone 2005, 65. Cone admits that "Carson portrayed the science of the day in such dense detail that much of the 388-page book is too unwieldy, even today, for most readers to comprehend" (Cone 2005, 66).

3. Carson's attack on DDT is the centerpiece of CEI's harsh rhetoric. Carson's research has become the world's conventional wisdom on DDT, but for CEI its negative effects on humans is unproved. DDT had been effective against malaria, but since its removal, malaria has become a vicious reality today—killing more than 1 million people a year and making 300 million seriously ill (<http://www.rachelcarsonwaswrong.com>).

4. *Environmental Defense Fund v. E.P.A.*, 160 U.S. App. D.C. 123, 489 F.2d 1247 (1973).

5. See the Waddell (2000) anthology, *And No Birds Sing*, for an in-depth review of *Silent Spring's* significance.

6. Professor Melba Vélez of Grand Valley State University contributed the first draft of this section ("Conceptual Perspectives") and advised on the chapter elsewhere.

7. The distinctive approach of communitarianism can be seen by comparing it to the virtue theory of environmental ethics rooted in the Aristotelian tradition (Kawall; Sandler 2007).

8. DeLuca (2011) argues that a commitment to the wilderness is still central: "Engaging the world from the orientation of the event of wild(er)ness is absolutely essential in this moment of myriad issues" (430).

9. Utilitarians as sophisticated as Peter Singer are not mechanistic but clear-headed social critics. Singer's *One World: The Ethics of Globalization* (2004) includes a major section on climate change/global warming, and he gets beyond political and economic perspectives to make it a moral issue raised by globalization. He rightly critiques the state-centric view and searches instead for principles that most people can agree on, for example, that we should treat others as we wish to be treated ourselves. He warns against giving political priority to short-term interests. But the critics are right that the book's achievements are modest and that he sees problems as piecemeal rather than systemic. Douglas Doepke correctly objects to "the book's safely liberal framework," that is, not getting beyond market reforms, better democracy, and more generous foreign aid. Similarly, John Stuart Mill wrote mostly in procedural terms when he described utilitarianism, rather than taking on the structural and institutional issues that exist outside of particular actions or rules.

10. For a book of essays that makes justice central to global environmental issues, see Sandler and Pezzulo (2007); see also Crocker and Linden (1997). DeLuca (2011) describes the complications of making moral issues central in environmental action. The Environmental Justice Movement has had "many important successes" but in the end cripples long-term sustainability (415).

11. Sen and Chakrabarti (2010) describe local projects "to achieve environmental justice" in India and the United States. All of them are poor communities suffering from severe environmental pollution. In each case, local initiatives and involvement are the source of change.

12. As described in the Introduction, the word *ubuntu* is derived from the Zulu maxim *umuntu ngumuntu ngabantu*, translated as "a person is a person through other persons." *Ubuntu* is not merely African, but embodies a fundamental truth about the human species (Masolo 2004).

13. For a list of practical suggestions and recommendations, see Msafiri 2007, ch. 5.

14. Challenging the mainstream media to "focus on real stories, not entertainment pablum," Jason Kawall (2010, 127) is understandably upset that CNN cut its entire science, technology, and environment staff in December 2008 (see Brainerd 2008).

15. Ignoring these tragic effects, Rand Paul argues that mountaintop coal removal is a net positive. "It enhances the land" (McMorris-Santoro 2010, 1).

16. ABC's *20/20* program, "A Hidden America: Children of the Mountains," hosted by Diane Sawyer (February 2009) is helpful for classroom instruction on the social costs of coal mining in central Appalachia (ABCNewstore.com:*20/20*:A Hidden America).

17. Sachsman, Valenti, and Simon (2010) give an in-depth account of environment reporters in the first decade of the twenty-first century. The Center for Environmental Journalism, established at the University of Colorado in 1992, illustrates one attempt to enrich the training of journalists through interdisciplinary work with units across the campus.

18. See Knight (2010) for a detailed and widely referenced counterargument that environmental concerns were prominent in news content from 1890 to 1960.

REFERENCES

Berry, Wendell. 1975. "Think Little." In his *A Continuous Harmony: Essays Cultural and Agricultural*, 71–85. New York: Harcourt Brace Jovanovich.

——. 2001. *Life is a Miracle*. Los Angeles: Counterpoint Books.

Bosso, Christopher J. 1987. *Pesticides and Politics: The Life Cycle of a Public Issue*. Pittsburgh, PA: University of Pittsburgh Press.

Brainerd, Curtis. 2008. "CNN Cuts Entire Science, Tech Team." *Columbia Journalism Review. The Observatory Online*, December 4.

Brooks, Paul. 1980. *Speaking for Nature*. Boston: Houghton Mifflin.

Buhs, Joshua B. 2002. "The Fire Ant Wars: Nature and Science in the Pesticide Controversies of the Late Twentieth Century." *Isis* 93 (3): 377–400.

Burns, Shirley Stewart. 2007. *Bringing Down the Mountains: The Impact of Mountaintop Removal Surface Coal Mining on Southern West Virginia Communities, 1970–2004*. Morgantown: West Virginia University Press.

Carson, Rachel. 1962. *Silent Spring*. New York: Houghton Mifflin.

Christians, Clifford. 2004. "*Ubuntu* and Communitarianism in Media Ethics." *Ecquid Novi* 25 (2): 235–56.

Cone, Marla. 2005. "The Unbroken Chain: Marla Cone on Rachel Carson's *Silent Spring*." *Columbia Journalism Review,* July/August: 65–66.

Cox, Robert. 2010. *Environmental Communication and the Public Sphere,* 2d ed. Thousand Oaks, CA: Sage Publications.

Craig, David. 2009. "Justice as a Journalistic Value and Goal." In Lee Wilkins and Clifford Christians, eds., *The Handbook of Mass Media Ethics*, 203–16. New York: Routledge.

Crocker, David A., and Linden, Toby. 1997. *Ethics of Consumption: The Good Life, Justice, and Global Stewardship*. Lanham, Md.: Rowman and Littlefield.

DeLuca, Kevin Michael. 2011. "Truths, Evils, Justice, and the Event of Wild(er)ness: Using Badiou to Think the Ethics of Environmentalism." In George Cheney, Steve May, and Debashish Munshi, eds., *The Handbook of Communication Ethics*, 414–35. New York: Routledge.

Doyle, William S. 1976. *Strip Mining of Coal: Environmental Solutions*. Park Ridge, N.J.: Noyes Data.

Irland, Lloyd C. 2007. *Professional Ethics for Natural Resource and Environmental Managers: A Primer*. New Haven, CT: Yale School of Forestry and Environmental Studies.

Jamieson, Dale. 2008. *Ethics and the Environment: An Introduction*. Cambridge, U.K.: Cambridge University Press.

Johannsen, Kristin, Mason, Bobbie Ann, and Taylor-Hall, Mary Ann, eds. 2005. *Missing Mountains: We Went to the Mountaintop But It Wasn't There*. Nicholasville, KY: Wind.

Kawall, Jason. 2010. "The Epistemic Demands of Environmental Virtue." *Journal of Agricultural and Environmental Ethics* 23: 109–28.

Killingsworth, M. Jimmy, and Palmer, Jacqueline S. 1992. *Ecospeak: Rhetoric and Environmental Politics in America*. Carbondale: Southern Illinois University Press.

Knight, Jan E. 2010. "Building an Environmental Agenda: A Content and Frame Analysis of News about the Environment in the United States, 1890–1960." Ph.D. dissertation, Scripps College of Communication, Ohio University.

Kuhn, Thomas. 1962. *The Structure of Scientific Revolutions*. Chicago: University of Chicago Press, rev. ed. 1970.

Lear, Linda. 1997. *Rachel Carson: Witness for Nature*. New York: Henry Holt and Company.

Leopold, Aldo. 1987. *Sand County Almanac and Sketches Here and There*. New York: Oxford University Press.

Lytle, Mark Hamilton. 2007. *The Gentle Subversive: Rachel Carson, Silent Spring, and the Rise of the Environmental Movement.* Oxford, U.K.: Oxford University Press.

Masolo, D. A. 2004. "Western and African Communitarianism: A Comparison." In Kwasi Wiredu, ed., *A Companion to African Philosophy*, 483–98. Oxford, U.K.: Blackwell.

McMorris-Santoro, Evan. 2010. "Rand Paul: Controversial Mountaintop Removal Coal Mining Isn't So Bad—It Enhances the Land." *TPM*, July 29.

Msafiri, Aidan G. 2007. *Towards a Credible Environmental Ethics for Africa: A Tanzanian Perspective.* Nairobi, Kenya: CUEA Publications.

Murphy, Priscilla Coit. 2005. *What a Book Can Do: The Publication and Reception of* Silent Spring. Amherst: University of Massachusetts Press.

Norwood, Vera L. 1987. "The Nature of Knowing: Rachel Carson and the American Environment." *Signs: Journal of Women in Culture and Society* 12 (4): 740–60.

Nussbaum, Martha C. 2001. *Upheavals of Thought: The Intelligence of Emotions.* Cambridge: Cambridge University Press.

Pacey, Arnold. 2003. *The Culture of Technology.* Cambridge, MA: MIT Press.

Perschel, Robert T. 2004. *The Land Ethic Toolbox: Using Ethics, Emotion, and Spiritual Values to Advance American Land Conservation.* Washington, D.C.: Wilderness Society.

Reece, Erik. 2006. *Lost Mountain: A Year in the Vanishing Wilderness—Radical Strip Mining and the Devastation of Appalachia.* New York: Riverhead.

Sachsman, David, Valenti. JoAnn, and Simon, James. 2010. *Environment Reporters in the 21ˢᵗ Century.* Piscataway, NJ: Transaction Publishers.

Sandler, Ronald. 2007. *Character and Environment: A Virtue-Based Approach to Environmental Ethics.* New York: Columbia University Press.

Sandler, Ronald, and Pezzulo, Rhoeda, eds. 2007. *Environmental Justice and Environmentalism: The Social Justice Challenge to the Environment Movement.* Cambridge, MA: MIT Press.

Sen, Ranen, and Chakrabarti, Sharadindra. 2010. "Wither Imperatives of Environmental Justice." *Current Science* 98 (4), February 25: 476–77.

Shabecoff, Philip. 2002. "The Environment Beat's Rocky Terrain." *Nieman Reports* 56 (4): 34–36.

Singer, Peter. 2004. *One World: The Ethics of Globalization.* New Haven, CT: Yale University Press.

Smith, Michael B. 2001. "'Silence, Miss Carson!' Science, Gender, and the Reception of *Silent Spring.*" *Feminist Studies* 27 (3): 733–52.

Steingraber, Sandra. 2010. *Living Downstream: An Ecologist's Personal Investigation of Cancer and the Environment.* Cambridge, MA: De Capo Press. [first edition published in 1997]

Taylor, Charles. 1989. *Sources of the Self: The Making of the Modern Identity.* Cambridge, MA: Harvard University Press.

Waddell, Craig, ed. 2000. *And No Birds Sing: Rhetorical Analyses of* Silent Spring. Carbondale: Southern Illinois University Press.

Ward, Ken, Jr. 2004. "Using Documents to Report on Mountaintop Mining." *Nieman Reports* 58 (2): 12–14.

CHAPTER 8

✦

Stormfront and the Ethics of Hate

More hate groups are recruiting more members and gathering more strength now than ever before in American history reports the Southern Poverty Law Center. SPLC director Mark Potok was quoted by NPR: "We have absolutely explosive growth of these groups in 2009, and we have now found continued growth through 2010." Potok attributes the growth to a bad economy, the reach of the Internet, and changing racial patterns.[1]

Stormfront is the most popular Internet website of the white supremacy movement. Founded by Don Black in 1995, it is a sophisticated forum, offering special pages for homemaking, education, entertainment, philosophy, and classified ads. Youth and children will find testimonials written by peers who long for pure Caucasian culture and identity. Much of the rhetoric echoes the plain-song style of an oppressed minority, a David facing the Goliaths of pluralism and integrationism. Race-mixers are to be pitied for failure to understand (as only white supremacists can) what made America strong. *Stormfront* projects, in many of its materials, an image contrary to the military 𝔖𝔱𝔲𝔯𝔪 𝔲𝔫𝔡 𝔇𝔯𝔞𝔫𝔤 implied in its name and by its Fraktur type font. We suspect, without firsthand knowledge, that its founding circle has discovered that even its strident target audience enjoys recreation, raising children, and holding decent jobs. Relentless militancy—the founding vision—has given way to a culture-building, family-friendly, "ordinary American" familiarity that still taps latent racial fears. *Stormfront* appears to offer an antidote, however ill-conceived, to the postmodern permissiveness that feeds a youth culture of dropouts and weaklings.

Don Black is a former Grand Wizard of the Knights of the Ku Klux Klan. Born in Alabama, he got his start in white nationalism as a teenager working on political campaigns and distributing literature, for which school authorities censured him. After earning a degree in political science from the University of Alabama, he took over the Klan at age 25 when David Duke resigned in 1978. Soon after, he was sentenced to three years in federal prison for plotting a military-style takeover of the Caribbean island Dominica. This brazen piracy intended to create one spot on earth where racial purity could be showcased.

During his imprisonment, Black learned computer programming. When he started *Stormfront*, he had the savvy to include library links, articles and books, and substantial material on the Populist Party, which Black represented in a U.S. Senate race in the late 1980s. Recently Black's political affiliations have broadened to support the Council of Conservative Citizens and the Libertarian Party. Is it possible that *Stormfront* could become a political force in mainstream American politics?

Other hate groups may not be as technologically advanced as Black's *Stormfront*, but their number is on the rise, mirroring the dramatic growth of the World Wide Web. As access to the Internet became less expensive and creating web pages much simpler, the number of websites and web visitors has grown exponentially. *Stormfront* was the only publically known site in 1995; researcher Marc Knobel of the Council of Jewish Institutions in France estimates the number of hate websites worldwide to be nearly 60,000 at present (Cohen-Almagor 2010, 105). Bulk mailings to a few hundred were always difficult and largely ineffective, but hate websites have millions as their potential audience. On average, 36,000 people visit *Stormfront* each day.

The Southern Poverty Law Center has identified 200 other active Ku Klux Klan sites besides *Stormfront*. Together they defend "the superiority of the White race" and warn against diluting it with inferior races. Jews are vilified as Satan's people, and immigration is condemned as an "uncontrolled, outrageous, and unprecedented plague." In addition, the number of websites for the National Association for the Advancement of White People (NAAWP), founded by former Klan leader David Duke, has mushroomed and energized the so-called "Klan without robes."

Numerous neo-Nazi websites promote the anti-Semitic racism of Adolf Hitler's Nazi party. Many of the sites are devoted to Holocaust revisionism, denying the murder of Jews in World War II. In addition, many neo-Nazi skinheads such as the Oi! Boys and Hammerskin Nation have websites saturated with racist hard rock music.

The websites of religious hate groups are flourishing, too. Congregations of Christian Identity are virulently racist and anti-Semitic. They claim that today's Jews are not descended from Old Testament Jews but are Satan's creation and that Jews and blacks are viruses seeking to destroy the purity of the Aryan (white) race. The World Church of the Creator (WCOTC) calls nonwhites physiologically inferior, subhuman "mud people." The site for White Aryan Resistance (WAR) rails against the nonwhite birthrate, massive immigration, and racial intermarriage. Other religious sites are anti-Catholic and anti-Muslim or violently antiabortion. Alex Curtis's Nationalist Observer website features his "Tribute to Jewry," that is, "Jew New York City" decimated by an atomic bomb.[2]

Such hate speech is contradicted without exception by all major ethical theories. For virtue ethics, vitriolic hatred is patently wrong. Kant's principle that humans ought to be treated as ends in themselves does not tolerate physical or psychological abuse. In utilitarian ethics, white supremacy/black inferiority produces too much harm and benefits only a misguided few. And for communitarian ethics, Internet hatred, as in real life, is the polar opposite of flourishing community. But beyond condemnation, communitarianism calls for all personal,

Hate and love: a KKK wedding ceremony (© Michael Norcia/Sygma/Corbis).

educational, and policy efforts to combat hate speech, using anything but vengeful and aggressive means that contravene good ends.

Because hate speech is built of the principle of moral exclusion, communitarian ethics confronts it directly. Moral exclusion occurs when individuals or groups are perceived as outside the boundaries of fairness and justice. Rights can be denied in law and human dignity in ethics to barbarians and aliens who threaten racial purity. The targeted group is innately evil, a social menace, so segregation or eradication is necessary to prevent harm to the social order. Hitler is the archetype of moral exclusion. For the Christian Identity Movement, "killing a Jew is like stepping on a cockroach." Associations with vermin, excrement, animals, and the devil are standard rhetoric here, much as they were in the Rwanda genocide.

With healthy membership in the human community as the primary value for communitarianism, moral exclusion is its radical opposite. Internet hate not only inflicts harm to individuals but also erodes the tolerance and open-mindedness necessary for democratic societies to function (Cohen-Almagor 2006). Since Don Black started *Stormfront*, hate groups have created Internet websites as virtual communities existing in isolation from and opposition to the existing order. Internet technology enables the recruiting and maintaining of hate groups that are "educated" and trained for protest or violence. Reports, handbooks, and Internet links on urban guerilla warfare, terrorism, grenade launchers, and building bombs are effective in expanding and satisfying the membership. Communitarian ethics helps us pay special attention to the communal dynamics of moral exclusion.

GOOD AND BAD IN PUBLIC LIFE

To embrace the good, one must know the boundaries of the bad. To be able to see the significance of another person, one must have felt the isolation that comes from being a stranger. Exclusion and embrace are the ying-yang of all relationships.

Think of the communities you identify with. When you say, "I'm from Idaho," you also mean in part that you are not from New Jersey. You may have passed through Hackensack, but you claim no part of it as important to your personality or identity. When you say, "I'm a liberal," you also mean to say, "I'm not favorable to tax breaks for big corporations and I don't support politicians who are." Each claim is an incitement to action. You care for Idaho potato growers, but ignore Newark-based executives. How very natural, normal, and universal. Out there somewhere are people whose preferences balance yours. To find them, all you need do is visit Jersey. They like Rutgers, you like Nez Perce. They like the coast, you like the mountains. You may disagree with those knotheads, but you are not trying to push them into the sea.

Theologian Miroslav Volf notes that living is choosing. We embrace and we exclude (1996). We define ourselves by liking and opposing, choosing and discarding—from sports teams to flavors to ethnicities, regions, religions, and ideas. The communities in which we live gather our preferences and create boundaries to keep preferences intact. We like to be broad-minded, just not stupid broad, not naïve or gullible. We do not mind sharing a neighborhood with diverse people, but we prefer that Gestapo-types keep their distance. And we resist being labeled "Gestapo" for feeling that way. Volf reminds us that attitudes about those who live far away make all the difference. Even those distant people oblige us toward openness and the possibility of embrace. "Instead of seeking to isolate ourselves from other groups by insisting on our pure identity, we should open ourselves to one another to be enriched by our differences.... Guests should be welcomed in, and we should pay visits to our near and distant neighbours so that through cross-fertilization our respective cultures can thrive, correcting and enriching each other" (Volf, 1995, 204).

Philosopher Charles Taylor adds that nonrecognition or misrecognition (identifying someone as a terrorist because of his or her citizenship, for example) is a form of oppression, "imprisoning someone in a false, distorted, and reduced mode of being" (1994, 25). "Imprisonment" manifests most clearly in social behavior that turns into moral exclusion that divides the social world based on judgments linked to race and ethnicity (Appiah 1994, 149). We build ethical systems on bundles of emotive forces, the philosopher David Hume advised. How can we master those emotive forces so that, at the end of the day, we may reckon that our choice has been "open," with all its vulnerabilities, rather than "closed," with all its fears? And it should be noted how difficult this "openness" can be when your intention is to do it sincerely. The little classic *48 Laws of Power* outlines how to appear virtuous, all the while working your purposes on the vulnerable other. For example, Law 43 advises that "seducing others is to operate on their individual psychologies and weaknesses. Soften up the resistant by working on their emotions, playing on what they hold dear and what they fear. Ignore the hearts and minds of others and they will grow to hate you" (Greene 1998, 367). So you see, this business of exclusion and embrace can be tricky. If you follow Volf and do it sincerely, you risk a failure in which you may forever doubt whether you were "coming off" as one of Greene's loonies, or as Black himself must "come off"—in order to lure so many into a movement that plays fully on fear while appearing to provide the answer to it.

HATE AS A WAY OF SPEAKING

Some words are so charged with ethnic or racial emotion that most people use them only when the expression of hate is clearly intended. "Nigger," "Kike," and "Wop" are charged with negative valences. The use of such words is impolite at the least, offensive "fighting words" more often. The City Council of New York in 2006 went so far as to resolve that "nigger" would not be used inside its jurisdiction. Why? The N-word recalls our worst national failure and its residue of suspicion and animosity still evident in business, entertainment, and politics. The election of the nation's first African American head of state has raised the tenor and subdued the humor of these national suspicions. We recognize hate speech as a slur, insult, diminution—language that establishes a barrier the other cannot overcome. Hate speech separates by conditions of birth, castigating nature, as well as an entire people's history and heritage. Hate speech today is intentional nastiness barely cleaned up with populist rhetoric. It is total rejection based on conditions unchangeable. It is acting out in language what would be criminal to act out physically, the eradication of a group for no reason other than natural membership in it.

Where diverse cultures meet, hate speech is volatile and disruptive. Imagine billboards on your campus featuring common hate words. Who would attend such a school, who would walk those grassy pathways and subject themselves to public slur and cynicism? Who would do chem lab with a partner who openly despises your family? University campuses recognized the problem, of course, because anything that can be said will be said on a university campus. Many institutions passed rules forbidding hate speech in order to promote social environments where learning could be done free of the emotional tension hate kindles. Those universities' regulations, however noble their purpose, ran afoul of a tradition of American free speech and were abandoned by order of the courts.

By 1991, more than 300 universities in America had hate speech codes, yet instances of hate speech had increased, since 1986, by 400 percent, with 80 percent of incidents still unreported (Uelmen 1992), perhaps because codes were the new barometer and hate speech became identifiable. With codes or without, intimidation and harassment is rife on university campuses. The recent dustup (actual physical confrontation but no serious injuries) between the General Union of Palestinian Students and College Republicans at San Francisco State University is but an example of the inability of campus administrators to adjudicate "free speech" without quite clearly picking sides and exposing some constituents to "shut up or take what's coming" (Cravatts 2009). In America, we can despise the despisers, but we cannot stop their speech. Private universities are exempt from the ban on hate speech; some still enforce codes. Most of these codes prohibit speech or conduct that creates an "intimidating, hostile, or offensive educational environment." Some codes ban "general harassments and threat" without further specifications.

The famous case of the planned (but never held) Nazi march in Skokie, a largely Jewish suburb of Chicago, shows the three-ring legal circus that ruling against hate presents. Only the threat of bodily harm, which the state could not prevent, kept the American Nazis and their swastika off Skokie streets that day. Officials there felt legally obliged to permit an event, which they could not guarantee would happen safely and without violence (Downs 1985).

Hate speech has irony—and meanness. Until it shut down in 2009, the popular website JuicyCampus.com was filled with hate speech, all anonymous posts. You could say all the forbidden words there because the Internet's impenetrable mask kept your identity private while your animus went universal. From the ultimate bad-mouth no one knew who was talking. To support civility and decency, a campus in southern California voted to disallow JuicyCampus on its servers. The stark self-censorship made national news (USA Today 2008). The vote to block the site came from student leaders, the very demographic JuicyCampus wanted to reach.

Perhaps JuicyCampus fans believed their freedom was something new. Not so. America has a distinguished record of racial, ethnic, and religious hate speech. America in the 1920s was ripe with public bigotry and vitriol against African Americans, Catholics, and Jews. During the quiet administration of President Calvin Coolidge (1923–29), the Ku Klux Klan marched for the first and only time in the nation's capital. Henry Ford, one of the richest men in the country, publicly accused Jews of corrupting industry with their banking cabal and culture with their jazz (Walker 1994, 17).

At the same time, however, one of the nation's most effective free speech advocates was born, the American Civil Liberties Union. Quickly the ACLU rushed to the defense of socialists, communists, and others whose speech rights were under threat from federal power. When the city of Toledo forbade the sale of Henry Ford's anti-Semitic newspaper, the *Dearborn Independent*, the ACLU took the city to court, winning injunctive relief against bans in Toledo and Cleveland. No friend of hate speech, the ACLU was nonetheless a dear friend of the First Amendment, which it has promoted many times as a national right trumping any legal assault on talk per se, no matter how brazen or intimidating. Thus, the ACLU, sworn enemy of government censoring a minority voice, has as a consequence been champion to those whose speech advocates positions that most ACLU members abhor.

Such are the conflicts broiling in a country that poses as the world's exemplar of government "of the people, by the people" yet struggles to define who "the people" are, given social, cultural, racial, and other common social divisions. That struggle is at the heart of this chapter's concern. Robert Bellah, in his classic study *Habits of the Heart* (1985), called America a "culture of separation." The fragmentation in which media present the world to us "undermines the sense of overall purpose in the lives of individual persons" forcing them to seek a "foothold in reality" by looking to self rather than the world outside self: "Such preoccupation with personal identity makes it difficult to see that the lives we lead make a difference for the common good" (Hollenbach 1994/95, 18).

Persons bewildered, firm ground sought in identity, little confidence in conflicting social messages, values riddled with hypocrisy, heightened sense of need to come to terms with intractable contradictions—failure of the common life. Does this sound like your university experience?

WHY NOT BAN IT?

Surely a government with the power to regulate every vegetable packed on a truck for interstate shipment can do something about words that divide and inflame? Government can ban what words it will. If you think not, say the word "bomb" within earshot of an airport TSA official, call it a joke, and watch your life become very stressed.

The Supreme Court has faced speech boundaries several times since 1919, none with greater impact than the case of Benjamin Gitlow, arrested for criminal anarchy in New York in 1919. Gitlow was part of a Socialist Party effort to protest what it called the bourgeois war on Europe. To make the protest effective, Gitlow published and distributed 16,000 copies of the "Left Wing Manifesto" and other leaflets projecting Communist ideology as superior to all other political plans. In 1925, on appeal from his conviction, the Supreme Court affirmed. In the words of Justice Sanford:

> It is a fundamental principle, long established, that the freedom of speech...does not confer an absolute right to speak...whatever one may choose...or an unrestricted and unbridled license that gives immunity from every possible use of language.[3]

Boundaries to freedom of speech must and do exist, Sanford said. How had Gitlow's speech crossed them? Sanford resorted to metaphor: "A single revolutionary spark may kindle a fire that, smoldering for a time, may burst into a sweeping and destructive conflagration" (*Gitlow*, at 669). State power, the Court concluded, rightly "protect[s] the public peace and safety" before sparks become flames, before words escalate to active violence, before people get hurt and property damaged, before the state loses control. Sanford was asserting that peace trumps speech, when speech is likely to incite a breach of peace. For Gitlow's communist propaganda, substitute racially charged speech, or cartoons of the Prophet Muhammad, or salacious and hurtful words posted anonymously on a university billboard. The result, if such words could carry a sum, would be additional bad tidings, raw feelings, and deep social distrust. Hate speech is not worth it, the court seemed to say. When common sense or basic human sympathy breaks down, the state steps in, Sanford promised.

Basic human sympathy? Is this some older-era village-green feeling that late-night comedians rip apart for laughs? If "sympathy" kept the lid on discourtesy in times past, it also kept women in their place and sustained other oppressions deemed discourteous and disruptive. If sympathy is author to rigid roles and myopic social sensitivities, to that we say good riddance. Yet before you write off sympathy, consider the argument made by James Q. Wilson, a commonsense naturalist who wonders why people really are so nice (1993, 24). Fundamental to the species, Wilson claims, are four learned survival virtues that now define and guide the moral quest. First among them, he insists, is sympathy. Humans feel for each other, Wilson asserts, in ways no other animals do. We are not instinctively sympathetic—not like bees or ants—but emotionally connected in varying degrees. Sympathy is universal. Even in the least sympathetic environments—war, for instance—agreements of human sympathy require opposing armies to treat prisoners and civilians decently, even sustaining their lives as the add-on cost of battle. Wilson recalls that America was aghast when Kitty Genovese, struggling with a thug on a street in Queens in 1964, called for help, pled for rescue, but was ignored. Kitty died. The *New York Times*' headline reported, "Thirty-Eight Who Saw Murder Didn't Call the Police" (March 27, 1964). This breakdown in human sympathy shocked the nation. People told police investigators they thought someone else was paying attention and who knows what is really underway out there?

(The mayor of Milwaukee was recently assaulted when he pulled out his mobile phone to call 911 for a woman in the state fair parking lot screaming for help. Her assailant took a metal pipe to the mayor [*USA Today*, August 8, 2009, A3].)

We are not like that, Wilson knows (and he claims we all know). We are not calloused and uncaring. We have not descended to the level of the degenerate Romans who found entertainment watching gladiators (Bok 1998, 15). We know better than that and feel with better impulses. Our connective tissues are stronger. The lives of people count for us (even the lives of pets and trees). We are by evolution's grace sympathetic organisms, Wilson contends. When Lincoln appealed to the "bonds of affection" linking a fractured nation in his First Inaugural in March 1861, he knew that even his oath to defend the Constitution would never abrogate his sense that the secessionists were errant siblings, not aliens or beasts (Miller 2008, 21):

> We are not enemies, but friends. We must not be enemies. Though passion may have strained, it must not break our bonds of affection. The mystic chords of memory…will yet swell the chorus of the Union, when touched again…by the better angels of our nature.

We care for each other's person and welfare. We do, and must. Why then do we hate?

GITLOW'S DISSENTERS

Sanford's opinion was law in 1925, but moments later, its very foundations were shaken by the dissent of two justices weary of lip service to First Amendment promises. History knows Justices Holmes and Brandeis as the great dissenters. Certainly this dissent was the reason. Holmes wrote for both:

> It is said that [Gitlow's] manifesto was more than a theory, that it was an incitement. Every idea is an incitement. It offers itself for belief and if believed it is acted on unless some other belief outweighs it or some failure of energy stifles the movement at its birth.… If in the long run the beliefs expressed in proletarian dictatorship are destined to be accepted by the dominant forces of the community, the only meaning of free speech is that they should be given their chance and have their way. (*Gitlow*, at 673)

Was Holmes conceding the argument to Gitlow? No, Holmes found no virtue in socialist politics and never believed such notions had even a remote chance of success. Perhaps because he believed socialism impotent, Holmes would enable its argument in the great American open marketplace. If a few (and likely only a powerless, feeble few) took it up, their campaign would pose no threat to the forward progress of America. Let those bumbleheads try to persuade us. Nothing lost.

Would Holmes allow the same logic for words like those in *Stormfront*? Holmes's "dominant forces of the community" were Caucasian business barons of the 1920s, bureaucrats in the administration of Calvin Coolidge, entrepreneurs like Henry Ford. Holmes's brethren on the bench, skillful former corporate attorneys, knew that the real business of America, as Coolidge aptly put it, was business.[4] Not likely that these "forces" would capitulate on premises as close to the heart of their investments as Gitlow proposed. But another premise loomed large here.

Racism endures in America. Many organizations exploit fear of racial differences. The Nationalist Movement seeks to "take our country back" from all manner of non-Caucasian peoples and organizations (Barrett, 2008). The New Century Foundation claims that black people are more dangerous than white people, more prone to violence, more likely to need imprisonment for the safety of the peace-loving populace. The Foundation's book, *The Color of Crime* (1994), claims to document the integrity of law and the relative lawlessness of black and Hispanic people. The National Alliance attracts members around the world based on gentile European ancestry. Its publications call Hitler the greatest man of our era. Jews are blamed for inflation, media brainwashing, and government corruption, with blacks depicted as criminals and rioters. Books and speeches by Hitler, Joseph Goebbels, and the American neo-Nazi George Lincoln Rockwell are displayed and promoted. The Holocaust story is seen as a conspiracy of exaggerations, half-truths, and outright inventions. The New Century Foundation's rhetoric is charged with exclusion and counter-history, though it appears at first glance a more businesslike, less cultic operation.

Stormfront itself may seem civil in comparison. *Stormfront*'s blogs are magnets for fanciful turns, supportive quotes, and aphorisms too numerous to catalog here, except for this example, which readers may interpret however they choose: "The two most common elements in the Universe are hydrogen and stupidity" (Ellison, 2001, 6). To give itself historical weight, the website features statements from aviator Charles Lindbergh (1939):

> We can have peace and security only as long as we band together to preserve that most priceless possession, our inheritance of European blood, only so long as we guard against dilution by foreign races. It is time to turn from our quarrels and to build our White ramparts again.

The World Church of the Creator is anti-Christian, anti-Jewish, and anti-nonwhite, but the Creativity for Kids website promotes white pride and is loaded with educational materials for children. The Hammerskin nation website, geared to teens and young adults, uses links to youth music, cutting-edge Internet graphics, and chat forums (Cohen-Almagor 2010, 104–5). But with or without a user-friendly patina, the message is an unrelenting white-supremacy racism.[5] You have to wonder how much the diet of family-friendly graphics makes the racism seem acceptable.

SHOULD HATE SPEECH BE SUPPRESSED?

White race blogs offer three general impressions. First, those in the movement perceive that their opinion is suppressed, ignored, and disrespected by a wider culture amuck in global propaganda. Schools do not honor their views; school textbooks fail to write history as they see it. Mainstream politicians crave their support but publically repudiate their opinions. Mainstream media are hopelessly feminized, Semitic, and adversarial. The courts, once stalwart defenders of racial values, now promote values alien to the movement. The racists' only allies are liberals whose loyalties to liberalism are so consistent that they will fight for the right of opponents to articulate foolishness, all in the name of freedom.

Legal scholar Franklyn S. Haiman (1993) is one such reluctant ally. Haiman understands the injury hate speech can induce. He opposes such speech, with fury no doubt. His liberal credentials are manifold, his writings consistent and clear: the proper response to bad speech is more and better speech, not legal suppression.

Suppressing the verbal or symbolic expression of group hatred does not make the attitudes that give rise to such expression go away. Except where words present the likelihood of immediate and serious physical harm, the proper antidote to bad speech is good speech. To use the force of law against bad opinion is to risk an evil far greater than inflammatory language. The evil that would undo us is the intermingling of morality and law that would make courts and judges arbiters of the good, as well as arbiters of the peace.

Second, those in the movement are keen to expand race hate rhetoric to metaphysical proportions. No problem is localized; every instance of race engages a seemingly cosmic struggle for survival and moral victory. Race is not a matter of tax money to refurbish a blighted urban school; it is instead a conspiracy to deflect all wealth away from rightful holders into the rapacious grasp of the undeserving. In this regime of race hate, there can be no political solutions, only territorial ones. The cosmic crisis presented by race requires two distinct universes. Peace is achieved only when borders are erected and enforced. (We should not discount the psychological catastrophe of race-haters who, once in their own theoretical world of sameness, are no longer confronted with their objects of hate. What now to do with their undirected hostility?) Best-case scenarios are not a return to race-based privilege, or political hegemony as depicted in classics such as *Sounders* or *The Autobiography of Miss Jane Pitman*. The solution proffered by white-race broadcast and print propaganda is simple disappearance: Dark skin must go away.

Given the movement's belief that its truth has been suppressed by holier-than-thou activists falsely claiming the moral high ground, those con artists of equality see further dialogue as a sign of weakness and surrender. Further, if solutions have nothing to do with elementary recalibrations of social entitlements, and everything to do with fundamental distinctions of value based on race heritage, then political compromise is hopelessly stalled. It is not worth the trouble.

These realities present the third impression: no viable solutions exist. The movement is energized on itself, not on treasured outcomes. The movement is its own reward.

We cannot quickly dismiss the dire implications of this analysis. Hate speech represents a social movement without resolvable goals. The speech of race hate perpetuates itself by increasing its volume, maximizing its apocalyptic forecasts, and fueling its own twisted passions. As a social movement, it shares political equivalence with the dreaded LRA of northern Uganda who have terrorized millions for over two decades with no declared political end-point, no reasons or aspirations, except to keep on terrorizing. In their wake are thousands of traumatized victims and thousands more in shallow graves. American racists are not supporting such armed violence today, but the rhetoric leads to inevitable conflict against entrenched forces stubbornly resisting the obvious facts of color and heritage.

Communitarians understand that people do not manage well when rhetorical intimidation hovers in the ether above them, when, as in the docudrama *Mississippi Burning*, rumblings in the night threaten to end what little stable peace their pathetic patch of earth may have tenuously achieved. What is to be done?

Robert Fortner (2009, 342) has shown how media may be signalers of evil, critics of evil, or dupes of evil. He reports the worst recent examples of media inciting violence (Radio RTML, Rwanda), but the more difficult circumstance for news journalism is the coverage of evil that fosters more of the same. Terry Anderson, a journalist held for five years in Lebanon, believes that even media coverage of terrorist organizations legitimizes them: "In my opinion, the very reporting…is a first victory for the terrorist" (Fortner 2009, 342). The problem of hate speech compounds merely on the possibility that its discussions prompt more of it, its depiction in entertainment formats make it palatable, its analysis in public forums spreads its shadowy insinuations of ethnic righteousness. Perhaps the best recourse is to pay no heed.

A DIFFERENT WAY FORWARD

This book presents what some might call an impossible counter-scenario. We may be mocked for waving a peace flag while antagonists gnash their teeth ready for war. The solution described in these pages may look amateurish, lame, the folly of idealism untested by the grit of life on the street. Okay, hang with us anyway.

We propose communitarian dialogue and reconciliation. We propose a change of outlook, tactic, and heart.

Communitarian dialogue changes the emphasis of a conversation. We no longer argue for equal time; we insist on active listening as a prelude to serious talk. We are not advancing a beleaguered check and counter-check on epithets and name-calling, a steady reduction in the temper of war-words. We recommend voluntary quiet, a time for no words at all, a time for rhetoric to settle. Then what to do with soundless time? Perhaps the mere presence of the other will begin a process that tainted logic and strenuous rights-claiming cannot. Begin with the dialogue of silence. Of course, the communitarian solution will always finally engage in a flow of words that reach for new social solutions. Reconciliation is never achieved silently. But first, allow silence to reckon with presence.

Communitarian dialogue will start when an alternative set of irrefutables replaces those just noticed. First, one's status as victim must be challenged. We discover that we stand together in culpability, and together in responsibility for change. In a place where dialogue is practiced with sophistication, the Maasai say: *Irorie amu miany eye*. It translates, talk to him for he will not stop dying. In communitarian dialogue, we reckon with the futility of arrogance (the belief that all fault is with the other) and the illusion of isolationism (the belief that trouble is best solved by living alone). We reckon with common moral miscues, and deeper, all-to-common relational failures. We are not victims, but co-perpetrators. We are not faultless, but co-conspirators. Our rhetoric has been death-directed. We must change together.

Communitarian dialogue refuses the escalation of race hate. Simple refusal. Communitarians believe that race hate may be cancerous and malignant, but not terminal. Available solutions, though distant, are a hope that communitarian dialogue embraces as prima facie evident. Argue until blue (even blue with rage), yet the hope is not diminished. With that hope always at the table, we give our best effort anticipating an outcome that affirms the deep humanity of the other and finally, our mutual recognition that bonds more or less invisible link our futures in ways we once disparaged. Race hate is not a cosmic certainty. It is, in the communitarian way, a removable though belligerent barrier to a better future of cooperation and mutual support.

If you choose a communitarian future, do not expect smooth winds on easy seas, as if adversaries will fade away in the light of your inclusive kindness and persistence. Our social world is more complex than that.

In the 2008 presidential campaign, race hate reared its fury tempered by the honor of pulpit and office. The Rev. Jeremiah Wright, pastor of candidate (later president) Barack Obama's church in Chicago, became YouTube's most watched personage, now famous for his flaming condemnations and vilifications of white society. Such rhetoric is political poison, and candidate Obama had no choice but to explain his own response to it.

In a speech on March 18, 2008, which some claim was path-breaking for its courage, the first viable African American candidate for the presidency of the United States both rejected the race hate of his spiritual mentor and embraced, even celebrated, the kindness he had known from this man during his own years of maturation. Senator Obama could no more disown the Rev. Wright than his own white grandmother, he said, who had her own issues with race and sometimes made them public. Later, as the Rev. Wright continued his diatribes unabated, candidate Obama did in fact denounce him, as political winds required.

Did race play a role in the Democratic and then national presidential campaigns of 2008? To think not would be stupid. Yet through it came what may be a new public reality in America's effort to deal with its history of race-based legal and economic inequality. That story is still too fresh, too much underway, for comment here. Readers, you will do it.

Communitarian dialogue directs its effort not to containment of hate speech within well-defined federal guidelines (there are none), but to a mutual recognition that hate speech is a road to perdition (to borrow Sam Mendes's 2002 movie title) and therefore emotionally and politically unprofitable. Hate speech makes the soul shrivel. Its consequences, to use the language of utility, are a lesser good, or better, no good at all. No one prospers, including the *Stormfront* regulars, where hate speech rules. The social complexity that diversity brings to a nation of immigrants and natives (the former long ago displaced the latter as power base) cannot find the good by setting wrong standards for the good. Kantian deontology stipulates the rational mind as ground to recognizing that universal law is the right and proper way to guide social progress. Hate speech finds no passage there; its mind speaks gibberish to reasoned people of all backgrounds.

Communitarian dialogue proposes a realistic alternative to cope with race hate's deeply embedded appeal. That alternative is to recognize the other as a person, to organize social effort to points of mutual well-being, and to shed the strategy of posting and defending the "rights of man" elaborated by notions of individual autonomy. The assertion of individual rights also leads to perdition, for we are not atoms in a chaotic, competitive universe. We are selves bound together in mutual need, complementing each other in the effort to build a culture of flourishing human growth. Our talk should reflect who we are, people knitted in mutuality who thrive when personal energies are directed to improving the life of someone else without regard to epidermal hues. Communitarianism is a strategy to make relationships strong. When we practice that, we discover that right action sustains life, and "works of love" (Kierkegaard) validate themselves as genuinely good.

The communitarian turn also presses past the First Amendment to include and embrace the equal protection of law and due process of law secured in the Fourteenth Amendment (1867), applied to the states as a sidebar in *Gitlow*. Without equal protection, the right to speak is softened by majority power, made to serve those who own the technology, bent away from minority voices. Access is denied, the history of communications technology teaches. Communitarian theory follows George Fletcher's argument that the post–Civil War amendments, particularly the Fourteenth, was a "second Constitution" that built organic nationhood, the equality of all persons, and popular democracy—needed correctives to the individual freedom and republican elitism that typified the original constitutional terms. "The postbellum constitution emphasized not freedom from government but equality under law," a document that announced a "second founding" of the then 37 united states (Fletcher 2001, 217).

MAKING CHOICES

Faced with hate speech, one might say, "Just look away. Be a good non-consumer. Strangle the market by boycotting the product." Averting the eyes as a strategy relieves you of complicity. You cannot be a hatemonger if you pay no heed to hatemongering.

At the same time, mere avoidance of the message seems like a "nonstarter" moral solution. There will always be an audience for racism. This contemptible residue of the "better angels of our nature" will not peter out by the loss of individual nonparticipants. Perhaps the opposition's falloff will embolden purveyors by creating the impression that the weaker side is abandoning the field. Averting the eyes gives a pass to hate speech: we tolerate when we should oppose.

Communitarianism offers a better response, not in the form of a definitive public policy, but by an orientation that exposes the fallacy of discounting another's humanity, and raises for all people the mutual obligation to become co-conspirators in friendship.

That friendship can be hard won. The acclaimed film *American History X* presents the story of two brothers, skinheads filled with white rage, who finally understand that "hate is baggage. Life's too short to be pissed off all the time" (*American History X*). In a school paper project confessing his reversal, the protagonist Danny Vinyard concludes with Lincoln's words, reminding his stunned followers—young, bigoted, distrustful—that strained passions ought not "break the bonds of affection" that people across any divide should feel and live by. It was Vinyard's coming to truth in the shadow of a giant who set that truth in immortal lines.

Let us appeal here to a communitarianism approach found far away from Lincoln's Washington or Vinyard's Venice Beach. Benezet Bujo has described a community confronting its problems, facing its differences, working toward a cooperative future (2001). Bujo calls the process a palaver—a meeting of community stakeholders to hear each other's stories, reckon conflicting claims, and move forward together. Bujo, a Congolese scholar and Catholic priest, calls palaver the traditional African process for strengthening mutuality while adjusting policy to meet requirements of corporate prosperity. Yet not only prosperity—in Bujo's rural African setting, survival is never taken for granted. Without the palaver, a village disintegrates; its fragments are insufficient to the demands of nourishing a next generation; the village becomes exhausted and overwhelmed. In this sense, Bujo advances past the liberal "marketplace of ideas" where truth emerges by virtue of the rationality and persistence of listeners and speakers. The "marketplace" may be a liberal fiction grafted onto Plato and the Sophists, whose dialogic method held within it the "hope that nasty talk will call forth countervailing words of equal force and greater wisdom [as when] contraries clash to reveal some high truth" (Peters 2005, 65). For Bujo, survival is the goal and higher truth perhaps a nice afterthought.

In the West, social safety nets are considerably better established. Few citizens of Western democracies starve; few die of disease unattended. The West suffers its disparities, shortages, and unequal access, but for most people (the vast majority) life-sustaining help is not far away.

Hate speech, however, brings us closer to Bujo's world. Hate speech brings intimidation and nullification to the doorstep, to the highways, to the offices and shops where people conduct daily business. Hate speech looms in play lots and pulpits, close to our sanctuaries and our recreation. Our music carries its rhythm; our politics uses a tangled rhetoric. Hate speech is communication, unique to human symbol-makers, that severs capacity to coexist and threatens existence itself.

Palaver cannot be forced by legal mandate. Its dynamic of patient listening and slow-burn consensus-making requires formidable first-order commitment.

We must honor palaver to practice it well. We must train youth to do it. Mediators and advocates who come to know palaver are the teachers of tomorrow and the leaders of consensus-building. Our common task is to subordinate the indifference of casual acquaintance and the disaster of premeditated hate by making an effort to hear, honor, and negotiate the stories of a big village aiming at a better future.

It remains almost a footnote to ask: Is it morally okay to hate the hater, to speak angrily about the one whose cadence and lyric is detestable? Stephen Kershnar raises the question—can hatred of the hater be a virtue? In his study of Batman's hatred of criminals, Kershnar advances Aristotelian virtue as normative, then concludes that "hatred is an appropriate attitude toward persons who maliciously cause others to suffer.... Good persons should not feel benevolent toward evildoers who intentionally hit, poison, or kill others" (2008, 34). Of course, Batman must hate in order to be Batman. His hate is part of his tragic legacy, his mystique. But should hate cross over to real people as a proper response to hate-filled advocates of harm.

That it will is certain. Nazis do not march (or threaten to march) in Skokie without kicking up hate for their hideous historical associations. People are beings with a full range of emotions. Communitarianism maintains real warrant, not an abstracted ideal, for emotion per se. Communitarianism is not a campaign to eradicate intense and fierce responses to the bitterness of entrenched, institutionalized hate. Communitarianism will not, however, let hatred be the last word—even hating the haters. Public discussion cannot end there. If it does, there is no community to gather tomorrow. Hating the hater is intermediate only, a passage, not a destination. Communitarianism insists that when the last criminal in Gotham is locked up, Batman's posture must change even toward the bad guys.

Stormfront and its progeny lead to no civic solution at all, but must be led by those whose destination is peace. Hating the hater perpetually is not communitarian strategy. Even *Stormfront* fanatics must be approached as persons invited to the palaver, first to learn how social progress is done, then to add their say, a new perspective shaped by the crucible of encounter and embrace.

NOTES

1. The NPR report was released on February 23, 2011. <http://www.npr.org/2011/02/23/133970226/new-report-higher-hate-group-count-than-ever?sc=emaf.>
2. The best video for presenting these details on hate groups is the HBO production narrated by the Southern Poverty Law Center's Morris Dees, "Hate.com: Extremists on the Internet."
3. *Gitlow v. New York*, 268 U.S. 652 (1925), at 667.
4. The famous line was spoken by President Calvin Coolidge in Washington, D.C. on January 17, 1925.
5. Racism on the Internet in various countries is monitored by the International Network Against CyberHate founded under Dutch law in 2002 <http://Jugendschutz.net>.

REFERENCES

American History X, <http://www.imdb.com/title/tt0120586/>.

Appiah, K. Anthony. 1994. "Identity, Authenticity, Survival: Multicultural Societies and Social Reproduction." In Amy Guttman, ed., *Multiculturalism : Examining the Politics of Recognition*. Princeton, NJ: Princeton University Press, 149–64.

Barrett, Richard. 2008. "Change out of Crisis." <http://www.nationalist.org/speeches/government/change.html>.

Bok, Sissela. 1998. *Mayhem*. Reading, MA: Addison-Wesley.

Bujo, Benezet. 2001. *Foundations of an African Ethic*. Nairobi: Paulines.

Cohen-Almagor, Raphael. 2006. *The Scope of Tolerance: Studies on the Cost of Free Expression and Freedom of the Press*. London: Routledge.

———. 2010. "In Internet's Way." In R. Fortner and M. Fackler, eds., *Ethics and Evil in the Public Sphere*, 93–116. New York: Hampton Press.

Cravatts, Richard L. 2009. "Hate Speech at San Francisco State University." <http://www.americanthinker.com/2009/02/hate_speech_at_san_francisco_s.html>.

Downs, Donald. 1985. *Nazis in Skokie*. Notre Dame, IN: University of Notre Dame Press.

Ellison, Harlan. 2001. "Introduction." In S. Mark Young, Steve Suin, and Mike Richardson, *Blast Off : Rockets, Robots, Ray Guns, and Rarities from the Golden Age of Space Toys*. Milwaukie, OR: Dark Horse Comics, 6–8.

Fletcher, George P. 2001. *Our Secret Constitution*. New York: Oxford University Press.

Fortner, R. 2009. "The Media in Evil Circumstances." In L. Wilkins and C. G. Christians, eds., *The Handbook of Mass Media Ethics*. New York: Routledge, 340–52.

Greene, Robert. 1998. *The 48 Laws of Power*. New York: Penguin.

Haiman, Franklyn S. 1993. *"Speech Acts" and the First Amendment*. Carbondale: Southern Illinois University Press.

Hollenbach, David. 1994/95. "Civil Society: Beyond the Public-Private Dichotomy." *The Responsive Community: Rights and Responsibilities* 5:1 (Winter), 15–23.

Kershnar, Stephen. 2008. "Batman's Virtuous Hatred." In Mark D. White and Robert Arp, eds., *Batman and Philosophy: The Dark Knight of the Soul*. Hoboken, NJ: Wiley and Sons, 28–39.

Kierkegaard, Søren. 1995. *Works of Love*. Translated by V. Howards and Edna H. Hong. Princeton, NJ: Princeton University Press.

Lindbergh, Charles A. 1939. "Aviation, Geography, and Race," *Reader's Digest*, November, 64–67. <http://www.stormfront.org/forum/t51642/>.

Miller, William Lee. 2008. *President Lincoln*. New York: Knopf.

New Century Foundation. 1994. *The Color of Crime*.

Peters, J. 2005. *Courting the Abyss*. Chicago: University of Chicago Press.

Taylor, Charles. 1994. "Politics of Recognition." In Amy Guttman, ed., *Multiculturalism: Examining the Politics of Recognition*. Princeton, NJ: Princeton University Press, 25–74.

Uelmen, Gerald. 1992. "The Price of Free Speech: Campus Hate Speech Codes," *Issues in Ethics* 5:2 (Summer) <http://www.scu.edu/ethics/publications/iie/v5n2/codes.html>.

USA Today. 2008. "Campuses Work to Ban Gossip Web Site." February 2.

Volf, Miroslav. 1995. "A Vision of Embrace: Theological Perspectives on Cultural Identity and Conflict," Ecumenical Review 47:2 (April), 195–205.

Volf, Miroslav. 1996. *Exclusion and Embrace: A Theological Exploration of Identity, Otherness, and Reconciliation*. Nashville, TN: Abingdon.

Walker, Samuel. 1994. *Hate Speech: The History of an American Controversy*. Lincoln: University of Nebraska Press.

Wilson, James Q. 1993. *The Moral Sense*. New York: Free Press.

CHAPTER 9

Edward Bernays and Public Relations as the Engineering of Consent

"The public be damned!"

With those four words, William Henry Vanderbilt, the richest man in the world, articulated a truism of economics and offended millions of Americans. Vanderbilt's statement also illustrated the need for public relations, both in the sense of offering statements to the media designed to encourage conversation rather than provoke irritation and in the sense of bridging the chasm between big business and the public.

The nineteenth-century railroad magnate's offensive statement may have been unjustified, but it was not gratuitous. His outburst followed a question put to him by a reporter for the *Chicago Daily Tribune* about complaints from the public following the cancellation of an unprofitable train route (Hatch 1882, 12). Vanderbilt believed that businesses succeeded by providing quality service to paying customers, but he also understood that staying in business required solvency. Businesses were not charities. A laissez-faire capitalist who held that the public would benefit from unrestrained competition among self-interested businesses, Vanderbilt gave a simple answer when the reporter asked whether he ran limited express trains for profit or for public service: "The public be damned!" Vanderbilt's statement confirmed the public's worst suspicions about rapacious business in the Gilded Age. Five years later, in 1887, the public responded to the railroad industry's contemptuousness by having Congress create the first federal regulatory agency, the Interstate Commerce Commission.

It is fitting that the term "public relations" first appeared in the inaugural *Year Book of Railway Literature* published in Chicago, where Vanderbilt gave his infamous interview (Robinson 1897, p. iii). Indeed, the railroads became early believers in the usefulness of public relations. In 1906, PR patriarch Ivy Lee sent out one of the earliest press releases on behalf of the Pennsylvania Railroad, reporting an accident in Atlantic City, New Jersey, that claimed the lives of fifty people. Lee also persuaded the railroad to transport reporters to the scene of the accident. These efforts at transparency generated goodwill for what in other circumstances could have been devastating news for the railroad. Six years later, the Pennsylvania Railroad hired Ivy Lee full time, making him the first corporate public relations executive.

These experiences in early corporate public relations in America taught powerful lessons to Edward Bernays, PR's first major theorist. Bernays taught the first university-level public relations course (in the Journalism Department at New York University), wrote the first book in the field (*Crystallizing Public Opinion*), and worked as the first self-proclaimed public relations counselor, all in 1923. He understood that the public was to be engaged, never dismissed, and that wise corporations were proactive, neither reactive nor silent (Cutlip, Center, and Broom 2000, 150). He would call his science of shaping public opinion "the engineering of consent," a process that he championed as both ethical and democratic (Bernays 1947). Indeed, Bernays, whom *Life* magazine named one of the 100 most influential Americans of the twentieth century, believed that public relations was both exclusive and socially essential, a profession that required a deep understanding of social psychology and a commitment to the highest standards of conduct.

COMMITTEE ON PUBLIC INFORMATION

Bernays was six years out of college and had worked as a magazine editor and a theater publicist in New York when the United States entered the war in 1917. Twice he tried to enlist for military service, but his poor eyesight and flat feet kept him from active duty. So he did the next best thing: He joined the government's new Committee on Public Information, which assigned him to the New York Office of the Foreign Press Bureau.

Established by President Woodrow Wilson in 1917, the Committee on Public Information (CPI) was the first extensive propaganda agency run by the U.S. government. The CPI had three purposes: (1) to mobilize public support for Americans fighting in the war, (2) to provide the public with ample information about the war, and (3) to reduce conflicting reports about the war by coordinating information that the public received. Muckraking journalist George Creel was appointed director of the CPI, and what became known as the Creel Committee went right to work.

The CPI used several complementary strategies to mobilize public support for Americans fighting in Europe. One strategy was to publish pamphlets, a lot of them, on many different subjects (Aucoin 1998, 492). Some of the pamphlets used the Great War (it was not called World War I until World War II began) as an occasion to explain what democracy meant. Others showed that the war was being fought "to make the world safe for democracy," or opposed U.S. isolationism, or defended American intervention in the European war. Pamphlets with titles such as *Conquest and Kultur: Aims of the Germans in Their Own Words* portrayed Germany as authoritarian, militaristic, and ruthless. Still other pamphlets offered practical ways that ordinary citizens could help America's war effort, including purchasing war bonds and keeping a lookout for German spies.

Another medium that the CPI found useful was public speaking coordinated on a national scale. Broadcasting was still a few years in the future, so the CPI used the most effective means of live transmission that it had at its disposal: It organized speakers across the country to deliver short patriotic and war-related speeches in movie theaters, houses of worship, and other meeting places. The community-based speakers, called Four Minute Men, received weekly instructions from the CPI. By the end of the war, thousands of Four Minute Men had spoken to millions of Americans.

The CPI left no stone unturned in its effort to mobilize public support for the war. It created a Bureau of Cartoons to influence newspaper cartoonists across the nation. In its weekly bulletin, the Bureau of Cartoons provided themes and captions for cartoonists to consider using: promoting enlistment, for instance, or recycling—whatever the CPI believed would support the war effort. There were even Bureaus of War Expositions and State Fair Exhibits. Most famous of all media were the visually powerful CPI posters. Some promoted thrift: "Food is ammunition—don't waste it." Others advertised Liberty Bonds: "Beat back the Hun with Liberty Bonds." And many took direct aim at the enemy. "Remember Belgium," read one such poster, illustrated with a background of flames and a German soldier dragging an unwilling girl by her hand in the foreground.

Besides promoting American involvement in Europe, the CPI worked to keep the public up to date about developments in the war. Seeing itself as the clearing-house for information about it, the CPI's Division of News produced more than 6,000 news releases and published the government's first daily newspaper, the *Official Bulletin*. Another division supplied feature articles about war efforts to magazines and Sunday newspapers. And the Division of Film sent photographs to newspapers and magazines and produced newsreels and movies for America's movie theaters. (The 1918 production *Pershing's Crusaders* was the Division's first feature-length film.) The CPI understood that the more it could fill news channels with reliable, official information, the less it would have to contend with reports that raised questions about America's military involvement in Europe (Vaughn 1998).

Because the Great War was indeed a world war, the CPI told America's stories far beyond America's borders. With three branches—a Wireless-Cable Service, a Foreign Press Bureau, and a Foreign Film Division—the CPI's Foreign Section had offices in more than thirty countries. Bernays, who directed the Export Section and co-directed the Latin American Section of the Foreign Press Bureau, saw his work as "psychological warfare" (Ewen 1996, 162). He convinced American multinational firms such as Ford and International Harvester to distribute pamphlets on U.S. war aims overseas and to put posters in the windows of their American offices abroad. He had postcards sent to Italian soldiers at the front to boost their morale and he had leaflets dropped behind the German lines to sow dissent. He organized rallies at Carnegie Hall featuring dissidents who advocated freedom from Austria-Hungary. And to counter German sympathy in Latin America, Bernays had U.S. propaganda printed in Spanish and Portuguese and inserted into periodicals sent there (Tye 1998, 18–19).

"The work I did for the CPI," Bernays later reflected, "gave me the first real understanding of the power of ideas as weapons and words as bullets" (Cutlip 1994, 165). The weapons and bullets Bernays learned to use at the CPI launched his career in public relations. Former CPI colleague Carl Byoir paid Bernays $150 a week to help Lithuania, which seceded from Russia at the end of World War I, gain recognition by the U.S. government. Bernays set about his new task with characteristic gusto. He sent short articles about Lithuania to newspapers to use as filler. He produced longer feature articles about Lithuanian music, Lithuanian theater, Lithuanian sports, Lithuanian business, and Lithuanian food. "Each story contained the message that Lithuania, the little republic on the Baltic, the bulwark against Bolshevism, was carrying on a fight for recognition in accord with the principle of self-determination laid down by President Wilson," Bernays explained. "This theme would appeal to Americans' identification with liberty and freedom" (Tye 1998, 157). With positive articles about Lithuania appearing in hundreds of newspapers across the country, Bernays had little difficulty soliciting supportive editorials and telegrams to send to U.S. Senators. In 1922, the United States formally recognized the Republic of Lithuania as an independent country (Cutlip 1994, 166).

PROPAGANDA

Bernays explained his PR philosophy in his seminal 1928 book *Propaganda*. The book's short opening paragraph is astonishing. "The conscious and intelligent manipulation of the organized habits and opinions of the masses is an important element in democratic society," Bernays asserted. "Those who manipulate this unseen mechanism of society constitute an invisible government which is the true ruling power of our country" (37). In just two sentences, Bernays seemed to confirm the suspicions that people have about public relations—that it is manipulative, that it is secretive, and that it works.

In Bernays's eyes, propaganda is essential to all societies, democratic and otherwise. Following the writing of the British physician Wilfred Trotter, whose 1916 book *Instincts of the Herd in Peace and War* said that human beings instinctively suppress their individuality to follow the will of the group, Bernays argued that group behavior needs to be recognized and directed to beneficial goals. Bernays believed that society, left on its own, has the tendency to become chaotic, irrational, and dangerous. Fortunately, society seldom becomes completely dysfunctional because its leaders consciously mold public opinion, mostly without the public knowing or, for that matter, even caring very much. Indeed, Bernays maintained that it is perfectly acceptable to use propaganda to create order out of chaos as long as it is not used for unethical ends.

To Bernays's way of thinking, we are happy living with the illusion that we control the decisions that we make on a daily basis. But so many choices are being made beforehand that few real decisions are ours to make. Bernays referred to such control as "the invisible government," and he gave examples in an array of human endeavors including business, politics, women's activities, education, social service, art, and science. One example is a man who is making a stock purchase. Why he chooses one stock over another is a matter of what Bernays calls "a mélange of impressions stamped on his mind by outside influences which unconsciously control his thought" (1928, 73). The railroad stock that he buys is on his mind because it was in yesterday's headlines, it once served him a good dinner on one of its fast trains, it is known for its honesty and its good treatment of its workforce, and it has shares owned by J. P. Morgan. These factors, all of which are under the control of others, lead the man to make his choice. He only thinks that his choice is independent.

True to his roots at CPI, Bernays saw nothing inherently sinister about propaganda. He traced the use of the term to the year 1627, when Pope Gregory XV created the Office for the Propagation of the Faith to oversee Roman Catholic missionary work around the world. Thus, the word "propaganda" originally meant propagation, not deception or manipulation. Commenting on a dictionary definition of propaganda as the systematic effort to gain public support for an opinion or a course of action, Bernays pointed out that any negative connotations were late arrivals to a neutral term. "Propaganda is only good or bad depending upon the merit of the cause urged and the correctness of the information published," Bernays said (1928, 48). Twenty years later, after another world war cemented the negative characteristics of propaganda permanently, Bernays adjusted his vocabulary. He still advocated the strategic and skilled molding of public opinion, but he began referring to propaganda as "the engineering of consent."

Insisting that manipulation of public opinion is inevitable even for democracies, Bernays proposed that democratic societies face the fact that public opinion requires management. For Bernays, free enterprise is a mirage; so is the kind of renaissance knowledge required for informed decision-making on myriad complex issues that all of us face in contemporary society. That scenario may not appear to be entirely democratic, but it is a fact that we have to live with, according to Bernays. "This invisible, intertwining structure of groupings and associations is the mechanism by which democracy has organized its group mind and simplified its mass thinking," he said. "To deplore the existence of such a mechanism is to ask for a society such as never was and never will be" (Bernays 1928, 44). Thus, the question is not whether public opinion is managed, but rather how it should be managed and by whom. Modern democracies do not leave propaganda to chance. They turn to public relations professionals who follow ethical principles as they mediate among the various constituencies. With approval of our leaders, they help guide us toward desirable goals. "The engineering of consent is the very essence of the democratic process, the freedom to persuade and suggest," Bernays said (1947, 114).

One desirable social goal was equal treatment of African Americans, the primary mission of the National Association for the Advancement of Colored People. Hired to promote the NAACP's national convention in 1920, Bernays and his wife and PR partner Doris Fleishman sought to attract the greatest amount of attention for the organization. The meeting was to be held in Atlanta with an impressive roster of black and white civil rights leaders, which made the event

Doris Fleishman and Edward Bernays: The First Couple of Public Relations (© Bettmann/ CORBIS).

newsworthy. But to guarantee that *The Atlanta Constitution* gave the meeting coverage on the front page, Fleishman persuaded the mayor of Atlanta to attend the convention and convinced the governor to put the state militia on alert, given the volatility of race relations at the time. This careful and imaginative planning led to prominent newspaper coverage in Atlanta and across the nation, boosting awareness of the NAACP's fight against racial discrimination (Bernays 1928, 148–50; Tye 1998, 125).

Bernays thought of public relations not as an art, but as a science based on testable hypotheses about human behavior. He derived much of his approach from Sigmund Freud, his uncle and his major intellectual influence. Freud taught Bernays that scientific observation can yield keen insights into human behavior and that much human motivation is unconscious. To these principles, Bernays added his own conclusion: that identifying unconscious desires gives the upper hand to those who want to wield influence. Indeed, Bernays was so confident in his PR program that he claimed results could almost be guaranteed. In certain cases, he said, "We can effect some change in public opinion with a fair degree of accuracy by operating a certain mechanism, just as the motorist can regulate the speed of his car by manipulating the flow of gasoline" (1928, 71–72). It helped, of course, if the target audience did not know that it was being persuaded.

In *Propaganda*, Bernays provided example after example of stimulating a desire that would allow people to think that they were choosing the product apart from external influence. That is, creating the right conditions is the key to public relations success. To increase the sale of pianos, for example, Bernays said that he would do more than simply advertise them. Instead, he would set out to promote the desire for a music room in the home. His campaign would have famous decorators design music rooms to be exhibited to celebrities in the world of music and, of course, the press. Influential architects would include music rooms in their upscale house plans. More and more homeowners would want to create their own music room, which they would furnish with a piano. The condition precedes the sale (1928, 77–79).

Bernays followed a similar process when the Beech-Nut Packing Company hired him to boost its sluggish bacon sales. Increasing advertising was not the method for Bernays, who understood that this strategy would simply shift sales from one company to another in the short term. Bernays looked instead to increasing the desire for bacon in general. He paid a New York physician to canvass his professional colleagues to see if they favored light or hearty breakfasts. When the vote came in for hearty breakfasts, newspapers and wire services promoted the story, and sales of bacon and eggs soared. Bernays used this success to contrast "the old-fashioned propagandist," who would take out full-age advertisements to promote the price, taste, and nourishment of bacon in the hope of breaking through consumer resistance, with "the new salesman," whose reliance upon social psychology would lead him to secure the endorsement of doctors because the new salesman understands that so many people depend upon physicians for guidance about health. Because of "the psychological relation of dependence of men upon their physicians," Bernays said that it was a matter of "mathematical certainty that large numbers of persons will follow the advice of their doctors" (Bernays 1928, 76; Tye 1998, 51).

Perhaps his most famous example of creating conditions that produced desired results occurred after Procter and Gamble hired Bernays in 1923 to promote Ivory soap. His inspiration for creating the condition of desire for Ivory soap came when a sculptor wrote to Procter and Gamble asking for a large block to Ivory soap to carve. The result was the first National Soap Sculpture Contest, with cash prizes and copious publicity for huge blocks of Ivory soap carved to look like the Empire State Building, say, or William Howard Taft. Bernays changed contest eligibility from "all walks of life, regardless of age" to students from fourth to twelfth grade in order to get kids to ask for Ivory Soap, something they had never done before. For decades afterwards, a million bars of Ivory soap were purchased annually so that children could enter the soap-carving contest. No telling how many more bars of Ivory soap went into bathtubs and showers as a result of this contest (Tye 1998, 56–57).

If Bernays had an Achilles' heel, it was his own ego. PR practitioners grew tired of his self-promotion and his repeated name-dropping, especially of his famous Uncle Sigmund. Nobody doubted that Bernays was creative, talented, hard working, and tireless, but his self-aggrandizement was hard to take and his exaggerations came from a bottomless superiority complex.

No other Bernays success story illustrates his penchant for embellishment more than the celebration of Light's Golden Jubilee in 1929. How the fiftieth anniversary of the invention of the electric light by Thomas A. Edison was to be celebrated was a matter of some debate until Edison's friend Henry Ford took charge, spending $3 million on the jubilee. Bernays was hired to help with promotion by General Electric, the jubilee's junior partner.

The publicity was profuse. Newspapers reprinted 50-year-old articles announcing Edison's invention. Luminaries including Albert Einstein and General John J. Pershing wrote tributes. George M. Cohan composed "Edison—Miracle Man." The U.S. Post Office issued a stamp commemorating Electric Light's Golden Jubilee.

A who's who assembled in Dearborn, Michigan, where Edison's laboratory had been re-created. President Herbert Hoover was there; so were Marie Curie, Charles Lindbergh, J. P. Morgan, John D. Rockefeller, Jr., Will Rogers, and Orville Wright. From the lab, Edison reenacted his famous experiments as an NBC radio announcer breathlessly narrated: "Will it light? Will it burn? Or will it flicker and die, as so many previous lamps had died? Oh, you could hear a pin drop in this long room. Now the group is once more about the old vacuum pump. Mr. Edison has the two wires in his hand; now he is reaching up to the old lamp; now he is making the connection. It lights!"

The event was a success, and praise for Bernays poured in afterwards. The *Atlantic Monthly* said, "Henry Ford was supposed to be the manager of the show, but the man who set the stage and pulled the strings attached to all the dignified marionettes was Edward L. Bernays."

Yale University psychologist Leonard Doob praised Bernays's work as "one of the most astonishing pieces of propaganda ever engineered in this country during peace time." Bernays capitalized on this publicity. A circular from his office asked, "Will any of your clients celebrate important anniversaries in 1930?...If our experience in handling the public relations aspects in the Light's Golden Jubilee and other clients interests you, we should be glad to discuss with you the anniversary possibilities of your clients."

Bernays had worked hard on media relations for Light's Golden Jubilee, but it was Henry Ford who arranged to bring Edison and his lab to Dearborn, and the prominent guest list was Ford's, not Bernays's. In fact, Henry Ford grew so irritated with Bernays's repeated attempts to appear in photographs with Hoover and Edison that he told one of his advisors to "get Bernays the hell out of here or I'll have [him] thrown over the fence." Undaunted, Bernays allowed himself to be praised for the work of others. Bernays repeatedly referred to Light's Golden Jubilee as his "greatest triumph" (Cutlip 1994, 205–7; Tye 1998, 63–69).

AMERICAN TOBACCO COMPANY

The year after *Propaganda* was published, George Washington Hill, president of the American Tobacco Company, hired Bernays to help him increase market share by reaching women, who at the time represented a largely untapped customer base. Except for some college women and a few women who had lived overseas or who had worked in factories during World War I, most women did not smoke. Women smoked only one out of ten of the cigarettes that Hill produced, and he wanted to increase sales by increasing this percentage.

To make smoking more attractive to women, American Tobacco's Lucky Strikes appealed to women's desire to be slim. One of American Tobacco's advertising campaigns urged women to "reach for a Lucky instead of a sweet." Bernays's earliest work on this account followed the logic that cigarettes fostered slimness by suppressing appetite. He identified beauty with thinness by supplying fashion editors with numerous photographs of slender models in designer dresses. He also furnished newspapers with articles in which dentists advised substituting fruit, coffee, and cigarettes for sugary desserts that caused cavities (Tye 1998).

But Bernays believed that there had to be stronger appeals to potential women smokers, so he went to psychoanalyst A. A. Brill for advice. The good Freudian explained that cigarettes signified inequality between the sexes: Cigarettes were acceptable pleasures for men, but taboo for women. From this consultation with Dr. Brill, Bernays conceived of cigarettes as "torches of freedom" for women who, having recently won the right to vote and being eager for greater equality, could be persuaded to smoke as a sign of liberation from patriarchy.

Inspired by his new insight into the psyche of women, Bernays went to work designing one of his most famous publicity stunts. He hired several fashion models to march in New York's popular Easter parade and, on cue, to light a

Lucky Strike. Meanwhile, Bernays let a number of press photographers know that women activists would protest the taboo against smoking in public by lighting their "Torches of Freedom" on Fifth Avenue. The press release, which appeared to come from the women, said, "We are doing this to combat the silly prejudice that the cigarette is suitable for the home, the restaurant, the taxicab, the theater lobby but never, no, never for the sidewalk." The press release also told the photographers that the women would smoke their torches of freedom publicly from 11:30 a.m. to 1:00 p.m.

The press took the bait. Models lit Lucky Strikes at the appointed place and time and photojournalists took pictures. The next day, April 1, 1929, the *New York Times* published a photograph of the feminist demonstration with the caption "Group of Girls Puff at Cigarettes as a Gesture of 'Freedom.'" Wire services enabled newspapers near and far to do the same thing. More women smoked publically and sales of cigarettes to women climbed.

Pleased with his torches of freedom stunt, Bernays tried to refine his persuasion. The torches for freedom promoted women's smoking in general, not a particular brand, even though the models smoked Lucky Strikes. Bernays wanted to promote the primary brand of his employer, so he investigated women's feelings about Lucky Strike cigarettes only to learn that they disliked the forest green color packaging. But having spent years with brand imaging, American Tobacco refused to change the color. Bernays needed another strategy. If the problem was green, then the solution was to change the way women felt about that color. So Bernays began to promote green as the new popular color. Bernays promoted green social events, green home and wardrobe fashion, and green store window displays. And his efforts paid off. The color green grew in popularity in the early 1930s. American Tobacco was so pleased with this campaign that it paid Bernays a bonus (Sobel 1978, 96).

Sometime after the Surgeon General declared cigarettes carcinogenic in 1964, Bernays expressed regret for his role in promoting smoking: "No reputable public relations organization would today accept a cigarette account, since their cancer-causing effects have been proven" (Bernays 1986, 115). Had he known the dangers of smoking cigarettes, he said, he would have refused to work for a tobacco company. But Larry Tye, Bernays's biographer, reported that Bernays was not as innocent as he tried to appear:

> Whatever his attitude in public, at home he did all he could to persuade his wife, Doris, to give up her pack-a-day habit.... Anne, his younger daughter, recalls that when her father found a pack of her mother's Parliaments "he'd pull them all out and just snap them like bones, just snap them in half and throw them in the toilet. He hated her smoking." (Tye 1998, 48)

Having read early research reports that connected smoking to cancer, Bernays tried to keep his family away from cigarettes even as he promoted them in his work. He also advised his client to be prepared to dispute and discredit scientific studies on the negative effects of smoking. Publicly, though, Bernays was positive, even aggressive. And Bernays, a nonsmoker who lived to be 103 years old, always took great pride in his public relations campaigns on behalf of cigarettes.

UNITED FRUIT COMPANY

In no other episode of Bernays's storied career was his CPI training more evident than in his work for United Fruit Company, forerunner of Chiquita Brands International. Headquartered in Cincinnati, Ohio, and having operations on six continents, today's Chiquita Brands has 23,000 employees, mostly based in Central America. Chiquita Brands' history includes decades when it treated supplier countries such as Guatemala as "banana republics," a pejorative label for Central American countries ruled by a small group of elites who kept their wealth and political control by allowing powerful outside corporations to exploit the country's servile labor force and export commodities (especially bananas). In the early 1940s, United Fruit Company president Samuel Zemurray hired Bernays to help expand market share for the company that already dominated U.S. banana sales. In characteristic fashion, Bernays launched a multidirectional public relations campaign. He promoted bananas as an aid to digestion by having United Fruit fund research and by printing 100,000 hardback copies of a book about bananas and digestion and sending them to physicians, librarians, and newspaper and magazine editors. Bernays also promoted the strategic dimensions of United Fruit's "Great White Fleet" of ships that transported troops and supplies, as well as bananas. Bernays made sure to promote bananas where they would be noticed—in hotels, to the food service of railroads, airlines, and passenger ships, and to manufacturers of cakes, cookies, ice cream, and candy. By 1950, bananas had replaced apples as America's favorite fruit, and they continue to dominate the fruit consumption of today's Americans, who eat a per capita average of 75 bananas every year.

To promote United Fruit's role in Central America, Bernays traveled to its operations in Guatemala. He found the conditions disturbing there. Native employees were poorly paid, had no chance of advancement, and were required to show respect by removing their hats whenever one of their Anglo bosses passed by. "Good will to all groups toward fruit company is poor," Bernays reported. He recommended treating the Guatemalan workforce better, but to no avail. United Fruit management was concerned about the price of bananas, not the conditions and the pay at the company's plantations (Tye 1998, 164).

But United Fruit was facing more than low morale in Guatemala. Sweeping democratization was afoot. An uprising in 1944 ended the military dictatorship of General Jorge Castañeda and ushered in the reforms of the populist Juan Arévalo. The new president built schools and hospitals, allowed laborers to unionize, and redistributed land confiscated from German sympathizers during World War II. Arévalo's successor, President Jacobo Arbenz Guzmán, went even further. To help remedy Guatemala's unequal land distribution—less than 3 percent of the country's population owned 70 percent of its arable land, only 12 percent of which was cultivated—he confiscated 1.5 million acres of uncultivated land and redistributed it to 100,000 poor families. More than 200,000 acres of this land had belonged to Guatemala's largest landowner, United Fruit (Tye 1998, 165).

These measures were just the beginning. Arbenz planned to build a high-way to compete with the train system controlled by United Fruit and a second port to compete with United Fruit's shipping facilities at Puerto Barrios. He also wanted to purchase 177,000 more acres of uncultivated land owned by United Fruit for just $3 per acre, the value that United Fruit claimed on its tax forms (Tye 1998, 166).

United Fruit responded by paying Bernays $100,000 per year to protect its Guatemalan operations. Bernays's advice: Convince the U.S. government that Guatemala was on the verge of becoming a Soviet satellite. Bernays prepared the groundwork for this accusation by persuading influential magazines such as *Time*, *Newsweek*, the *Atlantic Monthly*, and the *Nation* to publish articles about Guatemala's growing communist activities. And he led an all-expenses-paid fact-finding expedition of representatives from such media as the *San Francisco Chronicle*, the *Cincinnati Enquirer*, the *Miami Herald*, and the *Christian Science Monitor* to Guatemala. Bernays promised the journalists that they would be free to do whatever they needed to do to get the true story about Guatemala, and he pro-vided as much assistance to them as he could. They obliged by reporting about the alarming development of communism in Guatemala. Bernays's biographer Larry Tye said that "he managed to win over the reporters while convincing them that he was merely an honest broker of facts" (1998, 172).

Proclaiming the threat of communism so close to the U.S. border was an effective strategy in the early 1950s, the peak years of the Red Scare at home, when McCarthyism was in full swing. Through a revived front organization called the Middle America Information Bureau, Bernays commissioned a comparison of political speeches by key Guatemalan leaders with those of leaders of the Soviet Union to highlight similarities. At the same time, Bernays relentlessly supplied the wire services, *Meet the Press*, and New York newspapers with tips and insider infor-mation from United Fruit sources in Guatemala. The effect was to make the public interests of the United States match the private interests of United Fruit. United Fruit and the U.S. government became close allies. The next step seemed logical, given the growing perception that communist rule in Guatemala was imminent: In June 1954, 200 CIA-trained soldiers led by exiled army officer Carlos Castillo Armas—what Bernays called an "army of liberation"—entered Guatemala, and with U.S. support, seized control of the country. Bernays's work for United Fruit had paid off handsomely.

PUBLIC RELATIONS AND COMMUNITARIANISM

By justifying propaganda as a practice essential to democratic societies, Bernays introduced ethics and community into the discussion of public relations. This rela-tionship is appropriate because public relations is a communication activity that participates in communities—for better and for worse. Indeed, communication scholar Kathie Leeper has observed that "community is the basis for determining and affirming our basic values and...the focus of our responsibilities" (1996, 168). Quoting Bernays, who said "public relations is the practice of social responsibility" (Leeper 1996, 175), Leeper argued that public relations is ethical when it promotes community bonds. She identified three values—democracy, fairness, and truth-telling—as characteristics of public relations that strengthens community.

As Bernays and recent observers such as Leeper have understood, public relations can enhance democratic processes by adding voices to the marketplace of ideas. Traditional print and broadcast media have a great say in setting the public's agenda for discussion. They cover important social and political issues, health, business, sports, and myriad other subjects of concern to the public. But traditional media cannot be expected to think of everything—and the public would not want to leave agenda setting only in the hands of the gatekeepers of traditional media—so public relations practitioners have an important role to play. By introducing subjects, issues, and points of view into the public media that would otherwise be downplayed or absent, they expand dialogue, helping citizens to reach more informed decisions about matters of importance to them.

But the presence of public relations does not automatically increase democratic deliberations. Indeed, many critics point to public relations as a major corruptor of democratic processes. As a strategic enterprise, public relations does not simply inject an overlooked viewpoint into public discussion. PR targets key audiences to maximize its influence and it seldom announces itself in order to appear as an unsponsored participant in public affairs. And because PR can be costly, it tends to favor institutions and well-heeled individuals; grassroots concerns can easily get overlooked in an environment in which paid professionals clamor for their clients' attention. If the public becomes disabused by the strategies and inequalities that public relations can introduce into the marketplace of ideas, its faith in public processes can diminish, thus reducing democratic participation.

To keep public relations on the prosocial side of the democratic ledger, Bernays advocated licensing from 1953 until his death in 1995 (Bernays 1953). Being a public relations counselor should mean more than a title on one's business card, Bernays complained. It should show capability and community mindfulness. "Under present conditions, an unethical person can sign the code of PRSA, become a member, practice unethically—untouched by any legal sanctions," Bernays observed. "In law and medicine, such an individual is subject to disbarment from the profession....There are no standards....This sad situation makes it possible for anyone, regardless of education or ethics, to use the term 'public relations' to describe his or her function" (Bernays 1986, 139).

Bernays did not want to restrict the free speech of people who performed public relations functions as American citizens. Nobody would need a license to create a blog or send a news release to a TV station or host a fund-raising event that would attract media coverage. What Bernays wanted to restrict was the commercial use of the title "public relations counselor," which he defined as "the practitioner, a professional, equipped by education, training and experience to give counsel to client or employer on relations with the publics on which the subject depends" (1986, 35). Bernays went on to identify four functions that the public relations counsel performs:

1. analyzing "the relations of the subject and the publics on which it depends, for its social goals,"
2. identifying "the adjustments and maladjustments between the subject and these publics,"
3. recommending "attitudes and actions necessary to attain the social goals," and
4. interpreting "the subject to the public" (1986, 35).

The public relations counsel "functions on a two-way street," Bernays said, interpreting "public to client and client to public" (1986, 36).

Bernays failed to sell the idea of licensing public relations counsel as a sort of registered trademark. His biggest impediments were the Constitutional guarantee of free speech and court cases that prohibit the licensing of occupations simply to raise standards or to decrease competition. Seen in the light of the First Amendment, the proposal to license public relations counselors seemed draconian: Bernays appeared willing to deny people's right to express themselves in order to prevent a minority of unethical practitioners from sullying the trade. Instead of licensing, public relations relies upon the accreditation program of the Public Relations Society of America for professionalism. Since 1964, this voluntary program has publicly identified the organization's most knowledgeable, experienced, and principled members as APR (Accreditation in Public Relations). No doubt the APR program is a step in the direction of professionalism, but it is far from the legal quality control mechanism that Bernays advocated. After all, membership in PRSA is voluntary and so is the APR program. APR may add status to one's career, but it does not prevent those whom Bernays complained lacked training, education, or ethical behavior from working as public relations counselors (Cutlip, Center, and Broom 2000, 155–56). This point was driven home in 1986, when, of all people, the president of the Public Relations Society of America avoided censure for ethical violations simply by quitting the organization when he was under investigation by the Securities and Exchange Commission for insider trading (Plumley 1989). After leaving PRSA and signing a consent decree with the SEC, Anthony Franco continued to serve as chairman and CEO of Franco Public Relations Group in Detroit until his retirement in 1993.

The democratic concept of equal representation sometimes conflicts with the normative principle of promoting community health and life. For this reason, Bernays advised PR counselors to refuse the business of clients they believe to be dishonest or whose products are poor, harmful, or in competition with another client. His own work with American Tobacco Company notwithstanding, Bernays advised PR counselors to avoid working for clients that compromised their duty to society.

Simply encouraging individual public relations practitioners to represent honorable clients is no way for PR to realize its professional potential, according to Sherry Baker. This approach conceives of PR practitioners as experts for hire whose primary responsibilities are to maintain their expertise and to apply it on behalf of clients, whose only responsibility is to state (and pay for) the service they desire. Because this conception ignores the broader community, Baker proposes that PR practitioners make a covenant with the community, pledging publicly to serve PR clients without harming other members of the public. If commitment to this pledge among the public, PR practitioners, and clients evolved into the expectation that PR cultivates vital relationships across the community, then public relations would move much closer to the professional status that Bernays desired for the field (Baker 2002).

In her discussion of cause-related marketing, Patricia Parsons agrees with Sherry Baker's philosophy: "what is important to the ethical practice of public relations is that there be mutual benefit to both the organization and the cause, and that the promotion be honest" (Parsons 2008, 116). Parsons uses breast cancer awareness as her example. Finding a cure for breast cancer is certainly a high-profile, noble cause. But publicity for this cause obscures the fact that heart disease kills more women in the developed world than breast cancer does, fails to mention its high overhead (the Canadian Breast Cancer Foundation received just 59 percent of funds raised from the "run for the cure"), and ignores pertinent information including the fact that Breast Cancer Awareness Month was the brainchild of Imperial Chemical Industries, which owned Zeneca, the company that produces chemotherapy drugs used to treat breast cancer. Parsons advises, "After taking a heartfelt look at these ethical issues, if breast cancer 'awareness' is still where you believe your money is best spent for the community—then it's the right decision." But she is skeptical. "Given my own family background, I'd be the first in line to support finding a cure—but more awareness? I don't think so. Besides, I'm told that there are more people employed in the cancer business today than there are people with the disease—and the morbidity statistics are only getting worse" (Parsons 2008, 116).

TRANSPARENCY

Because community requires truth-telling and disintegrates with deceit, PR counselors need to perform their work with maximum transparency. Here again some of Bernays's work serves as a negative example—particularly his use of front organizations and third-party testimonials to disguise public relations activities. Instead of honest debate that leads to democratic decisions, misleading information is coercive, motivated commonly by a lack of trust in the judgments of others.

Indeed, honesty can be a thorny issue for public relations counselors who are committed to community. The nature of their work—the fact that they represent one client instead of another—can make them believers in a cause or a product and dismissive of alternatives. This partiality shows that they work hard for a client in which they believe, but community-mindedness can give even diehard devotees

CHAPTER 9 • Edward Bernays and Public Relations   165

some perspective. At the very least, respect for others can motivate public relations counselors to be honest so that they earn the trust of the communities they serve.

Transparency has intrinsic value for truth-seeking and truth-telling because it enables discussants in the public sphere to know the motives and intentions of the other participants. Stephanie Craft and Kyle Heim call it "an indispensable element of public accountability and a necessary condition for promoting public trust in institutions" (Craft and Heim 2009, 221–22). The Public Relations Society of America "Code of Ethics" expresses the need for transparency this way: "Open communication fosters informed decision-making...which in turn builds trust with the public by revealing all information needed for responsible decision-making." Through transparency, professional communicators show respect for persons because disclosing our interests and purposes enables others to think and act with integrity. Deceiving or hiding our intentions, however, manipulates others by treating them as means to an end (Plaisance 2007). As Thomas Bivins observes, "Ethical persuasion requires that the people being persuaded have all the facts they need to reflect critically on a situation and make an informed decision. That includes the identity of the persuader and her motivation. Without that complete information, we are being effectively manipulated" (2008, 237).

DOING IT RIGHT

Bernays himself was more interested in getting the results he wanted than in transparent deliberation. He acknowledged as much when he said, "If you can influence the leaders, either with or without their conscious cooperation, you automatically influence the group which they sway" (1928, 73). When Bernays appealed to ethics, he spoke in utilitarian terms. His concern was the greatest benefit with only minimal harm. When he considered the overall consequences good, he concluded he had done the right thing. Instead of an ethics of consequences, communitarianism is a duty ethics in which public communicators have an obligation to promote the common good. Rather than focusing on professional decisions and values as Bernays did, communitarian ethics emphasizes community decisions and values.

Consequentialism is known as a single-strand theory, and that is one of its strengths. To determine what is right action, consequentialism does not need to appeal to God or metaphysics or debate the nature of good and evil. Only the results matter: What is ethical is what produces the most desirable consequences. Calculating the consequences of the options open to us requires that we ask how much benefit and how much harm would result in the lives of everyone affected, including ourselves. Once we have completed these calculations for all relevant courses of action, consequentialism is obligated to choose the action that minimizes loss and produces the greatest amount of happiness.

But this explicit standard for guiding our ethical choices is also this theory's greatest weakness. Utilitarianism, as this approach to ethics is called, depends on measuring consequences accurately. But how do we always know what the results of our choices will be? Consequences are often blurred, and in the long term, we rarely know for sure. Who, for instance, can possibly calculate the social changes that we will face in the future decades in the wake of converging media technologies? Moreover, nearly every major public relations campaign has unintended consequences. And what if we "win the battle but lose the war," that is, promote the spectacular yields of high-technology agriculture, while land and water are being polluted in the long run? Consequences, the exclusive standard, are unreliable even when taken with the greatest care and competence.

Despite the difficulties with calculating the results—recognized by this theory's adherents—utilitarianism is the preferred system in democratic societies. Democracies operate with majorities, adding up individual votes to determine policies. Professions find consequentialism compatible in form with what they know. Public relations since Edward Bernays likewise finds it attractive to produce the greatest public good with the least possible harm. A practitioner-centered ethics—outlined in codes of ethics, personnel contracts, and company policy—is the prevailing definition of professional morality.

Communitarianism grounds public relations in the community, not first of all in the profession. How the moral order engages community life ought to be the focus, not first of all what public relations practitioners consider virtuous. Like all media professions, public relations is an institution of power whose decisions and policies can be self-serving, and practitioners defensive when criticized. Communitarianism challenges public relations counselors to focus on the moral life as a whole, such as justice, human dignity, and no harm to innocents.

The Public Relations Society of America "Code of Ethics" is wisely oriented to community. Truth as disclosure is a core principle of "open communication in a democratic society." "Preserving the integrity of the process of communication" is what the public expects. The PRSA code "supports the right of free expression" for social life to foster well, not good only for itself. When public relations counselors follow the same moral rules that the public does, a basis is established on which trust can be built.

In communitarian ethics, understanding is the key concept for public communication. The concept "information" is technology-centered—the data, facts, and reports made available by the electronic media. The idea of "knowledge" assumes a rational human being and has been shaped largely by the logic of mathematics and science. "Opinion" is generally seen as subjective and relativistic. For public life, George Gadamer replaces these terms with the idea of understanding. Understanding is normative for community life. It is not individualistic or dogmatic, but dialogic. Its essence is interactive communication through which humans interpret other cultures and enable collaboration among themselves. Language is a natural ability across the human race, and this everyday language, rather than the artificial language of science or technology, is the way of understanding for Gadamer. Words derive their meaning from the interpretive, historical context humans themselves supply. Language is, therefore, inescapably communal, the public agent through which people comprehend the world (Gadamer 1989; cf. Shin 1994).

In assessing public relations, communitarian ethics holds up understanding as the supreme value. For public relations agencies seeking to serve the public responsibly, do its policies and practices meet the standard of understanding? Do messages further the dialogue out of which understanding comes to life or subvert it? Do the persuasion campaigns for health care, business or government empower understanding or undermine reasonable decision-making? When Bernays argued for public relations as an "agent of democratization," he could only have meant "agent of understanding," though he did not use this term. All the tales of spin, partisanship, omission, and deception are obviously contrary to it. Public relations serves the public interest when its constructions of reality for a client affirm and abet the public's irrepressible search for understanding.

CONCLUSION

Two pictures emerge from our look at Edward Bernays and public relations. One picture is of the clever impresario who overcomes the obstacles he faces through adroit and imaginative manipulation of research, political will, and public image. Bernays got people to bring home the bacon; he even made smoking look good. He was, in other words, someone to have as an ally.

The other picture is of an innovator who wishes desperately, at times even against his own experience, to maintain an elevated ethic so that public relations would not devolve into what he warned so warmly about: the manufacture of consent. Bernays deserves our admiration for working diligently in the last part of his career to elevate the field above huckster and flack, to establish its credentials and give it a place of honor in democratic life. People who work hard to advance responsibility beyond themselves and their own contributions are true communitarians. They leave a legacy richer than themselves. They encourage another generation to press ahead toward the common good. Communitarian ethics reaches toward a high public ideal: service to others as prior to personal fame, fortune, or public esteem. That ethics surfaces occasionally in democratic life, and we celebrate it.

Bernays argued that public relations is central to democracy, but he did not address the fact that public relations counselors are hired, not elected. Public relations counselors are employees or independent contractors, not delegates. Indeed, the "invisible governments" that Bernays discussed sway public opinion mostly without the public's knowledge. But as Bernays pointed out, public relations plays an important role in community life. Acknowledging this fact, community-minded public relations counselors should be cognizant of the lives that they affect and humble enough to admit that they cannot always see what is best for everyone. This communitarian perspective should lead to ways of working inclusively, engaging the public in deliberations and activities that respect and enhance the life of the whole community.

REFERENCES

Aucoin, James. 1998. "Pamphlets." In Margaret A. Blanchard, ed., *History of the Mass Media in the United States: An Encyclopedia*, 491–92. Chicago: Fitzroy Dearborn.

Baker, Sherry. 2002. "The Theoretical Ground for Public Relations Practice and Ethics: A Koehnian Analysis." *Journal of Business Ethics* 35: 191–205.

Bernays, Edward. 1928. *Propaganda*. New York: Ig.

———. 1947. "The Engineering of Consent." *Annals of the American Academy of Political and Social Science* 250 (March): 113–20.

———. 1953. "Should Public Relations Counsel Be Licensed?" *Printers Ink*, December 25.

———. 1986. *The Later Years: Public Relations Insights, 1956–1986*. Rhinebeck, NY: H & M.

Bivins, Thomas. 2008. "The Future of Public Relations and Advertising Ethics." In Thomas Cooper, Clifford Christians, and Anantha Babbili, eds., *An Ethics Trajectory: Visions of Media Past, Present and Yet to Come*, 233–38. Urbana: University of Illinois-Institute of Communications Research.

Craft, Stephanie, and Heim, Kyle. 2009. "Transparency in Journalism: Meanings, Merits, and Risks." In Lee Wilkins and Clifford Christians, eds., *The Handbook of Mass Media Ethics*, 217–28. New York: Routledge.

Cutlip, Scott M. 1994. *The Unseen Power: Public Relations, A History*. Hillsdale, NJ: Lawrence Erlbaum.

Cutlip, Scott M., Center, Allen H., Broom, Glen M. 2000. *Effective Public Relations*, 8th ed. Upper Saddle River, NJ: Prentice Hall.

Ewen, Stuart. 1996. *PR! A Social History of Spin*. New York: Basic.

Gadamer, H. G. 1989. *Truth and Method.* Trans. J. Weinsheimer and D. G. Marshall. 2nd ed. New York: Seabury Press.

Hatch, Rufus. 1882. "Hatch on Vanderbilt." *Chicago Daily Tribune*, October 17, 12.

Leeper, Kathie A. 1996. "Public Relations Ethics and Communitarianism: A Preliminary Investigation." *Public Relations Review* 22 (2) (Summer): 163–79.

Parsons, Patricia J. 2008. *Ethics in Public Relations: A Guide to Best Practice*, 2nd ed. London: Kogan Page.

Plaisance, Patrick Lee. 2007. "Transparency: An Assessment of the Kantian Roots of a Key Element in Media Ethics Practice." *Journal of Mass Media Ethics* 22 (2–3): 187–207.

Plumley, Joe. 1989. "Ex-PRSA President Anthony Franco Gives Association Bad Public Relations." *Journal of Mass Media Ethics* 4 (1): 107–8.

Robinson, Harry Perry. 1897. *The Year Book of Railway Literature*. Chicago: Railway Age.

Shin, Kuk Won. 1994. *A Hermeneutic Utopia: H. G. Gadamer's Philosophy of Culture*. Toronto: Two for Tea Press.

Sobel, Robert. 1978. *They Satisfy: The Cigarette in American Life*. New York: Anchor Press/ Doubleday.

Tye, Larry. 1998. *The Father of Spin: Edward L. Bernays and the Birth of Public Relations*. New York: Henry Holt.

Vaughn, Stephen. 1998. "Committee on Public Information." In Margaret A. Blanchard, ed., *History of the Mass Media in the United States: An Encyclopedia*, 155–57. Chicago: Fitzroy Dearborn.

CHAPTER 10

⚘

United Negro College Fund and the Advertising Council

In 1972 a copywriter named Forest Long created a tagline for what would become one of the most successful public service advertising campaigns in American history: "A Mind Is a Terrible Thing to Waste." Long worked for Young & Rubicam, a prestigious New York advertising agency. Their client was the United Negro College Fund (UNCF), an organization dedicated to advancing higher education among minority students by funding scholarship programs and providing financial support to historically black colleges and universities. The project was UNCF's first major public service advertising campaign, designed to generate much-needed economic support, as well as to inform the public about the continuing importance and unique role of its member institutions (Fujinaka 2000, 1823).

Prior to the campaign, UNCF requested assistance from the Advertising Council, a nonprofit organization founded by leaders of the ad industry to provide free advertising and marketing services to noncommercial causes deemed to be in the national interest (O'Barr 2006). The Council connected clients with supporting agencies like Young & Rubicam, which volunteered their time and expertise to create appropriate campaigns that exceeded the abilities and budgets of the organizations served (Chambers 2009, 108). By the late 1960s the Ad Council had overseen many successful projects, from Rosie the Riveter during World War II, to Smokey Bear for forest fire prevention and environmental awareness to Keep America Beautiful.[1] However, its support for the UNCF was the first time the Ad Council had taken on a nationwide campaign primarily for African Americans (Gasman 2007, 170).

After settling on the new slogan, UNCF and Young & Rubicam launched a series of ads in print, as well as on radio and television. Rather than perpetuate the often-divisive politics of the era and present African Americans as charity cases, the spots promoted basic values of fulfilling potential, advancement through hard work and thrift, pride in achievement, providing fair opportunity, and social responsibility. For instance, the television piece "Disappearing Mind" emphasized that education provided individuals with the chance to make an impact they never otherwise could. African Americans were presented as agents of their own uplift. With an education they could contribute to the good of society. One print ad featured a monkey wrench; the accompanying text remarked that with an education, this mechanic's tool could have been a stethoscope or computer. Another advertisement said, "We're not asking for a handout. Just a hand." The radio spot "Accomplishments," meanwhile, recounted many little-known first achievements made by African Americans, including ice cream and open-heart surgery (Fujinaka 2000, 1826–27). Ads featured such prominent alumni of historically black colleges as Martin Luther King, Jr., singer Leontyne Price, and Atlanta mayor Maynard Jackson.[2]

With an average of $10 million annually from the Ad Council in pro bono services throughout the 1970s, the UNCF campaign worked. During the first five years of "Mind," donations doubled (Gasman 2007, 187, 191). By the 1990s the UNCF series had so saturated public consciousness that three out of four Americans recognized the United Negro College Fund's slogan (Fujinaka 2000, 1827). In pragmatic terms, "A Mind Is a Terrible Thing to Waste" helped transform the United Negro College Fund from a small organization known to philanthropists and charitable foundations into a nationally recognized and increasingly effective force in American higher education.

FREDERICK D. PATTERSON

No person was more central to the creation of the UNCF than Frederick D. Patterson. Born on October 10, 1901, in Washington, D.C., he was named after the famous abolitionist, Frederick Douglass. When his parents died soon after from tuberculosis, Frederick and his five siblings were split up, although an older sister, Bessie, eventually became his guardian. Upon Bessie's graduation from the Washington Conservatory of Music, she and Frederick moved to Texas, their parents' state and home to many relatives (Goodson 1991, 2–5).

Frederick Patterson enrolled in Sam Houston Elementary, a church-supported school where he often boarded when siblings moved around the region for jobs. After graduating eighth grade, he followed Bessie to the Prairie View Normal and Industrial Institute outside Houston, where she found a position teaching music and choir. Prairie View was a "normal" school that trained teachers using a two-year curriculum; it was also a land-grant institution for the state of Texas that focused on agricultural and technical productivity (Goodson 1991, 8–9). Patterson completed his studies there and then enrolled at Iowa State College to study veterinary medicine.

Like other African American students at Iowa State who were few in number (he was the only one in his program), Patterson worked regular jobs to support himself while studying full time. He also joined the Student Army Corps, which provided a subsidy for males who spent four years in the program. He and several other black students rented living quarters together because fraternities were still segregated at Iowa State. Remembering that he and a friend, the only two African American students among 1,500 in the Corps program, were made to eat separately from the others, Patterson said, "I learned a lesson I never forgot: how people feel about you reflects the way you permit yourself to be treated. If you permit yourself to be treated differently, you are condemned to an unequal relationship" (Goodson 1991, 18).

After commencement in 1923, Frederick Patterson accepted an offer to teach at Virginia State. By 1926 he returned to Iowa State for a year on a master's degree fellowship from the Rockefeller Foundation's General Education Board. Soon after receiving his master's, Tuskegee Institute asked him to join its faculty in veterinary science, and he began work there in 1928. A second GEB fellowship allowed him to earn a doctorate at Cornell University in 1931–32, thereby becoming the first Tuskegee professor to earn a Ph.D. degree—the doctorates of Robert Russa Moton and George Washington Carver, two of Tuskegee's most famous personnel, were honorary (Goodson 1991, 34–36). A year later he was promoted to director of the Department of Agriculture, after its leader was killed.

In 1935 Frederick Patterson replaced retiring Robert Moton as President of Tuskegee Institute. Tuskegee was in trouble at the time, running a deficit of $50,000 annually. Predictably, the majority of the new president's work became financial. Only 33 years old and lacking many of the wide personal and professional connections of his predecessors Moton and Booker T. Washington (Gasman 2007, 15), Patterson had to balance black and white faculty needs and perspectives along with those of largely white funders and board members. He often acknowledged the politics of his role: "I had to tread carefully. Some people had called both Booker Washington and Dr. Moton Uncle Toms. To some extent, I found that I too needed to bow to the exigencies of race relations" (Goodson 1991, 49).

By the early 1940s Frederick Patterson had settled into the leadership of Tuskegee Institute. Funding remained his top concern, as it was for other presidents of black colleges and universities. Because many of these schools were modeled on land-grant institutions, leadership also meant balancing educational quality with practical skills. Creating a five-year plan, whereby students could choose to work for the college in return for their education, helped translate deficits into a surplus. However, of necessity, Patterson began to think about changing the model and scope of fundraising for Tuskegee and its peer group. The Great Depression may have been a major factor for the decline in donations to education during those years (Gasman 2007, 18–19; Tucker 2002, 416), but the New Deal's implementation also gave wealthy philanthropists frustrated by what they saw as President Roosevelt's anti-business agenda a convenient excuse to withhold their contributions. Patterson began to look for other sources of support:

> The direction was moving from the control and contributions of a few to a larger giving constituency. The idea occurred that this was the direction of national philanthropy, with the masses brought in to contribute. Only by going beyond any immediate constituency such as alumni and trustees could a campaign have a national appeal. Could black colleges, perhaps through a united effort, make a case for the needs of black youth now being severely restricted and handicapped by lack of resources? (Goodson 1991, 64)

That realization would shape the rest of his life, as well as launch the UNCF.

THE UNITED NEGRO COLLEGE FUND

Frederick Patterson began to explore his ideas for expanding fundraising for black colleges in more detail. For some time he had written a weekly column, "Southern Viewpoint," for the *Pittsburgh Courier*. Looking for a topic one week in January 1943, he decided to make public some of his thinking. The resulting column, appropriately titled "Would It Not Be Wise for Some Negro Schools to Make Joint Appeal to Public for Funds,"[3] posited that

- the financial situation was even more dire for historically black institutions of higher education than for others;
- black colleges might become much more effective in fundraising if they made a unified appeal and then devised a fair method by which to divide gifts;
- the campaign could start with blacks themselves.

From what now is a classic in journalism, here are sample paragraphs:

> Private Negro colleges have carried the brunt of our educational effort for the Negro people of America. They educate to the extent of their means nearly 50% of those who receive college training. They have pioneered in areas, until recently, hardly possible in few if any state supported institutions.
>
> These Negro institutions may well take a cue from the general program of organization which seems to involve most charitable efforts today. Various and sundry drives are being unified with a reduction in overhead for publicity and in behalf of a more purposeful and pointed approach to the giving public.
>
> The idea may not be new but it seems most propitious at this time that the several institutions referred to [Atlanta, Dillard, Fisk, Hampton, Morehouse, Tuskegee], pool the small monies which they are spending for campaigns and publicity and that they make a unified appeal to national conscience. The nominal contribution of one dollar per person could be sought over the widest possible range. During these critical times, a unified financial campaign for several Negro colleges seems to be an idea worth toying with. (Patterson 1943, 7)

Tuskegee itself was spending $20,000 annually in fundraising but receiving only $40,000 per year in return. Another important issue was that HBCU presidents competed with each other by asking for donations among the same group of philanthropies. Therefore, during this period Patterson also set about writing the presidents of other HBCUs in order to gauge the extent of their current financial difficulties. The peers he contacted responded quickly, often revealing that their positions were even more precarious than Tuskegee's (Goodson 1991, 122–23).

With the responses in and a pattern emerging, Patterson called a meeting of black college presidents, eighteen of whom came to Tuskegee along with representatives from the New York marketing firm John Price Jones (with which

Tuskegee had worked in the 1920s). Although some attended skeptically, in the end the founders came away with three goals for the proposed college fund: raising funds for member colleges, promoting understanding of African American needs and problems, and setting an example of interracial cooperation. By 1944 when the United Negro College Fund officially incorporated, the ranks had swelled to twenty-seven member institutions and Frederick Patterson had received the public endorsement of John D. Rockefeller, Jr. Patterson was chosen to be the fund's first president, with William Trent, Jr. its first executive director (Gasman 2007, 22–25).

The creation of the UNCF entailed a dramatic shift in the way HBCUs conducted fundraising. Membership in the fund required being a private institution accredited by the Southern Association of Colleges and Schools or an equivalent. Member presidents first worked out a distribution formula whereby all colleges divided 40 percent of the returns equally, with the remaining 60 percent distributed according to the investment made by each institution. In this way, small colleges with fewer resources were favored to receive a higher share of the earnings (Goodson 1991, 127–28). Next, UNCF devised a solicitation policy where each president would raise funds for that person's own institution some years and would travel to cities on behalf of the UNCF in other years. Making headway was difficult at first. Presidents tended to violate the solicitation policy by fundraising only for their own school, as well as initially refusing to share with UNCF their school's full donor lists (Gasman 2007, 28).

Even so, the United Negro College Fund's first capital campaign beat all expectations. Spurred by donations of $25,000 each from the Rockefeller Foundation and the Julius Rosenwald Fund, the member institutions raised a matching $50,000 themselves and poured the combined money into an ad campaign aiming to raise $750,000. The 1944 campaign brought in $765,000, more than three times what the UNCF colleges had raised individually in the previous year. In addition, costs were reduced to less than 16 percent of the total raised, some 50–66 percent less than individual colleges normally spent on fundraising (Gasman 2007, 31–32). Corporations donated the largest percentage, although a record $106,000 came from individual African Americans, more than 84 percent of whom were first-time givers (Tucker 2002, 421). The UNCF had arrived.

Over the following decade the United Negro College Fund grew, though the proportionate division of its funds to a growing number of member institutions meant that financial concerns and constraints always remained at the fore. Throughout this period John D. Rockefeller, Jr. stayed closely involved with the Fund, providing donations, personal contacts, and expertise. For Rockefeller, the fund represented an individualistic mode of self-help for what he described as America's "Negro problem" (Gasman 2007, 35–47). Rockefeller recruited a mostly white leadership of fellow industry titans who emphasized values such as hard work, thrift, and independence. He sought individuals who, like himself, saw the UNCF "as a solution that neither undermined capitalism nor involved government intervention" (Gasman 2007, 43). Importantly, Rockefeller's approach led to mistrust of

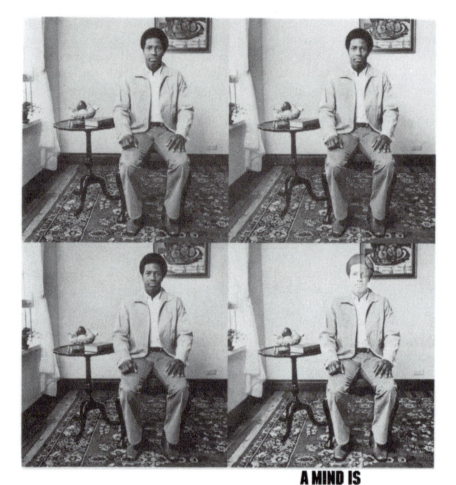

A MIND IS
A TERRIBLE THING TO WASTE.

People are born every day who could cure disease, make peace, create art, abolish injustice, end hunger.

But they'll probably never get a chance to do those things if they don't get an education.

We're educating over 45,000 students at 40 private, four-year colleges every year.

Most of these young people would never get to college on their own. Three-quarters need some kind of financial aid. Well

over half come from families earning less than $5,000 a year.

You can help us help more. By sending a check. Whatever you can afford.

Because we can't afford to waste anybody.

GIVE TO THE
UNITED NEGRO COLLEGE FUND.
55 East 52nd Street, New York, N.Y. 10022

advertising contributed for the public good

Ad Council poster, "A mind is a terrible thing to waste" (The Advertising Council, Inc.).

black leadership within the organization. He and other white leaders of the UNCF often openly doubted the African American staff's financial acumen. "Rockefeller Jr. and his associates kept a close eye on the operations of the Fund, effectively cementing white control of the organization during this time" (Gasman 2007, 58).

The U.S. Supreme Court's 1954 decision to desegregate American public education in *Brown v. Board of Education* changed this situation significantly. After the court overturned *Plessy v. Ferguson* on the grounds that "separate" was inherently unequal,[4] large sectors of public opinion began to adopt the view that historically black colleges were no longer useful in a society that was headed toward desegregation.

Having spent a decade building the case for the unique role of HBCUs to enable higher education for people of color, the UNCF now found it necessary to shift its justification. After the *Brown* decision, it halted its $25 million capital campaign, despite being already half way to the goal. The Ford Foundation and other major donors believed that continuing support of the HBCUs would support segregation. However, UNCF member presidents pointed out that many of their schools did not bar access to nonblacks; other institutions were the ones that had to change their policies to fit the new law (Gasman 2007, 101–5). Indeed, on the whole the UNCF and its members saw the *Brown* decision not only as a victory, but an opportunity for growth and a chance to become better, more competitive institutions (Chambers 2009, 106; Tucker 2002, 428).

Gradually the UNCF found new arguments to advance its case. First, their successful history and visibility positioned HBCUs as vital places to educate black students. Second, the UNCF reminded the public that the vast disparities remaining between white and minority populations in the United States made scholarships and institutional support even more critical to African American students. Third, by the late 1950s and now under the leadership of Benjamin Mays, the UNCF and its members also began to assert, if subtly at first, that white society, not them, held the keys to desegregation (Gasman 2007, 118).

The United Negro College Fund continued to evolve during the rise of the Black Consciousness and civil rights movements. In the late 1950s activism on black college campuses increased dramatically. With rare exceptions, UNCF member presidents supported sit-ins, protest marches, and other forms of nonviolent resistance conducted by more and more of their students—despite concern from many funders. Executive Director William Trent, Jr. released a statement emphasizing the UNCF's role in creating responsible leaders and trained workers, reserving the rights of each member college to manage the crises and trials of the movement. Funding initially declined over civil rights concerns, but ended up doubling annually between 1960 and 1966 (Gasman 2007, 125).

In 1966 Stephen Wright succeeded Benjamin Mays as leader of the United Negro College Fund. During this time the Black Consciousness movement started to modify the organization's fundraising messages. Advertisements still focused on corporate audiences and their preferences, but now also asked viewers to stand for equality. Descriptions of black students changed from industrious to intelligent (Gasman 2007, 128). The confidence gained from the Civil Rights Act, a plethora of legal decisions, and a growing sense of pride among African Americans increased openness in the UNCF's work and also increased control of the organization by its black leadership. This new boldness would launch the UNCF's involvement with the Ad Council, and the "A Mind Is a Terrible Thing to Waste" campaign.

THE ADVERTISING COUNCIL, A CAMPAIGN, AND ITS CONSEQUENCES

Soon after the United States entered World War II, the American Association of Advertising Agencies and the Association of National Advertisers created the War Advertising Council to help produce nationwide wartime public service announcements in addition to its commercial messages. As the United States' entrance into the global conflict began to look likely, leading advertising executives considered the implications for an advertising industry still slumping under the Great Depression. Most saw the looming war as a way to revitalize and insure renewed dominance of the industry in the American economy and public life. However, the War Ad Council's roots also lay in the successes and failures of the 1920s and 1930s, when advertising went beyond presenting products to molding opinion (Lykins 2003, 9). The War Ad Council was the indirect product of President Woodrow Wilson's Committee on Public Information, which he created in 1917 to help sell the American public on World War I (O'Barr 2006).

For the duration of World War II, the War Ad Council managed a variety of campaigns on behalf of government and industry, promoting war bonds and the Red Cross, warning citizens that "Loose Lips Sink Ships," recruiting women for the Women's Army Corps (WAC), and disseminating selective service information. After the war ended in 1945, the council renamed itself the Advertising Council and dedicated itself to producing governmental and other service-oriented campaigns on behalf of worthy clients. Over the following decades, the Ad Council's staff and volunteers became a key outlet by which to build Cold War consensus around American ideals such as free enterprise and individualism (Lykins 2003).

As the 1960s waned, the United Negro College Fund took on the new leadership of Vernon Jordan, who quickly set about furthering the changes Wright had made to the organization. Jordan was a turning point for the UNCF campaign. "No longer willing to submit to the agenda of white corporations, the message of the Fund challenged the status quo, held donors responsible, and brought to the fore the social ills of the United States" (Gasman 2007, 137). One key to Jordan's changes was his aggressive ramping up of the UNCF's publicity arm. Equipped with a large network of connections, he approached a friend in advertising named Joseph Mehan, who helped him persuade the Ad Council to take on UNCF as a client by arguing that African American higher education was in the national interest.

With the Ad Council's support, UNCF moved away from communicating in terms of potential losses for whites, or particular gains for African Americans. Instead, through the "Mind" campaign, UNCF began to secure "the middle ground, which suggests the extent of loss to both blacks and whites by projecting the cumulative effect of talent denied to the market; without aid, good ideas will go untapped, and 'we can't afford to waste anybody.' By focusing on the common good, the 'Mind' ads were highly successful; donations to the UNCF increased by 100 percent" (Gasman 2007, 187). The arguments began to focus on America's return on its investment. The "Mind" campaign appealed to the nation's common humanity and belief in educational opportunity. "Most important, the 'Mind' ads targeted the donor base as a single entity—U.S. citizens—and thus obviated the two-pronged approach used in the 1950s" (Gasman 2007, 194).

THE UNCF AND AD COUNCIL TODAY

Since this launch in the 1970s, the United Negro College Fund has continued to influence higher education on behalf of people of color. All the while it has kept its famous tagline: "A Mind Is a Terrible Thing to Waste." In 1999 the UNCF under William H. Gray III received $1 billion from the Gates Foundation, the single largest educational grant ever made (Roach 1999, 18). In 2008, the nation's 105 historically black colleges and universities comprised 3 percent of the institutions of higher learning in the United States, but still graduated 18 percent of African American undergraduates. Eight of the *U.S. News and World Report*'s Top 10 "Best Black Colleges" are UNCF member institutions. The Fund now manages over 400 programs for scholarships, mentorships, and internships, with over 8,000 scholarships annually in 900 American institutions (UNCF 2011). The UNCF's thirty-five years of the "Mind" campaign have been instrumental in raising over $2 billion. Three hundred and sixty thousand students of color at the thirty-nine UNCF member schools have received financial aid, and all the historically black colleges and universities have benefited substantially.

The UNCF still faces many serious challenges, however. Berger (2000, F6) has argued that the UNCF now has to navigate increasing media diversity and fragmentation in its fundraising campaigns. The Ad Council can no longer reach the entire American population through campaigns designed for the three major networks. In 2004 the *Journal of Blacks in Higher Education* (JBHE Foundation 2004, 28) reported that despite its success, UNCF's contributions to its member institutions are modest compared to the need. For example, "Harvard earns about as much on its endowment in three days as Howard does in an entire year. Each second Harvard earns $88, Howard earns 80 cents" (29). Harvard's return on endowment was about $2.8 billion annually, while Howard's (the largest endowment of the HBCUs) entire endowment was $317 million. In fact, twenty-nine of the HBCUs had endowments of less than $5 million in 2004 (28). A long road remains to be traveled before the UNCF secures economic parity with predominantly white institutions. Others realize, too, that the post-*Brown* questions of the historically black colleges' value in a desegregating nation still require an answer (Lowery 1994, 132).

It is worth noting that at least since the 1970s, some authors have criticized the Ad Council for promoting the economic and political status quo. In "The

American Economic System: The Gospel According to the Advertising Council,"
William Lutz summarized:

> This is the key to the function of the Ad Council, to keep power where it is now
> lodged while at the same time carefully cloaking the existence of any such power.
> Moreover, by its virtual monopoly of public service announcements, the Ad
> Council effectively prevents any opposing views from reaching mass audiences.
> By jamming the media with its views, the Ad Council not only manages to dis-
> tort, misdirect, and cover up, but it also manages to prevent any really critical
> views from receiving free and widespread dissemination. (1977, 861)

From this perspective, the UNCF could be perceived as accepting the power structures and capitalist ideology promoted by the Ad Council. What if maintaining
power structures, and glossing over tarnished reputations of powerful interests
such as the ad industry, were the real modus operandi of the Ad Council? Could
it be said honestly that it benefits the community? If not, what might that mean
for UNCF?

At the same time, the United Negro College Fund continues to promote
higher education by appealing to common hopes and interests in American
society. In 2006, the UNCF partnered with the Bush-Clinton Katrina Fund on
a multi-million-dollar campaign to provide emergency aid, as well as long-term
reconstruction assistance to HBCUs affected by Hurricane Katrina (Pluvoise,
2006). Michael Lomax, the Fund's current president and CEO, launched yet
another round of the "Mind" campaign in conjunction with the Ad Council in
2007, seeking to continue the successful tradition of appealing to the public's
fundamental humanity and young peoples' dreams of opportunity. Although
many have faulted the UNCF has been criticized from many sides over the years,
Gasman wisely concludes:

> If the UNCF is fed by capitalism, could anyone really expect it to be revolu-
> tionary? The organization's evolution may just be the logical conclusion of its
> founding premises: the mutual agreement on democracy and free enterprise as
> core American values and the understanding that education is the key to racial
> harmony and economic development. (2007, 200)

The Ad Council and UNCF probably have worked so well together for so long precisely because both, in communitarian style, seek to build from mutual agreement
about core societal values.[5]

The global economic crises of 2008–2009 brought new urgency to the UNCF's
mission, as well as a renewed emphasis on its venerable slogan. Continuing to
work with Young & Rubicam (via its subsidiary Landor Associates), in early
2008 the United Negro College Fund had revamped its organizational identity, deemphasizing the full name—considered outdated at best and pejorative by some—in favor of the acronym UNCF. "A Mind Is a Terrible Thing to
Waste" received even more prominent billing underneath the letters, as market
research continued to find it one of the most recognized slogans in American

advertising history. In fact, already by the mid-2000s the "Mind" campaign was so universally known it was voted by the American public to be one of only five slogans inducted into *Advertising Age's* Advertising Walk of Fame during its inaugural year, 2004.

Both the organization's internal revamp and the American economic crisis continue to prompt reconsideration of the UNCF's role in twenty-first-century America. For instance, UNCF has added "capacity-building programs" to its traditional lineup of scholarships and institutional support.[6]Also, the organization has developed partnerships with other minority education organizations, recognizing that definitions and perceptions of race and ethnicity continue to shift in the United States. Nevertheless, both the UNCF and its member institutions keep probing its strategy and priorities among these larger social changes. Some believe the UNCF needs to update its distribution formulas, which they assert work against smaller schools at the expense of large ones. Others are seeking new potential for cooperation between government and charities like the UNCF, as educational priorities continue to develop with a new federal administration and Congress (Stuart 2009).

Whatever its exact role in economic development within American free enterprise, the Ad Council's contribution beyond goods and services is historically significant. In 1943 when the UNCF was proposed, one of the three main goals highlighted this larger purpose: "promote understanding of African American needs and problems." Jason Chambers concludes:

> The advertising campaign for the UNCF not only brought more positive images of blacks to the nation's advertising landscape, it also helped initiate a national conversation about race and opportunity. The campaign has presented blacks as agents in their own advancement and as a group worthy of investment and support. (Chambers 2009, 106).

Beyond its work on behalf of the UNCF, over the past six decades the Ad Council has made other significant contributions to the national conversation on major social and environmental issues. The quality and impact of its work is perhaps reflected by the fact that several of its public service initiatives have been named to *Advertising Age's* Top 10 Campaigns of the twentieth century.

SOCIAL RESPONSIBILITY

The Advertising Council's public service campaigns and use of ad agency expertise for social causes are evidence of a communitarian thinking. "Take a Bite Out of Crime" for the National Crime Prevention Council and "Friends Don't Let Friends Drive Drunk" for the U.S. Department of Transportation are other famous public service initiatives. In fact, if its "time and labor were measured in billings, the Ad Council would be one of the largest agencies in the nation" (Chambers 2009, 108). The history of UNCF raises additional questions: What strategies work on the local and regional level to support social service and public issues? What examples from other democracies demonstrate marketing toward a communitarian framework?[7] What kind of organizational structure and culture are necessary for advertising to emphasize community service?

In communitarian democracy, the media should empower public life. Public communication cultivates shared interests and common goals. Citizens are taken seriously in clarifying and resolving public problems. Outside the government and market, the media do not merely report on civil society's organizations and activities but seek to enrich and improve them. Schools, religious organizations, families, voluntary associations, NGOs, citizen-action groups—these dimensions of civil society facilitate democratic life. Social values and people's worldviews come to expression in and through them. Involvement in civil society helps the public come to terms with political and consumer issues themselves, rather than reduce them to problems for politicians to solve. The Ad Council's "Mind" campaign has tangibly benefited education. It represents the largest contribution to the education of students of color outside federal and state government support. Instead of serving only the market, it demonstrates how advertising as an institution can serve civil society.

A specific way of asking about advertising and social responsibility is through the "Future of Public Media Project" funded by the Ford Foundation. The project's questions have centered on the way today's technological revolution is changing public knowledge and action:

> Social networking and other Web 2.0 tools, do-it-yourself media (DIY), and new shared platforms, such as Wikipedia, are not only creating new opportunities for media to spur public knowledge and action but changing the terms of mass media as well. How will new participatory platforms evolve to serve the needs of democratic politics? (Aufderheide and Clark, n.d., p. 2ii)

Publics create themselves by communication, and "communicating about shared problems...builds a group's awareness of itself as a public. In this context, public media are those media that aim to increase public knowledge and cohere and mobilize audience members" (Aufderheide and Clark, n.d., 3; see Clark and Aufderheide 2009). Just as news and entertainment media play a critical role as public communication, advertising can use its expertise and finances to support agencies involved in public causes. Nongovernmental organizations such as Human Rights Watch, Amnesty International, and the Global Campaign for Women's Human Rights understand human rights history, specific abuses, and strategies for action. Pro bono support can make a crucial difference in bringing their expertise into the public forum. An alliance with international nongovernmental associations such as Doctors Without Borders, Friends of the Earth, International Red Cross, Greenpeace, and World-Watch on Deforestation can also facilitate democracy on the national and local levels. Through them and their numerous counterparts, the Ad Council—or local and regional coalitions of advertising agencies—can identify and promote the moral conditions of democratic life.[8]

ETHNIC DIVERSITY

The communitarian perspective emphasizes public service advertising, the Ad Council, and pro bono assistance to charitable organizations. In a broader sense, communitarianism inspires the kind of commitment to diversity that the Ad Council's support for UNCF exemplifies. In the social responsibility version of communitarian ethics developed by the Hutchins Commission in 1947, the media are challenged to give "a representative picture" of a society's diversity. For Charles Taylor (1994), a community's diverse components need to be recognized; they all should contribute their voice and participate in action for democratic societies to be credible. In Paulo Freire's (1970) terms, when social groups have developed a critical consciousness, they will "speak a true word" about their condition and enrich public dialogue.

But difficult issues in advertising and ethnic diversity need to be overcome to better serve the common good. These problems can be summarized under three related but distinctive headings:

1. *Packaging*: Advertisers study groups to determine their cultural features and preferences, not to understand them for their own sake but to use these findings to sell products. Audiences are not seen as people but as means to someone else's ends.[9]

   > To interest advertisers in supporting Spanish-language broadcasting, Latinos were identified, that is, called into question as a lucrative, untapped market. The broadcasters had to convince advertisers that Latinos were desirable consumers, that Latinos were a large enough group with enough spending power to make it a worthwhile target market. (Christians et al. 2011, 157)

   Packaging sometimes devalues culture and exploits it rather than celebrating it. The media sell their audiences to advertisers; the goal is not first of all to represent cultures authentically. Targeting specifically to Latina/os or African Americans can be seen as exploiting unique people groups. As Dwight Brooks reminds us, "it is through the discourses of advertisers and their clients that the categories of consumers get established" (1995, 34).

2. *Stereotyping*: Advertising tends to stereotype a minority's way of life and culture. U.S. Latina/os are more than people dancing salsa (cf. Valdivia 2003, 399–418) and serving mojitos; but that is what television ads often depict. Advertisements frequently characterize Asian Americans as polite and passive. Hispanics are portrayed as sexual and scandalous. If these reductions help in promotion, advertisers assign such portrayals to that specific group of people. Ads typically use cultural cues to describe who specific products are for, but using these cues perpetuates the stereotype and slows social progress. Hispanics, for example, are homogeneously bound into a culturally defined niche. "Latinos—be they Cuban, Mexican, or Puerto Rican—came to be identified in the marketing sense as a nation

within a nation, possessing a distinct culture, ethos and language. They become identified as Spanish-speaking" (Christians et al. 2011, 158). Differences within ethnic groups are reduced for the purpose of marketing efficiency.

3. *Representing*: What distinguishes a group of consumers from a group of citizens? Can success in appealing to one hurt the other? Is there an ethical way to construct both "realities"? How might the content of advertising change when representing a group vs. marketing products to it? The issue is complicated by the fact that the commercial media landscape is designed to attract those with "consumption potential."

Marketing responsibly to a diverse group can be difficult. Successful advertising requires targeting toward a group's characteristics and selling that cluster as a product. The almost impossible challenge is for culturally specific marketing to promote the human dignity of the targeted group. Advertising's language of marketing, of business-building, tends to obscure the language of human agency unless there is a total commitment to the ethical principle of human dignity.

The "Mind" campaign succeeded because it communicated the shared humanity of a group traditionally marginalized within American higher education. Despite the UNCF's early support from white industrialists who in some ways sought to shape its message to their own political views, especially in opposition to Roosevelt's New Deal, Young & Rubicam's work tapped the educational values promoted by the HBCUs on their terms. While the UNCF's focus has broadened over the years as its influence has grown, the pithy headlines of its public service announcements continue to connect the distinct challenges minority students often face to society at large, thereby affirming both their equality and value. Promoting human dignity is the genius behind the Ad Council's ongoing UNCF campaigns, and its spectacular achievements are models for advertising as a whole.

VIRTUE ETHICS AS ALTERNATIVE

Virtue ethics has a long tradition in philosophy, since the days of Confucius (551–479 B.C.) and Aristotle (384–322 B.C.). Despite the major contributions to ethical theory and professional morality made by virtue ethics, communitarianism calls for a new generation of media ethics that is more explicitly multicultural. The complexities of ethnic diversity point to the limitations of virtue ethics and recommend communitarian ethics instead. There is no magic answer for bringing ethnically diverse communities into their own, but communitarian ethics opens the most fruitful pathways.

For virtue ethics the important issue is living well, developing capacities that are distinctive to us as human beings. For Confucius and Aristotle, the question is what dispositions or virtues I should acquire. They become settled over time through education and habit, and together are the character traits that we need to be exemplary human beings. Our character according to Aristotle is the ground of our practical wisdom. *Phronesis* as he called it, is "the disposition that allows us to deliberate correctly not in general but in a given situation" (Sanders 2003, 38). In Aristotle's words, "virtuous conduct gives pleasure to the lovers of virtue" (*Nicomachean Ethics*, 1099a: 12) "because their desires are in harmony with their reason" (Sanders 2003, 16; cf. 27–39).

Virtue ethics explains a great deal about the UNCF and the Advertising Council. Frederick Patterson insisted on a cooperative approach in founding it. Forest Long of Young & Rubicam made a strategic decision about the campaign theme that undoubtedly reflected his character. Other executives over the history of the Advertising Council promoting pro bono work were probably motivated likewise. It is possible that some developers of Spanish-language advertising have not reduced the Hispanic population to consumers but have wanted their culture to flourish. However, a transformation of packaging, stereotyping, and representation will not be accomplished by individual decision-makers. Even if the numbers of virtuous media executives, writers, and programmers were multiplied, the institutional policies and social structures that make ethnic diversity difficult would remain in place.

Communitarian ethics likewise calls for courageous leaders in the media who do not see ethnic audiences only as markets. Communitarianism applauds those who reject stereotypical language. Good leaders are expected to make a difference in company practices. But communitarian ethics shifts the focus to the audience, to ethnically diverse communities themselves. When advertising devalues cultures and exploits them, the primary challenge is for those communities to resist and redefine themselves. Like preventive medicine, when body life is healthy, attacks on it have less impact. When dialogue internally is strong, negative messages from without do not penetrate a community deeply or permanently.[10]

Paul de Silva, President of Canada's A4One Media, promotes the communitarian ideal (2009, 51–55). As the host of the CBC television series "Neighbourhoods" on Toronto's multicultural communities, he complains that Canadian television does not reflect the ethno-cultural diversity of Canadian society. He emphasizes the importance for democracy of all people speaking in their own voice regardless of cultural background. But "barriers created by a legacy of racism and exclusion and the particular economic realities of television in Canada," severely limit access to the public media, even though Canada is "an officially constituted multicultural society" (2009, 51).

De Sliva endorses conscious efforts to increase the presence of what he calls "racialized communities" in advertising, and in entertainment such as CBC's *Little Mosque on the Prairie* and Omni/Rogers's *Metropia*. He calls for the Canadian Association of Broadcasters to assist in training its members and to provide resources for program production. But in communitarian style, he emphasizes the importance of developing alternative infrastructures within professional associations so diversity can be rich. He sees lobby groups as representing the issues.

He calls for sustainable discourse within ethnic communities on solutions and alternatives.

De Silva knows that individuals with power are responsible and that media transmissions must be held accountable. But the focus throughout A4OneMedia is on interactive communication, on the ethnic groups' identity and belonging. Overcoming a sense of exclusion and marginalization within racialized communities is the overall task of democratic life in communitarian terms. In this spirit, the "U40 World Forum" has issued its "Vision for 2030," affirming that cultural diversity is crucial to human progress. With support from a wide range of professionals in thirty-four countries, the U40 World Forum highlights the active involvement of civil society in achieving this vision.[11]

CONCLUSION

Despite some shortcomings, public service advertising is preeminently communitarian because it "mobilizes the public to take action for the good of the community" (O'Barr 2006, 1). Public service advertising uses marketing strategies developed for selling commercial products and services to persuade citizens to act in society's interest, both for solving problems and for enhancing its quality.

The United Negro College Fund is a classic example of advocacy in communitarian terms. Inspired by a concern that communal life prosper, the Ad Council became involved in the UNCF during the social upheavals over civil rights. Such public service campaigns are an important dimension of advertising's history and continue to manifest the communitarian ideal on both the local and national levels.

NOTES

1. Smokey Bear and his famous slogan, "Only You Can Prevent Forest Fires," began in 1944. Smokey Bear is "one of the most recognizable figures in America, ranking alongside Mickey Mouse and Santa Claus. 99% of Americans recognize Smokey" (O'Barr 2006, 15).
2. For classroom instruction, television and print ads are available online at "A Mind Is a Terrible Thing to Waste" or <http://www.UNCF.org> and elsewhere. For four ads rated the best, see <http://www.ilovetvcommercials.com.psa3>.
3. The full text of the article is reprinted in both Goodson 1991 (Patterson's autobiography) and Gasman 2007 (Appendix A). An electronic version of the document is also available for download directly from the UNCF web site, at the following URL: <http://www.uncf.org/history/default.asp>.
4. *Plessy v. Ferguson* is the landmark Supreme Court decision in 1896 that upheld the constitutionality of racial segregation. Segregation even in public accommodations such as the railroad was permitted under the doctrine of "separate but equal."
5. See Omachonu and Healey (2009) for an analysis of minority ownership and communitarianism's role in achieving it.
6. "Capacity-building programs" refer to a category of financial support given to nonprofit organizations—in this case the HBCUs—to increase their effectiveness and fulfill their mission.

7. A recent example of transnational work on public service advertising is Lannon (2008). He explores this genre in the context of the United Kingdom, where the British government is the third largest advertiser by pounds spent.

8. Stefan Landsberger (2009), an expert on historical propaganda in the People's Republic of China, adds a global perspective by examining the role of public service announcements as extensions of a propaganda tradition. Their social purposes reflect that legacy, though mixed with advertising benefits for firms that sponsor or underwrite their creation. Among other insights, Landsberger recognizes that PSAs are often disregarded by viewers if they resemble traditional commercials. In prior decades they were typically trusted by Chinese viewers, but are now usually ignored.

9. Báez (2008) documents that Latina/os "are increasingly desired as a niche by transnational industries" (258). Thirty-eight million Latina/os in the United States saw their purchasing power increase 30 percent between 2003 and 2006, triggering substantial growth in Hispanic advertising.

10. "Dialogue" is interactive but oriented to verbal, unit-by-unit, rational exchange. The "Mind" campaign and the others sponsored by the Ad Council are visual communication. For an adequate analysis of the way "human visual behavior" works in professional practice and everyday life, see Newton (2001, ch. 2) and Williams and Newton (2007). The visual is "a form of human experience with primal and symbolic components that affect and shape our lives in profound but often imperceptible ways" (105). The photographic image "resulting from observer–observed interaction" assumes "a place in reality formation" based on "yet other heart and minds—those of anyone looking at the image" (Newton 2001, 44). As Newton and Williams (2007) describe the ways the human mind processes visual images, the ethics of representation takes on complexity and depth beyond our mainstream linear models (see Newton 2001, chs. 4–5, 8).

11. Established in Paris in June 2009, the U40 World Forum includes cultural professionals, civil society activists, members of national commissions for UNESCO, government representatives, and university professors.

REFERENCES

Aufderheide, Pat, and Clark, Jessica. n.d. *The Future of Public Media*. A Future of Public Media Project. Funded by the Ford Foundation, 1–13. <http://www.centerforsocial-media.org>.

Báez, Jillian M. 2008. "Mexican (American) Women Talk Back: Audience Responses to Latinidad in U.S. Advertising." In Angharad Valdivia, ed., *Latina/o Communication Studies Today*, 258–81. New York: Peter Lang.

Berger, Warren. 2000. "Source of Classic Images Now Struggles to Be Seen." *New York Times*, November 20, F6.

Brooks, Dwight E. 1995. "In Their Own Words: Advertisers' Construction of an African-American Consumer Market, the World War II Era." *Howard Journal of Communications* 6 (1–2) (October): 48.

Chambers, Jason. 2009. "A Mind Is a Terrible Thing to Waste: The Advertising Council, the United Negro College Fund, and Educational Access for African Americans." In O. Vernon Burton and David O'Brien, eds., *Remembering Brown at Fifty*, 105–16. Urbana: University of Illinois Press.

Christians, Clifford, Fackler, Mark, Richardson, Kathy Brittain, Kreshel, Peggy, and Woods, Robert. 2011. *Media Ethics: Cases and Moral Reasoning*, 9th ed. New York: Pearson Allyn and Bacon.

Clark, Jessica, and Aufderheide, Pat. 2009. *Public Media 2.0: Dynamic, Engaged Publics*. A Future of Public Media Project, White Paper, funded by the Ford Foundation, 1–43.

de Silva, Paul. 2009. "Television, Public Sphere, and Minorities." *Media Development* 4: 51–55.

Freire, Paulo. 1970. *Pedagogy of the Oppressed*. New York: Seabury.

Fujinaka, Mariko. 2000. "United Negro College Fund." *Encyclopedia of Major Marketing Campaigns*, 1823–1827. Detroit: Gale Group.

Gasman, Marybeth. 2007. *Envisioning Black Colleges: A History of the United Negro College Fund*. Baltimore, Md.: Johns Hopkins University Press.

Goodson, Martia Graham, ed. 1991. *Chronicles of Faith: The Autobiography of Frederick D. Patterson*. Tuscaloosa: University of Alabama Press.

JBHE Foundation. 2004. "Endowment Wealth: The Huge Disadvantage of the Black Colleges." *Journal of Blacks in Higher Education* 44 (Summer): 28–29.

Landsberger, Stefan. 2009. "Harmony, Olympic Manners, and Morals—Chinese Television and the 'New Propaganda' of Public Service Advertising." *European Journal of East Asia Studies* 8 (2): 331–55.

Lannon, Julie, ed. 2008. *How Public Service Advertising Works*. London: World Advertising Research Council.

Lowery, Mark. 1994. "50 Years and Going Strong: The Nation's Largest Scholarship Pool for Black Americans Celebrates its 50th Anniversary, While Bracing Itself for Future Change." *Black Enterprise* 25(2): 132.

Lutz, William D. 1977. "'The American Economic System': The Gospel According to the Advertising Council." *College English* 38 (8): 860–65.

Lykins, Daniel L. 2003. *From Total War to Total Diplomacy: The Advertising Council and the Construction of the Cold War Consensus*. Westport, CT: Praeger.

Newton, Julianne H. 2001. *The Burden of Visual Truth*. Mahwah, NJ: Lawrence Erlbaum.

O'Barr, William M. 2006. "Public Service Advertising." *Advertising and Society Review* 7 (2): 1–17.

Omachonu, John O. and Healey, Kevin. 2009. "Media Concentration and Minority Ownership: The Intersection of Ellul and Habermas." *Journal of Mass Media Ethics* 24(2–3), 90–109.

Patterson, Frederick D. 1943. "Would It Not Be Wise for Some Negro Schools to Make Joint Appeal to Public for Funds?" *Pittsburgh Courier*, January 30.

Pluviose, David. 2006. "Presidents Bush, Clinton Reach Out to Katrina-Devastated HBCU's Through 'Wave of Hope' Campaign." *Diverse: Issues in Higher Education* 23 (15), September 7.

Roach, Ronald. 1999. "UNCF's Gray Way." *Black Issues in Higher Education* 16 (September 30): 18.

Sanders, Karen. 2003. *Ethics and Journalism*. London: Sage Publications.

Stuart, Reginald. 2009. "UNCF Wrestles with New Economy, Old Issues." *Diverse: Issues in Higher Education* 26 (6), April 30.

Taylor, Charles K., et al. 1994. *Multiculturalism: Examining the Politics of Recognition*. Princeton, NJ: Princeton University Press.

Tucker, Shuana K. 2002. "The Early Years of the United Negro College Fund, 1943–1960." *Journal of African American History* 87 (Autumn): 416–32.

UNCF. 2011. Annual Report. *A National Commitment: 40 Years of Putting Minds to Work.* <http://www.uncf.org>.

"UNCF Launches African American Education Campaign." 2007. *Sacramento Observer*, 44 (20), May 3–7, G3.

Valdivia, Angharad. 2003. "Salsa as Popular Culture." In Angharad Valdivia, ed., *A Companion to Media Studies*, 399–418. Oxford, U.K.: Blackwell Publishing.

Williams, Rick, and Newton, Julianne. 2007. *Visual Communication: Integrating Media, Art, and Science.* Mahwah, NJ: Lawrence Erlbaum.

PART III

Entertainment

CHAPTER 11

⚹

Deep Throat and the Ethics of Mediated Sex

Had this book been titled, "The One Thing You Need to Know about Great Sex," sales would be ten times greater, at least in university bookstores. But not a single university instructor would put it on a reading list, despite the upsurge such a title would bring to enthusiastic reading of class assignments.

Everybody takes an interest in sex. Few people are satisfied with their sexual potency, and many imagine their lives would be happier—their spirits lighter and their moods cheerier—if sex were better for them.

Into this cauldron of desire and deprivation comes an industry of producers, writers, talent agents, marketers—purveyors of mediated sex who are all essentially offering the same title—"The One Thing You Always Wanted to Know about Sex." Even if we used such a title to entice you to read these pages, you would know that we had stolen it from 10,000 prior productions.

The film *Deep Throat* is now a museum piece, a relic of the sexual revolution. Yet it represents a cultural icon, standing in for all the films, books, and magazines that brought to an end American silence about sex and introduced a creative, open, and surely abusive conversation concerning humankind's best unkept secret. Produced in 1972 by Lou Perry, the film starred a then unknown actress named Linda Lovelace and a third-tier actor, Harry Reems. Director Jerry Gerard found Reems doing bit parts in the National Shakespeare Company, and Lovelace came to the film likely coerced by her husband Chuck Traynor, who handily pocketed Lovelace's $1,250 fee. If reported revenues are accurate (do you believe mafioso accountants?), *Deep Throat* was the most profitable film of all time. If not that, it is still one of the most famous. The *New York Times* cited it as the progenitor of "porno chic." Its title will live forever as the pseudonym chosen by *Washington Post* editor Howard Simons for the Watergate investigation source, W. Mark Felt, whose confirmations and advice to reporters Woodward and Bernstein toppled the Nixon administration. *Deep Throat* was rated X by the MPAA for oral, anal, and vaginal sex acts.

If you expect this chapter to be a rant against skin flicks, we are going to surprise you. Our first witness will be the distinguished professor at Harvard Law, solicitor general of the United States, and state supreme court justice. His credentials to address the topic (of free speech, not porno chic per se) are manifold, and the country has often depended on his wisdom.

The eminent Charles Fried articulates the classical liberal position that the varieties of sex one engages in should be the result of personal choice as long as those choices do not infringe on the rights of another. For consenting adults, the state, even the cultural mores that undergird state authority, should have no decision-making power. Fried (2007, 59) echoes John Rawls's notions of justice as fairness when he insists that all of us have the right to choose our values and sexual practices as long as those choices are consistent with the rights and capabilities of others making similar choices.

Sex slavery, then, could not survive scrutiny, nor could the widespread practice of parents arranging the nuptials of children, taking from them the choice of marrying at all. Urban prostitution-rings, the kind described in Luke Bergmann's *Getting Ghost* (2008), present a kind of unfair bargaining platform with intimidation and drugs the pressure points. But commercial sex per se should pose no inherent problems, provided all parties can negotiate freely. According to Fried, Amsterdam's sex trade does it right.

Fried's chapter on sex begins with a quotation that smacks of animality only because of the rhetoric a dominant culture has built around ideals of heterosexual monogamy as the norm. "Love is nothing but the exchange of two fantasies and the contact of two epidermises" (2007, 124). What could be more practical and morally innocent?

In Fried's political climate, sex should be a commodity of exchange not unlike other vital human services subject to government regulation. Addictive drugs are rightly certified by federal overseers. Doctors are licensed. Universities are granted the right to issue degrees by agencies that certify that those degrees meet established thresholds of human knowledge. If all this can be regulated by government, let government appropriately regulate the sex trade, he argued.

If you want to build a house, you need a permit. Not just any structure is permitted. Economies related to sex should likewise be free to establish value on level playing fields where bidders are protected from exploitation but not from stupidity or desire, these being the motivations for all kinds of questionable transactions, from fast food to overpriced coffee. Media sex, so much safer than physical contact, deserves wide berth and infrequent regulation, roughly akin to the open climate that *Hustler* publisher Larry Flynt has made his personal crusade. The state has minimal reason to regulate media sex and nearly no capacity. Witness the difficulty of prosecuting antipornography laws today. Better to permit liberty and personal choice than to suppress, which eventually leads to residual problems and proliferation of crime. Consensual sex is "just about as close as you can get to the irreducible heart of self-ownership" Fried insists (2007, 125). Fried notes that communitarian critics of an open marketplace for sex wrongly judge sex to be a trust granted by the culture/state for use as prescribed (2007, 138–39).

Joining Fried in celebrating an open marketplace for sexual material are contemporary anticensorship feminists and public advocacy agencies such as the American Civil Liberties Union (ACLU). Feminists have been divided on the value and deficits of pornography since the 1970s when antipornography feminists worked toward restriction in Minneapolis and Indianapolis. Neither effort succeeded. In the wake of these failed projects, another voice of feminism began to advocate the value of pornography as a form of liberation for women, particularly lesbians, who rejected old stereotypes of pornography hurting women (who are not that weak) and, after all, many women choose to find and articulate their own sexuality through media. One of those product lines, the Black lace series, achieved some market success as pornography "written by women and marketed to women" (Wyatt and Bunton 2009, 154). Femme Productions, begun by former pornography actress Candida Royalle, provides an "emotional context and motivation for sex" (Berger, Searles, and Cottle, quoted in Wyatt and Bunton 2009, 154.) Women should support these projects, advocates claim. In the absence of any definitive social science data proving a connection between pornography use and illegal behavior, the ACLU insists that government has no role in proscribing sexually oriented media. To open that gate, even a little, is to permit a vocal minority to impose "their personal political or moral values on others" (ACLU, quoted in Wyatt and Bunton 2009, 153).

Old Kantian notions that prolific sex is bad and duty requires puritan restraint—that is now the butt of jokes, not a seriously argued moral option. A universal law concerning sex? Ridiculous. We cannot even find standards for who, when, or how. Rather than trying the impossible, that is, finding common understandings of acceptable and "bad" mediated sex, the only option—and the choice that turns male hegemony back on itself—is "free and unfettered erotic expression" (Hardy, quoted in Wyatt and Bunton 2009, 154).

Fried gives intellectual clarity to the common and quite popular notion (especially among youth and young adults) that sex, which does not victimize, spreads no disease, and creates no underclass, is sex we should all be free to choose. Certainly the creation and enjoyment of films such as *Deep Throat* and the profit to be enjoyed from their reception falls into this cluster of economic transactions ...if Fried is right.

FRIED IS NOT THE LAW

Deep Throat was a sensational box-office success and established the structure of the porn-film industry. Although estimates on its total viewership and revenue vary, the 61-minute movie is conservatively estimated to have grossed more than $100 million from a $25,000 production cost (Lane 2000, 29).[1] Its stunning commercial success initiated porn as big business and spawned the "porno chic" trend of the early 1970s. However, *Deep Throat*'s debut also marked the point when pornography itself became narrative and generated a host of litigation that helped redefine pornography's legal standing in the United States.

In 1966 the U.S. Supreme Court established a new, three-part definition of obscenity: any obscene work had to be of "prurient interest" to an individual, "patently offensive," and "utterly without redeeming social value." Critics' fears were realized in the following years, when on that basis the Warren Court overturned more than thirty obscenity convictions. Emboldened in the late 1960s and early 1970s, pornographers created more graphic material, leading up to *Deep Throat*'s success in 1972. Yet by 1973 the high court was led by Chief Justice Warren Burger and composed of several new Nixon appointees. In *Miller v. California*,[2] the Burger Court adjusted the definition of obscenity, replacing the individual standard with a community one, and changed the "without value" clause to lacking "serious" value. This decision, along with prosecutions of several people involved in *Deep Throat*'s production, eroded the number of theaters willing to show adult films. As a result, the 1974 *Deep Throat* sequel found much less commercial success (Lane 2000, 27–32).

In other ways *Miller v. California* arrived too late to change the trajectory of the growing U.S. porn industry. Magazines featuring nudity, such as *Playboy* (1953) and *Penthouse* (1965), were already largely accepted by mainstream society. So-called "stag" films of earlier decades had spawned feature-length films. Estimates of the porn industry's profits during this period suggest that revenues rose sharply into the hundreds of millions of dollars (Bakker and Taalas 2007, 104). While the *Miller* decision made pornographers more cautious, it did little to reduce the amount of material. Instead, it prompted new avenues of distribution, with emerging technology the key.

Development and release of the videocassette-recording format in 1975–76 changed pornographic film distribution channels. Print pornography succeeded after *Miller* in part because it was relatively anonymous and easy to distribute. So too video allowed publishers to create, transfer, and distribute moving images with a similar low impact on communities—the new standard of obscenity (Lane 2000, 33). Videotape also reduced costs significantly over traditional film production, further increasing profits. Throughout the 1980s and 1990s, the pornography industry continued to use technological advances in the production and distribution of adult films. The increasing popularity of cable television provided new avenues to convey pornography directly into homes, making its consumption even more discrete. The development of DVD recording continued to decrease costs and facilitated production.

The development of the Internet and related technologies created another seismic shift in the distribution and production of pornography. Readily available pirated material plus the tube industry's plentiful free soft porn, was biting into the porn industries revenues, reported Jon Swartz in 2010 (Swartz 2010, 3B). The $13 billion annual industry sales went into a tailspin, so to speak. Moreover, the anonymity provided by accessing porn on the Web has continued to erode the few remaining public aspects of its consumption. Therefore, obscenity laws based on community standards may no longer be relevant, since technology has largely severed any links between porn and communities by reducing its consumption to a private, individual act.

Only with respect to children has the law been minimally effective. The Children's Internet Protection Act links federal funding for public libraries to filtering software that prevents children from exposure to blocked material. Adults using those systems may ask that filters be disabled. As soon as CIPA became law in 2000, a federal suit challenged its constitutional basis. But the Supreme Court finally determined that protecting children in public libraries was okay by the First Amendment, that the federal mandate did not threaten a librarian's professional judgment, and that the rights of adult users were not unduly encumbered by the process. The inconvenience to librarians did not outweigh the gains rendered to children who are saved from exposure to material beyond their level of maturity.

In an era when any inconvenience can become a federal issue, especially around the essential rights that we have come to define so carefully, the allowance shown by the court to the ambiguous and contested needs of children was a surprise. It is still true that in the United States, alongside a hard-won freedom to express nearly every expressible opinion, there is a residue of optimism that protects the welfare of children until they can capably exercise their individuality and choose for themselves, bearing also the full panoply of consequences. Children are inherently and legally communitarians in our framework of justice. Only adults may break ties of mutuality and with arbitrary abandon choose whatever the heart wants. If in the process anyone becomes a victim of his or her own choice, we say, almost lackadaisically—your problem, not mine.

VICTIMLESS? INNOCENT?

Has the law provided well for persons interested in buying mediated sex? Have media producers come close to providing consumers with surrogate experience reasonably close to what happens when sex happens? If so, all may be well. Why then disrupt the flow of goods? Customers want, suppliers provide. Win-win. But virtual sex is not as clean as that. We miss a big part of the wider moral landscape if we think that Professor Fried's open marketplace settles the matter.

Linda Lovelace tells her story, for instance, in stark moral terms, none of it with happy endings. Late in her short life (she died in 2002 at the age of 53), she claimed her husband Chuck Traynor coerced her performances. In 1986 Attorney General Edwin Meese conducted hearings on the pornography industry in America. Lovelace told the Meese Commission: "During the filming of *Deep Throat*, actually after the first day, I suffered a brutal beating in my room for smiling on the set...the whole crew was in one room, there was at least twenty people partying, music going, laughing, and having a good time.... I figured out of twenty people, there might be one human being that would do something to help me and I was screaming for help. I was being beaten.... Nobody, not one person, came to help me" (*Attorney General's Commission* 1986, 205). In the *Toronto Sun*, Lovelace claimed, "There was a gun to my head the entire time" (*Toronto Sun* 1981). The accumulated evidence of the Meese Commission reveals that Lovelace's sense of

Deep Throat star Linda Lovelace with husband and manager Chuck Traynor (© Condé Nast Archive/Corbis).

victimization was felt by many others caught up in the production of pornography (*Attorney General's Commission* 1986, 197).

Linda Lovelace was born Linda Susan Boreman in the Bronx in 1949. Raised in Catholic schools, Boreman gave birth to a son in 1969. Linda's mother convinced the young mother to give up the child for adoption, and subsequent emotional trauma led her to "escape" to New York City where she married Traynor in an ill-fated relationship. He introduced her to acting in short "stag" features. A year later, Boreman became the queen of porn in *Deep Throat*. A couple of sequels never matched *Deep Throat's* success, but stills in *Playboy* and *Esquire* kept her in the market.

In 1974, Boreman was arrested for possession of cocaine. That year her two biographies appeared, each an attempt to revive stardom. Six years later, after Boreman had befriended feminist activist Andrea Dworkin, she wrote *Ordeal* and changed her story dramatically. She portrayed Traynor as a pimp who threatened her at gunpoint, beat her often, and watched her so closely she could not escape. She told legal scholar Catherine MacKinnon: "I literally became a prisoner. I was not allowed out of his sight, not even to use the bathroom. He slept on top of me at night, he listened to my telephone calls with a .45 automatic pointed at me. I was beaten physically and suffered mental abuse each and every day" (MacKinnon 2006, 18).

Boreman parted ways with Traynor and married Larry Marchiano in 1974, had two children, and divorced in 1996, claiming Marchiano was alcoholic and abusive. Her second biography, *Out of Bondage* (1986), led to several speaking appearances in which she condemned the porn industry as callous and exploitative.

Tragedy dogged her. In April 2002 a car rollover put her in the hospital, where on April 22 life support was turned off with her grown children and ex-husband Marchiano at her bedside. In a 2005 interview, co-star Harry Reems categorically denied that Lovelace was ever coerced or threatened. Her antiporn crusade was just another attempt to get money. He said, "Nobody ever forced her to do anything" (Interview 2005).

ARE THERE THINGS WE SHOULD NOT KNOW?

Boreman's story is tragic. Outside of porn she found a life, but never peace. Relationships frayed. Her story turned and twisted such that we finish it wondering, what really happened? Clearly, happiness never did.

Should an industry be condemned because one of its children is lost?

We do not reckon harm this way. Children get lost riding school buses; we do not keep children home from school because of that. You can argue that Lovelace was an adult when she began her career in porn film. Not a wise adult, but still of age to make decisions and be responsible for the bad ones. She should have known the risks before she took the plunge, as we would say about any risk behavior. She did know, but she refused to count the cost.

Literary critic Roger Shattuck raises the question that offends postmodern sensi-bilities left and right. Are there things we should not know? (Shattuck 1996, 302) Even with respect to sex, he wonders. According to Shattuck, history has two meta-narra-tives: love and power. The love narrative undergirds belief in a moral universe where generosity and sacrifice make sense, where duty and justice are reasonable motives for conducting life. The power narrative seeks gain without calculating human cost. There remains little reason to consider other people, since death is inevitable. Take what you can from whoever is vulnerable to your advances, the power narrative teaches. Then Shattuck applies his two themes and big question to scientific inquiry. Is there scientific knowledge that so tilts the mind's capacity toward power that, even if the love theme were preferred, the will cannot disregard the temptation toward power. Does genetics, the code of life, represent such knowledge? With genetics, a beneficent researcher turned bad could commandeer the future of humanity. Or nuclear energy—its destructive capacity, its fear factor? What might working knowledge of human heredity or uranium's power lead "good people" to do?

Turning to literature, Shattuck wonders, are there stories so dark, so absent of love, so morally raucous that the telling of the tale opens portals in the heart that are best unexplored? We know from many hard cases of dangerous tales that "one man's vulgarity is another's lyric" (Harlan 1971). Indeed, no standard of "good" art and "bad" art can possibly survive the test of variable tastes and diverse opinions. Even then, is there any good or only evil to be harvested from the darkest tales? In Shattuck's rendering, the stories of the Marquis de Sade are so excessively heinous, so sexually and violently perverse, that we could do well to keep silent about them. You will note that the word "sadist" and "sadistic" derive from his name.

Sex is thrilling and most stories would be flat indeed if the dance of romance were purged. Sex is so human, its pursuit and fulfillment universally treasured. Sex is so connected to every other human motive that dramatic tension itself would disappear if sexless stories were vogue. Yet, Shattuck warns, are there things we should not know?

CAN SEX GET DULL?

Do we risk losing the thrill if we settle for silliness or worse, sexual violence? Anthony Lane's *New Yorker* review of *Deep Throat* and the 2005 documentary *Inside Deep Throat* suggests we do face that risk, and the *New Yorker* has never been called prudish. Lane notes that an early scene in the original has two memorable lines. "Helen," Lovelace says, "there's got to be more to life than just screwing around." But in fact there seems not to be. Well then, adds Lovelace, "There should be bells ringing, dams bursting, bombs going off." Finally, Lane admits that this pacesetting sex film fails at all points to do what mediated sex is intended to do: evoke sexual excitement. He advises, "The movie is numbly, grindingly, trouser-saggingly dull. If you want arousal, get in your car and drive very slowly over a speed bump" (Lane 2005, 97). His comments preview a recent VH1 "how to find love" spoof hosted by Flavor Flav, with Bret Michaels, Tiffany, and Chris and Adrianne. When a reporter asked Adrianne why such huge cable audiences care to watch this stuff, she replied, "They have no life" (Keveny 2008, D1).

It seems that you can grow weary of the world's most persistently fascinating topic. Of course, each viewer will have a different tolerance threshold and will know when to turn off the set, computer, or screen. Each one will know his or her personal capacity for the quick, senseless humor of porn. Each member of the vast worldwide audience for porn will make rational choices, give or take, to maximize benefits (arousal) and minimize losses (boredom with all of it, or the soul drenching perversity of its Sade side).

This way of thinking leads along the road paved by the open marketplace's most used asphalt: caveat emptor, let the buyer beware. It is the lyric sung by our first advertising and mass-marketing specialists, the operetta of capitalism. It is the dance of the entrepreneur, newly alive with a product never before conceived and sure to be gladly received at checkout counter displays everywhere. If it satisfies a need, buy. If not, don't. Caveat emptor. Professor Fried would say to each rational consumer, make your choice. It is a strongly utilitarian argument.

Utility seeks the greatest good for the greatest number. Utilitarians believe that pleasure and pain are the two great motivators. Bentham (1789) introduced his moral theory with clarity and precision:

> Nature has placed mankind under the governance of two sovereign masters, pain and pleasure. It is for them alone to point out what we ought to do, as well as determine what we shall do. . . . They govern us in all we do, in all we say, in all we think. . . . In words a man may pretend to abjure their empire: but in reality he will remain subject to it all the while. (p. 1)

Freedom to choose one's pleasures and pains apart from interfering courts (civil or ecclesial) is the social vision of libertarians worldwide, from Fried to Ayn Rand with many variances among them. Wendy McElroy, for example, concludes after hundreds of interviews with professional sex workers (1995, 1): "Pornography benefits women, both personally and professionally." She dismisses academic feminists with their porn-as-male-culture stuffiness along with feminist freethinkers who reckon as Fried does that rational beings deserve freedom of choice. Better and truer to social reality, McElroy says, is the stronger feminist claim: erotic experience is good for women. On balance, it offers happiness.

Utility is not immune to pain. In fact, pain must never have the stronger play in utilitarian ethical reasoning. If all users and producers of pornography emerged with Boreman's grim tale, even utility would condemn it. But Boreman is an anomaly, Most users enjoy it. How do we know, besides McElroy's interviews? Look at the market. Pornography offers excellent prospects for profitable distribution, no matter legal deterrents. Markets matter in utilitarian ethics. Markets measure extent, proximity, durability, and purity of universal sovereign pleasure. Is there a better way than this, anywhere?

Sissela Bok's small classic, *Mayhem*, asks why we so often choose entertainment that contains values and behaviors that cannot be universalized. Of all people, the Romans should have known better, she writes. Their entertainment devolved into making humans into beasts, forcing death on some and killing on others, all the while metastasizing their own moral malignancies until great Rome fell to woodsmen with axes and sledges.

Bok summarizes the four effects of media violence: increased aggression by heavier viewers; a strong sense of fear and social distrust; desensitization to real violence; and increasing appetites for stronger violence as lesser levels grow mundane. Anyone can look at these effects and say, "No, not me. I've got it under control." The "not me" response is so common that researchers have named it the Third Person Effect, and it appears to be just as common as the four effects of entertainment violence that Bok (1998, 56–58) identifies. Is pornography related sufficiently to violent programming to listen again to Bok's appeal? Many think so (Saunders 1996).

Rather more dramatic results show up in research done for the Attorney General's Commission. Desensitization, increased appetites, and real aggression were strongly correlated with exposure to pornography. This research plus the testimonies of leaders and producers in the pornography industry led psychiatrist Park Elliott Dietz (one of the commissioners) to write that "pornography is a medical and public health problem because much of it teaches false, misleading, and even dangerous information about human sexuality" (*Attorney General's Commission* 1986, 489). Dietz was moved by the appeal of Andrea Dworkin, who challenged the Commission to "go and cut that woman down and untie her hands and take the gag out of her mouth...for her freedom" (ibid., 492). Maybe there is more to this gig than late-night, no-fuss sexual fantasies. Even if the rhetoric sounds alarming (and Dworkin was happy to compare the campaign against pornography with the antislavery movement), people can be hurt by this stuff, some unawares.

Catherine MacKinnon asks, "How many women's bodies have to stack up here even to register against male profit and pleasure?" (MacKinnon 1993, 22). Her question challenges the notion that half of the people should have legal rights to vent sexual fantasies at the expense of the other half.

The Meese Commission came under intense criticism for the composition of the eleven commissioners, the one-sided testimony of those they met with, and for ninety-two recommendations, even though the gist of those recommendations would have tightened clamps on child pornography, a version of this seedy business no one supports. The Commission was certainly identified with social conservatism, and with the backlash against the 1970 Commission on Obscenity and Pornography, which found no antisocial effects (Wyatt and Bunton 2009, 151).

Clinical psychologist Mary Pipher describes adolescent girls "coming of age in a more dangerous, sexualized and media-saturated culture" than ever before (Pipher 1994, 12). She observes that "our culture is deeply split about sexuality."

Media value sexual spontaneity, while therapists and public health professionals warn that casual sex can kill (ibid., 206). In the middle of lived experience that can satisfy or swallow you whole, here is mediated sex that may desensitize you or frighten you or turn you into a hormonal Mr. Hyde. Who is to know until you have tried it, and then, perhaps, you are scarred or hurt. Pipher seeks a way out for girls becoming women, a way around the risks of hurt beyond repair.

These liberal, sophisticated, and concerned women want change in our social treatment of youth, judgments of beauty, and the pressure posed by media to understand sexual intimacy as just one more experience on the road to satisfaction. Women are clearly considered victims here, and the maleness of the highest courts protecting sexual media and pornography is duly noted. So far, however, no one has described how to protect from abuse and still permit Shakespeare on the shelves and Sarah Jessica Parker on the screen. That is because there are no clear lines to be drawn between mediated sex that is okay and mediated sex that is not okay. "I know it (obscenity) when I see it," wrote a confounded Justice Potter Stewart in 1964. No one has expressed the complexity any clearer since, save perhaps for Ellen Willis: "What I like is erotica, and what you like is pornographic" (Assiter 1993, 155).

COMMUNITARIAN SEX

Ayn Rand, rest easy. Readers, relax. Communitarian theory is not a thinly veiled academic attack on personal freedom. The big eyes of Big Brother are not watching you. Communitarianism is not a campaign against your opinion, your tastes, your craziness, or what loyal followers of the Grateful Dead call your riff against the great gorilla (Auxier 2007, 112).

Communitarianism recognizes that humans are sexual creatures who seek to celebrate and enhance sexual experiences through story and art. In many forms and levels of sophistication, the energy, passions, and satisfactions of sex must be rehearsed and made vibrant. This theme is one of a very few that cannot be allowed to die. To fortify sexual experience, communitarianism widens its social responsibilities and expands its accountability, while disallowing sex as a threat to vulnerable persons.

Is this possible? A prison guard was recently prosecuted for using his position to extract favors from a reluctant but finally compliant female inmate, who eventually complained to authorities. Not a single civil libertarian protested the guard's prison sentence; not a single objectivist (Rand's term) slammed the female prisoner for prudishness. The public simply responded, "About time, serves him right." Why? Because common sexual morality does not allow power to overrule permission or bribery to transact intimate favors. Good sex, right sex, is always consensual and freely chosen. Communitarianism adds that sexual intimacy, like any other human activity, carries social implications and ought to be accountable to moral norms. Sex that assaults or threatens is out of bounds. Sex that diminishes a partner's humanity is unacceptable. Sex that objectifies women, turns women from persons to icons or contractors, is sex that must justify itself—especially to women—before it receives social approval and sanction. Where sex threatens to obstruct even normal human development (as in pedophilia), communitarians work to turn desire toward pro-human purposes.

Mediated sex, the kind you buy in a book or video, is distinguished by its lesser impact and subtler effects. Mediated sex does not create children. It does not spread AIDS. It does not draw women into the agonizing decision to abort. Its impact is scientifically controversial, and likely quite varied in any case based on a person's chemistry and psychology. Judith Reisman has stated that porno-graphic visual images imprint and alter the brain, triggering an instant, involun-tary, but lasting, biochemical memory trail" (Reisman, in Wyatt and Bunton 2009, 159). But such remarkable claims often fail to convince in the same way Meese Commission data budged few open-market freedom fighters toward tighter media scrutiny. Communitarianism does not, in the end, stand with *Playboy* freedom in photo, word, moving image, or computerized verisimilitude. Even mediated sex must account for itself to community norms that treasure life and progeny.

Think about it. CBS-TV seeks ratings as any other business seeks customers and sales. The MMA (Mixed Martial Arts) offers a new (lower) level of sporting fun, so on to the Saturday night schedule it goes. Weird, bearded big dudes wail on weird, bald big dudes, and red becomes the golden color of higher ratings. While a few fans cheer, a chorus of TV critics protests this "human dog fighting" and calls on CBS to salvage what bottom-barrel respect it may have left. But markets soon turn MMA from marginal to mainstream. Critics grow quiet, the *real* big dudes (owners, producers, financiers) relax and enjoy. Are we adjusting, or losing our capacity to discern and adjust?

DEEP THROAT RECONSIDERED

Is it possible that mediated sexual themes and action can be funny, scary, odd, bizarre, oppressive—and still find communitarian approval? Yes, obviously. Linda Lovelace's stardom was none of that, because she did her thing with a gun at her head, she claimed. But in the hands of a better writer, someone with a hint of healthy sarcasm or a capacity for humorous social protest, the film could have been offbeat, illuminating, and educational, as prison dramas sometimes educate the uncaught about life behind bars. *Deep Throat* in better hands could have worked themes that smacked against stereotyping or sexual monotony. *Deep Throat* was not produced with brilliance, hence its themes did not sustain baseline values and its ongoing survival in rental markets is more about being first than about filmic greatness.

Communitarian emphasis on relationships insists that power, oppression, and extortion give way to reconciliation, participation, and cooperation. This trajectory is grounded in the commitment of each member of the community to the other, to life and prosperity, as best the group can define and discover it. These choices are as old as ethics itself. From the first stories and art, people have found their bearings in relation to others. Are those friends or competitors? Will they learn my language or shackle me? Do I trust them? Communitarianism stands in a long line of world-views that offer as a first principle: treasure the other, develop the relationship, bear the other with kindness, intend good not harm. Alternative approaches have long histories, too. The competitive model was captured in theoretical terms by social Darwinists who saw every human interaction as a grab for scarce resources in the inexorable quest of living creatures to keep on living. The power model was captured in the thought of the Friedrich Nietzsche, who calculated that "supermen" prosper while the weak and virtuous (those sickly love-your-neighbor types) are doomed to servitude. Of course, there is a model of human relationships that so fears the other that it seeks to kill it. We discussed that model in chapter 8. *Mein Kampf* is their handbook and Hitler their ideologue, though many other notorious bandits could stand-in for him. Nature will have its way is also a popular thesis made into an ethic for human interaction by Richard Dawkins's *The Selfish Gene*.

Where did Linda Lovelace find herself? What ethic shaped her life and the fictional character she made immortal (at least until now)?

Communitarians advise this: there is a better way. Find your identity in positive relationships that presume commonality and friendship. Work toward the prosperity of others as a means of sensing and finding, even securing, your own happiness. Go so far as to allow that your own happiness is not your life's great goal. Rather, the others whom you love—their happiness first—oddly but inexorably comes back at you, most of the time. When it does not—when you suffer—that too may be part of a life well lived. Suffering, if it comes, is not necessarily bum luck or a break in cosmic order. It may simply be the cost of a larger relational commitment: you may endure pain for someone you love.

Communitarianism with sexual feelings finds expression in ways that, at the end of the day, accrue to the joy and happiness of all, even the wider circle of non-intimates who nonetheless celebrate intimacy and support it with appropriate communal resources. This take on sexual happiness will engage longer-term commitments, no doubt, than many encounters played out in mediated sex, and with actual happiness at a higher, more sustainable peak. Good news, right? Sustainable sexual happiness. Not the kind Lovelace portrayed. Not the kind that celebrates physical hurt, emotional trauma, cynicism, or scars that do not heal. Not the kind where abandonment is a suitable endgame. Not the kind that hides everything from public view. Communities of love celebrate sex that is powerful, sustainable, and restorative. Such sex does not collapse under its own burden of hurt and disappointment. Sexuality rightly practiced gets better, not boring; it grows ever stronger in the direction of the other's needs and desires, finding every good reason to keep faith with the beloved and with the community to which that love owes its social moorings.

CONCLUSION IMPOSSIBLE

The Enlightenment, with its insistence on individual rights, created a vacuum at the very center of the person. Enlightenment individualism presumed that knowledge operated like a sculptor chiseling patterns on the brain. If media conveyed Fact A, the brain would record and possibly recall A. If democrats (who respect persons and their rights) were to make reasonable choices based on A, then A could not (indeed, should not) be denied them. Moreover, the neoliberal state should have no power to decide whether Fact A was significant to persons within its domain. Persons alone have that choice, the theory goes. Only that way is the power of the state ultimately accountable to free citizens capable of self-government.

Likewise, for sexual practice. Apart from broad-based rules embedded in a culture's traditions, sexual practice in the neoliberal state is "my call." Besides, in a complex culture perhaps no one knows what the traditions are. Despite our many opinions and varying cultures, no, you cannot show up to class naked. You must not engage in acts of intimacy in public. Low-stimulation acts are negotiable, but full-power sex is still private. These traditional rules are up for definition and criticism, but they change slowly and you know what they are, like them or not. The rest is up to you. Shakespeare and *The Titanic* both demonstrate that no authority can control actual sexual practice. In the end, sex is a personal choice.

Communitarians believe Enlightenment theory has missed the brass ring on many important issues, this one included. Rather than the Enlightenment's "personal choice," communitarians recommend a better epistemology of love.

In personal choice Enlightenment terms, I am a consumer out there to maximize benefit at minimum cost. To the extent that sex (or mediated sex) is judged a benefit, I pursue satisfaction without running afoul of the law, health, or social taboo (if I get tagged a playboy or girl, future engagements become more arduous, increasing cost and diminishing payoff). In communitarian choice— the epistemology of love—sexual satisfaction is a powerful incentive to nurture the very thing we want most, intimacy and belonging, a relationship of openness, commitment, and happiness.

This high goal is difficult to achieve, and often, our greedy side wants satisfaction now. So there is pornographic fantasy with no risk of HIV and no emotional baggage to hamper the next adventure. Communitarianism is about relationships that work in the direction of life and prosperity. Choosing pornography means not regarding those women or men as persons who deserve respect or regard. "They" are usable. "They" are expendable. "They" are the not-people, respect unrequited.

If we choose to experience and develop sexuality using the epistemology of love, our choice of book—magazine—film should point us in the direction of human respect and nurture of the other. That is not to say we are without strong personal desires, but appetites are framed in terms of relationships, not in terms of appetites. The epistemology of love recognizes social obligations and support networks that meet and sustain sexual pleasure and commitment. These obligations are not for old folks too tired to care, but for us, to the degree we are past adolescent whining and gratification now. We must nurture relationships of many kinds if we are to find happy, lasting love. To set our sights on this love, follow it, learn of it, and to incorporate it into our hearts and heads is a social process directly related to the relationship we care most about. Seeing Linda gasp in pleasure is a false icon of love. Contributing to Linda's own false-love world is to deny her our respect and to impoverish her own quest for love. We owe Linda some measure of love because she is a person. Using her is false-love, not-love, as her screen image is a false icon of love. We will choose wisely, if it is love we want, what media icons and images we enjoy.

And so communitarianism sets a direction and enables a better, safer, happier landing for love seekers—which includes nearly all of us. The "One Thing We Need to Know" may still be elusive, but its opposite—what we do not need to know—is clear as day.

NOTES

1. By way of comparison, Francis Ford Coppola's *The Godfather*—also released in 1972 and considered by the American Film Institute the twentieth-century's second-best movie—brought in about $134 million during its initial U.S. theater run, from a $7 million production cost.
2. *Miller v. California*, 413 U.S.15 (1973).

REFERENCES

Assiter, A., and Carol, A. 1993. *Bad Girls and Dirty Pictures: The Challenge to Reclaim Feminism*. London: Pluto Press.

Attorney General's Commission on Pornography: Final Report. 1986. Nashville, TN: Rutledge Hill Press.

Auxier, Randall. 2007. "A Touch of Grey." In S. Gimbel, ed., *The Grateful Dead and Philosophy*. Chicago: Open Court, 97–116.

Bakker, Piet, and Taalas, Saara. 2007. "The Irresistible Rise of Porn: The Untold Story of a Global Industry." *Observatorio* 1: 99–118.

Bentham, Jeremy. [1789] 1823. *An Introduction to the Principles of Morals and Legislation*. London: Oxford.

Berger, R. J., Searles, P., and Cottle, C. E., eds. 1991. *Feminism and Pornography*. New York: Praeger.

Bergmann, Luke. 2008. *Getting Ghost: Two Young Lives and the Struggle for the Soul of an American City*. New York: New Press.

Bok, Sissela. 1998. *Mayhem: Violence as Public Entertainment*. New York: Addison-Wesley.

Braiker, Brian. 2007. "Hard Times for the Porn Industry." *Newsweek,* February 7.

Fried, Charles. 2007. *Modern Liberty and the Limits of Government*. New York: W. W. Norton.

Hardy, S. 2000. "Feminist Iconoclasm and the Problem of Eroticism." *Sexualities* 3 (1): 77–97.

Harlan, John. 1971. Court Opinion in *Cohen v. California*, 403 U.S. 15.

Interview: Harry Reems. 2005. February 11. <http://www.moviehole.net/20056169-exclusive-interview-harry-reems>.

Keveny, Bill. 2008. "Realities of Love Revealed." *USA Today*, 16 May, DI.

Swartz, Jon. 2010. "Free Porn on 'Tube Sites' a Turnoff to Industry Profits," *USA Today*, 2 March, 3B.

Lane, Anthony. 2005. "Oral Values." *New Yorker*, February 28, 96–97.

Lane, Frederick S., III. 2000. *Obscene Profits: The Entrepreneurs of Pornography in the Cyber Age*. New York: Routledge.

MacKinnon, Catherine A. 1993. *Only Words*. Cambridge, MA: Harvard University Press.

———. 2006. *Are Women Human? And Other International Dialogues*. Cambridge, MA: Belknap.

McElroy, Wendy. 1995. *XXX: A Woman's Right to Pornography*. New York: St. Martin's Press.

Pipher, Mary. 1994. *Reviving Ophelia: Saving the Selves of Adolescent Girls*. New York: Ballantine.

Reisman, Judith A. 2004. Testimony before the United States Senate, Subcommittee on Science, Technology, and Space of the Committee on Commerce, Science, and Transportation on "The Brain Science Behind Pornography Addiction and the Effects of Addiction on Families and Communities," November 18. <http://www.drjudithreisman.com/archives/Senate-Testimony-20041118_Reisman.pdf>.

Saunders, Kevin W. 1996. *Violence as Obscenity: Limiting the Media's First Amendment Protection*. Durham, NC: Duke University Press.

Shattuck, Roger. 1996. *Forbidden Knowledge: From Prometheus to Pornography*. New York: Harcourt, Brace.

Stewart, Potter. 1964. Concurring opinion in *Jacobellis v. Ohio*, 378 U.S. 197.

Toronto Sun. 1981. "Linda Lovelace's Allegations." March 20. <http://www.spiritus-temporis.com/deep-throat-film-/linda-lovelace-s-allegations.html>.

Wyatt, W., and Bunton, Kris E. 2009. "Perspectives on Pornography Demand Ethical Critique." In Lee Wilkins and Clifford G. Christians, eds., *The Handbook of Mass Media Ethics*, 149–61. New York: Routledge.

CHAPTER 12

☙

Russell Means: Oglala Sioux Activist

South Dakota's Pine Ridge Sioux Reservation was a site of despair and frustration in 1973. Most of the adults on the reservation were unemployed, rates of suicide and alcoholism were high, healthcare was substandard, and poverty was relentless. But the newly elected tribal leader, Dick Wilson, seemed more interested in helping his family and friends than in improving conditions for those he was elected to serve. "There's nothing in tribal law against nepotism," said Wilson, who formed a tribal security force who watched, bullied, and even beat his opponents (Wilkinson 2005, 144). After an effort to impeach Wilson failed, his opponents rallied.

On the night of February 27, 1973, American Indian Movement (AIM) activists and several hundred supporters occupied the site of Wounded Knee, inside the Pine Ridge Reservation.[1] AIM leaders including Dennis Banks and Russell Means seized the local trading post, museum, church, and other buildings—along with several hostages from the few white families living nearby. Reservation participants set up roadblocks throughout the surrounding area, and teams led by Vietnam veterans began to patrol the countryside. Others alerted media outlets across the Midwest to the occupation. By the following morning, the FBI, Bureau of Indian Affairs (BIA), and representatives of several other federal agencies surrounded Wounded Knee. A siege had begun.

Wounded Knee was chosen because it was the site of the last armed conflict between American Indians and the federal government, where in 1890 the U.S. Seventh Cavalry killed over 150 Lakota women, children, and men. According to Means,

> Wounded Knee would always remain the haunting symbol of the white man's murderous treachery and of our nation's stoic grief. At Wounded Knee, on ground consecrated with the blood of our ancestors, we would make our stand. At Wounded Knee, as nowhere else, the spirits of Big Foot and his martyred people would protect us. (1995, 253)

Media coverage exploded. Journalism crews from a multitude of American and international organizations soon arrived only to discover that what had appeared to be a sudden, even shocking, takeover by AIM had deep roots in contemporary and historical events. As Robert Allen Warrior notes, "One of the first lessons journalists learned at Wounded Knee, and they came in droves from around the world, was that they were arriving very late to a story that had deserved their attention much earlier" (1997, 69). The previous year, Russell Means and Dennis Banks led the Trail of Broken Tears caravan across the United States to Washington, D.C., where they occupied the BIA's offices in an effort to make the Nixon administration consider twenty key demands for American Indians. That fall, Means and others organized rallies in Scottsbluff, Rapid City, Custer, and Sturgis, South Dakota. In Custer, a white man, David Smitz, was acquitted of killing an Indian named Wesley Bad Heart Bull even though he had confessed to the crime.

Any initial hopes for an efficient resolution at Wounded Knee dissipated as the occupation ground into a standoff. South Dakota senators George McGovern and James Abourezk arrived to negotiate, but left without success. Little progress was made between the parties, although all hostages were soon released. (In a television interview during the siege, all of those detained at Wounded Knee denied they were held against their will.) AIM asked for enforcement of the government's 1868 treaty with the Oglala Sioux, but federal agents refused.

When supplies within Wounded Knee started to dwindle, small shipments of food, medical aid, ammunition, and other provisions were dropped into the site by plane and smuggled in on foot. Small arms fire erupted regularly between the two groups; protesters used shotguns and rifles while federal forces had armored personnel carriers. Activists inside the sandbag embankment declared Wounded Knee an independent Oglala nation and began issuing passports in Lakota.

Over the following two months lawyers, negotiators, and other representatives for both sides gradually moved closer to an agreement. Meanwhile, on March 26, U.S. Marshal Lloyd Grimm was shot and paralyzed from the waist down. On April 25 and 26, respectively, AIM supporters Frank Clearwater and Lawrence (Buddy) Lamont were fatally shot by federal agents. Fearing even more violence, Oglala elders and federal negotiators came to an agreement in the first week of May whereby AIM protesters would stand down in return for hearings on the 1868 treaty and on grievances against the BIA. On May 8, after 71 days, AIM and its supporters withdrew peacefully from Wounded Knee.

The standoff was over, but its consequences echo still today. For the first time in history, the same story appeared every night on network television for ten weeks. Such saturation coverage was not repeated again until the 1991 Gulf War, "Operation Desert Storm," and later with the trial of O. J. Simpson in 1995. Although it produced little political or economic benefit, Wounded Knee is considered a tipping-point in American Indian history. After nearly two centuries as U.S. citizens, Native Americans began establishing their voice. The protestors and their supporters at Wounded Knee confirmed that "we are Indians; we should be who we are." Although the leaders' decisions and actions during the occupation were often controversial, Wounded Knee sparked a communitarian revival of Native American languages, culture, religion, and education.

Russell Means (© Bettmann/CORBIS).

LIFE AND ACTIVISM

Russell Means was born in 1939 at Pine Ridge, the eldest son of Walter Means and Theodora Feather Means. Both parents were educated in BIA boarding schools. In 1942 the family moved to Vallejo, California, where Walter began work as a welder in Mare Island's navy shipyard. Laid off after the end of World War II, the family briefly moved to Huron, South Dakota, but in 1946 returned to Vallejo where his father resumed work at Mare Island. Russell usually spent summers with relatives in South Dakota.

In 1954 the family bought a home in San Leandro, south of Oakland, and that Fall Russell entered San Leandro High School. As an outsider among the white athletes and social elite of San Leandro, he began to despair over the prevailing racism against American Indians of the 1950s. Means skipped school with increasing frequency, often ending up in trouble. Eventually his parents sent him to live with an uncle in Winnebago, Nebraska. He left school while there, and in 1956 he returned to San Leandro, graduating in 1958. He enrolled in Oakland City College, but soon dropped out and made ends meet dealing drugs. He subsequently moved to Los Angeles, then San Francisco, working as a printer, dance instructor, and night watchman. At one point Means even lived on the streets, homeless.

Things began to change in March 1964. Means joined his father in the first takeover of Alcatraz Island by Indians. The Bureau of Prisons had vacated Alcatraz Penitentiary the previous year, and American Indian organizers claimed the island under an 1868 government treaty that provided Indians with surplus government land. Although the claim was quickly dismissed in the San Francisco press and later in the courts, the incident revealed to him for the first time the potential power of direct action (Means 1995, 106). Subsequently, facing increased pressure to provide for his second wife and their unborn child, Means began to work as a traditional Indian dancer, traveling around the West and Midwest to participate in four-day *wacipi* (dances). In 1965 he returned to college at Iowa Tech, and in 1967 received a scholarship to Arizona State University in Tempe. Later that year he began work as director of management information systems at the Office of Economic Opportunity on the Rosebud Reservation in South Dakota. Soon, however, the Means family entered the BIA's relocation program for vocational training and job placement and headed to Cleveland, Ohio.

By April 1969, seeing the need to help Cleveland's local American Indian community solve problems they faced in an urban environment, Russell Means and several partners founded the Cleveland American Indian Center (CAIC). By the end of the year he fell in with Dennis Banks and Clyde Bellecourt, the Minneapolis-based founders in 1968 of AIM, and quit his accounting job to focus full time on Indian organizing. CAIC began a series of programs to benefit local Indians, from a burial program to scholarships, job training, and pension assistance. Means also established a second chapter of AIM based at the center, the Cleveland American Indian Movement.

Indian activism gained critical mass in the years leading up to Wounded Knee. Beginning in November 1969 American Indians occupied Alcatraz for nineteen months. Banks, Bellecourt, Means, and others from AIM spent much of the Fall 1970 occupying Mount Rushmore to assert a claim to the Lakota's sacred *Paha Sapa*, the Black Hills of South Dakota. That November Wampanoag activists publicized a day of mourning at Plymouth Rock, Massachusetts, to commemorate the "true" story of Thanksgiving. During the protest AIM members boarded the *Mayflower II*, a replica of the original ship, and covered Plymouth Rock itself in red paint. AIM's exposure—and notoriety—grew exponentially. It developed into a national organization with an official policy of helping other Indian groups only when invited in. Russell Means was elected the first national coordinator. He later recalled:

> Far more important than these personal experiences was the historic groundwork laid during the early 1970s. That was the period following Alcatraz, which had inspired Indian imaginations and brought young Indian militants together by making them realize they could call on other Indians for help. It was a time when there was a stream of national publicity about AIM's activities, the first examples in this century of Indians speaking up and standing up for themselves, of showing pride in their heritage by wearing distinctive everyday dress....I knew this was our time. Indians were breaking out everywhere; we were on the verge of something big, it was all going to happen soon—and I was part of it. (1995, 178)

In the wake of Wounded Knee, Dennis Banks and Russell Means, among hundreds of other American Indians arrested, each faced thirteen felony counts at trial. The Wounded Knee Legal Defense/Offense Committee, led by lawyers such as Larry Leventhal and Ramon Roubideaux, attempted to change the trial's focus from alleged criminal activities conducted by the AIM activists to the underlying political issues related to the 1868 Fort Laramie Treaty between the federal government and the Oglala, as well as Article Six of the U.S. Constitution. The government treaty, signed to end the war with Red Cloud, had promised the Lakota ownership of the Black Hills, as well as rights to use land in Montana, South Dakota, and Wyoming. In the end, presiding judge Alfred Nichol dismissed all charges on grounds of prosecutorial misconduct.

It was a Pyrrhic victory. Means and Banks were released (although a series of other charges remained pending for both men); but without a verdict no legal precedent was created. The court did not order the federal government to return vast parts of the West to Native Americans. Meanwhile, ongoing violence occurred at Pine Ridge.

Other trials of AIM activists continued in the following years. Dennis Banks was convicted on assault and riot charges for AIM's 1972 actions at Custer, South Dakota; before sentencing, he went underground. Russell Means continued to organize protests throughout the Midwest but was eventually convicted on charges relating to riots in Sioux Falls and sentenced to four years. In the months before his sentence began, he joined Dennis Banks's Longest Walk, during which thousands of supporters marched on Washington to press for redress against the government sterilization programs of Indian women. (Following enactment of the Family Planning Act of 1970, the Indian Health Service initiated a campaign to sterilize Native American women. Between 3,400 and 70,000 Native American women were sterilized in the 1970s, depending on whether you trust figures from the Government Accounting Office or Lehman Brightman, a Lakota who investigated this issue [Johansen 1998].) Means entered prison in 1978 and was released on parole in August 1979. During his term, he read philosophy widely, from Plato and Aristotle to Locke, Rousseau, and Marx. He also survived a fifth attempt on his life.

Upon his return to Pine Ridge, Means began to focus again on economic advancement of Indian nations, refashioning AIM into an enduring not-for-profit agency. With his brothers, he helped build the first independent health clinic on Indian lands at Porcupine, South Dakota. He prepared business plans to manufacture goods such as pick-proof locks, as well as to utilize geothermal energy on reservations. A grant from the Corporation for Public Broadcasting funded a new AM radio station for Pine Ridge. KILI radio spread throughout the Great Plains, beamed by repeaters from reservation to reservation. In 1981 Means' Black Hills Alliance founded Yellow Thunder Camp, a permanent traditional settlement deep in the Black Hills. Envisioned as a spiritual youth camp, the idea was that the whole community, rather than only a few dedicated individuals, would engage in teaching. In its early years Yellow Thunder drew international news attention and became a popular celebrity cause among American liberal groups. More importantly, it was a site where Indians could reconnect with the land and their roots. Despite numerous legal challenges by the U.S. Forest Service, the camp survived for six years.

In the mid-1980s Russell Means became more overtly involved in elective politics, despite his complaint that voting is a tool for majority rule, not real change (Means 1995, 441). Having lost the election for tribal leadership of Pine Ridge in the reservation's 1974 elections, he made a second attempt in 1984 on a political platform labeled True Revolution for Elders, Ancestors, Treaties, and Youth, or TREATY. Shortly before voting occurred, an Oglala executive committee removed his name from the ballot on the grounds of his South Dakota conviction. He appealed its removal to the Oglala Tribal Supreme Court and eventually won, but too late for the reservation's election process.

Soon after, Larry Flynt, the notorious publisher of *Hustler* magazine, contacted Means and asked if he would join him in a run for the Republican nominee for president that year. Flynt wanted to attract attention to First Amendment rights, and after consultation with other American Indian activists, Means agreed. The partnership soon broke down, however, and Means moved on. By 1987 party insiders invited him to seek the Libertarians' 1988 presidential nomination. Means campaigned through 46 states, opposing President Reagan's spending policies and Washington bureaucracy while advocating a platform of individual liberty, self-determination, and minimal government. In the end, Congressman Ron Paul edged out Means by three delegates at the primary convention. In 2002 he attempted unsuccessfully to get on the gubernatorial ballot in New Mexico as an independent.

One day in 1991 a Hollywood casting director phoned to ask if Russell Means was interested in a role in the upcoming film *The Last of the Mohicans*. He auditioned and was cast as Chingachgook, the title character. It was a revelation. Although he faced daily racist behavior among a few crew members on the set, Means saw that acting offered a new way to change society:

> I hadn't realized I was an artist until I became an actor. In Western civilization, actors, poets, painters, sculptors, musicians, singers, and other artists are always first to recognize the need for social change. After them come intellectuals who grab hold of their ideas and put them in a form educated people can understand. Finally, when the people who live and work on the land join in, a revolution has a chance of succeeding. I love being an artist—it fits in with being a revolutionary.
>
> The movies offered me something else, too—a better way to get messages about my people to the world.... Working from within that tremendous venue of expression, I could become an agent for change. (1995, 517)

More parts followed, including *Natural Born Killers* and the voice of Chief Powhatan in Disney's *Pocahontas*. He starred in the HBO documentary, "Paha Sapa: The Struggle for the Black Hills." He began to act in several television broadcasts, including such documentaries as "Incident at Oglala" and "Images of Indians." He narrated "Wounded Heart: Pine Ridge and the Sioux." TREATY Productions followed in 1993, dedicated to creating CD-ROMs, short films and documentaries, magazines, books, television shows, and animated children's series. The same year he recorded his first music album on Soar Records, "Electric Warrior."

In 1995 he followed up with "The Radical," released on his own American Indian Music Company imprint. Since then his creative career has been ongoing, notably including starring roles in *Black Cloud* (2004), a film about a Navajo Olympic Boxer, and *Pathfinder* (2007), a tale of Norse and American Indian conflicts in northeastern North America centuries before Columbus.[2]

Long known as a captivating orator, Russell Means also continued to lecture and teach around the United States and abroad. In 1995 he published *Where White Men Fear to Tread: The Autobiography of Russell Means* with Marvin J. Wolf. The book is now in its tenth printing. Its Appendix (545–54) also contains his most famous speech, "For America to Live, Europe Must Die." Given at the Black Hills International Survival Gathering in July 1980, it was widely reprinted in periodicals such as *Mother Jones*. In this major critique of the political left, Means decried the revolutionary potential of Marxism as a mere continuation of Eurocentric, linear thinking, the ultimate successor of Newton and Hegel. He argued that this tradition only served to further abstract spiritual existence: "Marx put Hegel's philosophy in terms of materialism, which is to say that Marx despiritualized Hegel's work altogether" (1995, 547). Europe's intellectual leaders created a conflict between *being* and *gaining*, the latter allowing Europeans to develop an expansionist culture. "Being is a spiritual proposition. Gaining is a material act."

For Means, real revolution lies in removing the rationality that led Europeans to an overemphasis on civilization (and subsequent denigration of indigenous peoples). For him, without this acknowledgement American Indians cannot rediscover their true place in the universe's natural order.

> There is the traditional Lakota way and the ways of the other American Indian peoples. It is the way that knows humans do not have the right to degrade Mother Earth, that there are forces beyond anything the European mind has conceived, that humans must be in harmony with all relations. The European materialist tradition of despiritualizing the universe is very similar to the mental process which goes into dehumanizing another person.... Terms like progress and development are used as cover words here.
>
> When I use the term European, I'm not referring to a skin color or a particular genetic structure. What I'm referring to is a mind-set, a worldview that is a product of the development of European culture. I want to hammer home this point. What I am putting out is not a racial proposition but a cultural proposition. There is no racism involved in this, just an acknowledgement of the mind and spirit that make up culture. Caucasian is the white term for the white race; European is the outlook I oppose. (1995, 551–52)

Widely praised for its rhetoric, "For America to Live" appeared in a 1993 edition of the *100 Greatest American Speeches*.

Means also continued to promote international activism for the rights of indigenous peoples worldwide. Already in 1974 he and other AIM members founded the International Indian Treaty Council (IITC) as an NGO directly linked to the United Nations. IITC's work included regular interaction at U.N. headquarters in New York. One of the results of this ongoing exchange was a four-day conference in Geneva, Switzerland on first peoples. Over 130 organizations attended, including 35 U.N. member states, and the meetings resulted in the formation of the U.N.'s Working Group on Indigenous Peoples. In 1985 Means traveled to Nicaragua to investigate the conflict between U.S.-backed Contras and Sandinista revolutionaries who took over the nation's government. His work there focused on documenting the plight of the coastal Miskito Indians. In September 2007 the United Nations passed the Declaration on the Rights of Indigenous Peoples (Agenda Item 68. 07-49830E 100907).

Viewing the U.N. declaration as the fulfillment of IITC's mandate since 1974, in December 2007 Russell Means led the Lakota Freedom Delegation to withdraw from all treaties and agreements between the United States and the Lakota people. The Delegation continues to insist on an independent, sovereign territory, named the Republic of Lakota—with Means officially the Facilitator. It is based on an 1851 treaty map covering parts of North and South Dakota, Montana, Wyoming, and Nebraska—including the Black Hills. The concept of a self-governing nation is considered to be affirmed by treaties, case law, and the Constitution.

Reaction to the withdrawal has been mixed at best among American Indian communities for a variety of reasons. Many American Indian leaders are especially hesitant to endorse withdrawal from treaties. However, Means and the Republic of Lakota continue to press for sovereignty, as well as diplomatic relations with other nations. In a 2008 interview by the *New Internationalist* magazine, Means commented that the withdrawal was inspired by the Declaration on the Rights of Indigenous Peoples, and because the United States was one of only four nations that voted against the measure[3]:

> In the 20th century we tried armed struggle again. It didn't work.... We tried protesting. We tried petitioning. We tried voting for Democrats. We tried the courts. We tried every way imaginable to try to get some kind of redress. We are at risk of disappearing as a people. The colonial apartheid system does not work for us. (Bauer 2008)

As he summed it up two years later while conducting a peaceful—though rhetorically bombastic—South Dakota "fish-in," ignoring the legal limits for catching fish to promote Indian rights: "You only have treaty rights if you exercise them" (Berry 2010).

Russell Means's focus on education has also evolved. After Yellow Thunder Camp closed in 1987, Means developed a total immersion pedagogy of education inspired by a visit to traditional Maori schools in New Zealand. The TREATY ("True Revolution in Elders, Ancestors, Treaties and Youth") Total Immersion School and Ranch, to be located on the Pine Ridge reservation at Porcupine, aimed to restore Lakota identity by focusing on the community's language, culture, arts, and oral tradition—what Means called the three Ls of education: look, listen, and learn (http://www.treatyschool.org). Means planned a greenhouse for the school that would be tended in part by students who would raise produce both to be sold and to be donated to local senior centers. And the nonprofit Open Hand Studios began creating an online system using oral wisdom and community-based learning to teach Lakota youth their language and culture. The aim of both was to raise young people who "thrive as engaged citizens grounded in, living out, and passing on their cultural values"—whether living on the "rez" or elsewhere (http://www.openhandstudios.org).

But Means has raised too little money so far to build and operate the school, and most Lakota parents cannot afford to send their children there. "We're losing our language, and nobody cares," Means complained recently. The momentum to develop the TREATY Total Immersion School and Ranch slowed in 2011 after Means was diagnosed with inoperable throat cancer (Garrigan 2011, B1).

POLITICS OF RECOGNITION

Wounded Knee and Russell Means's activism since then illustrate what communitarian Charles Taylor calls the politics of recognition. Based on democracy's commitment to providing everyone with equal access to the procedures of democratic institutions, Taylor asks, "Is democracy letting its citizens down, excluding or discriminating against them in some morally troubling way, when major institutions fail to take account of their particular identities?" (Taylor et al. 1994, 3). In what sense should our specific cultural and social features as American Indians, African Americans, Buddhists, Muslims, the physically disabled, or children, publicly matter? In principle, democratic citizens share an equal right to education, police protection, political liberties, religious freedom, and health care. Does each citizen's voice also need recognition? Should universities and colleges that are circumspect about equal opportunity in admissions and the classroom, for example, also provide cultural centers and specialized curricula for underrepresented students of color? Should Lakota schoolchildren insist on learning in their native language? According to Taylor,

> A number of strands in contemporary politics turn on the need, sometimes the demand, for recognition. Nonrecognition or misrecognition can inflict harm, can be a form of oppression, imprisoning someone in a false, distorted, and reduced mode of being. Due recognition is not just a courtesy we owe people. It is a vital human need. (1994, 25–26)

Taylor considers recognizing multicultural groups politically as one of the most urgent and vexing issues on the democratic agenda. As a professor of philosophy at McGill University in his native French-speaking Quebec, active in politics, Charles Taylor often debates the issue of recognition within the Canadian context. A fundamental dispute in Quebec, and at Wounded Knee and in Russell Means's activism, is over the politics of identity. And this foundational question about the character of cultural identity needs resolution for community life to remain vital over the long term.

Rather than shutting off cameras in fatigue at the end of the Wounded Knee standoff, happy the ordeal was over, and presuming the dispute had been resolved, communitarian ethics probes this event to consider the complex issue of recognizing people of color in democratic societies. Russell Means's various efforts to give Native Americans a voice and provide platforms for meaningful action are attempts to work out a multicultural politics. As its first president—though, by his own admission, sometimes confused at a young age about good leadership— Means saw AIM as a national stage for Native Americans to speak for themselves. The communitarian principle for AIM is not its political effectiveness as an organization, first of all, but whether it gives Native Americans the recognition they deserve in a democratic society. Quality education is a prime need in the Pine Ridge reservation, but Means is correct that this education must bring to life Lakota language and culture.

Introducing John Rawls's *Theory of Justice* (1971) and *Political Liberalism* (1993) helps to clarify Charles Taylor's communitarian perspective. Rawls (1921–2002) was the greatest American moral and political philosopher of the twentieth century. His "justice as fairness," argued against utilitarianism, leads him to a commitment to American Indian equality parallel with communitarian ethics. When situations are inherently unequal, statistical averages are unfair and appeal to the majority often gives lip service to the minority. Rawls recommends his classic "veil of ignorance," asking that all parties step back from real circumstances into an "original position" behind a barrier where social differences of race, class, gender, education, and age are suspended. Behind the veil, no one knows how he or she will fare when stepping into real life. In this state of imagined equality, Rawls argues, we inevitably seek to protect the weaker party and minimize risk. In case we emerge from the veil of ignorance on the wrong side of the tracks, priority goes to the most vulnerable.

Two principles will emerge as consensus during hypothetical negotiations in the original position (Rawls 1999, 379). The first one calls for an equal system of maximum political liberty for everyone. Each person must have the largest political liberty compatible with a like liberty for all. The second principle involves all social goods other than liberty and allows inequalities in the distribution of these goods only if they act to benefit the least advantaged members of society. For American Indians at Wounded Knee and Russell Means's activism, Rawls's original-position strategy ensures that minority rights are taken seriously; those rights are given equality instead of secondary status.[4]

As reflected in the first principle—equal liberty for all—Rawls advocates political liberalism. Communitarians have opposed his egalitarian democracy. Charles Taylor, for example, argues that Rawls's liberalism assumes an overly individualistic conception of the self. Democratic life cannot be reduced to individuals exercising autonomous choice (Taylor 1985, ch. 1). For Taylor and other communitarians such as Michael Walzer and Alasdair MacIntyre, moral outlooks are not the product of individual choice. The social values to which we are committed— "equality" in Rawls's case—are not invented by self-sufficient entities. Whatever has value arises among those sharing a certain form of life. Communitarian ethics centers on the complexities and narratives of everyday existence.

Rawls's political focus contrasts with the more wide-ranging sociocultural sweep of communitarianism. Rawls's "justice as fairness" emphasizes governance. He sees his two principles as applying to the basic social institutions—courts, government organizations, and markets. His concern is whether the law and policies that define the property claims and rules that make up the marketplace are just. Thus, Rawls became the intellectual father of a legal innovation, affirmative action. He appropriately received the National Humanities Medal in 1999 from President Clinton for "helping a generation of learned Americans revive their faith in democracy." Rawls distinguishes questions of how to live from constitutional and legal questions (1993, 11). He wants the latter "political conceptions" to go forward without paralyzing "comprehensive conceptions." In his words, "political liberalism moves within the category of the political and leaves philosophy as it is" (1993, 375).

Communitarian ethics includes the political dimension of geographical communities. Community discourse includes explicit attention to the problems and solutions of administering our common life. But communities are not primarily political. Robert Bellah et al.'s *Habits of the Heart* (2007, 71–75) speaks instead of "lifestyle enclaves" in which our identity and well-being are fashioned. The communitarian perspective includes communities of memory, as faith communities and ethnocultural groups often are. Community means personal interaction, where face-to-face life together nurtures civility and trust. Community also includes those educational systems where rewards and benefits are shared and classroom loyalties value the whole more than individual success. These various community formations are sometimes at odds with a commitment to public affairs, but are needed together for human flourishing.

Given communitarianism's dense understanding of human life, it is not fixed politically on a "well-ordered society" as is Rawls. Certainly communitarianism includes the Bureau of Indian Affairs, the tribal leadership of Pine Ridge, and the senators from South Dakota in its analysis of Wounded Knee. It pays attention to Russell Means's failed attempts to gain political office. It assesses AIM's political protests, such as its dispute with the government over the Alcatraz penitentiary. But beyond the political, communitarian ethics puts on the agenda narrative (news and documentaries and Means's films), religious life, indigenous arts, and cultural concepts such as tribal sovereignty. All of these dimensions of community life need to flourish.[5]

CIVIL DISOBEDIENCE AND SOCIAL PROTEST

Wounded Knee is a showcase event for understanding civil disobedience and news coverage or documentaries on social protest. The highly charged symbolic drama unfolding on Pine Ridge during early 1973 captivated news audiences in the United States and abroad. Opinions vary widely today over the accuracy and efficacy of news coverage of the siege, its aftermath, and origins. But as Robert Allen Warrior noted, a month into the occupation a Harris poll found that more than 93 percent of Americans were following events at Wounded Knee (1997, 71). "Although Wounded Knee climaxed a series of actions by American Indian activists," Robert Warrior observed, "it was really the first moment in which the press devoted sustained attention to Native issues" (1997, 69). As the AIM movement progressed through the 1970s and beyond, leaders like Russell Means and Dennis Banks continued to make press coverage a key organizational goal.

The moral dimension of our life together always needs nourishing, and prophetic leaders often use dramatic events to make the issues of justice transparent. All ethical systems accept civil disobedience, though in different degrees and in various formats. In healthy communities, the conscientious objector is welcome or at least taken seriously. Under these constraints, and when conditions are urgent, communitarianism endorses protest for social justice that honors civility.

Although civil disobedience at Wounded Knee led to anti-communitarian violence, the events were represented by a few reporters who thought in communitarian terms. NBC's Fred Briggs used charts and photos to describe the trail of broken treaties that shrank the vast Indian territory to a few small tracts. CBS's Richard Threlkeld understood that AIM really sought a revolution in Indian attitudes. ABC's Ron Miller got inside the daily experience on the Pine Ridge Indian reservation to see what was happening through the eyes of Pine Ridge citizens themselves. Although it frequently turned sensationalistic, AIM created a national stage from which the broadcast media could represent the issues with the clarity that enabled audiences to think and act responsibly.

The best documentary of the National Poetry Film Festival for 1990, *Ghost Dance,* sets AIM's 71 days in the context of the slaughter of Lakota Chief Big Foot and 150 of his people at Wounded Knee Creek on December 29, 1890, by the U.S. Army. Most of those killed were followers of the Ghost Dance religion, which believed the old way of life could be resurrected. In *Ghost Dance* the story of their journey came back to life and their dream was renewed on this location eighty-three years later. Earlier Dee Brown in his classic, *Bury My Heart at Wounded Knee* (1970), had described the relations of American Indians, tribe-by-tribe, to the federal government from 1860 to 1890. *Ghost Dance* opens a veranda on that historical record.

Native American feature films and documentaries continue to create encounters for social protest and justice. In 1992 Val Kilmer, of Cherokee descent and active in American Indian organizations, starred in *Thunderheart* alongside respected Indian actor Graham Green. Kilmer played an Indian FBI agent forced to confront the difficult legacy of his heritage when assigned to investigate murders on a fictional reservation near South Dakota's Black Hills.

The first feature ever produced by a Native American team was *Smoke Signals* in 1998. Released to near universal critical acclaim and winner of both the Filmmaker's Trophy and Audience Award at the Sundance Film Festival, the film was based on two short stories by Sherman Alexie that explored the lives of two young men confronting a history of alcoholism and abuse after the death of a parent. Other important documentaries from indigenous perspectives include Discovery Channel's *How the West Was Lost* and *Trail of Tears: A Native American Documentary Collection.*

Communitarianism makes room for values and beliefs alongside politics and economics. In this sense, these documentaries and feature films that engage our worldviews and call for their transformation give us direction for meaningful, long-term sociocultural transformation.

THE GOLDEN RULE

The way social protest has been represented in the media, from Wounded Knee to *How the West Was Won,* reminds us that communitarianism is normative. It shows us how to deal ethically with unrest, protest, and civil disobedience. Turned into an ethical principle, the communitarian ethos is reflected in the golden rule (cf. Battles 1996). "Do to others as you would have them do to you" is the ethical norm for acting and thinking in communitarian terms. In fact, almost all discussion of ethics in violent contexts refers to the golden rule as the best guide for morally appropriate action.

The rule of reciprocity between others and oneself seems unarguable, the natural way to live harmoniously in human community. But its brevity and simplicity obscure its radical implications. It proceeds from the assumption of human dignity; in thinking about and living the golden rule we regard others as basically like ourselves. Thus, when followed it produces a "community of good will." As an ethical principle for American Indian leaders and organizations, it rejects hostile actions and verbal abuse even under conditions of conflict and oppression. For media institutions, the golden rule promotes a world in which cultural diversity is embraced.

The Amish of Nickel Mines, Pennsylvania, captured world headlines after five schoolchildren were killed and five injured in a deranged murder-suicide in October 2006. The communal Amish were compassionate and forgiving, refusing to act out of revenge. They visited the killer's widow and family, and brought meals and comfort. On the day of his funeral, more than half of the mourners were Amish. They were gracious throughout, neither hateful or victimized. Out of the shock and trauma of the tragedy emerged forgiveness—freely, readily, authentically. Journalists were "astonished by what they heard and saw.... Amish grace soon eclipsed the story of schoolhouse slaughter" (Kraybill et al. 2007, 48, 54). The Amish response inspired news commentators and their audiences: "This is about living our lives with a courage that understands that survival lies in reaching out, not striking back" (55). "The core of Amish culture is community" (93) and the Amish of Lancaster County nurtured it, taught it in their schools, celebrated it in worship, and practiced it. Forgiveness was embedded in their culture, swift and obvious, not a calculated choice.

The Native American group that most clearly embodied the communitarian ideal operating through the golden rule was the Indian Ecumenical Conference

(IEC). Founded in 1969, for more than two decades this influential movement among American Indians worked for social change differently from the militant activists (Treat 2003). Instead of confrontations at Wounded Knee, the Northwest Coast Fish-ins, and the Alcatraz occupation, the IEC during the 1970s and 1980s promoted spiritual revitalization and social change from the grassroots. As noted above, Russell Means in his "For America to Live" address lamented the loss of spirituality among Native Americans. He argued that European Christianity had intruded on American Indian animism. That was one issue as the IEC gathered thousands of people each summer in the Canadian or American Rockies, but the overall concern was for reinvigorating the spiritual dimension of American Indian culture. The IEC was dramatically intertribal, promoting interreligious dialogue in the belief that indigenous peoples must offer their own solutions to social problems and could do so most effectively when their religious life was strong.

TRIBAL SOVEREIGNTY

Over the last two decades, American Indians have experienced a growing sense of tribal sovereignty. The passage of the Indian Gaming Regulatory Act (IGRA) in 1986 has contributed to it as casinos become successful legally and economically. And Indian sovereignty "has increasingly surfaced in environmental disputes between tribes and states over air and water quality standards; grazing; treaty-based hunting, fishing and gathering rights; and mining, to name a few" (Loew and Mella 2005, 102). The Supreme Court has repeatedly affirmed tribal sovereignty beginning with *Cherokee Nation v. Georgia* (30 U.S. 1), which in 1831 established the rights of Indian tribes to govern their own internal affairs as so-called "domestic nations." States are prevented from interfering with those rights. As the *Reporter's Guide to Native America* puts it: "The United States recognizes the tribes' right to form their own government, determine membership, administer justice, raise taxes, establish businesses...and regulate resources and the conduct of tribal members on tribal land" (Native American Journalists Association, n.d., 7).

But tribal sovereignty is a cultural matter far deeper than self-government. It means tribal identity, rootedness in history, and shared values within geographical boundaries. And this social philosophy is often misunderstood by reporters and misrepresented in the media. "For non-Indian communities whose futures intersect and intertwine with those of tribal communities, it is vitally important to understand the dynamics of how Native people view their sovereignty and the land" (Loew and Mella 2005, 102–3). With mainstream media generally reflecting a utilitarian and neutrality worldview, it is no wonder that Native Americans have been "sharply critical of news coverage about their issues," complaining that it often "lacks historical and cultural context." Tribal sovereignty "is rarely invoked and almost never explained" in the news media (Loew and Mella 2005, 103, 105). As *Wisconsin State Journal* reporter Ron Seely put it, "Today, when many of us speak of Wisconsin's Native Americans and their cultures, we hardly get beyond gambling and casinos and a litany of stereotypes" (2003, 1).

Communitarianism recognizes that beliefs about the world hold peoples together, and that ceremonies and religion and language are not marginal but central to a community's distinctiveness. Tribal sovereignty is not feared, but understood appreciatively. Communitarianism supports those indigenous media that reflect tribal distinctiveness. Whether reporting on air and water quality, sacred sites, gaming, or fishing and hunting rights, many local radio and newspapers typically begin and end with tribal sovereignty. *Indian Country Today*, both in print and online, is involved in ethnic issues on Indian reservations, but tackles human rights problems more generally, too. Native interpretations of politics, law, history, economics, and religion are rooted in a clear sense of place; the land embodies their identity and culture. The Lakota scholar Vine Deloria, Jr. resonated with tribal self-determination in publishing *Custer Died for Your Sins,* and it became the first of several essential texts for developing American Indian studies as an academic discipline. Mohawk author Joel Monture, a former professor of the Institute of American Indian Arts and expert on indigenous beadwork, has published an acclaimed children's book, *Cloudwalker,* that gives poetic voice to the challenges faced by Indian youth.

American Indian journalists have also reflected a communitarian philosophy. Tim Giago, an Oglala born on Pine Ridge, in 1979 became the first American Indian reporter in South Dakota journalism, with a weekly column in the Rapid City *Journal* called "Notes from Indian Country." (Now his column is distributed nationally online and in print by McClatchy News Services). In 1981 Giago founded the *Lakota Times,* the first independently owned-and-operated native paper in the United States. In 2007 he was inducted into the South Dakota Newspaper Hall of Fame, and on the occasion, James Carrier, the Rapid City *Journal* editor who first hired him, noted: "Giago's paper was a steady rain every Wednesday. Meetings, menus, basketball scores, election results—people stood in line and snatched papers from carriers' hands just to read about—themselves! For once, there was something about Indians in a newspaper beyond drunks and welfare and violence" (2007, F1–F2).

Giago went on to found the Native American Journalists Association, work in television, and even challenge South Dakota Governor George Mickelson in 1990 to replace Columbus Day with Native American Day. Mickelson responded by doing so, and the new holiday was approved by the state legislature.

Giago continues to critique, provoke debate, and care for native pasts and futures in his work. He also publishes the *Native Sun News* in Rapid City; his articles in 2010 alone addressed Indian mascots in high schools, high rates of suicide among native communities, racial discrimination among Native American veterans, lack of healthcare funding on reservations, and more. But perhaps most communitarian of all, Tim Giago has played a singular role in the education and training of dozens of young American Indian journalists, and he calls "his proudest achievement the staff he's nurtured" (Carrier 2007, F2).

In all of these examples from much of Means to Giago, there is not unrelenting confrontation without newness, not monochromatic accounts but writings that are nuanced and complex, and ones that American Indians claim as their story. Paulo Freire (1970) puts it this way: The oppressed must speak the true word and initiate the revolution themselves, rather than presume that social transformation arises first of all from the oppressor's philanthropy or altruistic change of heart.

CONCLUSION

If journalism, entertainment, and working the streets are the vehicles, recognition the content, the golden rule the ethical principle, and language the method, the aim of communication in a multicultural context is the creation of dynamic harmony. The Western democratic tradition of voting is superficial for Russell Means because it is simply a tool for the majority. Instead, communitarian ethics, in addition to educating, uses the public media to build convergent views on the issues. AIM's strategy of loose collaboration reflected the traditional values of Oglala elders who lead by consensus, not majority opinion. The end is not simply to create a winning idea or strategy to be pursued, by force if necessary, but to increase balance and move closer to the natural order. "Instead of believing that the universe depends on what we think, we teach that we must use our hearts to achieve harmony with our fellow creatures" (Means 1995, 414). Put another way, proper communication moves human existence from what Means calls Eurocentric *making* back to its proper place of *being*.

The result of this collaboration is community-building. Wounded Knee and Russell Means's activism have brought other Indian struggles—such as those of the Miskito in Nicaragua—into the fold. The right to self-determination claimed so vocally at Wounded Knee implies a responsibility to listen to others and help them achieve equality. Means's and AIM's continuing involvement with the United Nations through its Working Group on Indigenous Peoples and its Declaration of Indigenous Rights makes it clear that whether in protest or news or entertainment, ethical communication adds rather than subtracts. Although sometimes misdirected, AIM's campaign for justice demonstrates, on balance, that oppressed peoples have indispensable contributions to make for the rest of humanity.

> What Wounded Knee told the world was that John Wayne hadn't killed us all. Essentially, the rest of the planet had believed that except for a few people sitting along highways peddling pottery, there were no more Indians. Suddenly billions of people knew we were still alive, still resisting. (Means 1995, 277)

The long career of Russell Means shows that fierce cries of protest can reverberate in communitarian terms. Communitarian ethics is normative, an ideal that shows us the pathway to follow but always an aspiration not fully achieved. Under Means's leadership, the communitarian goals are local voice, harmony within people groups, responsibility for others, and flourishing in one's native home. True to form, AIM and Means are not the last word on Native Americans achieving these goals, but their legacy gives the next generation hope.

NOTES

1. On May 11, 2009, "Wounded Knee" was shown on PBS as a documentary in its film series of five episodes on Native Americans, *American Experience—We Shall Remain*. It includes archival footage from 1973, along with present-day interviews with Dennis Banks and Russell Means. It is suitable for classroom instruction, though a group calling itself "The Wounded Knee Victims and Veterans Association" has accused PBS of glorifying AIM and disregarding the real victims—the residents of Wounded Knee.

2. For a complete filmography of Russell Means's acting and other media work, see <http:www.russellmeans.com>.

3. About two years after that interview took place, President Barack Obama endorsed the declaration in December 2010, on behalf of the United States. The United States was the last signatory out of the original four nations who voted against the U.N. Declaration on Human Rights, as the governments of Australia, Canada, and New Zealand already had endorsed the statement by early 2010. The effect on policy and legal actions of the four nations' endorsements remains to be seen. Some indigenous rights groups plan to utilize the endorsements in legal challenges, although the U.N. resolution itself is nonbinding.

4. For a careful analysis of Rawls, and extended application to journalism ethics, see Plaisance (2009, ch. 4) and Ward (2010, ch. 3, *inter alia*).

5. In Part II of his *Theory of Justice*, Rawls extends "justice as fairness" beyond political governance. He deals with justice between generations and civil disobedience, for example. Elsewhere he attends to immigration and nuclear proliferation in terms beyond policy. However, all such extensions start from his two principles that characterize a well-ordered society under favorable circumstances. This reduction makes "justice as fairness" helpful but not definitive. Martha Nussbaum's *Frontiers of Justice: Disability, Nationality and Species Membership* (2006) is a comprehensive review of Rawls as the West's most sophisticated approach to social justice, while unable to resolve the fundamental questions of physical and mental disability, the nation-state in a global world, and restricting ethics to the human species.

REFERENCES

Battles, Jeffrey. 1996. *The Golden Rule.* New York: Oxford.

Bauer, Shane. 2008. "Divorcing the US." *New Internationalist* 410, April 1. <http://www.newint.org/features/special/2008/04/01/lakota/#>.

Bellah, Robert, Madsen, Richard, Sullivan, William M., Swindler, Ann, and Tipton, Steven M. 2007. *Habits of the Heart: Individualism and Commitment in American Life,* 3d ed. Berkeley: University of California Press.

Berry, Carol. 2010. "Russell Means, Fish-In Activist, Asserts Treaty Rights and Discounts Both the RNC and DNC." *Indian Country Today*, January 12. <http://www.indiancountrytoday.com/politics/27912599.html>.

Brown, Dee. 1970. *Bury My Heart at Wounded Knee.* New York: Holt, Rinehart & Winston.

Carrier, Jim. 2007. "South Dakota Indian Journalist Gave Voices to a People Long Ignored." *San Francisco Chronicle Sunday Insight,* December 31, F1–F2.

Freire, Paulo. 1970. *Pedagogy of the Oppressed.* New York: Seabury.

Garrigan, Mary. 2011. "Russell Means has Looked Death in the Face Before." *Bismark Tribune*, August 19, B1.

Johansen, Bruce E. 1998. "Sterilization of Native American Women Reviewed by Omaha Master's Student." <http://www.ratical.org/ratville/sterilize.html>.

Kraybill, Donald B., Nolt, Steven M., and Weaver-Zercher, David L. 2007. *Amish Grace: How Forgiveness Transcended Tragedy.* San Francisco, CA: Jossey-Bass.

Loew, Patty, and Mella, Kelly. 2005. "Black Ink and the New Red Power: Native American Newspapers and Tribal Sovereignty." *Journalism and Communication Monographs* 7 (3) (Autumn): 99–142.

Means, Russell. 2008a. <http://www.russellmeans.com>.

———. 2008b. <http://republicoflakotah.com>.

Means, Russell, with Wolf, Marvin J. 1995. *Where White Men Fear to Tread: The Autobiography of Russell Means.* New York: St. Martin's.

Native American Journalists Association. n.d. *A Reporter's Guide to Native Americans.* Wichita, Kan.: Wichita Eagle.

Nussbaum, Martha. 2006. *Frontiers of Justice: Disability, Nationality and Species Membership.* Cambridge, MA: Belknap Press.

Plaisance, Patrick. 2009. *Media Ethics: Key Principles for Responsible Practice.* Thousand Oaks, CA: Sage Publications.

Rawls, John. 1971. *A Theory of Justice.* Cambridge, MA: Harvard University Press [revised edition 1999].

———. 1993. *Political Liberalism.* New York: Columbia University Press.

———. 1999. *Collected Papers.* Edited by Samuel Freeman. Cambridge, MA: Harvard University Press.

Seely, Ron. 2003. "Native Americans Have Been Stewards of Wisconsin Land for Centuries." *Wisconsin State Journal,* October 5, 1.

Taylor, Charles. 1985. *Philosophy and the Human Sciences: Philosophical Papers,* vol. 2. Cambridge, MA: Cambridge University Press.

———. 1992. *The Ethics of Authenticity.* Cambridge, MA: Harvard University Press.

———. 1999. "Conditions of an Unforced Consensus on Human Rights." In J. R. Bauer and D. Bell, eds., *The East Asian Challenge for Human Rights.* Cambridge, U.K.: Cambridge University Press, 124–44.

Taylor, Charles, with Appiah, K. A., Habermas, J., Rockefeller, S. C., Walzer, M., and Wolf, S. 1994. Edited and Introduced by Amy Gutmann. *Multiculturalism: Examining the Politics of Recognition.* Princeton, NJ: Princeton University Press.

Treat, James. 2003. *Around the Sacred Fire: Native Religious Activism in the Red Power Era.* New York: Macmillan Palgrave.

Ward, Stephen J. A. 2010. *Global Journalism Ethics.* Montreal: McGill-Queen's University Press.

Warrior, Robert Allen. 1997. "Past and Present at Wounded Knee." *Media Studies Journal* 11 (2): 68–75.

Wilkinson, Charles F. 2005. *Blood Struggle: The Rise of Modern Indian Nations.* New York: W. W. Norton.

CHAPTER 13

✍

Norman Lear's Comedic Commentary

In 1970, the CBS television network was poised for big changes. CBS was the ratings leader with such popular prime-time programs as *The Ed Sullivan Show*, *The Beverly Hillbillies*, *Green Acres*, *Family Affair*, and *Mayberry R.F.D.*, but the audience for these shows tended to be rural, older, and less affluent, a far cry from the ages 18–49, upscale, urban demographic that television programmers were coming to covet. To change its reputation as the "Country Broadcasting System," CBS executed what became known as its rural purge, cancelling shows with an undesirable audience, however popular they may have been at the time. *Green Acres* actor Pat Buttram complained that "CBS canceled everything with a tree" (Gitlin 1985, 203–20).

One beneficiary of this transformation in attitudes toward audience was Norman Lear. Lear began his career in television as a writer in the early 1950s, eventually writing material for such leading entertainers as Danny Thomas, David Susskind, Ed Sullivan, Jerry Lewis, and Dean Martin. In 1959, Lear teamed up with producer Bud Yorkin to form Tandem Productions, which produced such 1960s movies as *Never Too Late* and *Divorce American Style*, as well as television specials for Danny Kaye, Henry Fonda, and Andy Williams.

The television series that would change Lear's career forever had an inauspicious beginning. Norman Lear came up with the idea for his new program in the late 1960s when he was watching the popular BBC sitcom *Till Death Us Do Part*. The British program featured the white working-class crank Alf Garnett, who spouted racist, antisocialist, and other contrary opinions to his wife, daughter, and unemployed socialist son-in-law. Believing that the bickering Garnett household portrayed family life more realistically than what American television was broadcasting, Lear decided to adapt the Garnett family for an American audience—using more than a dash of memories of clashes with his own father. Lear recalled, "My father called me the laziest white kid he ever met, and I would scream at him that he didn't have to put down a race of people to call me lazy. Then I was the stupidest white kid" (Keveney 2009, D3).

In 1968, Lear produced a pilot episode of *Justice for All*. ABC liked the pilot with Carroll O'Connor and Jean Stapleton as Archie and Edith Justice well enough to order a second, but this one, renamed *Those Were the Days*, excited no interest at ABC. But once it was shopped at CBS, the rest was history. CBS ordered thirteen episodes and aired the first episode of the show now called *All in the Family* in January 1971 as a midseason replacement for *The Governor and J.J.*, a comedy about a bumbling widower governor and his charming and competent "first lady" daughter. Within a year *All in the Family* was not only the Nielsen ratings leader, but it also appealed to both baby boomers and their parents, making it a success demographically as well. *All in the Family* would dominate television for several seasons and lead to popular and critically acclaimed spin-offs such as *Maude*, *The Jeffersons*, and *Sanford and Son* (Edgerton 2007, 276).

ALL IN THE FAMILY

All in the Family features Archie Bunker, an outspoken, bigoted dockworker who sings the show's nostalgic theme song, "Those Were the Days," and finds fault with whatever departs from the simpler times that he longs for. "Guys like us we had it made—those were the days," Archie sings. Almost everything departs from the world order that Archie imagines. The equal-opportunity loud-mouth is suspicious of whatever is not white, Christian, male, and heterosexual—anything unlike him—so from his overstuffed chair in his living room, Archie denigrates Jews, nonwhites of every hue, ethnic groups, and progressive creeds. His outspokenness is matched only by his ignorance, which is evident in his frequent malapropisms. "No bum that can't speak poifect English oughta stay in this country...oughta be de-exported the hell outta here!" Archie says about immigrants. About the death penalty, Archie proclaims, "It's a proven fact that capital punishment is a well-known detergent to crime." And he tells his wife that God made "one true religion ...which he named after his son, Christian—or Christ, for short" (Leong, n.d.).

Archie Bunker's wife is Edith, a gentle and deferential, if often ditzy, woman. Archie calls her a "dingbat" and orders her to "stifle" herself whenever she disagrees with him. The home's peacekeeper, Edith is observant, accepting, and wise about people's motivations. She seldom stands up to Archie, but when she does, she is authoritative. When, for instance, Archie learns that Edith's recently deceased cousin Liz was lesbian and claims that God hates homosexuals, Edith scolds Archie for his narrow-mindedness and for presuming that God is as intolerant as he is. In another episode, Edith, under strain from both menopause and Archie's browbeating about vacation plans, loses her temper. "Stifle!" she tells a flabbergasted Archie. "I said stifle and I mean stifle. Stifle, stifle, stifle! We're not going to Disney World or any other world!" ("Edith's Problem").

Archie and Edith's daughter is Gloria. Married to Mike Stivik, Archie's political opposite, Gloria works to put her husband through college. Like her husband,

Gloria is politically knowledgeable and liberal, but as Archie's "little girl," she tries to mediate between her liberal husband and her conservative father. Mostly, though, Gloria serves as a foil for jokes, as in the following exchange:

ARCHIE: Can you believe a family of midgets by the name of the Bambinis came by to look at the house?

GLORIA: No.

ARCHIE: Sure. You couldn't tell the parents from the kids until the old man lit up a cigar. They was walking around here talking about lowering all the door knobs.

GLORIA: I hope you didn't say anything to hurt their feelings.

ARCHIE: No, I think anything I said went right over their heads.

("Quotes from *All in the Family*," n.d.)

Gloria's husband is Mike, called "Meathead" by Archie because of his intellectualism. Mike is Archie's opposite: educated, ethnic (Polish-American), countercultural, and politically liberal. With conservative Archie and liberal Mike living under the same roof, arguments erupt constantly. In one classic exchange, Archie rails against minorities: "If your spics and your spades want their rightful share of the American dream," he says, "let 'em get out there and hustle for it like I done."

"So now you're going to tell me the black man has just as much chance as the white man to get a job?" Mike asks.

"More, he has more," Archie answers. "I didn't have no million people marchin' and protestin' to get me my job."

"No," Edith says. "His uncle got it for him." ("Quotes from *All in the Family*," n.d.)

During the first season, an African American family moves to Queens next door to the Bunkers. Archie is displeased, not just because of the Jeffersons' race, but because George Jefferson is just as racist as he is. George Jefferson so dislikes "whities" that for a long time he refuses to set foot in Archie's house. "George Jefferson is the only black guy I know that calls Abe Lincoln a honky," Archie observes ("Memorable Quotes for '*All in the Family*,'" n.d.).

In season five, Archie's union votes to strike, his income plummets, and Archie lets Edith look for a job. The only one she finds is at George Jefferson's dry-cleaning store. George is reluctant to integrate his all-black staff, explaining that they "will think she owns the store and the honkies will think we bleached the help," but he finally consents just to spite Archie. For his part, Archie tells Edith that accepting the job will look like charity, not legitimate work. Edith responds, "If I don't take this job, we'll have to go on welfare. On food stamps. What do you call that?" ("The Bunkers and Inflation," Part 3).

With the Jeffersons next door, Archie has plenty of opportunity to express his racism. Much of the exchange between the Bunkers and the Jeffersons focuses on Lionel, George Jefferson's college-educated son, who is good friends with Mike. In one scene, Archie tells Lionel to stop spending time with his niece.

The Bunkers and the Jeffersons in *All in the Family* (© Bettmann/CORBIS).

"I have you into my house, there, you break bread with me and then you go and do a thing like this," Archie complains. "Thank you very much, Lionel."

"You mean me taking out Linda?" Lionel asks.

"Yes," Archie says.

Lionel answers, "Oh you don't have to thank me for that, Mr. Bunker. I'd do it again but she's leaving tomorrow."

"Let's cut the funnies," Archie scolds. "You know what I'm saying to you. I'm saying that youse guys ought to stick with yourselves."

Lionel gets in the last word. "You mean guys ought to stay with guys?"

("Memorable Quotes for '*All in the Family*,'" n.d.)

Issues that *All in the Family* raised—including race, homosexuality, and feminism—had previously been absent from U.S. network television comedy. Indeed, before 1971 nothing like *All in the Family* had ever been seen on American television, a medium in which language was never off color, injustices were individual and temporary, and sexuality was hetero and so chaste that married couples slept in separate beds. In the first season alone Archie slurred "black beauties," "pollocks," "spics," "wops," "the tribe" (Jews), "pinkos," and "fairies." Network censors tried to screen out such words, but Lear insisted that they were essential to the dialogue. He wanted the bigotry on the show to be visceral to get people to think seriously about prejudice and discrimination.

In the second season, the network tried to stop Lear from producing an episode about male impotence. As difficult as it is to believe in an era replete with TV ads for drugs to treat erectile dysfunction, impotence was a subject deemed unsuitable for broadcast television. In 1965, an episode of the popular hospital drama *Ben Casey* about male impotence employed euphemisms because network censors would not allow the term to be used. But Lear was able to overcome network objections to produce "Mike's Problem," which wrestles with problems that impotence—in this case induced by the stress of studying for final exams—can cause in a marriage.

All in the Family uses humor to deal with issues that are difficult to discuss, such as prejudice, crime, inequality, and disease. A typical episode begins with Archie being judgmental. His adamant pronouncements are exposed as ill-informed, and by the end of the episode he is left to face the limitations of his prejudice. However much the audience laughs at Archie's uninformed point of view, Archie is shown to be likeable despite his faults. In the final-season episode "Little Miss Bunker," for example, Edith's freeloading cousin Floyd asks the Bunkers to take care of his 9-year-old daughter while he is out of town. But Floyd is an alcoholic who has no intention of returning for Stephanie, so Edith and Archie have to decide what to do with the child. Archie suggests asking the police to take her away because he does not want to raise another child, and he tells Edith she is too old to raise a child. But when the Bunkers realize how much their niece needs a stable home, they decide to keep her with them. Archie's good heart wins in the end.

All in the Family debuted with a disclaimer that became the show's mission statement: "The program you are about to see is *All in the Family*. It seeks to throw a humorous spotlight on our frailties, prejudices, and concerns. By making them a source of laughter, we hope to show—in a mature fashion—just how absurd they are" (Campbell 2007, 10). Robert Wood, President of CBS, recalled the network's nervousness about the show's debut. "I had no idea at all what the fallout would be to *All in the Family*," he said. "I sent teletypes to all our affiliates and told them to bolster up their switchboards. I put on extra operators in New York City. I was expecting an avalanche of public opinion. I think we got eleven calls in New York City!" (Newcomb and Alley 1983, 176). Indeed, network telephone operators received only a thousand calls, well over half of which were positive (Staiger 2000, 83).

The gamble paid off. After a shaky first season, the show won Emmys for Outstanding Comedy Series, Outstanding New Series, and Outstanding Continued Performance by an Actor in a Leading Role in a Comedy Series, won by Jean Stapleton, who played Edith. The Los Angeles chapter of the NAACP bestowed its Image Award to *All in the Family* for contributing to positive race relations. The show began its second season at the top of the Nielsen ratings, and it stayed there for five years. The series lasted a total of nine years and continues to air in reruns today (Campbell 2007, 20–21).

One of *All in the Family*'s biggest fans was award-winning singer and actor Sammy Davis, Jr. Not only did he arrange his schedule so that he could watch the program, but he lobbied for months to make a special guest appearance on the show. And special it turned out to be. Sammy Davis, Jr.'s appearance on February 19, 1972, marked the only time in the program's nine-year run when a guest star appeared.

In "Sammy's Visit," Archie has begun moonlighting as a taxi driver. He happens to give a ride to Sammy Davis, Jr., who forgets his briefcase in Archie's cab. When he goes to Archie's house to retrieve the briefcase, Archie welcomes him nervously. But it does not take long for Archie's bigotry to surface. "You was born black," Archie tells Sammy Davis, Jr., "so you didn't have no choice about that. But, why'd you turn Jew?"

At another point, Archie makes a pronouncement about segregation: "If God had meant for us to be together, he'da put us together. But look what he done. He put you over in Africa, and put the rest of us in all the white countries."

Sammy Davis, Jr. replies, "Well, he must've told 'em where we were because somebody came and got us."

Gloria tries to smooth things over. "I'm sorry, Mr. Davis, sometimes my father says the wrong things," she says.

"Yeah, I've noticed that," Sammy Davis, Jr., replies.

Lionel Jefferson joins in, "But he's not a bad guy, Mr. Davis. I mean like, he'd never burn a cross on your lawn."

"No," says Sammy Davis, Jr., "but if he saw one burning, he's liable to toast a marshmallow on it."

Before Sammy Davis, Jr. turns to leave, he poses for a snapshot with Archie. On the count of three, Sammy Davis, Jr. kisses a very surprised Archie on the cheek. Then he tells Archie: "I can honestly say, having spent these moments with you, you ain't no better than nobody." Director John Rich won one of his three Emmys for this episode.

The popularity of *All in the Family* raised interesting questions about selective exposure in the minds of certain media researchers. Selective exposure—the observation that audiences attend to media that confirm their worldview—seemed at odds with the popularity of Lear's program, for if a large portion of Americans were prejudiced, and there was no reason to believe that they were not, then most Americans would have avoided the program. But *All in the Family* set TV viewing records. What was going on?

Psychologists Neil Vidmar of the University of Western Ontario and Milton Rokeach of Washington State University were determined to find out. They surveyed 370 North American adolescents and adults to see if their level of prejudice matched their reactions to *All in the Family*. What they found was sobering. Selective exposure was less of a factor than selective perception. Put simply, viewers saw the show differently. They demonstrated what researchers would come to call "polysemy," a diversity of interpretations. Many viewers understood *All in the Family* the way Lear had intended—as satire on bigotry. But many more said that the program was "telling it like it is." Highly prejudiced viewers tended to watch *All in the Family* more than those with low prejudice; they viewed Archie with admiration and thought that he won in the end. "*All in the Family* seems to be appealing more to the racially and ethnically prejudiced members of society than to the less prejudiced members," Vidmar and Rokeach concluded. "The program is more likely reinforcing prejudice and racism than combating it" (Vidmar and Rokeach 1974, 45–46).

Vidmar and Rokeach's research suggested that however honorable Lear's intentions, his program ended up reinforcing bigotry among a large portion of viewers. Lear, however, rejected this conclusion. He said, "I've never received a letter from a bigot or some somebody who agrees with Archie—and there have been thousands—that didn't somewhere say, 'Well, why do you always make Archie such a horse's ass at the end of the show?' It doesn't escape the notice of any of those 'right-on Archie' people that the point of view of the show is that the man is foolish—his bigoted attitudes harmful" (Newcomb and Alley 1983, 193).

But Lear also acknowledged that *All in the Family* did not diminish prejudice among bigoted viewers. "These people are not changed," he said. "There are people who write, 'I see a lot of my uncle in Archie, I see a lot of my neighbor in Archie.' I've never seen letters saying, 'I see a lot of myself in Archie'" (Newcomb and Alley 1983, 193).

Depending upon the subject of the joking, humor can be no laughing matter. Humor can hurt. Think of the times when you have heard someone excusing ridicule that humiliated someone by saying, "I was just kidding." The excuse may be true, but it often provides little comfort. Laughter can be the best medicine, but laughter can also express contempt. How can we distinguish good humor from irresponsible or cruel humor, not according to some laugh meter, but according to a humane moral scale?

Aristotle thought of humor as a virtue between the extremes of vulgar buffoons who "try to be funny at all costs" and the boorish and dour "who cannot say anything funny themselves and are offended by those who do." For Aristotle, the golden mean was found by "those who joke in a tactful way." Aristotle understood that comedy was a means of understanding problems in different ways. He referred to *eutrapelia*, by which he meant versatility. *Eutrapelia* meant rising above practical responses to problems so that we can see problems in a new light. Humor can spur creativity by approaching problems playfully (Morreall 2009, 23, 145).

But the playful disengagement that humor requires can be harmful, according to John Morreall, author of the philosophy of humor *Comic Relief*. Disengagement can trivialize problems, as if they are "no big deal." Or it can desensitize people, laughter replacing compassion. And most relevant to the discussion of *All in the Family*, playful disengagement can even promote prejudice: "Those who circulate racist and sexist jokes do it," Morreall suggests, "not by making truth-claims, but by being *indifferent* to the truth" (Morreall 2009, 106). Morreall notes that humor perpetuates objectionable stereotypes when it derides people without social status and power and when it perpetuates stereotypes of people that the social system marginalizes. As an antidote to such denigrating humor, Morreall proposes a simple ethical principle: "Do not promote a lack of concern for something about which people should be concerned" (Morreall 2009, 110). This principle articulates in a negative way the purpose behind *All in the Family*.

In his conclusion, Morreall explains that community is at the center of humor, that comedy celebrates community as it acknowledges social conflict. Comedy may use indirect tactics to confront serious issues, Morreall says, but it does so recognizing that we "belong in communities. We get by with a little help from our friends. Life isn't a solitary struggle, but a social adventure" (2009, 144).

Whatever influence *All in the Family* had on its viewers, the show had a marked influence on American television. It launched spinoffs including *Sanford and Son*, *Maude*, and *The Jeffersons*. It also served as inspiration for *Chico and the Man*, another program laced with ethnic humor, and influenced such socially relevant sitcoms as *The Mary Tyler Moore Show*, *M*A*S*H*, and *Good Times* (Staiger 2000, 21). "*All in the Family* really changed the face of television," recalled CBS President Robert Wood. "I always felt that the sketches on the *Carol Burnett Show* were a little more chic, the comedy on an ABC show a little smarter, a little sharper, because of *All in the Family*. It got television up on its toes and things became sharper and better. Comedy, I thought, had a much better edge to it. All of television benefitted for a period of five years and I think it did advance the entertainment level of television considerably" (Newcomb and Alley 1983, 176).

SANFORD AND SON

Norman Lear returned to the British well for his next successful series, *Sanford and Son*. Like the successful BBC sitcom *Steptoe and Son* from which Lear drew, *Sanford and Son* featured an outspoken, prejudiced junk shop owner and his son to comment on the day's social issues.

Sanford and Son, however, used an African American cast and was set in the Los Angeles Watts district. Actor-comedian Redd Foxx played Fred Sanford, a crotchety, conniving widower who lives with Lamont, his thirty-something unmarried son and partner in the salvage business. Plots typically involved one of Fred's get-rich-quick schemes or his imaginative efforts to keep Lamont from leaving him all alone to find a better life for himself. Episodes were chock-a-block with insults and one-liners and were likely to include one of Fred's fake heart attacks during which he clasped his chest, staggered, and cried out to his long-deceased wife, "I'm coming to join you, Elizabeth!" Holding the show together were the values of family, friendship, tolerance, and honesty.

But whatever the focus of the particular episode, race usually surfaced as an issue. For instance, in "Fred Sanford, Legal Eagle," Lamont tells Fred that he will pay the fine for a traffic ticket even though he got it unjustly. "If you had the green light," says Fred, "you can't get a ticket." "You can if the light is green and you're black and the cop is white," Lamont says.

In another episode, Lamont takes Fred, who has been suffering with a tooth-ache for two days, to a free neighborhood dental clinic ("Tooth or Consequences"). As they are sitting in the waiting room, Fred surprises Lamont by demanding to see a white dentist.

Lamont: What did you say?

Fred: You heard me, I want a white dentist.

Lamont: Well what makes you think you're going to get a black dentist?

Fred: You said it was a free clinic, didn't you? Where you think you're gonna find a black dentist? In Beverly Hills?

Lamont: Wasn't you the guy who told me once that you didn't want nothing white but milk?

Fred: Well my tooth wasn't hurting then. I want the best available dentist for my tooth. Now just by coincidence, the best dentist schools are of the white people, by the white people, and for the white people. Now don't it seem likely that the best dentist would be white? ("Memorable Quotes for 'Sanford and Son,'" n.d.)

However strong the writing about race for *Sanford and Son* may have been, it did not always measure up to Red Foxx's satisfaction. Complaining that the show lacked black writers and directors, creative talent who understood African American culture, Foxx left *Sanford and Son* at the end of the third season and the beginning of the fourth. For those episodes, his character was in St. Louis. Foxx returned to the program as part of a settlement of the lawsuit NBC filed when he left.

Sanford and Son was popular from its start in 1972. It ranked sixth in the Nielsen ratings in its very first season, rising to second in season two, behind only *All in the Family*. When NBC cancelled the program after its fifth season, it was tied for seventh place in the Nielsens. Red Foxx left *Sanford and Son* in 1977 for a more lucrative contract to star in ABC's *The Redd Foxx Comedy Hour*, a move on ABC's part that effectively put an end to one of its costliest competitors.

MAUDE

American television viewers met Maude Findlay as Edith Bunker's upscale cousin on *All in the Family* in 1972. Like Archie Bunker, Maude was outspoken, caustic, and domineering. Unlike Archie, though, Maude was upper middle class, educated, and socially progressive. Much of the spin-off program involves Maude's strident feminism and her political activism. Late in the series, Maude expresses the equal right for women to lead the country by running for and winning a seat in the U.S. Congress.

Maude is married to her fourth husband, Walter, an appliance salesman. They share their home with Maude's 27-year-old divorced daughter Carol and her 9-year-old son Philip. Walter appreciates Maude's social progressivism, but often employs his sense of moderation to calm Maude's relentlessness. Besides getting involved in politics and debating the legalization of marijuana, Maude experiences such personal issues as getting a facelift and experiencing menopause.

In a controversial two-part episode Maude becomes pregnant at the age of 47. She contemplates whether to have the baby despite the health risks that were possible at her age. After discussing the topic with her husband and her daughter, Maude decides to have an abortion. "When you were young, abortion was a dirty word," her daughter tells her. "It's not anymore." Pro-life viewers, anxious about the impending Supreme Court decision of Roe v. Wade, felt differently. They pressured two CBS affiliates into not running the episodes at all, and 32 CBS affiliates cancelled the two-part episode's summer rerun.

But the program was not simply a vehicle for liberalism. The program also poked fun at liberal thinking. In the third episode, for instance, Maude requested that her agency send a black woman as a replacement for the home's maid. Maude wanted to hire an African American in order to help right past injustices of discrimination. But Maude was uncomfortable assigning work to Florida, her new African American maid, because she felt that the labor was menial and demeaning. The first week that Florida worked at the Findlay's home, Maude went out of her way to treat Florida not as a maid but as a member of her household. But Florida found Maude's constant fawning condescending. Florida did not believe that her domestic labor was beneath her, and she simply wanted to do her work without being constantly reminded of the plight of her race. The perspective shift takes place during the confrontation and Maude is reminded of the true meaning of equality. Florida, while a poor black woman, still has the right to pursue work of her choice. Maude, with all her sophisticated progressivism, loses sight of true equality momentarily and is turned around by her more enlightened maid ("Maude Meets Florida," CBS 1972).

A mid-series episode involved Maude taking lithium to treat a manic-depressive illness. At the time, critics feared that the issue was too serious for a sitcom. Lear, committed to the responsible use of television, hired medical consultants to work on the script, and sought to increase the public's sensitivity to mental illness (Campbell 2007, 52).

Later the show tackled alcoholism. Maude and Walter were both heavy social drinkers, but when Maude woke up in bed with Walter's best friend Arthur after a night of drinking, both Maude and Walter swore off alcohol. Walter, however, could not stay sober, and in an alcohol fueled rage he slaps Maude and then suffers a nervous breakdown.

During its first four seasons on CBS, from 1972 to 1976, Maude ranked in the top ten of the Nielsen ratings. Beatrice Arthur, who played Maude, won an Emmy Award for Best Actress in a Comedy Series (Maude) in 1977. The show's popularity sank in season five and the show was cancelled in April 1978.

OTHER SUCCESSES

Other hit shows followed thereafter, including *All in the Family* spin-off *The Jeffersons*, *One Day at a Time*, and the soap opera spoof *Mary Hartman, Mary Hartman*. These character-driven family comedies that paid attention to social and political issues were unmistakable Norman Lear productions—which was no accident because until he left active television production in 1978 to focus on business and political concerns, Lear made a point of participating in the story conferences of every one of his series (Alley 2004, 1335–37).

CBS broadcast *The Jeffersons* for 11 seasons from January 18, 1975 through June 25, 1985, making it the longest running situation comedy in the history of American television. The show focused on George and Louise Jefferson, who moved from next door to the Bunkers in Queens to a swank apartment in New York's Upper East Side. Although *The Jeffersons* dealt with social issues such as racism and gun control, the program grew less political over time. But as one of the first programs to depict African Americans as wealthy, it paved the way for other programs, such as *The Cosby Show*, that portrayed African Americans as everyday people with everyday concerns. The race of the Jeffersons did matter—an African American maid being interviewed for a job at the Jeffersons' apartment asked, "Well, how come we overcame and nobody told me?"—but it was not the program's primary concern.

At the same time that *The Jeffersons* was on the air, Lear produced *One Day at a Time*, a sitcom about a divorced mother raising two teenage daughters and trying to reenter the job market. Like other Lear productions, *One Day at a Time* mixed humor with serious issues, which included virginity, birth control, premarital sex, infidelity, sexual harassment, alcohol, and financial stability. Besides being frank, Ann Romano, the mother, is fun and strong, yet vulnerable. In the show's pilot episode, Ann's 17-year-old daughter slams out of the house threatening to live with her father because Ann will not let her go on a coed camping trip. "For the first seventeen years of my life my father made the decisions and the next seventeen my husband made the decisions. The first time in my life, I make a decision, and I blow it," she cries (Campbell 2007, 152). But Ann, Julie, and Barbara learn, slowly but deliberately, to make choices that will help them lead fulfilling lives as women neither subservient nor reliant on men.

With *Mary Hartman, Mary Hartman* in 1976, Lear departed from his tried-and-true sitcom format, this time producing a five-day-per-week soap opera spoof. *Mary Hartman, Mary Hartman*—so named because Lear said that soap operas repeated everything—satirized the plots of soap operas, as well as the consumerism that they promoted. The main character, Mary Hartman, was a suburban housewife with family troubles that included an impotent husband, a flashing grandfather, and a sullen daughter. She lived in a world of chaos and violence where people were as likely to die by impalement on an aluminum Christmas tree as in a car accident. But her moral compass always points true north to consumer goods that will improve her life: a certain brand of coffee, maybe, or floor wax or toilet bowl cleaner. By the end of the first season, Mary Hartman appeared on a talk show, had a mental breakdown in front of a national audience, and ended up in a psychiatric ward, where she got to participate in the Nielsen Ratings.

None of the three networks would touch *Mary Hartman, Mary Hartman*. It required too much air time, it was too racy—there were frequent bedroom scenes, talk about sexual stimulation, and use of words such as "penis" and "vagina"— and it did not use a studio audience, so the viewers were never cued on when to laugh. Undaunted, Lear syndicated the program independently, selling the program to individual television stations that broadcast it outside of prime time. *Mary Hartman, Mary Hartman* soon became a critical, must-see success, proving Lear's belief that there was a ready audience for innovative television. What Lear did not foresee was the toll of exhaustion that the grueling production schedule would take on Louise Lasser, who played Mary Hartman. After making 325 episodes in just 16 months, Lasser called it quits and the program ended (Campbell 2007, 161–66).

Not all of Lear's productions were commercially successful. Between 1975 and 1978, five new series—*Hot L Baltimore*, *All's Fair*, *All That Glitters*, *Fernwood 2 Night*, and *America 2-Night*—were all cancelled after no more than one year. After a hiatus from TV production in the 1980s, Lear returned to television in the 1990s with *Sunday Dinner*, *The Powers That Be*, and *704 Hauser*, but all three quickly disappeared from the air. However, Lear's final involvement in television comedy was more positive. Lear consulted on various episodes of the animated program *South Park* and even provided the voice of Benjamin Franklin in the episode "I'm a Little Bit Country" in 2003.

Norman Lear left an imprint on a strain of television comedies that followed his impressive run. Although *Seinfeld* (1989–98), *Friends* (1994–2004), and most other popular TV comedies retreated from socially conscious humor, not all did. For more than twenty years, *The Simpsons* has been serving social commentary in animated form. And so has *South Park*, which Lear praised for "doing edgy, cause-oriented, problem-oriented cultural pieces" ("Norman Lear on TV.com" 2002). Lear also singled out *The Daily Show*, saying that Jon Stewart, like Bea Arthur on *Maude*, probes "the absurdity of the human condition" (Boucher 2009, D10).

Lear also affected black sitcoms. Before *Sanford & Son*, American television networks had broadcast only three situation comedies with primarily African American casts: *The Beulah Show* (1950–52), *The Amos 'n' Andy Show* (1951–53), and *Julia* (1968–71). So *Sanford and Son*'s six-season run was a welcome change, as were Lear's other two successful black sitcoms. *Good Times* ran for six seasons, and *The Jeffersons* set the record for the longest-running black sitcom at eleven seasons.

The success of Lear's black sitcoms, which ran altogether from 1972 until 1985, attracted attention from commercial networks, which broadcast numerous black sitcoms in the 1980s and 1990s. The most notable include *The Cosby Show* (1984–92), about the close-knit, affluent Huxtable family in Brooklyn; *Family Matters* (1989–98), about a middle-class Chicago family and the nerdy next-door neighbor; *The Fresh Prince of Bel-Air* (1990–96), about a street-wise teenager from Philadelphia living with rich relatives in southern California; and *Martin* (1992–97), about a mouthy Detroit media personality (Nelson 2009). The networks' attention to African American viewers, who comprise one-fifth of the audience of broadcast television, paid off in quality programming that added diversity to the airwaves and paid off handsomely in advertising revenues and syndication at home and abroad. Significantly, *The Cosby Show* led the Nielsen Ratings' for five straight years. It also defied the common wisdom at the time that comedies were so culture bound that they could not fare well in the international television market. *The Cosby Show* became a hot international commodity, commanding huge audiences in countries as diverse as South Africa, Denmark, Poland, Lebanon, and Israel (Edgerton 2007, 395).

But the golden era of black sitcoms is now past. Few black sitcoms appear on the major broadcast networks today. The animated *Cleveland Show* is an exception, but many of the voices in that program are those of white actors. Most black sitcoms appear on the BET and TBS cable networks, off the radar of most American television viewers (Miller 2009). Perhaps society's increasing cultural diversity will lead TV networks to answer the communitarian call that Norman Lear affirmed by committing themselves to projecting pictures that are inclusive of the society in which we live.

By 1981, Lear had created his classic sitcoms, but his politically motivated work was far from over. Televangelists had been coming on strong on television, attracting growing numbers of viewers, raising spectacular sums of money, and wielding political influence. Worried that televangelists were blurring the line between religion and politics, Lear began watching Jerry Falwell, Pat Robertson, and Jimmy Swaggart, thinking that he might make a movie about them called *Religion*, a comedy about two preachers, one motivated by God, the other motivated by power. What he saw on religious television appalled him. "They railed against the Supreme Court, the public school system, secular humanism—often with thinly veiled anti-Semitic and anti-Catholic intolerance," he recalled. "You don't wish Supreme Court justices dead with a bible in your hand as Swaggart once did. They exploited their followers' needs for their own ends, and insisted that federal law ought to embody sectarian beliefs" (Landy 1992, 18).

Although Lear insists that God and politics should not mix, he acknowledges that religious faith made important contributions to civil rights and opposition to the Vietnam War. But, he says, "there's an important difference. The Berrigan brothers and William Sloane Coffin [religious figures who opposed the Vietnam war] never suggested that you were a good or bad Christian depending on what you said about the war. Martin Luther King never said you were not a worthwhile Christian if you didn't agree with him. None of them ever said your compact with the Almighty was threatened by your politics" (Garvin 2007, 1).

Lear responded to televangelism by crafting an answer in the medium he knew best: television. He created a series of 30-second TV spots that told viewers that, no matter what TV preachers said, the quality of their faith did not depend upon their political views. The spots ended with the narrator saying, "That's not the American way." After University of Notre Dame President Theodore Hesburgh saw the spot, he put Lear in touch with several Protestant and Catholic religious leaders, who urged him to institutionalize this campaign. Thus was born People for the American Way, a nonprofit organization set up to promote Constitutional freedoms in opposition to the Rev. Jerry Falwell's conservative lobbying organization, the Moral Majority. According to its mission statement, People for the American Way's purpose is to educate Americans about the tenets that sustain American democracy: "pluralism, individuality, freedom of thought, expression of religion, a sense of community, and tolerance and compassion for others."

CONVERSATIONS

In democratic societies, change happens only after citizens complain, challenge, discuss, analyze, propose, debate, and vote. Conversation—sometimes calm, sometimes emotional—is what moves democracies. In this vein, Norman Lear's programs provided important grist for the mill. Watching a Lear production was likely to get people talking about race or gender or divorce or teenage sexuality or television itself. To be sure, Lear's comedies got people laughing, but they also got them thinking and talking. "I can't honestly say I can see anywhere where we changed anything." Lear has said. "But what I have are thousands of memories of people relating to me that we made them talk. And you know, the funny thing is, people are still talking" (Boucher 2009, D10).

Getting people to talk is probably Lear's greatest legacy, but Lear's effects on television comedy should be remembered, too. Before *All in the Family*, American sitcoms seldom raised sensitive issues. *Gomer Pyle, U.S.M.C.*, a show about a naïve marine recruit and his exasperated drill sergeant, aired from 1964 to 1969 during the height of the Vietnam War, yet it never even mentioned the war. The idea was to broadcast programs that did not offend audiences, so entertainment programming before *All in the Family* tended to be escapist. Because it dominated the ratings, *All in the Family* showed that television comedy could tackle serious issues without putting off the audience. *All in the Family*, *Maude*, *The Jeffersons*, and other Lear programs demonstrated this principle year after year, which helped create opportunities for other edgy prime-time sitcoms such as *M*A*S*H* and *Scrubs*.

Expanding the possibilities of television comedy is important in a society that watches as much television as Americans do, an average of three hours every day. There is nothing wrong with making or watching some escapist programming, which can be relaxing and entertaining. But infusing the time we spend watching television with issues of critical concern to the well-being of society adds social value to television viewing. And if this infusion can itself be artful and engaging, then the television experience is improved. That is Norman Lear's legacy, and that is why he was awarded the National Medal of Arts in 1999 by President Bill Clinton, who observed that "Norman Lear has held up a mirror to American society and changed the way we look at it" ("The Backstory," n.d.). Lear was also nominated for an Academy Award, honored with Emmy Awards and a Peabody Award, inducted into the Television Academy Hall of Fame, and given a star on the Hollywood Walk of Fame.

When asked whether his programs actually improved race relations, Lear has been dismissive. "If 2,000 years of the Judeo-Christian ethic hasn't seemed to help," he has said, "I would be some kind of fool if I thought my little half-hour sitcom was having that kind of effect. What I do know is people talked. That's always good" (Keveney 2009, D3). Lear acknowledges that his programs did not have a direct cause-and-effect relationship with their audiences, but that his programs spurred conversation. Conversations, one after another over time, create the context for change, and Lear not only helped make the agenda for our conversations more significant, but he showed how subsequent television could continue to inspire them.

In previous chapters the communitarian argument has stipulated that more and better conversation has inherent value. Stories are intrinsic to civilization. "We wouldn't recognize a community as human if it had no stories," writes Kwame Appiah (2006, 29) in his book subtitled *Ethics in a World of Strangers*. We grow as persons as we tell and evaluate the stories that define our values. We become "persons" as we define ourselves by connecting to others with words. "Evaluating stories together is one of the central human ways of learning to align our responses to the world. And that alignment of responses is, in turn, one of the ways we maintain the social fabric, the texture of our relationships" (Appiah 2006, 29). Conversation signals communal identity. As we share symbols and meanings, our vocabulary deepens.

One of the most revered scholars ever to teach and write in the field of communication studies built his reputation on conversation. James Carey's essays are rightly cited for their enduring scholarship, but when you find someone who knew him, talked with him, enjoyed conversation with him, then you will know something of this man that his printed words cannot tell (Fackler 2010, 110). One of Carey's key concepts was "acts of resistance." He understood conversation to be the bulwark of freedom against the hegemony exercised so commonly by political power against the conscience. In concrete terms, when any social force presumes it has the power to determine your conscience, your best defense (to keep yourself really you) is to start talking. "The task is to engage in 'acts of resistance' against the dominant discourse whatever its political origin or learning" (Carey 2000, 11).

Lear's characters engage in acts of resistance through comedic satire. It is a complex enterprise to use language to achieve an effect opposite to its conventional meaning. But in each instance of Archie's gruff belligerence, his character was communicating something quite different from his words. Active viewing is required for these meanings to gain their foothold. We must see Archie as an "act of resistance" to the sectarian, exclusive, and chauvinistic discourse that made Archie a cultural icon. Our own act of resistance may translate Archie into his antithesis in order to challenge the hegemony of prejudice and race on our consciences. In that sense we engage in an ongoing conversation that produces, maintains, repairs, and transforms our world (Carey 1989, 23).

Sometimes humor is communitarian by design. That is the case in Glasgow, Scotland, where the charity "Universal Comedy" offers comedy workshops to persons experiencing the alienation of unemployment, often with side effects of anxiety and depression. Funded by the National Lottery, the workshops put participants in groups of ten to work with professional comedians for eight weeks with the short-term goal of restoring their place in the broader community. By providing regular occasions for creative thinking and social interaction, the workshops help foster personal development and a sense of empowerment in their participants. The success of "Universal Comedy" has been such that it now offers workshops tailored to the needs of healthcare and social service organizations. "There are a lot of people who are unemployed and isolated from their communities and their outlook is very poor," says Patsy Morrison, "Universal Comedy's" founder and managing director: "Our workshops intervene and challenge this, but we do it in a way that's fun, sociable and creative and with a genuine understanding of the problems people face" (Diamond 2009).

Of course, there is always a butt of the joke in Archie's outbursts. He ridicules, he criticizes. The interpretive task mentioned above is crucial to Lear's humor, but Lear himself is not the butt of Archie's jokes. Lear depends on others, the butts so to speak, to forego first-level meanings and laugh at offensive slanders. What if humor becomes so pointed and bitter that the "butt of the joke" does not laugh? That has been a common criticism among feminists with respect to comedic portrayals of late adolescent men. Tucker Max's outrageous book/movie *I Hope They Serve Beer in Hell* unrelentingly objectifies and abuses women, for laughs, if you are not a woman, or if you can politely agree to forget all dignity, if you are. Catharine MacKinnon describes such "humor" in *Only Words* as learning that "language does not belong to you, that you cannot use it to say what you know… that information is not made out of your experience" (1993, 6). You hear and see the entertainment that others seemingly enjoy, but as the one offended, you can neither enter that experience nor critique it. You are silenced.

Communitarian ethics objects to classical liberal support for all words of all kinds in the interest of expressive freedom. Humor that kicks at the dignity of others is not the path to social maturity. Words intended to deflate or diminish an African American, in Archie's case, are not free-pass language, simply because they are words and not actions. The butt of Lear's humor, whatever the demographic, must be able to laugh along with Archie's audience if the humor is to have moral lift.

The law depends on the "rational person" test (an ideal that juries must imagine exists as they contemplate testimony and culpability)—likewise with ethical humor. If an African American who is self-aware, socially conscious, historically grounded, and who enjoys the full range of emotion can laugh at the end of the show, then Archie-type humor has passed the communitarian test. Communitarian ethics does not allow people to be deprived or diminished of dignity, and the judge of diminishment is not Lear or network executives, but the butts of the many jokes that comprise Lear's long career of humor writing. Let them laugh, or the humor has failed.

We think Lear does very well at humor that wins smiles from those whose ethnicity, religion, color, and gender are satirized. Few writers have Lear's skills and sensitivities. Perhaps that is why audiences have conceded to pay for entertainment from Tucker Max. A Norman Lear comes along all too infrequently.

REFERENCES

Alley, Robert. 2004. "Norman Lear." In Horace Newcomb, ed., *Museum of Broadcast Communications Encyclopedia of Television*, 2d ed., 1335–37. New York: Fitzroy Dearborn.

Appiah, Kwame. 2006. *Cosmopolitanism: Ethics in a World of Strangers*. New York: Norton.

"The Backstory." n.d. <http://www.normanlear.com/backstory.html>.

Boucher, Geoff. 2009. "Prime-Time Provocateur." *Los Angeles Times*, June 14, D10.

Campbell, Sean. 2007. *The Sitcoms of Norman Lear*. Jefferson, NC: McFarland.

Carey, James. 1989. *Communication as Culture*. Boston: Unwin Hyman.

———. 2000. "The Engaged Discipline." In National Communication Association, ed., *The Carroll C. Arnold Distinguished Lecture*. Boston: Allyn and Bacon.

Diamond, Pauline. 2009. "Something to Laugh About." *Community Care*, September 24, 30–31.

Edgerton, Gary. 2007. *The Columbia History of American Television*. New York: Columbia University Press.

Fackler, Mark. 2010. "Oral Culture as Antidote to Terror and Ennui." In Linda Steiner and Clifford Christians, eds. *Key Concepts in Critical Cultural Studies*. Urbana: University of Illinois Press, 103–14.

Garvin, Glenn. 2007. "Lear Recalls When Guys Like Him Had It Made." *Knight Ridder Tribune Business News*, May 13, 1.

Gitlin, Todd. 1985. *Inside Prime Time*. New York: Pantheon.

Keveney, Bill. 2009. "For Lear, These Were the Days." *USA Today*, June 9, 3D.

Landy, Thomas. 1992. "What's Missing from this Picture: Norman Lear Explains." *Commonweal*, October 9, 18.

Leong, Kristie. n.d. "Archie Bunker Quotes!" <http://www.associatedcontent.com/article/278713/archie_bunker_quotes_all_in_the_family.html>.

MacKinnon, Catharine. 1993. *Only Words*. Cambridge, MA: Harvard University Press.

"Memorable Quotes for '*All in the Family*.'" n.d. <http://www.imdb.com/title/tt0066626/quotes>.

"Memorable Quotes for '*Sanford and Son*.'" n.d. <http://www.imdb.com/title/tt0068128/quotes>.

Miller, Julie. 2009. "Who Is Killing the African-American Sitcom?" *Movieline*, September 30. <http://www.movieline.com/2009/09/who-is-killing-the-african-american-sitcom.php>.

Morreall, John. 2009. *Comic Relief: A Comprehensive Philosophy of Humor*. Malden, MA: Wiley-Blackwell.

Nelson, Dwayne C. 2009. "Top 10 Black Sitcoms of All Time." *Associated Content*, October 20. <http://www.associatedcontent.com/article/2286825/top_10_black_sitcoms_of_all_time.html>.

Newcomb, Horace, and Alley, Robert S. 1983. *The Producer's Medium: Conversations with Creators of American TV*. New York: Oxford University Press.

"Norman Lear on TV.com." 2002. <http://www.tv.com/norman-lear/person/19699/summary.html>.

"Quotes from *All in the Family*." n.d. <http://scenteddemented.com/allinthefamily.html>.

Staiger, Janet. 2000. *Blockbuster TV: Must-See Sitcoms in the Network Era*. New York: New York University Press.

Vidmar, Neil, and Rokeach, Milton. 1974. "Archie Bunker's Bigotry: A Study in Selective Perception and Exposure." *Journal of Communication* 24 (1), Winter, 36–47.

CHAPTER 14

✒

Reading the Romance and Popular Art

The most popular genre of novels in modern literature is the romance. Eight thousand new romance novels are published every year. In 2010 the global leader in romance fiction, the Toronto-based Harlequin Enterprises Limited, sold 130 million books in 114 international markets on six continents. As the *New York Times* puts it: "The romance reader is a little like the Asian carp: insatiable and unstoppable. Romance is now the fastest-growing segment of the e-reading market, ahead of general fiction, mystery and science fiction" (Bosman 2010, 1A).

But literary scholars scorn romance novels as lightweight women's fiction—disposable, formulaic, and brainless. Are the millions of women who read them passive and naïve? Are they victims of patriarchy? Professor Janice Radway, then of the University of Pennsylvania, had a hunch that romance readers enjoy "the titillation of seeing themselves, not necessarily as they are, but as some men would like to see them: illogical, innocent, magnetized by male sexuality and brutality" (Radway 1984, 4).

Radway decided to talk with romance readers to hear them describe their reading experiences. Radway's communitarian approach was novel: Instead of assuming that meaning lies in the text, she thought that the social context would show how people integrate a medium's values into their own. And her strategy was a game changer. Having become a cornerstone of the study of popular culture, reader-response has expanded to romance fiction in electronic form—soap operas and telenovelas, "the most popular genre of television drama in the world today and probably in the history of broadcasting," according to Robert Allen (2008, 8). Radway's influential analysis of reading raises a question for communitarian ethics: Does romance fiction—in novels, soap operas, telenovelas, and cyberbooks—promote ethical reflection, critique, and conduct?

RADWAY'S STUDY

Originally published in 1984, Janice Radway's *Reading the Romance: Women, Patriarchy, and Popular Literature* explains why so many women devour romantic fiction.[1] Radway studied forty-two female romance readers in a Midwestern town she called "Smithton." Her research centered on a bookstore employee who was the unofficial leader of the forty-two. "Dot Evans" began reading romances as a young married woman, under doctor's orders to do something for herself every day. By the time that she was reading a hundred books a month, Dot Evans found work at a bookstore, advising customers which romances to read and later circulating a newsletter about recent releases. The group of regulars who talked to Dot Evans about books became Radway's subjects.

All of the women were married and most had children. Half of them had education beyond high school and all lived in the suburbs and owned their own homes. Half of them read 1–4 books per week, one-third read 5–9, and the rest ten or more. They typically read a 200-page romance from cover to cover in one two-hour sitting. They saved longer books for the weekend, when they could take several sittings to get to the emotionally gratifying happy ending.

In sixty hours of interviews and three surveys, the Smithton women described their reading of romance novels as resistance to patriarchal demands placed upon them, as well as escape from the drudgery of their daily lives, and private enjoyment for themselves. Radway found that while these women devoted themselves to nurturing their families, they received little empathy and devotion in return. Romantic fiction, then, allowed escape from tiresome routines—"my time alone"— and supplied the tender heroes and willful heroines absent at home. In Radway's terms, the strong and independent heroines in romance literature enabled the Smithton women's fantasies to cut against masculine dominance. On one level the Smithton women read romance because of their taste for this kind of literature, but at a deeper level, they read to protest and engage their fantasies at the same time.

> The Smithton women were proud of the roles they play in patriarchal society. They were wives and mothers first and foremost. They found in romance novels an affirmation that patriarchy does, indeed, work. Romances promise that sensitive and tender men who will give up everything for their women really do exist. The women knew that the novels are not real life.... But in romance stories, they found a symbolic resolution of the tensions involved in patriarchy: True love is real, but the everyday nature of marriage is hard work, and meeting the daily needs of husbands and children and keeping up with housework is exhausting. (Alexander 2003, 203)

Reading fiction resolved tensions that were unresolved in real life.

Radway examined the language of readers because she believed that textual analysis alone could not explain how people actually read fiction. She complained that literary critics dismissed empirical investigation and relied on their untested intuitions to describe how readers find meaning in a text. Because readers interpret romance novels in multiple ways, Radway insisted that ethnography is essential to understanding the complex negotiations of meaning that occur when readers read (Radway 2009, 201).

Sarah Wendell, author of the blog smartbitchestrashybooks.com, at home with her Kindle and some favorite romance novels (© James Leynse/Corbis).

Radway also developed her perspective in feminist terms. Traditional criticism thought that romance novels suppressed women, who passively and uncritically absorbed messages that subjugated them. Radway criticized this perspective for wrongly supposing all women interpret what they read in the same way. According to Radway, this view assumes romance novels have one fixed meaning that women consume perfunctorily and submissively.

Radway responded to the overly generalized and problematic assumptions of both literary and feminist criticism by examining the economic and social situations of women who read romances. She questioned the participants about their definitions of romance and about their reasons for calling romance novels a success or failure. Then she used psychoanalytic theory to identify the kinds of pleasure these women derive from reading romances.

Reading the Romance has secured its place as a groundbreaking study because its themes resonate with communication scholars, feminists, and cultural critics. Not only did Radway challenge the stereotype of romance readers by investigating the reasons that women read them, but she addressed three long-standing debates in communication studies:

1. *High culture versus low culture.* Academic critics have traditionally distinguished between high art and popular art because they think that mass or popular culture is devoid of moral content or social value. Part of Radway's influence stems from her challenge to this assumption. Radway has helped debunk the view that the books and programs consumed by large segments of society necessarily appeal to our base instincts and inclinations—violence, gender and racial stereotypes, animal sexuality, and crude tastes. A traditional "high culture" typically assumes that popular art forms "reconcile readers to social domination" rather than provide occasions for education or liberation (Caputi 1986, 78).

   In the standard literary criticism that Radway opposes, the plots and characters of romance novels idealize heterosexuality as the model for intimate relationships and even accept violence against women by men. This criticism takes aim at the romance genre for story lines that depict a woman as being incomplete without the devotion of an aggressive man whose violence against the protagonist is a response to the heroine's overwhelming charms.

   Rather than wholesale rejection, Radway probes the contradictions within such narratives without presuming readers are uncritical. She insists on evidence from the practice of reading to understand why such narratives still captivate their audience. In the process of clarifying the social context of reading, Radway also undermines the assumption that the way women are socialized neatly determines the meanings they derive from what they read. Reading romance novels is not a simple process in which authors transfer intended meanings to readers. Instead of extracting a fixed message, readers negotiate and interpret texts in often unforeseen ways. Romance novels, in other words, engage readers actively. To summarize, Radway's work encouraged "a seismic shift in thinking about culture on both sides of the Atlantic"—from a high-literary definition of culture to an anthropological one" (Wood 2004, 148).

2. *Reading communities.* Traditional criticism considers reading to be an individual experience. Faced with the empirical evidence presented by the women of Smithton, Radway explained reading romance novels as a social process of meaning-making. She acknowledged that women read romance novels in the privacy of their homes and, by their own admission, the solitude of reading was a crucial incentive. But Radway insisted that the interactions between the readers and someone like Dot Evans were an equally significant part of their reading. How women relate to one another and discuss their reading affect how they interpret the texts.

3. *Subversion.* Despite the gendered and often stereotypical narratives found in most romance novels, many of the women in Radway's study articulated their own perception of reading as an act of opposition. Radway freely admits that reading romance novels is full of seeming contradictions beginning with resisting oppression by reading stories that dramatize female self-abnegation. The language of resistance used by the women of Smithton seems incongruous with the anti-feminist content of the novels, but Radway finds that, as in other acts of appropriation or opposition, readers always interpret texts, sometimes rejecting what they read and sometimes reconfiguring it.

   As Radway explains, the Smithton women consistently experienced reading as a way to put off the demands associated with their roles as wives and mothers. The women used the language of reading romance novels as a "Declaration of Independence" (Radway 1984, 14) in which they stepped out of their duties as caregivers and nurturers to focus on themselves. These readers used books to secure privacy, conversation, and companionship. The books come between family members and their readers, who temporarily declare themselves off-limits to all those who normally would impinge upon them for emotional support and maternal care. (Radway 2009, 208)

As with any groundbreaking work, Radway's study has been the subject of scrutiny and criticism. Some scholars have questioned whether Radway's immersion in the readers' culture prevented her from achieving critical distance from them and whether her friendship with the readers may have led them to say what they thought the ethnographer wanted to hear (Modleski 1986, p. xii). Other scholars have criticized her focus on middle-class readers, pointing out not only that social class influences how readers interpret popular literature but also that an emphasis on interpretations that resist oppression downplays hardships that people experience because of unequal access to social and economic goods

(Parameswaran 2006). As Ien Ang (1988) says, compensatory pleasure does not replace real needs.

These criticisms have led many scholars to refine Radway's approach to the study of reading, but they hardly detract from her pioneering effort. Radway proposed "the then radical, and now perfectly obvious, notion" that in understanding the agency of audiences, we must "study the members of those audiences to see what they get out of particular media and genres" (Valdivia 2006, 10–11). She showed that reading communities and subversion make a dichotomy between low and high art unacceptable.

SOAP OPERAS

Soap operas are the electronic equivalent of romance fiction, as Radway herself acknowledged in her 1991 review of her research ([1984] 1991, 11). Soap operas originated as dramatic serials broadcast on radio in the late 1920s and early 1930s that were sponsored by household goods and soap manufacturers—Proctor and Gamble, Pillsbury, Lever Brothers, and Colgate-Palmolive. These radio serials were broadcast in daytime hours for homemakers who were the primary market for the sponsors' products.

Soap operas no longer have this narrow programming and audience focus, but the general format continues—an ongoing narrative, with each episode a self-contained story but promising new developments tomorrow. Like romance fiction generally, they emphasize personal relationships, with sexuality, biological families (or professional ones in the medical soaps), and emotional and moral conflicts serialized in the context of the social issues of the day. Soap operas in the United States have been exclusively on television since November 1960, when the last radio network soap opera went off the air.

Soap opera scholar Robert Allen complains that soap operas are the "most parodied of all broadcasting genres" as though they are of interest "primarily or exclusively to uncultured working-class women with simple tastes and limited capacities." He argues that contrariwise, "the soap opera is one of the most narratively complex genres of television drama whose enjoyment requires considerable knowledge by its viewers" and whose appeal "for half a century has cut across social and demographic categories" (Allen 2008, 2; Allen 1985, 1995). In the United States today, for example, 3 million regular viewers are college students. And soap operas in Australia and New Zealand aim to engage teenage and young adult audiences with depictions of feminist, post-feminist, and "Girl Power" characters (Jackson 2006).

Hence, to ascribe the genre's pervasiveness to the medium's visceral power itself, or some inadequacy of viewers, misses the meanings soap operas create. The never-ending nature of the narrative gives viewers no moral resolution, freeing producers to introduce serious ethical and social issues without having to take an overt stance on them (Allen 2004, 253–55).

Ien Ang's critique of the famous 1980s evening soap opera *Dallas* approaches these shows from a perspective similar to Allen and analogous to Radway's position on romance novels. Ang argued that the traditional negative perception of mass culture ignores the enjoyment so common to viewer experience and therefore places our understanding outside "of the way cultural practices take shape in the routines of daily life. Thus it remains both literally and figuratively caught in the ivory towers of 'theory'" (2009, 182). Instead, soap operas must be investigated outside of "high culture" assumptions.

In a later analysis of *Dallas*'s impact among overseas audiences, Liebes and Katz reinforced Radway's perspective. In their research, soap opera ideologies were not simply projected to and received by viewers. Referencing both Ang and Radway, they conclude:

> Viewing escapist programs is not as escapist as it seems. In fact, viewers typically use television fiction as a forum for discussing their own lives. Concern over family, social issues, women's status, and so forth, are activated in response to these programs.... The value comes not from the program, but from negotiation with it. (Liebes and Katz 1990, 154)

Soap operas, like romance novels, are texts that audiences may debate, subvert, appropriate, resist, and share.

Soap operas dominated daytime broadcast ratings before and after World War II. By 1939, more than forty-five 15-minute serials aired weekdays between 10 A.M. and 4 P.M. on the four American radio networks (Hilmes 2006, 8). The genre spread to England with the advent of *Front Line Family*, which was created for the BBC's North American Service in order to encourage American entry into World War II (Hilmes 2006, 5). In 1948, twenty-five of the top thirty daytime programs were soap operas as were the ten highest rated (Allen 2008, 4).

The shift from daytime radio to television was difficult. Viewers needed to pay attention to a screen in one room, rather than listening to radio as background to daily routines. Actors had to perform visually and not merely read their lines. And production costs quadrupled. But by the 1960s, the 30-minute soap opera had established itself on network TV with CBS's *As the World Turns* (sponsored by Proctor and Gamble) leading the ratings. *Days of Our Lives* at University Hospital became a breakthrough hit for NBC and enhanced its daytime ratings through the late 1960s by featuring a "host of medical, emotional, sexual, and psychiatric problems in the show's first years, including incest, impotence, amnesia, illegitimacy, and murder as a result of temporary insanity" (Allen 2008, 6). ABC found its identity through *Peyton Place* as a twice weekly prime-time serial based on the novel by Grace Metalious and its film adaptation. It became the biggest prime-time hit of the 1964–65 television season.

The television soap opera's format of never-ending stories has been resilient. The longest story ever told, *The Guiding Light*, was heard every weekday on radio from 1937 to 1952 and aired on television (CBS) daily from 1952 to 2009. Of the four daytime soaps on network television at present, three of them have been aired every weekday for more than 35 years and *General Hospital* has been aired every weekday for nearly 50. The newest, *The Bold and the Beautiful*, started in 1987.

From the 1970s to the present, the television soap opera has undergone constant innovation. Soap operas face the perennial problem of its audience aging-out of the prime demographic group required by sponsors. Introducing new characters and social controversies to attract new viewers while retaining the loyal ones is a constant challenge. *The Young and the Restless* (CBS) and *The Bold and the Beautiful* (CBS) have been the most successful at responding to this challenge. The genre was invigorated in the 1980s by *Dallas* and the boom in programming soap operas during prime time. *Dallas's* "Who Shot J.R.?" episode attracted one of the largest television audiences ever. It also spawned prime-time imitators *Dynasty* and *Falcon Crest*, a spin-off *Knot's Landing,* and serialized dramas such as *Hill Street Blues.*

Although the number of working women has increased, daytime viewing has not changed very much. "Fifteen percent of core daytime viewers—women ages 18–49—were watching last season, a percentage that's unchanged from 20 years ago" (Levin 2011, 2D). But the shift to cable has been dramatic, with nearly half of the daytime viewership now watching cable TV. *Judge Judy* with 9 million viewers is the most watched cable daytime series. *The Oprah Winfrey Show's* 6.4 million viewers has led the ratings for daytime talk shows, and as she moves on to *Oprah's Next Chapter,* television scrambles to fill the void. Soap opera network audiences are in decline, with talk shows on cable cheaper to produce and younger audiences wanting "entertaining relevance—more talk and reality than scripted drama" (Levin 2011, 2D). Real-life celebrity soap operas on 24-hour cable news have been big since the O.J. Simpson trial. The *Soap Opera Digest*, with a circulation of 1.5 million helps viewers keep up with the plots and characters. The use of video recorders has led to soap operas being tape-recorded off the air more than any other genre. Hilary Estey McLoughlin, president of Warner Bros.' Telepictures Productions, speaks to daytime television programming after Oprah Winfrey with a soap opera inflection about "... real people overcoming adversity and transformation stories....Women connect with" this "kind of fodder" when there are "great storytellers" (Levin 2011, 2D).

TELENOVELAS

When Janice Radway reframed media messages as social events, she opened the door to a richer understanding of telenovas, a version of romantic fiction that seems to engender as many meanings as there are viewers. Telenovas are the most watched television genre on the planet. Anyone who has seen Spanish channels on cable television has likely watched at least part of a telenovela. Its trademarks—melodramatic and repetitive format, visual appeal, and airing frequency—represent a 50-year-old Latin American tradition that today has more vitality than ever. Telenovelas have become ubiquitous as even networks such as ABC have aired telenovelas like *Ugly Betty* during prime-time slots to English-speaking audiences. Telenovas are so popular that when the Spanish-language network Telemundo replaced prime-time telenovelas with remakes of popular English-language programs such as *Charlie's Angels* and *Starsky & Hutch*, its ratings plummeted (Barrera and Bielby 2001, 4).

The origins of the telenovela can be traced to the American soap opera, yet they differ in important ways. First, soap operas air for years or decades and their never-ending narratives center on the lives of several families and characters. In contrast, telenovelas air for a maximum of ten months (or between 120 and 200 episodes) and focus on two (mostly heterosexual) lovers and their journey to overcome adversity and be together. A second difference is the intended audience. Unlike soap operas, which have traditionally been broadcast in the mornings and afternoons for an audience of homemakers, telenovelas have always been prime-time entertainment meant to reach a heterogeneous audience. Accordingly, when initially adopted by Latin American countries, the soap opera format was modified to accommodate the preferences of male audiences that seek closure and resolution of conflict embedded in the narrative. This trend continues today, according to Tomas López-Pumarejo, as telenovelas include in their audience teenagers, immigrants, college students, and married men. "They are becoming more cinematic in plot, content, and visual complexity, and they have proven to be effective in dealing with sensitive social issues more profoundly than other shows" (2007, 199). Telenovelas have stayed current by balancing traditional family values and gender roles with today's social mobility and female empowerment.

Like romance novels and soap operas, telenovelas have been dismissed by academic critics as an inferior genre of mass culture. But following Radway's lead in *Reading the Romance*, research on telenovelas shows a different picture. Like the readers of romance novels in Radway's work, viewers often use telenovelas to facilitate cultural resistance and oppositional perspectives. López-Pumarejo has found that, more than simply working as tear-jerking Cinderella stories, many viewers see in telenovelas reflections of the national culture (2007, 206).

As a result of demand from Latin America, Europe, and Asia in the 1980s, telenovelas have become Latin America's number one cultural export (Barrera and Bielby 2001, 5). Part of their extraordinary success is because Globo (Brazil's leading exporter of telenovelas) and Televisa (Mexico) are vertically integrated conglomerates. But telenovelas are also inexpensive to produce and their ongoing storylines keep audiences coming back for more. Additionally, telenovelas are sold at different prices to maximize reach and distribution. Telenovelas continue to rise in demand and popularity in the countries of Eastern Europe (Jujnovic 2008). Israel and the Dominican Republic import more telenovelas than other countries (López-Pumarejo 2007, 198). Mexico's Televisa soap operas have topped the ratings in Korea, Russia, and Turkey. As public broadcasting shrinks in many countries around the world, nations with growing commercial systems acquire telenovelas to please a wide audience.

Many of the same dynamics are underway in Turkey where its racy soap operas are becoming big television hits from Morocco to Iraq. Dogan TV Holding, Turkey's largest media market, produces the soap operas *Gumus* (*Noor* in Arabic) and the steamy *Ask-I Memnu* and markets them throughout the Middle East. For Irfan Shain, Dogan TV Holding's Chief Executive, "it's all about local culture. Regionalism, not globalism, sells" (Kimmelman 2010, 2). Television critic

Sina Kologlu put the dramatic rise of Turkish soap operas in historic terms: "Years ago we took reruns of *Dallas* and *The Young and the Restless*. Asians and Eastern Europeans are buying Turkish series, not American or Brazilian or Mexican ones. They get the same cheating and the children out of wedlock and the incestuous affairs but with a Turkish sauce on top" (Kimmelman 2010, 3).

REALITY TELEVISION

Another genre of television illustrates the complex interplay of audience, economics, and fiction suggested by Radway's study of romance novels: Reality TV.[2] Rather than relying on traditional writers and cinematographers, reality television's cast members produce its intense, competitive, and dramatic programming. Jason Mittell observes:

> One of the most striking success stories in recent American television is the rise of reality TV over the past decade, a development that has led many commentators to assert that such programming is what viewers really want—or more cynically, what we ultimately deserve. (Mittell 2010, 86)[3]

Reality television has a complex history. *Survivor*, a game-like competition pitting cast members against each other with the backdrop of surviving on a remote island, arrived in Summer 2000 and is often considered the genre's breakout hit. Many shows utilized its juxtaposition of a very narrow reality with carefully managed outcomes, going all the way back to *Candid Camera* of the 1950s (Mittell 2010, 86–88). Shows of the 1990s like *Cops* and *America's Most Wanted*, as well as MTV's *Real World,* set the tone for the following decade's rapid growth. The quiz show *Who Wants to Be a Millionaire* appeared in 1999, and itself had roots in earlier game shows and televised contests.

The results were seldom pretty, but they fascinated viewers. *Survivor*, considered by many a classic but one of the tamer offerings of reality TV, features both physical hardship of weathering life as a twenty-first-century castaway, along with inevitable betrayal since only one winner can emerge. *Fear Factor* contestants were forced to face various scary or disgusting encounters for the chance to win a hefty cash prize. An episode might feature twenty- and thirty-somethings eating cockroaches, flipping a vehicle, or navigating beams high above the ground.

Reality TV has had its share of romance, too. Shows such as *The Bachelor* and *The Bachelorette* highlight one individual's quest for true love, with the protagonist sorting through several dozen prospective mates via a wide range of encounters, some fun, others romantic, many awkward as cast members are eliminated one-by-one. Tied to almost all of the shows are pervasive product placements and marketing.

In many ways, reality television offers the same mix of motivations, reliance on stereotypes, and life's quirkiness, as romance novels do. As Jason Mittell argues:

> One of the key features of reality television is that it constructs a vision of the "real world" that is highly selective and distorted....Reality television represents

America filled with highly attractive young adults who are obsessed with competition, greed, and consumerism to the point that they will eat bugs or marry strangers to win, with few ethical hurdles standing in the way of success. (2010, 93)

However, like Radway with romances, Mittell realizes—despite the economic logic underlying the production of both media—that it "would be a major mistake to assume that if meanings are present in a program, viewers must automatically adopt them" (Mittell 2010, 94). *Survivor* may bring up new considerations of the nature of loyalty, while *America's Next Top Model* could help viewers grapple with questions of stereotypes and beauty. Watching people overcome their anxieties on *Fear Factor* could inspire an audience rather than intimidate them. Programs like *The Bachelor* and *The Bachelorette* could engage viewers similarly to Radway's readers. Audience meaning-making is more active than we may think, even when watching people chew worms.

ONLINE ROMANCE FICTION

In *Reading the Romance,* the women of Smithton relied on local romance maven and bookstore employee Dot Evans for book recommendations. Today the Internet enables fans all over the globe to join online communities for sharing their enthusiasm for romances. Websites for discussing, reviewing, and marketing romance novels range from those created by fans and advocacy groups, to those of established and aspiring writers, to home websites of romance book publishers. Harlequin Enterprises Limited, for example, publishes over 110 titles a month in thirty-two languages. These books are written by some 1,200 authors worldwide. The website *eharlequin.com* stands out with its interactive features to shop, learn to write, blog, review, and read free digital novels. Membership perks include writing guidelines and a professional critique service for aspiring authors.

Titles themselves are now also widely available in electronic form. In addition to its online presence, Harlequin was one of the first large publishers to make its books available in the eBook format. In 2010, Harlequin also ventured into a new electronic publication medium: it announced that select titles would be available electronically in Japan on the Nintendo DS portable gaming system. It was the first non-Japanese publisher to do so. Other popular romance publishers like Avon, Dorchester, and Hatchette help promote their global presence with online sites that offer book recommendations and discussion forums for fans of the genre.

However much publishers of the genre strive to meet the increasingly interactive needs of readers, there can be little doubt that the online romance fiction revolution is being led by its fans. Popular blog communities like *Romantic Links*, *Romance Vagabonds*, *The Goddess Blogs*, *Romance Bandits*, *Trashionista*, and *Romancing the Blog*, provide space where fans freely indulge and share their experiences as romance readers. Websites like *starry.com* offer free novels and cyberbooks in their entirety in order to promote the work of authors not yet recognized by mainstream publishers.

Among such sites, *RomanceNovel.tv* continues to rise in popularity. Created in 2007 by two sisters as the first network for fans of the romance genre, it offers direct access to popular authors through video interviews, casual conversations, and online chats. The website features blogs, news items, reviews, links, discussion forums, and book excerpts from both new as well as established authors. The site also offers excerpts from forthcoming novels, and in 2009 added an online book club and discussion board. Though the medium differs from Radway's books, library chats, and discussion groups, readers are as active online as they have ever been throughout the history of romance fiction.[4]

FEMINIST MEDIA ETHICS

Radway approaches the social context of reading from a self-consciously feminist perspective. Although the happy endings in popular romance typically entail a male hero embracing an adoring heroine, the women did not inevitably accept conservative traditions. Radway suggested that "romances offer 'compensatory literature' which occupies a temporary therapeutic space in the everyday lives of women who carry the burden for the care of others within the oppressive patriarchal family" (Wood 2004, 150–51). Helen Wood contends that Radway's feminist commitment insists on a "raising of consciousness" and assumes that feminism "offers a superior set of solutions to the problems of ordinary women" (2004, 151). Radway struggles with the enigma of all participant observation— how to integrate the voice and values of the researched with the researcher's interpretation.

At the end of *Reading the Romance*, Radway called for renewed efforts to study audience responses to popular culture: "The very fruitfulness of the methodology employed here indicates that we may not yet understand the complexity of mass culture's implication in social life" ([1984] 1991, 220–21). Rising to this challenge, Radhika Parameswaran studied seven groups of women (17 to 21 years old) in Hyderabad, India, who meet to discuss romance novels. Because she situates her ethnographic audience studies deeply in history and social context, Parameswaran sees reading practices in India in terms of resistance, submission, and coping mechanisms, but she also identifies a "troubling resurgence of patriarchal nationalism based in religious fundamentalism" (2006, 324). By studying non-Western media experiences, Parameswaran is helping to develop what she refers to as "alternative knowledges of the non-West, knowledges that revise, revisit, and complicate the narratives that have been fashioned by European/colonial anthropologists and administrators" (2006, 316).

Radway and subsequent audience researchers practice person-centered feminist media ethics. Understanding the moral domain in the everyday experiences that people share, these feminist scholars focus on romance readers and viewers, not on neutral principles and abstract judgments. Judgments of responsibility and decency, feelings of approval and shame, acts of compassion and care—these form the moral ideals that are grounded in community understanding.

Linda Steiner develops a systematic overview of this person-centered feminist media ethics, its accomplishments to date, and its future in media studies (2009). In her summary, "feminist approaches to ethics challenge women's subordination, prescribe morally justifiable ways of resisting oppressive practices, and envision morally desirable alternatives that promote emancipation" (2009, 377). Beyond this agenda, Steiner advocates a multicultural feminism that respects differences of all sorts—one that incorporates "values (such as community) and responsibilities (such as caring) that historically are associated with women, without assuming all women around the globe are permanently, much less equally, subordinated, and pressed into patriarchal domestic, reproductive, and sexual arrangements" (2009, 377). Reading books, watching television and movies, and producing Internet stories are productive arenas everywhere for putting this kind of feminist ethics to work.

Norman Denzin proposes a feminist communitarian ethics that brings together the best of both worlds. Both feminism and communitarianism are dialogic in character and emphasize humans-in-relation. Both are committed to a morality rooted in human experience and everyday life, rather than an ethics of abstract principle and rigid prescriptions (cf. Christians 2004, 238–41). Feminist communitarian ethics recognizes that "multiple moral and social spaces or spheres ...exist within the local community" (Denzin 1997, 277). Various social structures (family, religious organizations, schools, and government) are included in this framework. Communitarianism ensures that the public is taken seriously, and the feminist perspective emphasizes crucial dimensions of that public—gender, race, and ethnicity.

Feminist and communitarian ethicists believe that persons grow as they relate to others. The diversity of individuals-in-relation is emphasized within social structures, and each of these social structures is given close attention. As Steiner notes, "Ethical schemas that work only for women, or only in the private or intimate domain, will not suffice—certainly not in the media professions" (2008, 209).

A feminist communitarian ethics sees itself as gender neutral, and it extends beyond adults to children. It recognizes that "scholarly discourse has demonstrated little interest in or patience for kids outside of certain conventions such as school, gangs, or deviant behavior" (King 2009, 138). Instead it might ask, as C. Richard King does, what it would mean for cultural studies to give kids' popular culture its due. In short, Steiner summarizes, "to be useful, media ethics must holistically take seriously these interrelated dimensions" (2008, 207).

Moreover, a feminist communitarian perspective informed by Radway does not reduce the interpretation of mass culture to individual experiences of it. The important question is the nature of the social-individual mix here. It is a commonplace that individual viewers come away from TV viewing or book reading with whatever they personally find worthwhile in it. Dorothea Schulz has examined imported soap operas and telenovelas in the nation of Mali with this issue in mind—how are individual experiences and cultural givens interrelational? She concludes that "spectators' engagement with media content does not exhaust the social significance of their media practices" (2007, 24). The narrative's structure and its viewers' collective experiences shape "preferred readings" of these television shows (2007, 28). Just as Radway carefully balanced the reality of romance novel themes with what readers took away, a feminist communitarian approach strives for a nuanced understanding of the individual resistance that is possible against powerful marketing or political concerns of the mass media.

MORAL LITERACY

Human communities exist through language, which makes interaction possible and defines our identity. Communities are knitted together linguistically. And language is infused with values, which means that our social bonds are moral claims. Humans use language to articulate their desires and dreams and to engage the world outside. People depict and explain what they consider meaningful; they do not hold beliefs separately from their communication about them. Higher values are discriminated from lesser ones in dialogue. Humans see themselves in terms of practices and ideas that they evaluate as more worthy or less important. Within communities, judgments are made about the quality of life. Our widely shared moral intuitions—respect for the dignity of others, for instance—are developed through discourse within a community. More than specializing in reason or helping humans meet basic needs, language represents values, beliefs, and norms—the human spirit.

Without a broad acceptance of some common values such as tolerance and human dignity, a viable social order is impossible. Because our public life is based on moral values, the media should help us examine and discuss the common good. Put another way, moral literacy ought to have priority as the media's mission. Communications in the social arena ought to stimulate the moral imagination. This language appears whenever public policy asks, "Do these programs have any redeeming value?"

Do we use romance media to help us traverse the moral landscape? Do they inspire conversations about moral issues in moral terms? Are the moral contours of their taken-for-granted worlds (daily chores, dinner prep, homework, dishwashing) illuminated in ways that encourage us to discuss them together? That is partly what Janice Radway found among her Smithton readers. Romances provided them with not just a respite from diapers and chores but also the desire to penetrate the physical and social surface to the moral dynamics underneath. In this sense, the romance media assist the process of moral articulation. Because communities are woven together by stories that invigorate their common understanding of good and evil, happiness and reward, and life and death, communitarian ethics uses this "invigoration" standard for evaluating the popular arts.[5]

Moral literacy usually emerges despite the intentions of television executives who see the audiences of soap operas as markets rather than as social or citizen groups. Publishers of romance novels have very specific guidelines for aspiring authors that stipulate the tried-and-true ingredients that are sure to sell to target demographics. But moral literacy can still find a place in that frame of reference because readers are incessant creators of meaning:

> Consciously or unconsciously, consumers of mediated representations are value seekers. We search for meaning, the worth, the authenticity, the purpose, and the usefulness of a representation for our lives. Some representations we deflect as irrelevant; some we make selections from, that is, we extract those elements we find interesting or relevant; some we accept uncritically. In all these instances, we are necessarily engaging in a dialogue about meaning, importance, and value (Japp 2005, 43)

Readers can find community in romance fiction. Some romance novels and soap operas have raised consciousness of anti-Semitism, racism, and gender discrimination. Telenovelas and online romance fiction have facilitated moral discernment by their insight into humankind and by affirming that history has purpose. Viewers, readers, and bloggers have found in the unique aesthetic capacities of romance fiction the means of empowerment toward moral literacy.

ETHICS OF MEDIA ENTERTAINMENT

Romance novels, soap operas, telenovelas, reality TV, and online fiction are all forms of popular culture that are mass-distributed without explicit concern for the quality of their moral content. But moral literacy finds a place in these media due to readers' constant creation of meaning. Why then is focusing on the ethics of entertainment worthwhile? Does not popular culture's persistent commercialism, tendency to simplify and titillate, and demand for broad appeal, reduce its value for ethical reflection?

Japp, Meister, and Japp (2005) provide two answers to these questions. First, entertainment media are familiar in that "popular art, for good or ill, has become our cultural thesaurus of everyday life, often the only common frame of reference across race, gender, class, and other social divides" (6). Second, popular culture "mirrors the world in which we live, demonstrates the difficulties of discovering and maintaining ethical standards in a postmodern, mediated, commercialized culture" (6). Popular art can provide a range of acceptable interpretations of everyday life. The entertainment arts "allow human beings to see themselves and their lives differently and to make changes based on those understandings" (Wilkins 2008, 252). As interpretive beings living with others, popular art—certainly the romance genre—is impossible to ignore.

Judging these answers to be satisfactory, what does a communitarian ethics of media entertainment emphasize?

Dialogue is one crucial component. Media narratives are not mere reflections of reality, but reconstructions of it. To process the hundreds of representations that we receive every day, as meaning-makers we engage those messages, holding tight to some while rejecting or bypassing others. Ethically speaking, Radway's groundbreaking work fosters moral literacy, at least in part, by acknowledging that romance readers actively construct their moral understanding of the books they read. Therefore, while the creators of mediated messages have responsibility, so does the public.

Given the new approach to popular culture that Radway represents, utilitarian ethics is unworkable. Focusing on consequences assumes the traditional theory of media effects that understands viewers as passive. This sender-message-receiver model is oriented to the sender, to an outside stimulus such as romance novels or television programs. "The basic model of media effects conceives of senders and messages as much more powerful than receivers in a communication system" (Mittell 2010, 362).[6] Calculating the consequences depends on the framework of causes and effects. Utilitarian media ethics tends to regard programs as stimuli that produce measurable results. The active audience model, on the other hand, "looks at the power of messages in relation to the power and practices of the viewers themselves" (Mittell 2010, 363; see 357–73). Audience interaction with media programs makes popular art a cultural forum rather than one simple uniform message. Communitarian ethics maps onto Radway's different understanding of mediated communication in a way consequentialism does not.

University of Edinburgh Professor Jolyon Mitchell demonstrates how the active-audience perspective validates communitarian ethics. Rather than focusing on the decisions of media producers, he explores how audiences can become moral agents. He argues for discerning readers and viewers who collectively examine and reframe violent news and entertainment. Learning the language of nonviolence goes beyond media analysis to participation in peace-oriented friendships and communities. In Mitchell's view, these are enriched by religious worship, where habits of nonviolence and forgiveness are experienced and nurtured (2007, 229). Faith communities can reframe media violence into a vision of peace.

A second major task for the communitarian ethics of entertainment is making sure that voices outside the dominant strands of popular culture are heard and encouraged. Popular culture tends to ignore possibilities beyond its main concerns, that is, to represent those artistic forms that resonate with the largest possible audience. Mass culture limits peoples' options for constructing their linguistic home (Bineham 2005, 20–21, 27). The communitarian approach, however, reaches beyond common-denominator programming. Its task is to insure that alternative meanings are available.

Walter Benjamin's classic essay, "The Work of Art in the Age of Mechanical Reproduction" (1955), puts this challenge in its most dramatic form. The technique of reproduction, as with radio and television soap operas, brings art objects close to a mass audience, but this process alters the images' quality. In Benjamin's terms, art's aura of authenticity has been destroyed by its being reproduced, with the copies simulating their own aesthetics at odds with the original. Despite these complications to the ideals of creativity and originality, communitarian ethics calls for popular art that opens up multiple worlds outside of its own technique. Otherwise one is resigned to mechanical art as reinforcing the status quo and keeping weaker groups out of power. Oral communications and the images they create are a community's lifeblood. Although images mechanically reproduced in a democratic society are of a different genre, communitarianism judges them by the same standard.

Aesthetic truth is a third feature of communitarian ethics in entertainment. Bill Moyers on PBS puts the promise of television in terms of its etymology: "The root word of television is vision from afar, and that is its chief value" (quoted in Patterson and Wilkins 2011, 285). Television, novels, online romance fiction, and other artistic forms of mass culture ideally help bring others, ourselves, and our worlds into sharper focus.

> Aesthetic truth has always had a metaphorical quality. Beginning with the work of the Greeks, the fictional renderings of drama were expected to reveal not the literal truth but that which is most difficult to come by—what Gandhi called "the truth of the human heart." (Wilkins 2008, 252)

At its best, popular art communicates truth about human culture. It discloses the hiddenness of our everyday life, its purpose and meaning. In communitarian terms, great art feeds the aesthetic imagination with morality and beauty, both of them appearing "as harmonious adaptations of the parts to the whole. Morality involves the subordination of one's desires to the overriding purpose of the morally good, while in beauty all particular details are harmonized in the unity of the aesthetic experience" (Dorter 2000, 45). When print and online romance fiction, soap operas, daytime talk shows, telenovelas, and reality television inspire aesthetic truth, they dignify human life. Integrating ethics and aesthetics fosters the formation of robust communities in technologically advanced societies.

CONCLUSION

Reading the Romance and its successors provide a theoretical framework with which to focus our analytic attention on print, visual and cyber media. Radway insists that interpretation spills outside of the text and into its social context. When reading and viewing are understood in the cultural terms that Radway and her legacy represent, our concern is not just the transmission of entertainment programs but human welfare.

Cultivating communities is the overall task of popular art. The artistic challenge is to promote an aesthetic where communities are primary. Communities in dialogue about the values that bind their members to one another should be the destination toward which mediated entertainment points. When communities are healthy, constructive political change takes place.

NOTES

1. Professor Melba Vélez of Grand Valley State University wrote the initial draft of this section, and also the first drafts of "Telenovas" and "Online Romance Fiction."
2. For a sophisticated analysis of these dynamics in reality TV, see Ouellette and Hay (2008).

3. This quotation refers to American television. For an examination of reality TV in the Middle East, both imported programs and local productions, see Ayish (2010).
4. Research is necessary to clarify internet relationships among romance fiction writers and readers, in order to compare them precisely to the Radway book-radio-television tradition. For review of the issues and strategies in online research, see Johns, Chen, and Hall (2004). The "Digital Ethnography" project at Kansas State University is breaking new ground in applying the research methods of anthropology to digital culture.
5. Schulz's analysis of Mali soap operas found that almost all Malian men distinguished between *filimu* [imported programs], not on the basis of geographical origin but in terms of their moral messages (2007, 26).
6. Professor Bagele Chilisa (2005) of the University of Botswana describes how the cause-effect model, presuming the passive viewer, discredits ways of knowing in communal societies. This unidirectional Western research methodology tends to favor the First World's thinking and subjugate indigenous knowledge systems.

REFERENCES

Alexander, Victoria D. 2003. *Sociology of the Arts: Exploring Fine and Popular Forms.* Oxford, U.K.: Blackwell Publishing.

Allen, Robert C. 1985. *Speaking of Soap Operas.* Chapel Hill: University of North Carolina Press.

——. 1995. *To Be Continued: Soap Operas Around the World.* London: Routledge.

——. 2004. "Making Sense of Soaps." In Robert C. Allen and Annette Hill, eds., *The Television Studies Reader,* 242–57. London: Routledge.

——. 2008. "Soap Opera." The Museum of Broadcast Communications. <http:www.museum.tv/archives>.

Ang, Ien. 1985. *Watching Dallas: Soap Opera and the Melodramatic Imagination.* Translated by Della Couling. London: Methuen.

——. 1988. "Feminist Desire and Female Pleasure: On Janice Radway's *Reading the Romance.*" *Camera Obscura* 16: 179–90.

——. 2009. "*Dallas* and the Ideology of Mass Culture." In John Storey, ed., *Cultural Theory and Popular Culture: A Reader,* 4th ed., 173–82. Harlow, U.K.: Pearson.

Barrera, Vivian, and Bielby, Denise D. 2001. "Places, Faces and Other Familiar Things: The Cultural Experience of Telenovela Viewing among Latinos in the United States." *Journal of Popular Culture* 34: 1–18.

Benjamin, Walter. 1979. "The Work of Art in the Age of Mechanical Reproduction." In his *Illuminations,* 3rd ed., 219–53. Translated by H. Zohn. Glasgow: Fontana/Collins. [original work published 1955]

Bineham, Jeffrey J. 2005. "The Construction of Ethical Codes in the Discourse and Criticism of Popular Culture." In P. M. Japp, M. Meister, and D. K. Japp, eds., *Communication Ethics, Media, and Popular Culture,* 13–40. New York: Peter Lang Publishing.

Bosman, Julie. 2010. "Lusty Tales and Hot Sales: Romance Novels Thrive as E-Books." *New York Times,* December 9, A1, A3.

Caputi, Jane E. 1986. Review of the book *Reading the Romance: Women, Patriarchy, and Popular Literature. Library Quarterly* 70 (January): 78–80.

Chilisa, Bagele. 2005. "Educational Research Within Postcolonial Africa: A Critique of HIV/AIDS Research in Botswana." *International Journal of Qualitative Studies in Education,* 18(6), 659–84.

Christians, Clifford. 2004. "*Ubuntu* and Communitarianism in Media Ethics." *Ecquid Novi* 25 (2): 235–56.

Denzin, Norman. 1997. *Interpretive Ethnography: Interpretive Practices for the 21st Century.* Thousand Oaks, CA: Sage.

Dorter, Kenneth. 1990. "Conceptual Truth and Aesthetic Truth." *The Journal of Aesthetics and Art Criticism* 84(1), Winter, 37–51.

Hilmes, Michele. 2006. "*Front Line Family*: 'Women's Culture' Comes to the BBC." *Media, Culture and Society* 29 (1): 5–29.

Jackson, Sue. 2006. "Street Girl: New Sexual Subjectivity in a NZ Soap Opera Drama?" *Feminist Media Studies* 6 (4): 469–86.

Japp, Phyllis M. 2005. "Representation as Ethical Discourse: Communicating with and about Mediated Popular Culture." In P. M. Japp, M. Meister, D. K. Japp, eds., *Communication Ethics, Media, & Popular Culture*, 41–63. New York: Peter Lang Publishing.

Japp, Phyllis M., Meister, Mark, Japp, Debra K. 2005. "Communication Ethics, Media, & Popular Culture: An Introduction." In P. M. Japp, M. Meister, D. K. Japp, eds., *Communication Ethics, Media, & Popular Culture*, 1–12. New York: Peter Lang Publishing.

Johns, Mark D., Chen, Shing-Ling, and Hall, Jon G. 2004. *Online Social Research: Methods, Issues and Ethics.* New York: Peter Lang.

Jujnovic, Marina. 2008. "The Political Economy of Croatian Television: Exploring the Impact of Latin American Telenovelas." *Communications* 33: 431–54.

Kimmelman, Michael. 2010. "Turks Put Twist in Racy Soaps." *New York Times,* June 17, 1–4. <http://www.nytimes.com/2010/06/18/arts/18abroad.html>

King, C. Richard. 2009. "Nurturing Racism: Taking Race and Kids (Popular) Culture Seriously." *Cultural Studies-Critical Methodologies* 9 (2): 137–40.

Levin, Gary. 2011. "Who Will Fill the Void Left by Oprah?" *USA Today,* May 25, 1D, 3D.

Liebes, T., and Katz, E. 1990. *The Export of Meaning: Cross-Cultural Readings of Dallas.* New York: Oxford University Press.

López-Pumarejo, Tomas. 2007. "Telenovelas and the Israeli Television Market." *Television New Media* 9: 191–212.

Mitchell, Jolyon. 2007. *Media Violence and Christian Ethics.* Cambridge, U.K.: Cambridge University Press.

Mittell, Jason. 2010. *Television and American Culture.* New York: Oxford University Press.

Modleski, Tania. 1986. *Studies in Entertainment: Critical Approaches to Mass Culture.* Bloomington: Indiana University Press.

Ouellette, Laurie and Hay, James. 2008. *Reality TV: Television and Post-Welfare Citizenship.* Malden, MA: Wiley-Blackwell.

Parameswaran, Radhika E. 2006. "Resuscitating Feminist Audience Studies: Revisiting the Politics of Representation and Resistance." In Angharad Valdivia, ed., *A Companion to Media Studies*, 311–36. Oxford, U.K.: Blackwell Publishing.

Patterson, Philip, and Wilkins, Lee. 2011. *Media Ethics: Issues and Cases*, 7th ed. New York: McGraw-Hill.

Radway. Janice, A. [1984] 1991. *Reading the Romance: Women, Patriarchy, and Popular Literature.* Chapel Hill: University of North Carolina Press.

———. 2009. "Reading the Romance." In John Storey, ed., *Cultural Theory and Popular Culture: A Reader*, 4th ed., 199–215. Harlow, U.K.: Pearson.

Schulz, Dorothea E. 2007. "Drama, Desire, and Debate: Mass-Mediated Subjectivities in Urban Mali." *Visual Anthropology* 20: 19–39.

Steiner, Linda. 2008. "Inclusive Gender Sensitivity: Reasoning through *Girls Gone Wild.*" In T. Cooper, C. Christians, and A. Babbili, eds., *An Ethics Trajectory: Visions of Media Past, Present and Yet to Come*, 203–12. Urbana: Institute of Communications Research, University of Illinois.

———. 2009. "Feminist Media Ethics," In Lee Wilkins and Clifford Christians, eds., *Handbook for Mass Media Ethics*, 366–81. New York: Routledge.

Valdivia, Angharad, ed. 2006. *A Companion to Media Studies.* Oxford, U.K.: Blackwell Publishing.

Wilkins, Lee. 2008. "The Future Ethical Issues of Entertainment." In T. Cooper, C. Christians, and A. Babbili, eds., *An Ethics Trajectory: Visions of Media Past, Present and Yet to Come,* 251–55. Urbana: Institute of Communications Research, University of Illinois.

Wood, Helen. 2004. "What *Reading the Romance* Did for Us." *European Journal of Cultural Studies* 7 (2): 147–54.

CHAPTER 15

✍

Art, Rage, Violence, Protest

Dude Freeman, a 16-year-old east-sider, and Rod Phelps, a 19-year-old west-sider, were two Detroit youth caught between friends, family, survival, drugs, and police. Subjects of a study in one of the country's most wrecked cities, their stories are about growing up with expectations of not surviving streets and social systems seemingly set against them. Author Luke Bergmann described how those systems worked:

> The [court] bureaucracy is so entrenched and every decision must move through clogged channels, kids may wait months for a decision about placement, sentencing, or adjudication that they expect "any day." Young people locked up [at Wayne County Juvenile] are simultaneously bored to stupefaction and racked with anxiety. Even as the days blur together, heavy with a sense of unknown imminence, things might shift unpredictably at any moment, as everyone goes to court, comes back, goes again to court, and comes back again to wait. (2008, 153)

Dude and Rod's stories—two lives of violent disappointments, too commonplace in American cities—caught even Bergmann by surprise. At the end, Bergmann, trained to observe and take careful field notes, simply writes: "I stood up slowly, still leaning against the car, and start to cry" (2008, 274).

If any environment screams for add-on moral virtue, this one does. Get Detroit 100 truckloads of justice, 200 of prudence. All the temperance in world warehouses, ship it express. And without C-130s loaded with courage, liberally dropped throughout the city, none of the rest makes a difference. Do the same for Gary, East St. Louis, Chicago, and New Orleans. Send leftovers to sun-soaked L.A., where everything began.

Ice-T was a member of the elite Army Rangers before he became a hip-hop and movie star. He took orders before becoming famous for cursing order-givers. Now at midlife, the music-rap phenomenon is best remembered for helping found the genre of "gangsta" rap—and for his anger at Daryl Gates, police chief of Los Angeles in the early 1990s, when the song "Cop Killer" was released. Police across the country felt under siege to a rage enflamed by the beat and passion of "one of rap's leading and most controversial figures" (Freydkin 1999).

Ice-T was born Tracy Lauren Marrow in 1958. His mother died when he was in third grade, his father four years later. After his father's death, family members sent Marrow to South Central Los Angeles to live with his paternal aunt—where he entertained friends and enjoyed the growing culture of hip-hop music. He attended South Central's Crenshaw High. And then, alternatives looking grim, Marrow enlisted:

> I got into the army because I had a kid and the army was an equal-opportunity employer. I was in trouble…and a lot of times people like that end up at a recruiter's office, tryin' to get their shit straight. So I went in there and I tried to roll with it. (Bennett 2006, 1)

After completing service in the Rangers, Tracy Marrow returned to Los Angeles and focused on building a life beholden to no one. Indeed, he is famously quoted as saying about his military duty, "I didn't like total submission to a leader other than myself." It seems eventually he found the leader he preferred.

In the early 1980s Marrow started to build a name on the street, calling himself Ice-T in homage to the legendary pimp-author Iceberg Slim. His plan upon leaving the army was to become a DJ and club promoter, but he made far more money as a hustler, stealing cars and pulling heists (Pinfield 2005). Eventually he began rapping at the Radio Club, which regularly featured hip-hop artists. He released his first singles in 1982–83, "Coldest Rap" and "Cold Wind Madness." Ice-T was also featured as an artist in two 1984 break-dancing films, *Breakin'* and *Breakin' 2*.

In 1987 Ice-T struck RIAA gold when his debut album, *Rhyme Pays*, went to No. 26 on *Billboard's* R & B charts. The iconic album, with its hit single "6 in the Morning," became one of the first true "gangsta" rap records. Produced by West Coast rap legend Africa Islam, *Rhyme Pays* was also the first hip-hop album released by Sire/Warner Brothers. Even more success followed with the genre-defining classics *Power*, which went platinum in 1988, and 1989's gold-status *The Iceberg/ Freedom of Speech…Just Watch What You Say*. By 1991, Ice-T and his crews were widely considered at their height: most hip-hop fans take that year's *O.G. (Original Gangster)* as his masterwork. Numerous critics gave the record four and five stars; on *Billboard's* Top 200 it shot to No. 9. (Hip-hop magazine *The Source* considers *O.G.* among the top 100 rap albums of all time.) In 1991, along with several other artists, he won a Grammy for Best Rap Performance by a Group. By the beginning of the 1990s Ice-T's rhymes, beats, and stage presence had transformed him into a music superstar.

The release of *O.G.* also introduced a new twist on Ice-T's earlier work: The record's "Body Count" track featured Ice-T's new hardcore punk/metal/rock band, Body Count. Ice-T and his friends grew up with rock, funk, and R & B as much as rap, listening to groups from Black Sabbath to George Clinton and James Brown (Pinfield 2005). Formed in 1990 by Ice-T and four friends from Crenshaw High, Body Count rose to prominence the following year after Ice-T arranged for them to play half of each of his contracted sets on 1991's inaugural Lollapalooza mega-tour. The band name referred to the LA news media's practice of reporting daily body counts from violence in South Central's neighborhoods.

Ice-T wrote "Cop Killer" in 1990, and Body Count made the song a staple of their well-received Lollapalooza act and through the end of 1991. Although

Ice-T was criticized in some rap circles—sometimes with a racial subtext—for his perceived switch in genres (even though all of the band's members were African American), the success led Body Count to the studio, where they laid down "Cop Killer" and other tracks into a full-length, self-titled album released in March 1992. Soon after, controversy over the song exploded.

The lyrics of "Cop Killer" are copyrighted and cannot be reproduced here, but they are widely known. Written from the perspective of a person who "loses it" and begins to hunt down police officers, Ice-T called it a "protest record [sung as if the performer] is fed up with police brutality" (McKinnon 2006).

In the first weeks after *Body Count*'s release, nothing happened. Late that spring, a jury in California acquitted white police officers who beat up African American LA-resident Rodney King. Sustained riots broke out in Los Angeles. In the aftermath of the riots that summer, a police officer in Texas brought "Cop Killer" to public attention via a police association newsletter. The Dallas Police Association and the Combined Law Enforcement Association of Texas (CLEAT) quickly launched a protest of the song, claiming it put officers in danger, and asked Warner Brothers Records to withdraw the album from distribution. CLEAT carried the campaign further, urging a nationwide boycott of all Time-Warner products. Police in Greensboro, North Carolina, announced they would not respond to calls from a store selling the record. Soon after, *Body Count* was removed from shelves in that store.

A nationwide reaction followed. President George H. W. Bush and Vice President Dan Quayle denounced the album. Tipper Gore, then active on issues related to media impact on children, condemned the song, comparing it to Hitler's anti-Semitism. Actor Charlton Heston, by then well-known in conservative political circles but not yet president of the National Rifle Association, protested by reading the lyrics of "Cop Killer" at a Warner Brothers shareholder meeting. Others defended "Cop Killer" as legitimate protest fully protected by the First Amendment (Sieving 1998).

And what did Ice-T think? In his bestselling 1994 book *The Ice Opinion*, Ice-T claims that the rap was to be "a metaphor for the dismembering of racism … whoever is still perpetrating racism has got to die, not necessarily physically, but they have to kill off that part of their brain" (168). The protest intended in Ice-T's in-your-face lyrics was to be a "warning, not a threat—to authority that says, 'Yo, police: we're human beings. Treat us accordingly'" (169).

In Ice-T's world, urban America—the ghetto or the 'hood—is a war zone. A community of citizen and state does not exist. He writes:

> When you're coming out of the ghetto you learn the cops aren't your friends, and you quickly realize they are the enemy.… Anybody in the ghetto can tell you the cops aren't there to "protect and serve."… You learn [that] by experience. (1994, 4–5)

As rage over "Cop Killer" grew, supporters lined up, too. Ice-T claims that 35,000 African American police officers "know I was saying the truth" (1994, 175). His fans, he claims, presumed the validity of the song's protest and "smiled and understood it" (1994, 169). Warner Brothers Records backed their artist, but felt the economic pressure. Finally, Ice-T himself removed the song from the album, with motives as curious as the song itself:

> I didn't have any fear about something happening to somebody on the street. ... If cops were out there doing an honest job, people wouldn't hate them so intensely. I was more worried about some lunatic hurting somebody at Warner Brothers or even about one of those cops going out and killing a cop and trying to pin it on me. (1994, 176)

The notoriety fueled sales of *Body Count*. After CLEAT's announcement, sales tripled in Texas. By August, the album jumped from No. 76 to No. 23 on *Billboard's* charts (Sieving 1998, 339–40), eventually selling over 500,000 copies. Although Ice-T pulled the song from later pressings, he replaced "Cop Killer" lyrics with the First Amendment in the album's liner notes.

Sieving points out that few, if any, outlets published more than bits and pieces of "Cop Killer's" lyrics. The song was never released as a single, nor did it receive radio play. No media coverage included the spoken-word introduction to the song, on which Ice-T stated "Cop Killer" was dedicated to cops who had hurt others out of hatred or prejudice. He concludes, "the public knew little, even during the height of the furor," aside from choice quotes from the chorus used by Ice-T's detractors (Sieving 1998, 343).

Ice-T's withdrawal of "Cop Killer" from later printings of *Body Count* marked the beginning of the controversy's end. In interviews during and after the controversy (and even today) the artist maintained that his focus was on corrupt, brutal LA police during the late 1980s and early 1990s. One typical response came when Ice-T appeared on the *Arsenio Hall Show*: "There's a lot of good cops out there, you know what I'm saying? I know a lot of police officers that are out there trying to do the right thing." Ice-T stood firmly behind his point: "Anybody who sympathizes with brutal police, I don't need them as a fan" (Hall 1992). Notably, on the same episode the host, Arsenio Hall, talked at length about the pressure he and his producers were under to cancel their interview with Ice-T.

Ice-T's career continued unabated after the "Cop Killer" episode simmered down. During the controversy itself, he appeared on the cover of *Rolling Stone*—as a cop dressed in blues and carrying a police baton. He left Warner Brothers records claiming the label did not force him out; the controversy made conditions so restrictive that he was unwilling to deal with Warner. Aggressive lyrics continued in the 1993 *Home Invasion*. Like its predecessors, it climbed the charts and eventually went gold at the RIAA. The album's title references what Ice-T maintained was the real cause of ire for people in positions of power: his music's invasion of thousands of white, middle-class homes, and the attempt thereby to break down traditional power structures. Other releases followed at a steady pace, two more going gold. On these albums Ice-T and his collaborators considered topics as diverse as the Gulf War, nuclear weapons, the death penalty, domestic violence, prison conditions, and drug abuse.

By this time Ice-T's superstardom—and notoriety— was such that he branched out into media other than music. In the late 1980s he produced the title song for

Ice-T on cover of *Rolling Stone* August 20, 1992. (Cover Image Courtesy of Rolling Stone, Issue Dated August 20, 1992 [Photo By Mark Seliger.] © Rolling Stone LLC 1992 All Rights Reserved. Reprinted By Permission.)

Dennis Hopper's movie about Los Angeles, *Colors.* In 1991 (the year before "Cop Killer") in the film *New Jack City*, he starred as a detective taking down a violent drug lord based in an apartment complex; he also produced music for the movie's soundtrack. More acting roles followed throughout the 1990s. In 1994 he played the protagonist in *Surviving the Game*, a homeless man lured with the promise of work and then hunted by a group of wealthy businessmen looking for the ultimate prey. Notably, he appeared as J-Bone, the leader of a band of off-the-grid rebels called LoTeks, in the 1995 big-budget release *Johnny Mnemonic*, a movie adaptation of William Gibson's cyberpunk short novel. Several television projects eventually led Ice-T to an ongoing role on the police drama *Law and Order: Special Victims Unit*, starting in 2000. Perhaps most ironically in a varied and by now decades long entertainment career, on *SVU*, Ice-T plays detective Odafin "Fin" Tutuola, a former undercover vice cop who transfers to a Manhattan police unit tasked with fighting sexual and other abuse crimes.

The 2000s also found Ice-T expanding into spoken word at universities such as Princeton and Harvard, as well as for Kansas State University's Martin Luther King Day celebration. In 2008, he began serving as orator for the Langston Hughes Project, a multimedia experience based on the poet's unfinished *Ask Your Mama: 12 Moods for Jazz*. The performance, created by University of Southern California jazz professor Ron McMurdy and with music played by McMurdy's quartet, uses jazz, images, and Hughes's poetry to explore African American struggles for social and artistic freedom.

PROTESTING INJUSTICE

No political movement happens until new currents trouble still waters. Politics tends toward status quo as wealth keeps itself safe and poverty fails to ignite the engine of social change. In that light, how is long-standing racial inequality to get the attention it needs apart from loudness that pricks consciences and stirs emotions?

Two ethicists troubled about protest and disorder have suggested a third way. In 1923 Martin Buber wrote the essays that became his classic book, *I and Thou* (1958). Buber explained two kinds of encounters. The common one, which he called I-It, is instrumental, efficient, and impersonal. Such transactions require the passing of information, but not an encounter between persons, which Buber believed was essential to establish genuine community. These latter encounters he called I-Thou. He used the reverential form of "you" to underscore the esteem the "I" renders to the other in genuine communication. Buber's *Thou* can be a person, a tree, even a piece of art. Will you take time to know it, or is a glance sufficient? Will you want to understand it, or use it for commerce or pleasure? How often have you heard a story about someone passing a stranger daily but never meeting the eyes or pausing long enough even for an initial greeting? The story of Kitty Genovese being stabbed in the Bronx while neighbors failed to come to her aid is still cited as a classic example of stupendously isolated people failing to show empathy (Wilson 1993, 36). Buber articulated a way toward fulsome human relationships, though his writings are sometimes categorized as "personalism" and put on the shelf, an early pastoral philosophy out of touch with urban realities.

Emmanuel Levinas adopted such a heightened regard for the Other (Buber's Thous) that ethics (how we treat Others) became the "first philosophy." For Levinas, the presupposition for understanding all reality was the primordial phenomenon of encountering the Other. His ideas, like Buber's, were forged in the crucible of Hitler's Third Reich. Both Buber and Levinas, Jews, survived to affirm the value of mutuality with an authenticity we cannot dismiss. Is it reasonable today to think so highly of others?

Author Lee Siegel (2008) begins his book on the Internet with a description of morning coffee: "I go to Starbucks, sit down, open my laptop, and turn it on. …Back in prehistoric time [maybe a dozen years ago] my attention faced outward. I might see someone I know, or someone I'd like to know" (16). All that outwardness is driven inward now. Siegel is surrounded by other people, all with their laptops on. "I can hardly see anyone else's face behind the screens" as public space formerly rich in social experience is contracted into "isolated points of wanting, all locked into separate phases of inwardness" (16). A 2010 study of 14,000 college students by the University of Michigan's Institute for Social Research noted a 40 percent drop in empathy since 1979, much of it in the last decade. Apparently the demands of online friendship are playing a crucial role in tuning-out others (Konrath, O'Brien, and Hsing, 2011).

Buber and Levinas remind us we are not alone, but inherently connected to others in ways that seek symbolic and dialogic expression. Such interdependence is much more unlikely nowadays as each of us dives into Internet relations, a social circle presented entirely on the small screen. Ice-T should be doubly frustrated. Not only is his 'hood made rough and criminal by the hierarchies of dominant modernity, but when his rap attacks Caucasian privilege with malfunctioning vengeance, all those white suburbanites have headphones on. Ice-T's yell and lyric must be shrill before anyone will pay attention.

But if Ice-T breaks through and his audience buys the message, to whom is he rapping—Thous or Its? Ice-T's frustration does not come in the language of Buber or Levinas.

> To understand where the rage and defiance in inner-city kids come from, you have to understand [that] even a strong-willed kid will have a difficult time giving a fuck when everywhere he looks…reinforce his feelings of helplessness. (1994, 3)

He speaks to youth in urban America with language meant to make sense there, among youth with no incentive to listen to socially sanctioned authority, an enemy Other.

Communitarian theory works both personally and institutionally. Communitarians acknowledge that Buber's Thou applies to subjects bigger and more distant than persons standing before us. Even then, when you imagine encountering a Thou, you anticipate a rich and deep conversation with an understanding friend. You never expect heart-to-hearts with a TV-ad pitchman or a stage entertainer. You know that the rhetoric of friendship in those settings is pseudo-intimacy. Your callback to the pitchman will reach an automated message center. If you try to reciprocate friendship to the stage performer, you will quickly face-off with the biggest bouncer that venue can hire. You know these things. Every well-socialized young adult gets it. Add race to the equation, and the likelihood of establishing a "common humanity" grows dim. "Kids don't know what color they are, but they learn. Sooner or later somebody clues them in.... As you get older, racism doesn't go away. It just builds and builds and builds" (Ice-T 1994, 133).

Does communitarian theory override these social barriers? No theory can make friendship happen. Communitarian theory, however, insists that no one be an It—treated as a tool, device, means to my personal happiness, or dismissed as irrelevant to my happiness. No one is outside the circle of "citizen" in policy debates, outside the circle of "neighbor" when you are getting business done, or outside the circle of "friend" when there is a need to be met. Communitarianism does not count its success by the number of people who get concert tickets, but by the breadth and depth of relationships formed and transformed at the event in all its parts.

The question for Ice-T is not box office or CD sales, but the cultural literacy his performance generates among people who need their racial eyewear cleansed. Can people leave his show with the sense they have been addressed, confronted, helped to see? Have Ice-T's lyrics built trust so that his message, however rough, can heal racial injustice and lead gang members and police sergeants toward mutual respect and civic cooperation? Ice-T is an entertainer, not a community organizer; a stage-man, not a social worker. His vision is to raise the tempo, not to craft public policy. His game is album sales, not school improvement. He writes:

> For now, I make records. That's my job. In those records, I draw parallels to the different degrees of anger people feel on the street. I give people an opportunity to see a lot of the problems without having to go through the actual violence. I make records from an enraged brother's point of view. The cops are lucky I believe in enlightening the mind more than I believe in violence.... It's up to you to change the system more than me. (1994, 195)

Greg Dimitriadis (1996) has chronicled hip hop's transition from "live performance" to "mediated narrative." Dimitriadis reveals that hip hop actually developed out of face-to-face relationships: "Hip hop culture originated during the mid-1970s as an integrated series of live community-based practices" (1996, 179). Rap began as social activity. It was (and is) created among friends, shared with others in "battles" of lyrical mastery and bragging rights over competitors. The young Ice-T, rapping away at Radio Club, was part of this tradition. Early hip-hop culture can be said to emphasize the I-Thou of Buber. But somewhere along the way, this tradition was replaced:

> The decentralized face-to-face social dynamic which marked early hip hop has thus given way to a different dynamic, one mediated by way of commodity forms such as vinyl, video and CD. These configurations have separated hip hop's vocal discourse (i.e., 'rap') from its early contexts of communal production, encouraging closed narrative forms over flexible word-play and promoting individualized listening over community dance. (Dimitriadis 1996, 179)

By the time of "Cop Killer," hip hop's commercialization was so complete that many of Ice-T's detractors directed their complaints against Warner Brothers.

The company was perceived as willing to discard public decency in favor of the vast profits a successfully marketed hip-hop album would provide (Sieving 1998, 346).

Despite his claim that he just "makes records," Ice-T did in fact reach many non-African Americans with his message of police brutality in "Cop Killer." The genius of his use of rock and punk and metal was that it made the African American experience of hopelessness more understandable to white young people:

> In disseminating white music with a black accent, *Body Count*—to a greater degree than Ice-T's rap material—teaches the suburban white teenager about social conditions far outside of his or her lived experience: a project of extreme importance in an increasingly multicultural, multidiscursive age. (Sieving 1998, 350)

And he demanded throughout 1992, and beyond, that America listen in just that fashion.

Body Count communicated to white youth not simply because of marketing but because its musicians grew up listening to and identifying with the same musical traditions enjoyed by their Other: punk, rock, and metal. The Black Sabbath and other rock pumping out of their stereos in high school was received, and helped them build a relationship with white kids far removed from South Central Los Angeles. Ice-T has collaborated with a variety of rock and metal bands, and noted the influence of punk in his own musical experience in serious and sometimes flippant terms: "What good is a rock and roll band if you don't get banned?" (McManus 2005). Body Count's lived experiences let them create a personal connection to Thous that transcended Warner Brothers' engagement of Its.

IS DISSENT THE RIGHT TACTIC?

Political rhetoric has become nearly void of humor and credibility. Political leadership has nearly no inventory left by which to confront the injustices. Thankfully artists and perhaps scientists still do. Ice-T can say what no Congressperson would dare. Ice-T can confront in your face. Communitarianism, as a condition of moral equity, wants to know if the faces confronted by his brash and seemingly violent lyrics can say, "OK Ice-T, I hear you, point well taken." Is there reciprocity in his lyric, a chance for the voice of the Other? About his own leadership, Ice-T appears shy to play role model: "Nah. Uh-uh. I haven't worked this hard to be pigeonholed. ... The type of role model they need [is] someone who tells them, 'Sure, you can hit everything'" (1994, 15).

William Lloyd Garrison was the nineteenth century's protest speaker par excellence. Editor of *The Liberator*, he had no patience with those who would compromise on the question of slavery. He held that no economic condition (slavery represented a capital investment) permitted even a day's delay in each slave's emancipation. He gave no quarter to the adroit political compromises of the Founding Fathers who managed to sell the idea of union by pushing the slavery question to the margins. To Garrison, the Constitution was "a covenant with death and an agreement with Hell" (Mayer 1998, 313). Of the great names of his day he cared only whether they recognized slavery's utter evil and promoted its immediate and complete discontinuation. Initially close to Frederick Douglass, he parted company over Douglass's irenic take on the Constitution. Garrison started a career in abolitionist publishing working on Benjamin Lundy's *The Genius of Universal Emancipation*, which he left when unable to pay a judgment for libeling a slave-ship captain. The lessons learned, however, never faded. His biographer quotes Garrison himself when naming the book: "I have need to be all on fire for I have a mountain of ice about me to melt" (Mayer 1998, front matter). Ice-T too has mountains of ice, though his metaphor and Garrison's are a century apart. For thirty years Garrison dodged death threats and never retreated "a single inch," as he promised he would not in his famous first-issue statement: "I will be as harsh as truth, and as uncompromising as justice.... I do not wish to think, or to speak, or write, with moderation ... AND I WILL BE HEARD" (Mayer 1998, 112).

Are these the words of a narrow-minded fanatic or a communitarian-type social reformer? The former are dismissed as zealots unequipped to deal with complex public policy. The latter are commonly stereotyped as consensus-driven moderates of the type Garrison despised. Surely Garrison's *Liberator* carried the torch of a committed antislavery advocate who would be the last to "dialogue" with ideological opponents. At the same time, he advocated important communitarian themes of enfranchisement at the margins, advocacy for the voiceless, confrontation with palliatives, and perpetual movement toward justice.

Elijah Parish Lovejoy edited the *St. Louis Observer* until May 1836, when he was chased across the Mississippi River after publically criticizing Judge Luke E. Lawless, who had determined that mob frenzy alone had caused a free black man to be lynched and burned; no one individual could bear blame or be indicted. The abolitionist Lovejoy saw that as terror masquerading as justice.

Once safely across the river in Alton, Illinois, Lovejoy again ran afoul of popular opinion. Illinois was a free state, but its businessmen just up-river from St. Louis knew commerce would not follow Lovejoy's biting rhetoric. In October, Alton's elders gathered to resolve: "We as citizens of Alton are aware that the Rev. E. P. Lovejoy still persists to publish an abolition paper to the injury of the community at large.... We now call on him ... and politely request a discontinuum of the publication of his incendiary doctrines" (Gill, 1958, 117).

Lovejoy responded, "The liberty of our forefathers has given us the liberty of speech.... Our duty and our high privilege [is] to act and speak on all questions touching this great commonwealth." Then with reciprocal politeness, he declined the community's resolution (Gill, 1958, 9). In less than a month the real incendiaries had torched the river warehouse where Lovejoy's press was hidden and killed the editor with five shotgun blasts.

American history is graced with the words of dissenters who defied communities in order to revive them. A contemporary dissenter (in the sense of one who sees past pretensions and calls communities to account), the African American scholar Cornel West describes "the oppressive effect of the prevailing market moralities" which lead to "a form of sleepwalking from womb to tomb, with the majority of citizens content to focus on private careers and be distracted with stimulating amusements" (2004, 27). West echoes the dissent that Ice-T frames in his own voice, that Garrison and Lovejoy framed in theirs.

Communitarians refuse to submit to a community that has chosen injustice as its keynote, whether obvious or ingrained and institutional. Majorities alone do not justify perpetuating a class system so clearly prejudiced as was American slavery, or the genocidal mania of a Nazi movement or the Stalinist pogrom. Majority strength alone does not compel communitarian allegiance. Life must be there, life and access to the benefits of life.

Jürgen Habermas describes democracy as the practice of "discursive ethics." Discourse ethics is dialogical, he claims. We develop moral judgment in conversation with people affected by loss, competing claims, institutional lethargy, corruption, danger, and arbitrary rule. Good judgment does not come pre-made in oracle or text. It is made in process. But the process must be aligned with reason and attentive to the reciprocity by which human society has always been distinguished, that is, the "public sphere." We are talking about media as a arena in which "individuals participate in discussions about matters of common concern, in an atmosphere free of coercion or dependencies (inequalities) that would incline individuals toward acquiescence or silence" (Warren 1995, 171). The public sphere must be a safe space to talk about what is unsafe in relations people are forming.

The Internet's anonymity has created safe spaces. Blogs are named but potentially all such names are fiction. The same for posts. An earlier chapter cites Juicy Campus where freedom to speak never implied the responsibility to be identified with an opinion or claim. Communitarians do not cheer for blogs as graffiti; communitarians recognize that speakers must own their words for the space between us—the mutuality of relationships—to fertilize and grow. Identity and word stand together for relationships to be trustworthy and open to reform.

Are Ice-T's lyrics, then, a democratic call to responsible action? There is nothing anonymous about Ice-T. He performs. He raises awareness and ire. He sticks social power centers with the pain of transparency and the sting of failing to perform for all the people. He speaks what he believes, no matter the footprint of his critique. Opposed to Ice-T were powerful voices representing law, the state, and significant professional associations. Other dissenters can identify easily.

SHOULD ICE-T RAP THOSE WORDS?

Augustine Chichuri, commissioner of the Zimbabwe Republic Police and spokesperson for Robert Mugabe, president of Zimbabwe, regularly threatens malcontents and perpetrators of violence with decisive action, using the full and necessary force of the state. And why not use force? Malcontents disrupt business. Street protestors dampen investor enthusiasm. Angry dissidents might hurt someone. "Necessary force" implies police restraint (no more force than necessary to keep the peace). Yet nearly every citizen knows exactly what Chichuri's threats mean. Dissent from Mr. Mugabe's way is itself a form of violence, according to Mugabe (and his Commissioner, who knows better than to dissent himself). Against such intransigence, the "power of nice" carries little impact. Happy alternatives to confrontation sound hollow ("We hope we've been able to convince you that there is another way, that being kind and considerate is an equally valid, more effective way to get ahead than being selfish and cutthroat"—ugh! (Thaler and Koval 2006, 118)).

Stephen Carter tackles the problem of dissent in American democracy in what he calls a "meditation on law, religion, and loyalty." He argues that "civic life requires dissent because it requires differences of opinion in order to spark the dialogues from which the community thrives and grows" (Carter 1998, 16). Carter argues that the nation's founding document, the Declaration of Independence, affirmed that consent was the basis of government authority, but that dissent was its prerequisite, and further, that a governing authority that failed to listen to consent was rightly opposed by dissenters. King George's agents were no longer legitimate authority on these shores, the Founders claimed. Carter worries that federal power in America has grown so ubiquitous that dissenting communities are at risk.

Few Americans today support Mugabe-style politics. Our democracy depends on wide permission to speak one's mind, and sometimes to offend. Always in democratic debate there is opportunity for buy-in. The listener is never condemned before the trial starts. Our entire political life depends on this practice of challenge, critique, and response. We ask only that dissenters not allow their passions to spill into destruction of property or threaten bodily safety. Otherwise, say what you will.

When Ice-T dissented in "Cop Killer," he used the verb *kill* and the obscene verb *fuck* in the imperative mood, and the defamatory noun *pigs* as a metaphor. Such a blatant call to violence was alarming, if not a direct threat. Yes, police face danger enforcing the law. In a country as large as ours, sworn officers take fire. Over the past ten years, more than 1,600 police officers have died in the line of duty. Each year, 16,000 are injured and 58,000 are assaulted (http://www.nleomf.org/facts/enforcement).

The confrontational work that police officers perform accounts for their losses at one level. Catching people involved in nefarious or violent behavior, ordering those people to submit to state power, then forcibly apprehending those who resist—this work is bound to raise the anger and anxiety of everyone engaged.

Yet another level must be considered, the racial divide and stigma that has plagued America since its founding. Race is complicated and the story of race in America beyond our scope. In Cornel West's analysis, the social and economic isolation of poor urban neighborhoods has produced a "lack of self-efficacy" especially among urban black males. West uses the most emotive and extreme terms to describe the nihilism, the "eclipse of hope," the "collapse of meaning of life," the "profound sense of psychological depression, personal worthlessness, and social despair that still describes racial minorities" (West 1993, 5). David Hollenback summarizes West's analysis as the "institutionalization of hopelessness" (2002, 15). Hopelessness as the normal path of life, hopelessness enforced by social structures, is perverse. When schools, social services, banks, employment agencies, and police departments regard you as a hopeless case, where is the break-out point?

Ice-T performs the break-out. He rages against an agency that, in his view, has institutionalized hopelessness. "Despite the frustration and anger I vent in my music, I have a great deal of hope for the future. When I meet with kids around the country, they all give me reason to be optimistic" (Ice-T 1994, 192).

Still, should Ice-T's lyrics enter the public sphere? Should people listen to "Cop Killer"? And remember, Ice-T in this chapter is a stand-in for many forms of social dissent.

Ice-T presents his message to several different audiences, but the two most volatile are police and urban black males. Seemingly at war, each armed and tense in an unsteady stand-off, these two appear ready for violence. Since death and violence cannot be the proper end of ethical behavior, our question for Ice-T becomes a question of means and ends. Does Ice-T will the death of police? Is killing a legitimate means to break institutional hopelessness?

To these, communitarianism answers, no. What of the performance then?

COMMUNITARIAN THEORY APPLIED

Interpretation is essential. Why should Ice-T's literal call for murder be interpreted as a cry of anguish and a plea for restraint when *Stormfront*'s racist messages (chapter 8) are rejected out of hand as hate speech? Why are one person's metaphors another person's fighting words?

The answer involves both context and community. If all of Ice-T's lyrics advocated murder, if Ice-T had not portrayed policemen sympathetically on the screen, if Ice-T had not explained his lyrics as hyperbole, there would be no reason to interpret "Cop Killer" as protest.

By contrast, *Stormfront*'s racism demands to be taken at face value. Nothing about *Stormfront*'s message leads a listener to imagine its meaning is different than what is actually said. *Stormfront*'s texts show no irony. No communities of interpretation recast *Stormfront*'s racism as healthy. Unlike Ice-T, who intended his lyrics to spur prosocial conversation, *Stormfront* intends its bigotry to beget more bigotry.

In a communitarian frame, Ice-T may perform his lyrical dissent if his two volatile audiences understand and affirm the imagery of his music and the connotative limits of his rhetoric. This mutual affirmation will not be easy. Police are not attracted to law enforcement as a profession because it affords manifold opportunity for artistic imagery and meaningful forays into metaphorical expression. The metaphors common to police work are basic. It will not be easy for police professionals to hear Ice-T and conclude, "He has a point there." Precinct chatter after Ice-T's performance will not likely focus on the aesthetics of Ice-T's penetrating vision of urban life. Nonetheless, difficult as the problem of interpretation can be, communitarian theory asks people who choose law enforcement careers to listen to the people they protect and serve. Listening requires the capacity, even the humility, to acknowledge that the Other speaks something significant.

Wisdom refuses a mindless literalism when art requires a broader context of meaning. Literalism can be truth's worst enemy. We do little to endear a friend if only literal meanings apply. The writer of the Psalms (17:8) refers to the wings of God without the slightest notion that such appendages give lift to the Almighty. Wisdom controls the interpretation of language, affording latitude in order to discover a truth embedded in image or likeness. Listening wisely is hearing an author/ singer's intent, not merely out-of-context dictionary definitions. W. E. B. DuBois, full of twentieth-century wisdom and passionate for change, urged crowds to be wise, alert, discerning. In a speech in August 1906, he said:

> We do not believe in violence...but we do believe in that incarnate spirit of justice, that hatred of the lie, that willingness to sacrifice money, reputation, and life itself on the altar of right....Our enemies, triumphant for the present, are fighting the stars in their courses. Justice and humanity must prevail. (Torricelli et al. 1999, 19)

Nor is the interpretive task an easy ride for the other volatile group of listeners, urban black males. Many will hear at Ice-T's performance a wealthy black man shouting feelings they understand well. But stepping back from the denotative meaning, reflecting and pondering the song's genuine connotative appeal—this is hard work for an emotionally invested audience. It is much easier, despite the enormous long-term costs, to take Ice-T literally. Quick responses to plain words must be resisted, of course. As this second group has no professional cadre (police have their captains and commanders, their civilian authorities), talented mentors are especially strategic for a truthful response to Ice-T's emotionally charged performance. Those mentors are among us—West himself, the renowned Archbishop Tutu, the great Martin Luther King, Jr., political leaders of color and civic virtue.

Perhaps we can learn from Ice-T. The young and the urban and police forces across the United States should read his work. His response in a 2005 interview is illuminating:

> If you believe I'm a cop killer, then you believe David Bowie is an astronaut. ...When you sing, you can sing from different perspectives. At the time, LAPD was totally out of control. The song ["Cop Killer"] was written a year before the Rodney King situation. So I was just letting people know that kids in the street were ready to go to war with the police. Eventually they did—there was a riot there. (McManus 2005)

Ice-T understands that literalism can kill. Context is not just important, it is crucial. Later in the same interview, he laughed lightly as he faced the irony of his words: "I also had a part of my life where I was a criminal. As a criminal, they were the opponent, so I was trying to beat them. Now I'm not a criminal and I need them to protect my house" (McManus 2005). Artists speak in metaphor, and to understand them requires knowing their context—and realizing that context changes.

Ice-T's rap finally confronts the paradox of liberal freedom. Widely held social values provide time-tested boundaries to the freedom cherished by all. John Durham Peters lays out this quandary in his astute study of censorship:

> Defending the speech we hate does not mean we need to learn to love it or think it is really good stuff. Refusing to make laws prohibiting speech and expression does not mean that speech and expression are necessarily free of ill effects. One can oppose censorship while maintaining a capacity for judgment about the value and quality of cultural forms. (2005, 9)

Peters's analysis of the liberal tradition shows that no one can stand still for long. Communitarianism is not a static paradigm, but answers Peters's conundrum by hoping even against history's grim lessons that human experimentation in symbol and word will find its way forward toward prosperity for all in the context of justice and peace. Communitarian discourse is not prim, proper, and stationary. It may sometimes be bold as a rap, as confrontational as a protest march, as moving as a eulogy. Communitarianism tolerates raucous disruption of the commonweal, provided the trajectory of that disruption is not chaos per se, but the social good. We are complicated symbolic creators one and all. Archie Bunker's un-politic humor carries important messages about social needs and change, but not all heard his humor in the same way. Yet through the storm of conversation, there is light.

In a communitarian frame, Ice-T carries responsibility for guiding all interested parties to responsible interpretation of his art. Communitarianism is not romanticism, where artists may fly to the winds of expressionism while careless (even cynically so) about who, if any, will understand them, the expression being everything. Romanticism is a workable thesis in a land that never was, a dream world removed from any street or tavern where police and citizen hang out in mutual distrust. Somewhere and at some time after Ice-T belts out his incendiary verbs and discourteous nouns, he must explain how those lyrics build trust and reshape hope. Performance art at Ice-T's level is founded on social institutions that channel his immense success. Those media too—social processes all—bear responsibility for creating new trajectories in law enforcement and urban recovery. The groups Ice-T raps for finally need to dance together. And Ice-T needs to be there with them.

And maybe, after a decades-long journey, he is. Applying this logic to "Cop Killer," communitarians find an unexpected surprise: empathy. More than sixteen years of commentary on his song cannot forget that Ice-T places himself in the shoes of a Thou. He tries to get at the despair that might lead someone to scream that a "pig" should die. At its heart, "Cop Killer" examines the breakdown of the I-Thou relationship.

Pop culture aficionados rarely fail to note the delicious irony present when the man who penned "Cop Killer" now plays an upright detective striving to protect civilians on NBC's *Law and Order*. In Ice-T's 2005 *Rove Live* interview, the host pointed out this seeming contradiction. Ice-T responded by sharing that his acting comes from his experience and perspective. (He has no formal acting training.) But then he went further:

> The character you see me play on *Law and Order* is not totally out of context. When I got the job, they said, 'Ice, you're not that fond of the police. Show us how to play a cop the way you wish they were.'
>
> And that's what you see every night on *Law and Order*. That's Ice-T, sending [to the viewer] how he feels cops should handle the situation.... If you think something's wrong, show [the rest of] us how to do it right. So that's what I try to do on the show. (McManus 2005)

Tracy Marrow, it seems, has come full circle.

ON THE WORLD STAGE

As this book nears publication day, the world reels with distrust and hatred between races and ethnicities. Zimbabwe's Mugabe has sung of race purity (against the colonizers) for almost three decades; his song has created chaos, death, and loss for Zimbabweans of every race. Many waited for his enflamed rhetoric to reach a community-building purpose and point. That never happened. Now Mugabe heads a ruined country, his legacy somewhere on par with Idi Amin of Uganda. He is a political performer stunted by the smallness of his own lyric.

Not all lyrics are small. At its best, hip hop has blended art and culture into guillotine critiques of social injustice, and powerful, indeed communitarian, glimpses into the I-Thou relationship. Many hip-hop artists follow the footsteps of pioneers like Ice-T, KRS-One, Afrika Bambaataa, Grandmaster Flash, Dr. Dre, Rakim, Ice Cube, and Public Enemy. Younger artists such as Talib Kweli and Mos Def—but two examples of many—are heirs to a rich tradition of language, interpretation, and music that still helps examine, critique, and build relationships among us neighbors of varying color and origin. These days one also finds Mos Def in movies like Michel Gondry's *Be Kind Rewind*, a recent ode to community-defined experience.

The music of calling out hopelessness also has shifted, spread around the world, and continues to respond to events. Although examples are diverse, one recent phenomenon is the development of Arab and Arab Diaspora hip-hop traditions. Supergroup Arab Summit's recent album *Fear of an Arab Planet* pays homage in its name to Public Enemy's classic, Grammy-nominated *Fear of a Black Planet*. Iraqi artist Narcicyst blends Arabic music traditions with the latest beats, covering them with lyrics that set fire to stereotypes while mixing in respect for Muslim lifeways and insights from his Master's thesis on hip-hop culture. In this growing, ever-shifting, but vibrant tradition one might consider the words of a music critic, who commented on Ice-T's follow up to *Body Count*, the 1993 album *Home Invasion*:

> As militant as *Home Invasion* is, as fully as it is the product of an artist under siege, it is still driven by an imagined ideal of racial harmony. Track after track…asserts that. It's a harmony in which people are judged not by their color but by their willingness to treat others with respect. (Decurtis 1993)

Federico Mayor, former head of UNESCO, writing a world-building tract at the turn of the millennium, notes our core problem in terms rarely voiced but easily recognized by anyone whose 'hood is hopeless and whose vision is social change:

> We cannot fail to observe the increase in soul sickness at the very heart of the most prosperous societies.…The heart itself seems prey to a curious void, indifference and passivity grow, there is an ethical desert, passions and emotions are blunted, people's eyes are empty and solidarity evaporates. (2001, 5)

Mayor goes on to describe contracts that address global crises in health, food supply, illiteracy, and human rights. His third contract is "cultural" (information technology, literacy, languages) and the fourth "ethical"—which this chapter takes as its concluding note.

At the end, Mayor calls for a new world commitment to peace. Economic and social development are the practical steps to this peace, which "leaves behind all forms of frustration, jealousy or rivalry and ensures that a spirit of solidarity and cooperation prevails over…power and competition" (2001, 460). How is this economic and social development to happen?

The Manifesto 2000 for a Culture of Peace and Non-Violence, written by Laureates of the Nobel Peace Prize, asks that youth of the world to pledge to:

> Respect the life and dignity of each human being without discrimination or prejudice;
> Practice active non-violence, rejecting violence in all its forms, especially towards the most deprived and vulnerable;
> Share time and material resources in a spirit of generosity;
> Defend freedom of expression and cultural diversity, giving preference always to dialogue and listening without engaging in fanaticism, defamation and the rejection of others;
> Promote responsible consumer behavior, to preserve the planet; and
> Contribute to the development of my community, in order to create together new forms of solidarity. (Manifesto 2000)

Communitarianism provides a framework for this initiative. Within this framework, artists sing their lyrics and audiences respond with intelligent action. Some of those ballads will echo the advice on public discourse given by the great democrat and Supreme Court justice William Brennan as he sent the forces of belligerent racial hegemony running for cover. Debate on public issues, Brennan wrote, "should be uninhibited, robust, and wide-open, and...it may well include vehement, caustic, and sometimes unpleasantly sharp attacks" (*New York Times v. Sullivan*, 376 U.S. 254 (1964)). Democracy's cadences are community-building, but not always friendly.

In democratic discourse, there is room on the stage for Ice-T's rap. In communitarian discourse, his point and purpose should be the generous gift of human dignity given to every sworn officer who upholds the rights under which Ice-T sings. Intact for the targets of his harsh verse, that gift will be intact for the rest of us, whatever hue we present in this world of many colors. To show the good purpose of his art, Ice-T should listen to critics and those offended by his offensiveness. More than any interpretation he might offer on the proper meaning of his music, listening would show good faith and proper aim.

Of course, we are speaking of history as if it were today, urging a music star toward ideals he has had years to practice or dismiss. But this guise of the historical present has its point in something quite important: reform happens. Yesterday does not determine tomorrow. Hopelessness so institutionalized that you want to scream in protest begins to break when you, today, relate to the Other in a way that respects the space between you as life-giving, people-affirming, treasured and not yet the way it should be. Movement toward communitarian goals thus begins.

REFERENCES

Bennett, J. 2006. "Interview: Ice-T." *Decibel*. September 1. <http://web.archive.org/web/20061020204850/http://www.decibelmagazine.com/features_detail.aspx?id=4908>.

Bergmann, Luke. 2008. *Getting Ghost: Two Young Lives and the Struggle for the Soul of an American City*. New York: New Press.

Carter, Stephen L. 1998. *The Dissent of the Governed: A Meditation on Law, Religion, and Loyalty*. Cambridge, MA: Harvard University Press.

DeCurtis, Anthony. 1993. "Ice-T Fires: Black Rage, Dope Beats." *Rolling Stone*, 653 (April 1), 51–2.

Dimitriadis, Greg. 1996. "Hip Hop: From Live Performance to Mediated Narrative." *Popular Music* 15 (2): 179–94.

Freydkin, Donna. 1999. "No Thaw for Rapper Ice T." *CNN*, October 27. <http://www.cnn.com/SHOWBIZ/Music/9910/27/ice.t/index.html>.

Gill, John. 1958. *Tide without Turning: Elijah P. Lovejoy and Freedom of the Press*. Boston: Starr King.

Hall, Arsenio. Host. 1992. *The Arsenio Hall Show*, "Interview with Ice-T." 8:01 min. Summer. <http://www.youtube.com/watch?v=c8WrXrwBSsc>.

Hollenbach, David. 2002. *The Common Good and Christian Ethics*. Cambridge, U.K.: Cambridge University Press.

Ice-T. 1994. *The Ice Opinion*. New York: St. Martins.

Konrath, Sara H., O'Brien, Edward H., and Hsing, Courtney. 2011. "Changes in Dispositional Empathy in American College Students over Time: A Meta-Analysis." *Personality & Social Psychology Review*, 15:2 (May), 180–98.

Mayer, Henry. 1998. *All on Fire: William Lloyd Garrison and the Abolition of Slavery*. New York: St. Martin's.

Mayor, Federico. 2001. *The World Ahead*. New York: Zed Books.

McKinnon, Matthew. 2006. "Hang the MC." <http://www.cbc.ca/arts/music/hangthemc-day2.html>.

McManus, Rove. Host. 2005. *Rove Live*, "Interview with Ice-T," 9:08 min. Week of July 3. <http://www.youtube.com/watch?v=k-esgVDqrLU>.

Peters, John Durham.. 2005. *Courting the Abyss: Free Speech and the Liberal Tradition*. Chicago: University of Chicago Press.

Pinfield, M. Host. 2005. *Sound Off*, "Ice-T." Episode 107.

Siegel, Lee. 2008. *Against the Machine: Being Human in the Age of the Electronic Mob*. New York: Spiegel & Grau.

Sieving, Christopher. 1998. "Cop Out? The Media, 'Cop Killer,' and the Deracialization of Black Rage." *Journal of Communication Inquiry* 22: 334–53.

Thaler, Linda Kaplan, and Koval, Robin. 2006. *The Power of Nice: Eight Ways to Kill the Business World with Kindness*. New York: Doubleday.

Torricelli, Robert, and Carroll, Andrew, eds. 1999. *In Our Own Words: Extraordinary Speeches of the American Century*. New York: Washington Square Press.

Warren, Mark E. 1995. "The Self in Discursive Democracy." In Stephen K. White, ed., *The Cambridge Companion to Habermas*. Cambridge: Cambridge University Press, 167–200.

West, Cornel. 1993. *Race Matters*. Boston: Beacon.

———. 2004. *Democracy Matters*. New York: Penguin.

Wilson, James Q. 1993. *The Moral Sense*. New York: Free Press.

Epilogue
Three Underlinings

In the ancient year of 1968, a one-time hit by Friend and Lover called "Reach Out of the Darkness" began with these lyrics and repeated them enough that the message was indelible:

I think it's so groovy now that people are finally getting together.

I think it's wonderful and how that people are finally getting together.

Back when it was groovy to say "groovy," there was hope that the social revolution of the 1960s would create a world less prone to violence and disconnect, more prone to peace and togetherness.

As this book was heading to production, *New York Times* columnist Thomas Friedman published an essay in which he compared the level of acrimony currently separating political camps in the United States with a similar dive among Israelis into villainous rhetoric preceding the assassination of Prime Minister Yitzhak Rabin in 1995. Then in Israel and now in the United States, Friedman (2009) observes "a different kind of American political scene that makes me wonder whether we can seriously discuss serious issues any longer and make decisions on the basis of the national interest." He titled this column, "Where Did 'We' Go?"

The hopeful dream of Friend and Lover did not last. Getting together is not what is finally happening.

This book urges a new approach that is after all not so very new, a good approach that is not so very easy to do. That approach is to find the space between people and imagine (again) how very important it is.

MUTUALITY

However independent we may be, we humans are social. We exist in time and space as persons in community. This observation should come as no surprise.

Even the reading of this book is fundamentally social, although you may have spent hours alone doing it. Consider: written by three with the assistance of many helpers, produced by dozens in a corporate network of specialists, promoted and reviewed by still others, likely assigned by a university professor, and on and on. And the solo time that you have spent with the book's stories and arguments was influenced by instruction you have received and by comments others have made. Writing and reading may be solitary activities, but they are made possible by the work of many others.

Because we are persons in community, many social philosophies have tended to emphasize one side or the other. The European Enlightenment produced an autonomous individual whose reason operated as a fundamental expressive force. For Enlightenment individualists, the world was composed of dualisms: subject–object, fact–value, material–spiritual. Galileo Galilei (1564–1642) was a central figure in the transition from medieval to modern science. He mapped reality in a new way, dividing nature into two famous compartments: primary (matter motion, mass, mathematics) and secondary (metaphysical, supernatural, values, meanings). In *The Assayer*, Galileo said, "This great book, the Universe…is written in the language of mathematics, and its characters are triangles, circles, and geometric figures" (1957, 238). Matter alone mattered to him; he considered all that was nonmaterial, immaterial.

Within a century, Isaac Newton could describe the world in his *Principia Mathematica* (1687) as a lifeless machine composed of mathematical laws and built on uniform natural causes in a closed system. The upper storey had dissolved. All phenomena could be explained as an outcome of an empirical order extending to every detail. Mystery and art were ephemeral, insignificant.

The fact–value split proposed and enacted by these giants of science led to a pervasive sense of individual autonomy. For Jean Jacques Rousseau, Europe's persuasive advocate of radical individual freedom, the highest good was the free self-determination of the human personality. Civilization's controls demean us, but free in a state of nature we are fulfilled (Derrida 1981).

The Enlightenment's autonomous self, separated from nature and from culture, is indifferent to moral standards. Alasdair MacIntyre notes that following the Enlightenment, we are unable to negotiate moral criteria or to understand the nature of community. Ethical discourse is in free-fall (1981, 245). We are failing "to get together" with the reality of our communal selves. We need to recover the space between, mutuality, the self in relation.

ORAL CULTURE

Recovering mutuality means making room for unmediated personal encounter. It means really talking with one another. After all, dialogue between persons is what bridges space between people. Recovering mutuality means producing oral culture, a force with the capacity to displace both individualism and artificial organicism where persons are lost in the whole.

Nearly as fast as someone can say "oral culture," the name of its most celebrated scholar, Walter Ong, comes up. Ong did most of his work on oral culture in West Africa, where communal life defined the traditions of village and tribe. A year before Friend and Lover released their hit song, Ong (1967) wrote, "Sound unites groups of living beings as nothing else does" (122). He went on to describe what for him was one of the most significant cultural rituals he had ever witnessed, the *oyenga,* a "drawn out, piercing shriek...high-pitched...sustained as long as breath hold out." A Catholic priest, Ong compared the *oyenga* to the bells in the Roman liturgy, but "more insistent and demanding, because it was voice" (1974, 150). Ong had been touched, deeply moved. However prominent poverty and corruption may have been in the recent history of the continent of Africa, Ong celebrated its more durable and hopeful oral traditions.

Of course, oral culture, so much a "reality" in African traditions, is hardly a revelation in North America, as if this continent were numb to it. Essayist Wendell Berry recalls an old social pastime called "sitting till bedtime." At the end of the day, work and chores done, neighbors would gather for stories, chatter, and apples (minimal food preparation and cleanup). Doing handcraft together, people would talk. Today, Berry muses, "most of us no longer talk to each other, much less tell each other stories. We tell our stories now mostly to doctors, lawyers, and psychiatrists, insurance adjusters or the police, not to our neighbor for their (and our) entertainment" (1990, 158).

Could a re-energized orality—a communal environment of talk that permits the honest question (revealing inconsistency) or the ridiculous joke (revealing pretense)—could an *agonistic* orality (Ong's term) support the recovery of mutuality and a transformation of the common good?

Some say new media such as the Internet are the answer. New means of democratized information sharing dispense with old forms, slow forms, monolithic and capitalized forms that once made celebrities of those who owned them.

The older media featured in this book can illuminate the dynamics of the new. Will limitless content serve the common good or fracture it? Build community or shred it? Have a conversation about these themes, and when that conversation happens, note well that it happened. Talk that shares the quest for understanding—that finds common cause and works for common prosperity—is good. It builds bonds.

UNIVERSALS

A clever observer may notice at this point what the great Paul Tillich (1954, 18) once taught the academic world: the most compelling foundation for ethics is ontology, the way things are put together, reality. But reality in the postmodern era is totally up for grabs. No one can assert its core and substance with any certitude. To do so seems like an affront to ethics, an arrogance unfamiliar with the *zeitgeist* of the new millennium. If you are under 25 years of age, this arrogance is a primal sin, unacceptable alongside the terrible "isms" of generations past. Yet, in fact, we do seek universals and they can be found, just perhaps not under the same stone your grandmothers turned over.

We point to the moral character of human life. All of humankind's effort to describe the good accepts moral resonance embedded in humanity. Every judgment of right and wrong is a human judgment, intrinsically so. Universally, we are moral beings, acquainted with obligation and responsibility, aware of freedom and possibility, each to a degree and altogether seeking to peel back the moral darkness and step closer to the light, variously defined in the multiple traditions that constitute culture.

The moral character of human life affirms its dignity, a quality recognized by all cultures. Human dignity is rightly treasured, cared for, and built up. It is wrongly terminated, cut short, or despised. It is the universal experience of humankind.

Communitarianism now begins to look good, compared to many alternatives. A justified ethics will acknowledge its value base as it resonates with the character of human experience. The resonance of communitarianism is evident even in the heated conversation that claims on this page may fire up. And following the heat, there will be meetings in campus hallways and campus pubs where you, with others, will find relief and refreshment celebrating the capacity to know at least this much (look around if you dispute it): community is how we celebrate; it is the situated reality of our human capacity to communicate; it is good.

In his essay "Standing by Words" (2005, 24–25), Wendell Berry notes "two epidemic illnesses of our times…the disintegration of communities and the disintegration of persons." Then he adds a third, the disintegration of language. Recovering language, he explains, will require that a speaker make a statement that clearly means something to others, and then "stand by it…believe it, be accountable for it, be willing to act on it." Such statements—repeated, varied, amplified, and transformed—comprise the human project of making our way, cutting our path. This "community speech" can be "wonderfully vital."

> This community speech, unconsciously taught and learned, in which words live in the presence of their objects, is the very root and foundation of language. It is the source, the unconscious inheritance that is carried, both with and without schooling, into consciousness—but never *all* the way, so it remains rich, mysterious, and enlivening. (Berry 2005, 33)

We might argue with Berry's insistence that the community speech he delights to describe is so "unconscious," as if beyond the capacity of the mind and person to reckon with, to intend, to take positive steps to find. We think it is not so cloud-covered that you cannot find it. This book represents one big, wordy effort to make community speech richer, better, clearer, and sharper. Iron sharpens iron, the ancient text says (Proverbs 27:17), so the purpose of this book is to help make yours razor-edged. As you work at it, a whole lot of groovy people will be listening and talking back, we hope.

REFERENCES

Berry, Wendell. 1990. *What Are People For?* San Francisco: North Point.

Berry, Wendell. 2005. *Standing by Words: Essays.* Washington, D.C.: Shoemaker and Hoard.

Derrida, Jacques. 1980. *Of Grammatology.* Baltimore, Md.: Johns Hopkins University Press.

Friedman, Thomas. 2009. "Where Did 'We' Go?" *New York Times.* <http://www.nytimes.com/2009/09/30/opinion/30friedman.html?_r=1>.

Galilei, Galileo. 1957. *Discoveries and Opinions of Galileo.* Translated by Stillman Drake. New York: Doubleday.

MacIntyre, Alasdair. 1981. *After Virtue.* Notre Dame, Ind.: University of Notre Dame Press.

Ong, Walter. 1967. *The Presence of the Word.* New Haven, Conn.: Yale University Press.

———. 1974. "Mass in Ewondo." *America* 28 (September): 148–51.

Rousseau, Jean Jacques. 1961. *Emile.* London: Dent. [original publication 1762]

Tillich, Paul. 1954. *Love, Power, and Justice.* New York: Oxford University Press.

Index